EDO KABUKI IN TRANSITION

三芝
居とも
ごみ
ぼ乃
ごど

EDO KABUKI
IN TRANSITION
FROM THE WORLDS OF THE SAMURAI TO THE VENGEFUL FEMALE GHOST

Satoko Shimazaki

Columbia University Press
New York

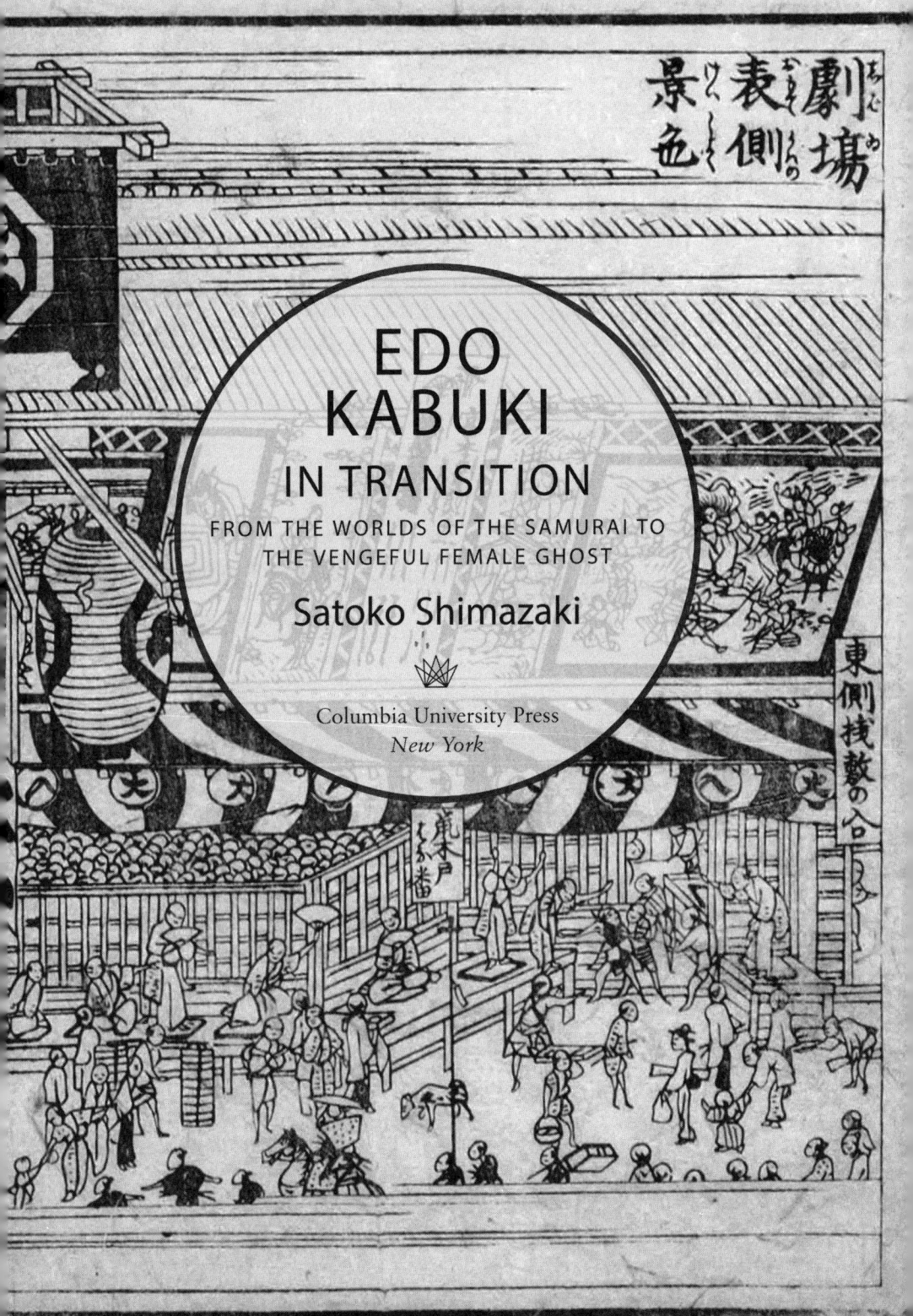

Columbia University Press wishes to express its appreciation for assistance
given by the AAS First Book Subvention Program and
Waseda University toward the cost of publishing this book.

Columbia University Press
Publishers Since 1893
New York   Chichester, West Sussex
cup.columbia.edu

Copyright © 2016 Columbia University Press
All rights reserved

Library of Congress Cataloging-in-Publication Data
Shimazaki, Satoko.
Edo kabuki in transition : from the worlds of the samurai
to the vengeful female ghost / Satoko Shimazaki.
pages cm
Includes bibliographical references and index.
ISBN 978-0-231-17226-4 (cloth : alk. paper)
ISBN 978-0-231-54052-0 (e-book)
1. Kabuki—History—19th century.   2. Japanese drama—
Edo period, 1600–1868—History and criticism.   I. Title.
PN2924.5.K3S365 2015
792.0952—dc23
2015027593

∞
Columbia University Press books are printed on permanent and durable acid-free paper.
This book is printed on paper with recycled content.
Printed in the United States of America

c 10 9 8 7 6 5 4 3 2 1

COVER DESIGN: Milenda Nan Ok Lee

COVER IMAGE: *(front)* Courtesy of Waseda University Tsubouchi Memorial Theater
Museum; *(back)* courtesy of the Idemitsu Bijutsukan, Tokyo

References to Web sites (URLs) were accurate at the time of writing. Neither the author
nor Columbia University Press is responsible for URLs that may have expired or changed
since the manuscript was prepared.

3 1327 00625 3181

CONTENTS

Acknowledgments vii
A Note to the Reader ix

Introduction 1

PART I
The Birth of Edo Kabuki

[1]
Presenting the Past:
Edo Kabuki and the Creation of Community 39

PART II
The Beginning of the End of Edo Kabuki: *Yotsuya kaidan* in 1825

[2]
Overturning the World:
The Treasury of Loyal Retainers and *Yotsuya kaidan* 97

[3]
Shades of Jealousy: The Body of the Female Ghost 150

[4]
The End of the World: Figures of the *Ubume* and the Breakdown of Theater Tradition 194

PART III
The Modern Rebirth of Kabuki

[5]
Another History: *Yotsuya kaidan* on Stage and Page 231

Notes 277
Bibliography 325
Index 349

ACKNOWLEDGMENTS

As with most first books that result from years of training, research, writing, and revision, I am indebted to more institutions and individuals than I can name. I can offer only an incomplete list of the people whose generosity made it possible for me to produce this book, and an inadequate expression of my gratitude to them.

I would never have entered a graduate program in Japanese literature in the United States if I had not had the good fortune to spend a year at Middlebury College as an exchange student in political science from Keio University, and had John Elder not been kind enough to supervise a clueless young woman with no background in the study of literature in an independent study course on Japanese poetics. His passion and encouragement first made me realize that I might be able to pursue a graduate degree in a subject that I had always loved.

The time I spent at Columbia University as a master's and doctoral student was a stimulating period of discovery, exciting challenges, and sleepless struggles to learn to write academically in a foreign language. Haruo Shirane was the ideal adviser, who always expected the best from all his students and who was and continues to be the most generous and encouraging mentor possible. I know that I will never be able to duplicate his skills as I advise my own graduate students, though I certainly try. I was also fortunate to work with Tomi Suzuki and Paul Anderer, who taught me so much during my years as a graduate student and have remained incredibly supportive ever since. Henry David Smith II gave me excellent feedback on an early version of one of the chapters in this book that I wrote for one of his seminars, and Gregory Pflugfelder, Samuel Leiter, and Andrew Gerstle provided invaluable comments during my dissertation defense that continued to guide me as I prepared this manuscript for publication. My fellow students at Columbia made my time there enjoyable and memorable. There are too many of them to name here, but I remember in particular the many long conversations about research that I had with my roommate Young-ah Kwon. And even after graduation, I have been blessed with the friendship of Linda Feng and Chelsea Foxwell, who read parts of my manuscript and gave me helpful comments from the perspective of specialists in other fields.

During the two and a half years that I spent doing dissertation research in Japan, I was fortunate to be able to work with Furuido Hideo at Waseda University and Nagashima Hiroaki at Tokyo University. In particular, I learned an enormous amount from Furuido Hideo's broad and deep knowledge of kabuki and his dynamic understanding of performance. I feel that everything I write is an attempt to fill in the outlines of ideas he has already intuited. I remember him telling his students never to miss a single kabuki production—advice I have taken to heart and tried to follow whenever I am in Tokyo. My research would have been impossible without the knowledge and experience I gained through working with theater ephemera and prints as a participant in the Yakusha-e Kenkyūkai (Actor Print Workshop) at Waseda University. I am grateful to Akama Ryō, Iwakiri Yuriko, Iwata Hideyuki, Kimura Yaeko, Matsumura Noriko, and Ōe Yoshiko, among others, for sharing their expertise. Ōtaka Yōji welcomed me into his seminar on *yomihon* at the National Institute of Japanese Literature, and Satō Satoru generously shared his knowledge of early modern illustrated fiction and his own collection of early modern books.

I continue to learn from students of theater and early modern literature with whom I studied in Tokyo, many of whom now teach at institutions in Japan. Umetada Misa, in particular, not only has been a great friend but has expanded my horizons and opened many doors for me during my dissertation research and beyond. This book would have looked very different without the help of people she introduced me to and the opportunities she created. Mitsunobu Shin'ya, Kuwahara Hiroyuki, Kaneko Takeshi, Matsuba Ryōko, and Kurahashi Masae have also answered questions and helped me locate materials as I revised the manuscript of this book. Satō Katsura, Abe Satomi, and Kodama Ryūichi have generously guided me to sources on modern kabuki, its actors, and the theater. Ellis Tinios, whom I first met when I was conducting dissertation research in Japan, has been a wonderful friend and mentor ever since. I have benefitted enormously from his generosity as a connoisseur of early modern prints and visual culture who is always eager to share his knowledge and the exciting materials he is continually discovering.

I had the good fortune to work with wonderful colleagues at the University of Colorado, Boulder. Janice Brown, Faye Kleeman, Matthias Richter, Antje Richter, and Laurel Rodd have all helped me in many different ways. I am particularly indebted to Keller Kimbrough, to whom I often turned for advice. Keller gave me many opportunities to grow as a scholar at an early stage in my career, inviting me to co-organize a joint conference and co-edit the volume that emerged from it. He also gave me excellent suggestions on my manuscript. At CU Boulder, I was also fortunate to work with Laura Brueck, Haytham Bahoora, Monica Dix, and CJ Suzuki, who formed a supportive community of young scholars.

The year I spent as a fellow at the Interdisciplinary Humanities Center at the University of California, Santa Barbara, was instrumental in allowing me to make progress on my manuscript. I am especially grateful to Kathcrine Saltzman-Li, who made it possible for me to spend a year there. She not only gave me very useful feedback on my project at different stages but helped me in many ways both small and large that have led me to where I am now. Luke Roberts replied to various questions about early modern history whenever I turned to him. I am also very grateful for the friendship and guidance of Michael Berry and Suk-Young Kim, who have kindly invited me to share my research at UCSB on several occasions.

At the University of Southern California, I have benefitted at various stages from the support and advice of my colleagues. I am especially grateful to David Bialock, Akira Lippit, Lori Meeks, Duncan Williams, Bettine Birge, and Sunyoung Park for sharing their experience and wisdom. I have always been encouraged by my talks with Brian Bernards and Youngmin Choe, colleagues at a similar stage in their careers.

Over the years, many people have made it possible for me to continue research work in Japanese theater archives. I am profoundly grateful for the friendship and guidance of Toeda Hirokazu and Tanaka Yukari.

Toeda Hirokazu helped me acquire an affiliation with the Waseda University Tsubouchi Memorial Theater Museum and arranged housing for my family at Waseda over the summer. He also paved the way for me to apply for a generous subvention for my book from Waseda University. My affiliation over the years with the Waseda University Tsubouchi Memorial Theater Museum has made it possible for me to entire archives and materials necessary for my research. Katō Norihiro and his wife, Katō Atsuko, whom I came to know when they visited UCSB, have become dear friends. Katō Norihiro also shared his writings and lecture notes with me when he came to give a talk at Colorado and helped my husband and me acquire housing at Waseda University one summer.

It is always a challenge for Japanese nationals to find funding to study for an extended period of time in Japan, and I am grateful to several institutions that created opportunities for me to do this. My dissertation research was made possible through the generous support of Columbia University and the Shinchō Foundation. The University of Colorado, the North East Asia Council of the Association of Asian Studies, the Shinsō Itō Center for Japanese Religions and Cultures, and the Visual Studies Research Institute at USC have all supported my research at different stages. The generous research funds I have received from the University of Southern California, as well as the subventions I was awarded by the Association of Asian Studies and Waseda University, have helped offset the production costs of this book.

In collecting images and acquiring rights to reproduce them, I was assisted by the staff of the Waseda University Tsubouchi Memorial Theater Museum; the Waseda University Library; the Department of Japanese Literature at Tokyo University; the University Library at the Tokyo University of the Arts; the National Institute of Japanese Literature; the National Diet Library; Nihon University Library; the Art Research Center at Ritsumeikan University; the East Asian Library at Princeton University; Tenri University Library; the Museum of Fine Arts, Boston; Zenshōan Temple; the Hyōgo Prefectural Museum of History; the Idemitsu Museum of Arts; the Tosa Yamauchi Family Treasures and Archives; Hirosaki City Public Library; the Tokyo National Museum; Hōsa Library, Nagoya; and the Tokyo Metropolitan Library. Satō Satoru gave me permission to use books from his private collection. I am also grateful to *Monumenta Nipponica* for allowing me to reprint part of a chapter that was published in the journal in a different form. In addition, I am indebted to the Waseda University Tsubouchi Memorial Theater Museum for giving me permission to use the image that appears on the cover of my book.

The anonymous reviewers for Columbia University Press gave me excellent feedback that helped me shape this book into its present form. It was a pleasure working with such a knowledgeable, talented, and dedicated group of people at Columbia University Press, starting with Jennifer Crew and Jonathan Fiedler, who made everything move forward smoothly. Margaret Yamashita put a lot of effort into editing my manuscript, and Irene Pavitt combed through the text with a meticulous eye at the final stage. Milenda Nan Ok Lee created a beautiful book with a great cover, and, last of all, Anne Holmes and Rob Rudnick produced a thorough index for the book.

My families in Japan and in the United States have been incredibly supportive throughout the many years that led to the publication of this book. My grandparents, Ikeda Teiichi and Mieko and the late Shimazaki Yuki, have always remained close to me despite the ocean that separates us. My parents, Shimazaki Fumio and Kiyoko, and my sister, Akiko, have from the start given me unwavering support, without which this book would not have been possible. Thank you for being there whenever I needed you. Helen and David Emmerich have been not only the best parents-in-law I could wish for but skilled editors who made countless suggestions on my work at different stages. Karen Emmerich, a dear friend and sister-in-law, read my manuscript with the most critical eye and made many excellent comments on it. My son, Theo, who was one day old when I heard that Columbia was planning to publish this book, makes everything worthwhile.

Finally, I would not have been able to write this book without the constant support and encouragement of Michael, who is my best friend, a stellar scholar, and a wonderful companion in life. Thank you.

A NOTE TO THE READER

Throughout this study, Japanese personal names appear in their original order of family name first followed by given or artistic name, except in citations of English-language materials. I also adopt the common practice of referring to many Japanese authors, especially premodern ones, by their given name. Tsuruya Nanboku IV, for instance, is abbreviated as Nanboku rather than as Tsuruya.

In order to make the text accessible to a wide readership, I have used the English translations of most Japanese titles and terms in the main text. The only exception to this rule is *Tōkaidō Yotsuya kaidan* (abbreviated as *Yotsuya kaidan*), which is the focus of this study. The original Japanese is given on the first occurrence and is used in endnotes and captions. When they are available, I have tried to use standard or existing English translations. Otherwise, all the translations in this book are my own unless noted otherwise.

In citing Japanese books published in premodern times, I follow the usual method of counting each leaf as one page with two sides, *omote* (front) and *ura* (back). I also indicate the fascicle number of the particular binding of the book that I used. Even when a book is unpaginated, as is the case with many theatrical ephemera and manuscripts, whenever possible, I have indicated the page using the leaf count.

EDO KABUKI IN TRANSITION

INTRODUCTION

YOTSUYA KAIDAN IN 1825: THE FLUID PLAY

At the end of the seventh month of 1825, the famous Nakamura Theater (Nakamura-za) in the heart of Edo (present-day Tokyo) staged the first performance of what is now known as the quintessential kabuki ghost play and, indeed, as one of the most popular works in the entire kabuki repertoire: Tsuruya Nanboku IV's (1755–1829) *Tōkaidō Yotsuya kaidan* (*The Eastern Seaboard Highway Ghost Stories at Yotsuya*). The production was an immediate sensation, and continued to thrill audiences for nearly two months with its gruesome violence, its spectacular special effects, and, above all, the phenomenal acting of Onoe Kikugorō III (1784–1849), the star for whom Nanboku had created the play. Substantially reworked productions of *Yotsuya kaidan* were staged about two dozen times in Edo during the remaining four decades of the early modern period (Tokugawa [Edo] period, 1603–1868), an impressive record for a play that started in the seventh month, which was a relatively unimportant time in the kabuki calendar. Furthermore, in modern times its script has been published more often than that of any other kabuki play. In retrospect, it is tempting to imagine that the fans gathered in the sultry theater on that late summer day in 1825 may have felt a frisson of excitement, sensing that they were watching something special in the history of kabuki theater. If they were astute enough, they may even have realized that they were witnessing not only the birth of a classic but also, as this book suggests, the beginning of the end of kabuki as generations of theatergoers had known it.

Stressing that first performance too much, however, is unwise. To romanticize it as an originary event is to risk falling into the trap of the textual imagination. Privileging it in this way invests it with meaning less as a particular moment in a long and shifting history of kabuki productions than as the first enactment of Nanboku's enduringly popular script. Such an approach subjugates the fluidity and evanescence of the production to a notion of repeatability guaranteed by the text's presumed stability. In fact, in many respects kabuki plays were not bound by their scripts: their content was malleable. So in order to grasp how early modern kabuki functioned as a theatrical form, we need to turn elsewhere, examining the traces it has left in the printed ephemera that defined its off-stage circulation.

If you were living in Edo in 1825, you probably would have seen pictures showing scenes from *Yotsuya kaidan* even before its first performance took place—indeed, even before the script had been written. For instance, kabuki theaters had poster-size advertisements known as "street playbills" (*tsuji banzuke*) printed at the start of each season that contained not only lists of the actors and their roles in upcoming productions but also pictorial representations of anticipated highlights. These large, woodblock-printed sheets were posted in places where people tended to gather and linger, such as bathhouses, barber shops, and street corners. If you had money to spare, you may also have bought your own copy of a playbill from a street vendor passing through your neighborhood. The writer Kyokutei Bakin (1767–1848) describes the irresistible allure these playbills held for him in his youth: "When, as a child, I heard the voice of someone selling playbills, I used to dash out of the house without even putting my sandals on properly."[1] If you were a patron (*hiiki*) of a particular actor or were one of the town officials (*machi yakunin*) who dealt with the theaters, you probably would have received a copy directly from the theater.

Produced cheaply, often in a rush, freshly printed playbills had a particular odor that came from the low-quality ink used to print them—a mixture of fermented persimmon juice and the soot produced when sesame or rapeseed oil is burned. For theater aficionados, this was the smell of the new theatrical season.[2] In a sense, a play began taking shape in the emotions conjured up by that smell and in the expectations the playbill created. In the case of *Yotsuya kaidan*, as you pored over your playbill, you would have learned that the play was going to be staged as part of a dual production with the classic *The Treasury of Loyal Retainers* (*Kanadehon chūshingura*, 1748). Thus you would have had two posters to pore over, because the production was evidently going to be divided between a "first day" (*sho'nichi*), in which the first half of *The Treasury of Loyal Retainers* and *Yotsuya kaidan* would be staged, and a "later day" (*gojitsu*) featuring the ends of the two plays.

Your curiosity piqued by these playbills, you may then have set out to get a more vibrant preview of the play at one of the stores in Edo that sold popular fiction and prints, where full-color depictions of actors in both forthcoming and ongoing productions, designed in the nineteenth century by the artists of the Utagawa school, were printed and sold in runs that could number in the thousands. Samples of these prints were hung facing the street, allowing passersby to take in a dozen or more at a glance. Perhaps your eagerness to see *Yotsuya kaidan* would have been stimulated by a lavishly colored triptych by Utagawa Kuniyasu (1794–1832) (figure I.1). In this unconventional triangular composition, the ghost of Oiwa, played by the handsome Onoe Kikugorō III, hovers over a burning wheel, grabbing her sister Osode with one hand and holding a baby in the other.[3] There is blood on both the baby's neck and Oiwa's mouth, suggesting that the ghost has been gnawing on the baby. The lower-left panel shows the servant Kohei, also played by Kikugorō. On the lower right, you see Oiwa's husband, Iemon, played by the star Ichikawa Danjūrō VII (1791–1859), brandishing his sword as he confronts his dead wife. All four of the adult characters are depicted using a systematized technique of stylized representation known as the "likeness" (*nigao-e*), making them instantly recognizable to an experienced viewer of prints. Generally published, at that time, in advance of the productions they advertised, these pictures offered fans sneak peeks of plays and of favorite actors as they might appear on stage.

Yet if you actually made a trip to the theater, you would almost certainly find that the content of the play diverged considerably from these advertisements. The dynamic image of *Yotsuya kaidan* presented in Kuniyasu's print, for instance, does not correspond to any scene appearing in later digests, actor critiques, or the various hand-copied scripts of the play that have survived. The preproduction print constituted no more than a tentative sketch of the play in the process of becoming. By

FIGURE I.1 Onoe Kikugorō III as Oiwa's ghost (*top*), Iwai Kumesaburō II as Osode (*center*), Onoe Kikugorō III as Kobotoke Kohei (*left*), and Ichikawa Danjūrō VII as Tamiya Iemon (*right*) in Utagawa Kuniyasu's triptych for the production of *Tōkaidō Yotsuya kaidan* at the Nakamura Theater in 1825. (Courtesy of Waseda University, Tsubouchi Memorial Theater Museum, 100-8767, 68, 69)

the same token, the actual production was most likely not divided neatly into two alternating parts, as the two street playbills implied. The Nakamura Theater issued a so-called follow-up street playbill (*oi banzuke*) featuring act 4 of *Yotsuya kaidan* with a start date of the ninth day of the ninth month. A note on this playbill announces that owing to the play's tremendous popularity, "we will be extending the production to the fifteenth and will stage it from the opening to the end of the ghost play's later day and even the night attack [from *The Treasury of Loyal Retainers*]."[4] The follow-up street playbill suggests that it was not until more than a month after the play opened that all five acts of *Yotsuya kaidan* were staged in some form, along with the end of *The Treasury of Loyal Retainers*. No concrete evidence remains to show how *Yotsuya kaidan* evolved over the course of its production or when the theater started introducing acts advertised for the later day. In fact, some parts of the play may never have been staged at all. Akama Ryō, who has compared various early modern scripts and ephemera, suggested that this may have been the case with part of act 4, included in modern editions.[5] Moreover, even if act 4 did make it to the stage, judging from the follow-up playbill, this segment likely appeared for only one week during the first production. The first day of *Yotsuya kaidan*, which ended with Oiwa's horrific death in act 2, attracted the biggest crowds during the play's forty-eight day run. Much of the text in the modern editions we are accustomed to reading from start to finish as a linear narrative was thus not part of the play viewed by those who attended the theater in 1825.

Today, almost two hundred years after *Yotsuya kaidan* was first performed, the reconstructed script of that production has been reified. Having assumed a relatively stable form in typeset editions, some of which were transcribed and annotated by the leading kabuki scholars of successive ages, it has come to stand for the entire history of the play. The script has *become* the play. In creating an "authoritative," composite text based on surviving manuscripts, none of which are in Nanboku's hand, scholars have given us quantitatively much more of the play than theatergoers could have seen in 1825.

In the play as it is known today, Oiwa is poisoned and disfigured by her neighbor and is cruelly betrayed by her husband, Iemon, who agrees to marry the neighbor's granddaughter. Then, after accidentally slitting her own throat on the blade of a sword, she repeatedly returns as a ghost to drive Iemon and the others responsible for her suffering to their deaths. The image of Oiwa's vengeful ghost, in particular, has acquired a place in Japan's cultural memory, having been reimagined any number of times in theatrical productions, films, television specials, anime, photographs, and various other visual media, as well as in novels and other literary works. However, this image of her, and the perspective on her story that it embodies, seems to have figured only briefly in the original production. The contemporary vision of *Yotsuya kaidan* takes as its point of departure an understanding of the plot and of the script as the authentic vessel for the play that simultaneously fetishizes and ignores the original production. By incorporating material from the entire duration of the production, modern scholarly editions have given us a *Yotsuya kaidan* that is much more "complete" than any experience of the play in 1825, but they paradoxically have also given us much less, by insisting on a fixity that is foreign to the play as originally staged. Audiences at the time knew very well that on the kabuki stage, nothing was ever fixed: if a kabuki play outlived its first production, it would inevitably be reworked, transformed into something new. By the same token, every production was inevitably a reworking, a transformation, of earlier material.

The idea that scripts are central to the theater and the reception of plays is deeply rooted in a specifically modern understanding of "performance" that emerged from a historical background in which texts, particularly printed texts, had come overwhelmingly to be regarded as the primary vehicle for transmitting knowledge. The connection between print and performance is evident in many areas. To take an abstract, rather academic, example, even something as seemingly verbally oriented as J. L. Austin's concept of the "performative utterance" assumes the a priori existence of a text, or a script broadly defined, as a condition for any cultural performance.[6] Early modern kabuki, in contrast, drew on and cultivated a markedly different understanding of performance and of the relationships between print and theater, script and play. In 1825, the kabuki play *Yotsuya kaidan* did not have the same ontological status as the play that circulates today, defined as it is through its embodiment in a typeset text. Two centuries ago, *Yotsuya kaidan* was less a fixed, scripted drama than an amorphous, changeable assemblage of kabuki conventions, of shared knowledge about actors and their lineages, and of various other cultural practices implicated in the construction of plays.

Sources indicating what actually took place on stage in Edo's theaters testify to the extreme fluidity of both kabuki plays and productions. This fluidity was first evident in the program of a day's performance. In contrast to current practice, early modern kabuki performances did not run by the clock, and they were timed and organized in ways that had nothing at all to do with the scripts of featured plays. Each performance was an all-day affair that could run for perhaps twelve to fourteen hours, though the precise length depended on the season or, more to the point, on the sun. Theaters opened before dawn and closed roughly at sunset. According to playwright Mimasuya Nisōji (1785–1856), a contemporary of Nanboku's, the drums signaling the start of the program generally sounded between 2:00 and 4:00 in the morning (*ake nanatsu*), and the show got under way before daybreak.[7] The beginning of the program did not, however, coincide with the beginning of the main play. On certain occasions, the first few hours were taken up by the performance of a playhouse's "house play" (*ie kyōgen*) and/or by ceremonial dances and skits (*bandachi* and *waki kyōgen*) performed by apprentice actors. This was followed by an "opening performance" (*jobiraki*) that also bore no relation to the advertised attraction, written by an apprentice playwright and performed by apprentice actors. All these were merely appetizers leading to the delicious entrées.

Fictional works show these early performances as enjoyed largely by visitors from the country who were not well versed in kabuki convention. A typical theater aficionado from Edo probably would have skipped most of the early-morning segments, unless the possibility of discovering new talent was of particular interest.[8] The main attraction—*The Treasury of Loyal Retainers* and *Yotsuya kaidan* in this case, both of which featured the stars Onoe Kikugorō III, Ichikawa Danjūrō VII, and Matsumoto Kōshirō V (1764–1838)—began much later in the day, after the opening segments had concluded and enough people had filled the theater. Even in the midst of the main plays, separate dance scenes or other historical plays could be inserted at intervals if, for instance, the stars felt the need to take a break.

The flexible structure of the day's program was only a small part of what made the theater so much more fluid than it is today. More important was the notion of the play that informed Edo kabuki. One way to think of kabuki theater is as a kind of entertainment similar to a festival. As the frequent discrepancies between preproduction advertisements and what actually appears to have happened on stage suggest, people did not necessarily go to the theater expecting to see the same scenes shown on playbills or actor prints, or even to see a particular play—not, at any rate, if we think of a play as a performance of a specific, settled script. One of the two major productions of the year, the "face-showing production" (*kaomise kyōgen*) of the eleventh month, is revealing in this regard. Its "cast playbill" (*yakuwari banzuke*)—a small booklet crammed with information about a production—typically advertised four different parts and listed the roles that the actors would be playing in each, even though in reality it was exceedingly rare for a theater to stage more than the first two segments.[9] This intentionally exaggerated presentation of the production captures something of the essence of Edo kabuki: the notion that a successful play could just keep going and going and that a big part of the pleasure of kabuki lay in imagining the actors in different situations. People did not attend the theater to witness a reenactment of a settled script; they went to participate in an ongoing event, to enjoy the feeling of being in the space of the theater as that event unfolded.

This was true of individual performances as well as of productions. Each production, even one with the same title as that of an earlier production, was in principle a new play. Each time *Yotsuya kaidan* was staged during the early modern period, it was not merely different—in the way that a fresh interpretation of *Waiting for Godot* is different—but also new. Scenes and effects in a play could be rewritten, subtracted, or added, or the whole plot could be reworked. Indeed, this could happen even during a single production. A popular play could continue for months, and often it would evolve over the course of the season. The second major production in the kabuki calendar, the "spring production" (*hatsuharu kyōgen*), is emblematic in this respect, since there was an expectation that it would continue, though in reality it often did not.[10] The first day of a production could be drastically different from its tenth day, twentieth day, and fortieth day. One legendary spring production of *The Great Hawk, the Splendor of the Soga Brothers* (*Ōtaka nigiwai Soga*), which starred Ichikawa Danjūrō II (1688–1758) and was staged in 1721 at the Morita Theater (Morita-za), continued for a stunning 280 days from the first month to the tenth month, during which time it continued to evolve as new acts were added.[11] Similarly, if a play was unpopular or if its popularity did not last, it could be canceled, modified, or partially replaced by an entirely new play. The number of extant follow-up playbills, which advertised new acts and other additions to productions, gives a sense of how often plays were altered. The logic behind Edo kabuki is perhaps best summarized in the verb that was used to describe the creation of a play. Unlike modern playwrights, who are said to "write" their scripts, playwrights in Edo "built" (*tateru*) a play, with each act serving as a building block. For example, the third act would be described as *mitate-me* (literally, "the third building unit").

Given all this, it is hardly a surprise that celebrated plays such as *The Treasury of Loyal Retainers* and *The Battle of Coxinga* (*Kokusen'ya kassen*, 1715), which have been read in classrooms around the world, were often not staged in their entirety in Edo. In fact, the very notion that a play *has* an "entirety" is a product of a textual imagination foreign to kabuki theater in this period. It is no coincidence that so many canonical history plays—including *The Treasury of Loyal Retainers*, *The Battle of Coxinga*, and *Yoshitsune and the Thousand Cherry Trees* (*Yoshitsune senbonzakura*, 1747)—originally derive from the puppet theater, in which both the creation and the reception of plays was much more textually oriented to begin with, or that the most famous domestic plays date from the nineteenth century and can thus be accessed through some form of insider script; very few scripts from earlier periods have survived. When we approach a kabuki play uncritically as a fixed text that can be consumed in accordance with our familiar relationship to the written word, we lose sight of the intangible, fluid aspect that was essential to the constitution of its meaning. It becomes impossible, for instance, to see the 1825 production of *Yotsuya kaidan* as an event and a potential caught up in the swirl of cultural systems that constituted Edo kabuki. Edo kabuki is part of a lost cultural imaginary; only fragments of its meaning have been gathered and preserved in text. Perhaps, then, we should put this in another, more positive light and say that when kabuki ceased to perform the communal function that I argue it originally had, textualization gave it a second life, thus allowing it to survive—albeit in a radically different form—to this day.

MODALITY AND MEDIALITY: PERFORMANCE AND PRINT

In this book, I am concerned partly with the different modalities in which kabuki has existed and with the location of its meaning. *Yotsuya kaidan* is a rare work that occupies a prominent position not only in the vanished terrain of the past but also in the present, in various forms that the play's modern textualization has made possible: productions, adaptations in film and other visual media, novels, and so on. Once a fleeting, communally constructed event, *Yotsuya kaidan* has now been canonized as a script more heavily scrutinized, edited, and anthologized during the twentieth century than that of any other kabuki play. This ontological duality causes all sorts of trouble for the scholar. One must draw on entirely different methodologies to explore, for example, the meaning of the play in 1825, when it was first staged, and its meaning exactly a century later when it was staged at the Kabuki Theater (Kabuki-za) in Tokyo. One approach is embedded in the characteristics of Edo kabuki as an urban entertainment, while the other must attend to the ways in which the institution of "literature" (*bungaku*) transformed kabuki in the modern period. One approach requires breaking away from the seemingly transparent access that written texts provide and rediscovering Edo kabuki as a cultural practice, while the other takes as its point of departure the creation of a textual mode of access. Viewed from another vantage point, however, the same duality that renders a diachronic consideration of *Yotsuya kaidan* so difficult also makes the play an ideal subject for exploring both the nature and the history of Edo kabuki itself, as well as the process by which Edo kabuki was reinvented in the twentieth century as a "traditional performing art" (*dentō geinō*). In order to understand the changing cultural and social roles that kabuki has assumed over the centuries, and specifically to understand *Yotsuya kaidan* in two radically different historical contexts, I pay careful attention throughout this book to both the modality of performance and the mediality of the play's reception, in forms ranging from woodblock-printed theatrical ephemera to the modern typeset script.

How do different medialities affect our reception of a cultural form? In *Publishing Drama in Early Modern Europe*, Roger Chartier invokes Florence Dupont's opposition of text as "monument" and text as "event"—which she used to mark the insufficiency of traditional visions of literature in treating the texts of antiquity—to think about plays in print and plays in performance.[12] The notion of the "monument" is rooted in a vision of the work as a fixed, stable text that a reader would experience alone and in silence. Such an understanding tends to privilege a static conception of an original, as opposed to the dynamism of the "event" constituted by a performance. As a product of both the institution of literature and the recasting of manuscripts into type via modern printing technologies, the kabuki scripts to which readers have access today lend themselves to a "monumental" reading, predicated as they are on the erasure of the fluidity of Edo kabuki. Consequently, in order to better understand the form as it was practiced in Edo, we must find a means to break away from the illusion of fixity promoted by the "monument" of the published script. One way of doing this, which is central to this book, is to learn from the mediality of theatrical ephemera and other printed objects that allow us to reflect on the nature of Edo kabuki as a process.

In the European context, the development of print and the circulation of printed scripts had a significant impact on the reception of plays and the understanding of theater. Particularly in Shakespeare studies, scholars such as David Kastan, in *Shakespeare and the Book*, and W. B. Worthen, in *Shakespeare and the Authority of Performance*, show how books contributed to the construction of the playwright as an author and how writing and printed scripts came to affect the meaning generated through performance. Early modern Japan witnessed an extraordinary expansion of the commercial publication of printed books and art. Just as they were in Europe, printed objects were an integral part of the culture of the theater. The nature of the relationship between print and the theater in Japan diverged enormously from that in Europe, however, especially in the case of kabuki.

In order to understand this, we must first grasp certain features of the role that print played in early modern Japan vis-à-vis its role in Europe. In the study of early modern Europe, Johannes Gutenberg's invention of movable type has received much attention as the occasion for a profound, if gradual, social transformation. In studies ranging from Marshall McLuhan's *The Gutenberg Galaxy: The Making of Typographic Man* to Elizabeth Eisenstein's *The Printing Revolution in Early Modern Europe* and Walter Ong's *Orality and Literacy: The Technologizing of the World*, print has been positioned as a radical agent of cognitive and social change. At the same time, careful investigations into the survival of manuscript and scribal culture, and the interaction of this culture with the culture of print, have complicated our view of this history, allowing us a more nuanced understanding of what is considered a revolutionary transformation.[13]

The situation in Japan was even more complex than that in Europe because after a brief period in the first half of the seventeenth century during which what are known as "old typeset editions" (*kokatsujiban*) were published, commercial publishers chose woodblock printing over movable type as the superior technology for mass-producing text. As Peter Kornicki discusses in *The Book in Japan*, woodblock printing had been in use in Japan for centuries before the early modern period, but only to produce Chinese and Buddhist books. In contrast, in the early modern period, the technology came to be used to reproduce on a mass scale what were essentially facsimile copies of manuscripts in all sorts of genres and on any number of topics.[14] Printing was thus deeply connected with what could be described as a scribal mediality. At the same time, even as printed books emerged as a familiar commodity during the early modern period, manuscripts also circulated on an unprecedented scale.[15] Given all this, and especially given the close affiliation of woodblock printing with scribal culture, we must be cautious when considering the nature of the changes wrought by the "print revolution" in Japan.

Discussions of the technology of print in Japan, including such important achievements as Kornicki's *The Book in Japan* and the more recent *Japan in Print* by Mary Elizabeth Berry, have delved into issues that resonate with the scholarly discourse focused on Europe. These include, for example, the relationship between printed texts and manuscripts, the role of print in both structuring and disseminating knowledge, and the impact of print on the creation of a sense of community. For the most part, these and other works on early modern print and book history in Japan focus primarily on the application of woodblock printing to the production of texts. It seems to me, however, that in early modern Japan, woodblock printing harbored, among its many other possibilities, something that set it fundamentally apart from movable type.

In Japan, woodblock printing was not only a means of mass-producing text. As Kobayashi Tadashi suggested, it was the commercial medium of choice for artists, who preferred it to painting, at least in Edo.[16] Many major Edo artists who produced ukiyo-e prints were also actively involved in book illustration. Early modern print culture in Japan is equally about text and image—about the creation of objects that today would be categorized as belonging to the separate disciplines of art and literature, or as straddling the two realms. Needless to say, the visual uses of woodblock printing have been studied by art historians, but this is an area that should be included in conversations about Japanese print culture and book history as well.[17]

Visual representations of plays in woodblock-printed materials serve as a crucial source in this book. As we saw in Kuniyasu's print for the 1825 production of *Yotsuya kaidan*, which offered the public a preproduction image of the actors who would appear in the play but not of a scene that would actually be part of it, woodblock printing contributed, above all, to the construction of the actor and his celebrity status. Actor prints were not the only medium that helped define actors' stardom by picturing them; almost every publication related to the theater was focused on the actors, particularly on their visual depiction. If the alluring scene in Kuniyasu's triptych inspired one to make the trip to the Nakamura Theater to see *Yotsuya kaidan*, one could purchase a cast playbill for the play at the theater or at one of its affiliated teahouses.[18] The first page featured an eye-catching array of actors' crests, whose precise arrangement in hierarchical order conveys a sense of lavishness (figure I.2). Other items of information included were the names and roles of the actors and the names of the chanters and playwrights. Along with the cast playbill, theaters and teahouses sold "picture-book playbills" (*ehon banzuke*) crammed with small, rough illustrations of the program's highlights that could be consulted during the play and taken

FIGURE I.2 The cast playbill for the production of *Yotsuya kaidan* and *Kanadehon chūshingura* at the Nakamura Theater in 1825 (1 *omote*). (Courtesy of Waseda University, Tsubouchi Memorial Theater Museum, *ro*-24-317)

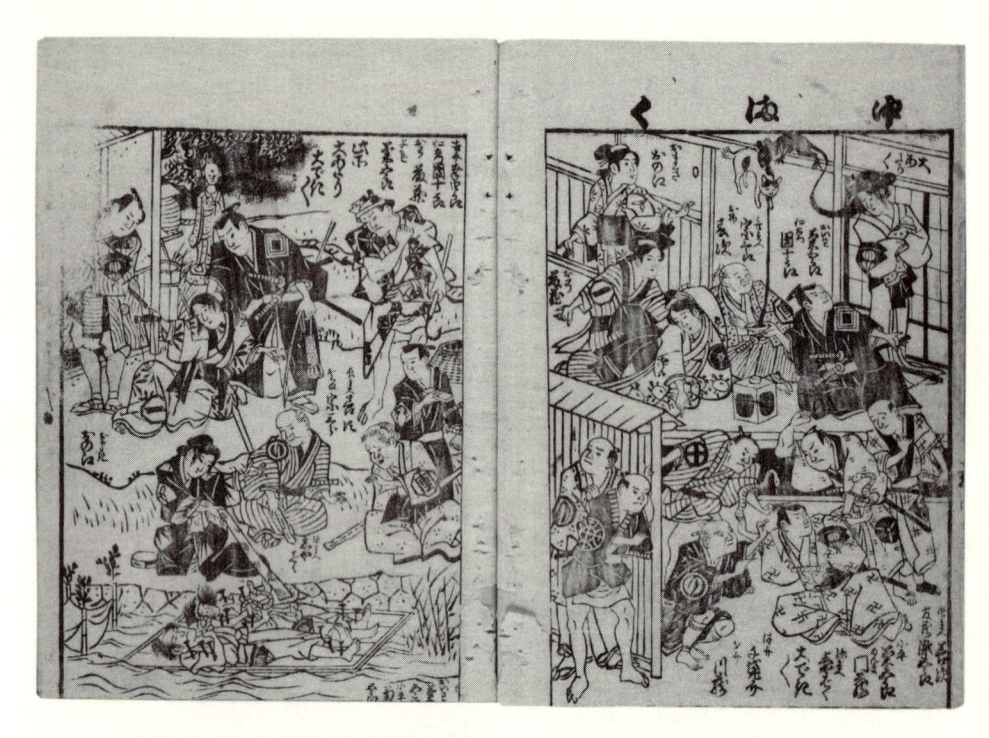

FIGURE I.3 The picture-book playbill for the production of *Yotsuya kaidan* and *Kanadehon chūshingura* at the Nakamura Theater in 1825 (5 *ura*). (Courtesy of Waseda University, Tsubouchi Memorial Theater Museum, *ro*-23-533)

home as souvenirs.[19] A spread from one of two such playbills printed for the original production of *Yotsuya kaidan* depicts scenes from acts 2 and 3: on the upper right, we see Oiwa, whose hair blends seamlessly with the fur of a rat that is biting a cat whose blood trickles down into Iemon's wedding cup. On the lower right, we see Kohei being bullied by Iemon's friends. The bottom of the left-hand page depicts a scene from act 3 in which Oiwa's and Kohei's corpses are floating down a river, each nailed to the opposite side of a door, though here they are depicted on the same side so that both bodies are visible (figure I.3). Picture-book playbills distinguished actors not by using likenesses, as in actor prints, but by marking them with their crests. The crowded pages thus served as a sort of miniature stage that could be imaginatively brought to life in the eye of a knowledgeable viewer.

To a certain extent, publications connected to the theater represent an anomaly in print culture because on the most basic level, they are not complete in themselves. The two-dimensional surface of the printed

INTRODUCTION

14

object gestures toward the bodies of the actors and the space of performance, taking meaning from them even as it helps give them meaning. These publications stand, as it were, in a dialectical relationship with the physical reality of the theater. This is perhaps most obvious in the visual depictions of actors, which literally trained the viewer's eye to look at actors in a certain way. Yet even a genre like the annual "actor critique" (*yakusha hyōbanki*), which includes few, if any, pictures, accomplishes something similar to the actor print or the likeness, participating in a verbal construction of actors' bodies. Perhaps the most enduring form of regular print publication associated with the theater—they were issued throughout the early modern period and even into the Meiji period (1868–1912)—actor critiques were published in the first month of each year. They evaluated the performances of notable actors in the three major cities during the previous year, taking up each actor in sequence according to his position in the hierarchy within each acting category. The format was a fictional conversation among stock audience members—the leader of the pack (*tōdori*), fan (*hīki*), so-called bad-mouther (*waruguchi*), and kabuki connoisseur (*migōsha*)—who discuss the actors' performances in each production, often in a favorable light, situating each actor in his lineage, considering the history of the roles he played, and comparing him with his predecessors.

If after seeing *Yotsuya kaidan* in 1825 one had bought the relevant actor critique, one would have found, flipping to the entry on Kikugorō III, who had played Oiwa and two other roles, that the participants in the discussion lavished praise on him for his performance of the ghost, finding that he did an even better job than his father did. In fact, as I point out in chapter 2, *Yotsuya kaidan* was specifically designed to feature Kikugorō and to evoke his performance lineage in every possible way; the actor critique's attentiveness to this issue merely reinforced this understanding. *Yotsuya kaidan* was less about the plot than it was about the meaning that Kikugorō and other actors created on stage through "twice-behaved behaviors" that drew on the memories of earlier generations. Every printed object associated with the play, including both those that preceded the production and those that followed it, was part of a process that shaped the Edo public's vision of the actors.[20]

Woodblock prints and woodblock-printed books put new images of actors into circulation in connection with almost every production. Discussions of print and theater in Europe, particularly those related to Shakespeare, have centered on the function that books and, in particular, scripts served as textual reconstitutions of plays. These tell us about the dual space that the play came to occupy in the age of print as a product of the stage and as a printed object—the mise-en-scène and its literary identity.[21] Even more importantly, they show us how movable type and discourse about print helped shape the reception of European theater in a manner that placed the playwright at the center. In the case of Edo kabuki, woodblock prints were considerably more important to the reception of the theater than any type of text and were incomparably more important than the script. For a long time, the theater does not seem to have relied on written scripts, and even after they became an important part of producing plays, they were rigorously kept from public view. With the exception of a few brief periods in the reception history of Edo kabuki, hardly any play texts were printed, a situation that differed considerably from that in Kyoto and Osaka. Instead, artists developed the technique of the likeness and produced massive quantities of prints to render immortal the figure of the actor, rather than the playwright. The technology of the likeness actually made it possible to envision the entire history of early modern kabuki through lineages of actors, including even those from the sixteenth century, whose faces were not recorded in prints from their own age. If scripts set in movable type created a reproducible version of Shakespeare's work and helped solidify the identity of the author and his imaginative world, woodblock printing in Japan—which was equally textual and visual—contributed, if anything, to the *suppression* of textual and literary modes of kabuki reception and to the promotion of reception focused instead on actors and plots. Woodblock printing helped construct the authority of the actors and the memories of their lineages so that kabuki plays would not become settled as texts but rather would be carried onward as processes residing in the memories of the actors' culturally defined bodies. This, above all, is what enabled a theatrical culture based in communal memory to continue for centuries.

Scholars in performance studies who deal with Japanese theater often cite the nō theater as an example of a form of nontextual theater centered on the training of the actor and the role of the school.[22] There is certainly an element of truth in this claim. But among the different types of traditional Japanese theater, nō is in fact among the most heavily textual—along with the puppet theater, whose texts were printed and sold for use by amateur performers—in that the circulation of texts for chanting practice (*utaibon*) was an indispensable feature of its reception. Nō texts circulated in both manuscript and printed form throughout the early modern period, which contributed to the establishment of the repertoire. Both the plots of nō plays and phrases and passages from them were thus widely available for incorporation into and adaptation to other performative and literary genres. This contrasted with the reception of Edo kabuki, which went in precisely the opposite direction.

All this changed in the modern period as intellectuals brought about a gradual shift in the location of authority from the actors to the playwright, which is a development I will explore through the specific case of *Yotsuya kaidan* in chapter 5. In 1825, however, *Yotsuya kaidan* was firmly ensconced in the modality and mediality of Edo kabuki. The play was not a fixed text, or even a fixed plot, but a performance based on established theatrical frameworks and actors' lineages—a leaky construction, less a freestanding structure than part of a large, ongoing cultural dialogue. I thus devote much of this book to situating scenes or moments from the 1825 production along a diachronic axis through the interpretation of visual ephemera and other sources, on the one hand, and an exploration of synchronic resonances across other genres, on the other. After working from three different viewpoints to understand what *Yotsuya kaidan* was in 1825, I then examine how the circulation of the play's meaning in the Edo context was transformed during the modern period.

REVISITING KABUKI AS A FIELD OF "SUBJUGATED KNOWLEDGE"

In this book, I am dealing with something like what Michel Foucault calls "subjugated knowledges," which he defines as a "whole set of knowledges that has been disqualified as inadequate to their task or insufficiently elaborated: naïve knowledges, located low down on the hierarchy, beneath the required level of cognition or scientificity."[23] The workings of the cultural system of Edo kabuki have been forgotten precisely because this system eluded inscription, leaving only traces of its existence and its nature in visual ephemera that came, during the modern period, to be overshadowed by the seeming completeness and reliability of the text—of scripts prepared by outstanding scholars using the best scientific methods of textual criticism.[24]

Edo kabuki plays are presented to us today in a form similar, say, to Shakespeare's plays, and it is easy to succumb to the illusion that analyzing the "monuments" of their texts gives us the most accurate knowledge of both the plays themselves and early modern kabuki more broadly. In reality, scripts conceal at least as much as they reveal, and in order to learn more about early modern productions, we must acknowledge those subjugated knowledges and try, as much as possible, to situate plays in the context of a culture of the theater that has been largely forgotten. Teasing out perspectives suggested by the ephemera that were so important to Edo kabuki will allow us to see kabuki in a new light, as occupying a central position in the early modern cultural field. In turn, this will bring early modern culture into more productive communication with the history of modern Japanese cultural production and will reorganize our understanding of how cultural forms from early modern Japan remained relevant, in different ways, during the Meiji and Taishō (1912–1926) periods.

Academic writings on early modern Japan tend to portray kabuki as a vibrant cultural form centered on commoners that was frequently in conflict with the censors, until it eventually became outdated in the Meiji period as successive waves of modernization swept the nation. Historians and scholars of early modern culture have been most active in defining kabuki in this light, as a resistant form, and their analyses have typically been based not on the content of the plays but on the types of sources that constitute dominant knowledge—above all, on government edicts relating to the theater.[25] This understanding does not necessarily accord with the views of kabuki specialists, whose research usually deals more with highly specific aspects of "content"—performance patterns, plots, and the careers of particular actors—and who have generally shied away from trying to define kabuki's larger social meaning during the early modern period.[26]

There is a good reason that kabuki specialists have been reluctant to engage in this kind of work. First, it is extremely difficult to generalize about kabuki in this period because there was enormous regional variation in almost every aspect of the form. Second, for much of the early modern period, very little textual evidence pertaining to the content of plays has survived. This is particularly true of productions in Edo before the 1780s, for which only a dozen or so scripts remain after the brief period in the late seventeenth century when works known as "illustrated prompt books" (*eiri kyōgenbon*) were published.[27] Uncomfortable as it may be to have to piece together arguments about the sociocultural role of kabuki in the absence of a substantial body of evidence, specialist scholarship does, in my view, need to address this issue, and this is one aim of this study.

Seen in isolation, the government bans and regulations that have often been invoked in discussions of kabuki's position in early modern society and culture, for instance, may present a slanted, official view that is disengaged from both the actual practices of kabuki theater and the way the theater was understood and enjoyed by theatergoers and the public at large. In his influential article "Bakufu Versus Kabuki" (1955), historian Donald Shively presents a powerful binary view of kabuki as a lowbrow form of entertainment for commoners that, while deemed unworthy of serious consideration, was nonetheless in constant conflict with the authorities. In Shively's view, kabuki was a theater of the townspeople, as opposed to nō, which was patronized by the shogun, the feudal lords, and the upper echelon of samurai. Thus, "from the start, the government was appalled at the popularity of kabuki and its disruptive influence" and expended a good deal of effort regulating the theater. Shively accounts for the fact that kabuki was allowed to exist at all, and in fact thrived throughout the early modern period, by suggesting that the authorities saw it as "like prostitution, a necessary evil."[28] This type of top–down perspective still dominates views of Edo kabuki as well as interpretations of early modern popular fiction.[29]

A few decades after Shively presented this basic perspective in English, the interpretation of kabuki came to be influenced by a powerful bottom–up perspective pioneered by Japanese scholars. Carefully selecting their examples, these critics offered a view of kabuki as a site for political expression and commoner resistance to authority. This discourse is perhaps best embodied in the notion of the *akusho* (evil place), which came to be used transhistorically and transregionally to analyze the social and cultural roles played by both the kabuki theater and the pleasure quarters. Hirosue Tamotsu's *The Idea of the Evil Place* (*Akubasho no hassō*, 1970) and *Evil Places on the Peripheries* (*Henkai no akusho*, 1973) were particularly influential in promoting this concept. In the wake of his work, the notion of the *akusho* has come to be invoked almost routinely in discussions of early modern kabuki theater.[30]

Looking back, however, it is clear that the concept is rooted in a view that positions culture in opposition to authority and thus seems to reflect the concerns of the late 1960s and the 1970s more than it does the early modern contexts to which the word *akusho* was actually applied. It is no coincidence that the 1960s and 1970s saw a celebration of nineteenth-century plays from Edo—specifically the bloody, chaotic, sometimes farcical revenge plays by Nanboku—in both films and productions by underground theater troupes. These films and productions and the publication of academic works on Nanboku and the culture of the Bunka (1804–1818) and Bunsei (1818–1830) periods constructed an image of kabuki as a politically subversive form, a kind of early modern counterculture.[31] This is not surprising, of course, as views of kabuki have generally been affected by the manner in which the early modern period as a whole has been conceptualized and narrated in relation to the national culture and history of the modern period.

In her essay "The Invention of Edo" (1998), Carol Gluck examines two crucial moments in the post-Meiji historiography of early modern Japan: in the 1920s and 1930s, the study of the Tokugawa period adopted a commoner-centered view of feudalism as the seed of civil society, while the 1980s witnessed an Edo boom as the city came to be reinterpreted as a decentralized, postmodern cultural space.[32] Both Marxist and postmodern views of Edo regarded early modern culture, including literature and theater, as reflecting the lives of members of the lower strata of society and as expressing the interests and attitudes of the common people—specifically, those interests and attitudes that placed the people at odds with the government. The discourse on *akusho* is a manifestation of this long-standing trend, born of a particular time.

As Moriya Takeshi persuasively demonstrated, the word *akusho* was originally used by members of the commoner class in Kyoto and Osaka to refer exclusively to the pleasure quarters. This usage emerged in the late seventeenth century just as commoners began engaging in the forms of entertainment available in the pleasure quarters, and they used the word to refer to the risks involved.[33] Moriya interprets *akusho* as a Buddhist term similar to *ukiyo*, a word that originally meant "depressing world" but came, during the early modern period, to be invested with a new meaning through the homophonic *ukiyo* (floating world), which evoked the ephemeral delights of the present. Like *ukiyo*, the word *akusho* appeared frequently in literature and popular culture. Examples abound in texts from Kyoto and Osaka dating from the Genroku period (1688–1704), notably in books in the genre conventionally known as *ukiyozōshi* (books of the floating world).[34] In these contexts, the pleasure quarters were imagined as a realm so enticing that it could easily lure a man into losing his head and thus everything else, as the term "*akusho* madness" (*akusho-gurui*) suggests. It is important to note, however, that the word *akusho* makes no appearance in legal documents. Instead, it reflected the perspective not of the government but of the new class of potential customers for the services on offer in the pleasure quarters. *Akusho* was a term that commoners applied to the pleasure quarters for their *own* sake, as a means of inoculating themselves against the catastrophic losses its temptations could occasion.

In using *akusho* to refer to kabuki as well as the pleasure quarters, Hirosue was not inventing a new usage out of whole cloth, however. In the late eighteenth and early nineteenth centuries, the word did come to be used in Edo to refer to both these places—though here, too, it was used by members of the target audience for these entertainments, not by the government.[35] Hirosue's view of Tokugawa culture as a topography characterized by the presence of two marginal "evil spaces" that served as sites of resistance to governmental authority was thus based in a dual redefinition of *akusho*. First, a usage of the term specific to a particular time and place was expanded to include the entire early modern period, and second, the sense of risk that the term carried for those with money to lose in the *akusho* was reinterpreted as an expression of official disapproval of the pleasure quarters and the theater. From the perspective of kabuki studies, these two shifts were important because together they enabled the invention of a new perspective on the entire history of kabuki and the social and cultural role it had played. This new perspective was both transhistorical and transregional in nature and was defined in terms of dominant knowledges, usually government documents.

As part of this reinterpretation, two tropes came to stand as emblems of the entire history of kabuki. The first was the image of the female performers whose imitations of the cross-dressing young men known as *kabuki-mono* (literally, "deviants") in early-seventeenth-century Kyoto had been identified retrospectively with the origin of kabuki theater.[36] The second was the raw depiction of urban lowlifes in the Bunka- and Bunsei-period plays (*kizewa* ["live *sewa*" or "true *sewa*"]) of Nanboku, who specialized in the depiction of gruesome murders, ghosts, and other

INTRODUCTION

incidents and characters at odds with conventional values in early modern Japan. Each of these two periods—the early seventeenth century and the early nineteenth century—has left a relatively rich archive of materials for study, both pictorial and textual. In the case of nineteenth-century Edo, scripts or copies of scripts, literary works relating to the theater, and actor prints have survived in numbers vastly greater than those for any other period of Edo kabuki. The selection of one trope from the beginning and one from the end of the history of kabuki—the first documented mainly by sources from Kamigata, the second by sources from Edo—gives the illusion of continuity and completeness, suggesting that kabuki can be understood as having an essential, transhistorical identity rooted in its attitude of resistance toward authority. Unfortunately, this image of kabuki begins to fall apart when one widens one's purview to include more than just these two tropes. Analyzing the history of the form by collapsing both two different times and the separate histories of two different regions from a perspective supposedly aligned with that of the shogunate gives a somewhat skewed image of kabuki.

Accordingly, I will try to move beyond this now ubiquitous understanding of kabuki by simultaneously broadening and narrowing my focus. On the one hand, I explore the specific "content" of productions and the social environment of kabuki, considering sources and elements as diverse as legal contracts, theater architecture, the annual calendar, and kabuki's incredibly rich interactions with other cultural forms and discourses. On the other hand, I have consciously limited my discussion to kabuki in Edo, since the content and construction of the plays, the relationship of the theater to print culture, the legal structures governing the theaters and the actors, and the production systems all were drastically different in Edo and Kamigata. Contrary to the view that has dominated English-language scholarship since the publication of "Bakufu Versus Kabuki," which held that early modern kabuki served as an outlet for popular resistance to shogunal authority, I argue that Edo kabuki in fact celebrated and drew on paradigms from samurai history and culture, gradually enabling a wider segment of Edo to internalize them both and thus contributing to the production of a new popular culture.

It is no coincidence that plays in the shogunal capital tended to draw on military tales and historical accounts that celebrated the shogunal lineage, especially the Seiwa Genji. Kabuki was a licensed business, and the people who earned their livelihoods from it had to be shrewd enough to comply with government regulations and make sure they continued to enjoy official protection even as they constantly introduced innovations calculated to attract the biggest audiences possible. The focus on plots that showed the shogunal lineage in a good light was presumably part of this balancing act. The result, however, was that Edo's licensed theaters came to play a significant role in the construction of communal knowledge and historical memory that referenced samurai history and culture but was shared by members of other classes as well. Kabuki created a sense of tradition—of the past as part of the present—for a new city that did not, at the start of the early modern period, have anything like the prestigious history and tradition of which Kyoto's residents were so proud.

The argument I am making is not merely about the role of kabuki in Edo. Rather, I am suggesting a different understanding of the manner in which kabuki functioned, proposing that it is best viewed as a cultural dialogue and a process. The modern textualization of kabuki, and its corresponding incorporation into a literary mode of understanding, has created a general image of kabuki as a somewhat obscure art form that lacked depth and thus was overwhelmed and supplanted in the modern period by new forms of theater. This view of early modern kabuki and its modern history has had a rather strange staying power, considering both how dismally attempts to "reform" kabuki have failed and that kabuki continues to draw larger audiences in Japan than any other theatrical form.[37]

In his essay "On the Power to Construct" (Kōseiryoku ni tsuite), collected in *The Origins of Modern Japanese Literature* (*Kindai Nihon bungaku no kigen*, 1980)—a seminal work on modern Japanese literature that is almost required reading for advanced students of Japanese literature in the American academy—Karatani Kōjin tries to account for the seeming lack of depth in premodern literature, especially in early modern works. Using the metaphor of linear perspective in art, he argues that our difficulty in perceiving a sense of depth in premodern art does not indicate the absence of depth but instead the premodern lack of a means of representing depth.[38] Although Karatani presents his argument masterfully, his generalization is perhaps most revealing for what it tells us about how impenetrable early modern cultural forms have come to seem, and how natural and easy it has become for us to reduce them to the status of silent "monuments"—and rather trivial monuments at that. Karatani's argument can be read as marking not so much the premodern lack of a means of representing depth in art as the lack of adequate categories by which to comprehend and engage with such premodern representations. From this perspective, the face of the kabuki actor becomes nothing more than a white, impenetrable surface. Only by subjugating the events and the cultural practices of the past to the hegemony of our categories, and especially our relationship to writing, has modern scholarship managed to maintain a boundary between premodern and modern and to fantasize the belated origin of a modern landscape, interiority, and the notion of transformative modernity.

FEMALE GHOSTS, GENDERED BODIES, AND EARLY MODERN SELFHOOD

This book examines such large issues as the social and cultural position of Edo kabuki and its creation of a shared historical memory; the role that theater can play in the construction of community; the different ways in which print, performance, and text participate in the reception of plays; and the question of how we conceptualize the transition from early modernity to modernity. Yet at the same time, it remains highly focused, addressing these big questions by circling back again and again to a single play, which it approaches from a variety of perspectives. This play is *Yotsuya kaidan*, and I consider both its first production in 1825 and its modern canonization. In my view, Nanboku and the kabuki productions he staged in the first decades of the nineteenth century—of which *Yotsuya kaidan* is the most famous—can be regarded as the best embodiment of the beginning of the end of Edo kabuki in the form it had assumed over the course of two centuries.

Nanboku became a playwright in an age when the theatrical conventions that had stood at the heart of Edo kabuki were beginning to lose their force and when the established historical frameworks known as *sekai* (worlds) that had long been central to the theater no longer played as important a role in the creation of shared historical memory and a shared culture. Nanboku's female ghosts offer us a window into these changes. Premodern Japanese theater often operated in a retrospective mode, summoning ghosts of the past so that they might speak to the present. A play was what happened when actors and spectators entered a communal performance space—be it a theater, a temple, or a riverbank—to share memories of well-known figures and scenes. Performance thus created a liminal space between this world and another. In fact, theaters were always home to spirits and ghosts from the past, as is suggested by the name of the underground structure of the kabuki theater that ran beneath both the main stage and the *hanamichi* (an elevated extension of the stage that passed through the audience, connecting the rear of the theater to the stage). It was called the "abyss" or "hell" (*naraku*).

In the late eighteenth and early nineteenth centuries, Nanboku added a new chapter to the theatrical tradition of representing spirits by concentrating on one type of ghost, of which Oiwa is the paradigmatic example: women whose jealous rage transforms them into a grotesque and frightening form. These women were not interested in reconciling with the past, or even in narrating their experiences; instead, they were consumed with a desire to act on the present. Female ghosts of this sort differed sharply from earlier kabuki representations of the dead and from jealous female demons in nō plays, in the extent to which they were associated with notions of the inherent defilement of the female body, including taboos associated with blood and pregnancy. Indeed, during the decades when Nanboku was active, vengeful female ghosts like Oiwa were ubiquitous in kabuki and in various other forms of cultural production in Edo, including most notably the genres of fiction known as "reading books" (*yomihon*) and "combined booklets" (*gōkan*). Nanboku's female ghosts were, I argue, one symptom of both the profound transformations under way in Edo kabuki and the larger cultural shift taking place at the end of the early modern period. The female ghost is thus a central theme in this study.

Nanboku rose to prominence quite late in his career—when he was already in his sixties and seventies—through his farcical, low-budget productions of horror plays (*kaidan kyōgen*) during the summer months, when theaters were ordinarily closed. Nanboku saw commercial potential in these months, when star actors usually took vacations to avoid the sweltering heat of the theater. He wrote ghost parts for the male-role actors Onoe Matsusuke I (later Onoe Shōroku I, 1744–1815) and Kikugorō III, incorporating stage tricks and devices from sideshows to surprise and frighten the audience. An actor critique that comments on the ghost play *Another Story of the Giant Princess Osakabe* by Shōroku

(*Matazoro Shōroku Osakabe banashi*), staged in the fifth month of 1814 at the Ichimura Theater (Ichimura-za), suggests just how frightening these productions could be, by quoting a child as having said, "I was so terrified I tried to get away, but the first-box seats, the floor, the standing area in back, and the closed-off spaces all were crammed with people. It was awful not being able to escape because of the huge crowd."[39]

The Otowaya guild—the Onoe acting family, to which Onoe Matsusuke I, Kikugorō III, and their successors belonged—developed specific techniques for performing ghost roles while acting in Nanboku's plays. Nakamura Shikaku II (1900–1981), who studied under Onoe Baikō VI (1870–1934), the grandson of Kikugorō III, explained that he had been taught special techniques for ghost roles: ghosts should be played, he said, in an empty, hazy state of mind so as to scare the audience, whereas *obake* (other supernatural creatures) ought to be portrayed with a scary face that nonetheless appeared somewhat comical.[40] The position of the actor's hands, posture, movements, and gait also changed depending on whether he was supposed to be a ghost or some other nonhuman creature. When playing a ghost, for example, the actor had to walk with the soles of his feet skimming the stage to give the impression that he was floating.[41] He also had to use a particular manner of speaking to emphasize the nature of the ghost as a human who had crossed over into the state of death.

Nanboku's and his contemporaries' interest in the defiled female body and the female ghost resonates in some ways with Mikhail Bakhtin's notion of the "grotesque body" and "grotesque realism" in medieval Europe. In *Rabelais and His World*, Bakhtin places great weight on the materiality of the grotesque body, associated with what he calls the "material bodily lower stratum" (eating, drinking, defecation and other forms of excretion, as well as copulation and pregnancy), framing it as the antithesis of the "classical body" of Renaissance Europe, which was regulated by and subject to the mind and intellect.[42] The grotesque body in Bakhtin's reading of Rabelais extends beyond the mere individual: "It is never finished, never completed; it is continually built, creates, and builds and creates another body."[43] This is a metaphor for a collective, social body that has the power to critique and subvert authority and the current order.

There is, however, a critical difference between the functioning of the grotesque body in Bakhtin's analysis and that of the ghost in early modern Japan: the former serves as a sort of gender-neutral collective consciousness, while early modern representations of the grotesque ghost are inseparable from the specific physicality of the female body. In early modern Japan, the female body was distinguished from the male body by its propensity to give rise to ungovernable, uncontrollable emotions. The female body harbored a tendency toward jealousy, toward the nursing of deep and primal grudges that prompted a withdrawal from the community. Whereas Bakhtin discovered a subversive potential in the return of the material body that had been suppressed by the intellect, the female body in early modern Japan was altogether different: preceding and, in fact, controlling the mind, it served as a privileged site for exploring a selfhood that was ordinarily impossible to dissociate from the ethics of class and household (*ie*) but could, under the right conditions, suddenly erupt into view, leading a woman into a nonspace outside the values of her community. At any moment, a woman might suddenly be seized by a fierce amorous or jealous obsession that would manifest itself in a bodily form. In nineteenth-century kabuki, this untamed excess of emotion had a fascination of its own that could easily overwhelm the interest of the framework known as the *sekai*, with its political and social valences, redirecting a play so that it came to focus on chaotic displays of jealousy and desire.

In this sense, my study might be read as an examination of how the trope of the unruly, defiled female body came to be used, because of the special position it occupied in understandings of affect as a property of the body to explore an emerging notion of the "subject." I situate nineteenth-century ideas about the female body in the context of long lineages of stories of monstrous transformations, often borrowing from popular Buddhist discourse that linked the female body to "bad" emotions such as lust, love, and jealousy. At the same time, it is important that the type of female body I consider through the trope of the nineteenth-century vengeful female ghost is, in a certain sense, disembodied. There was a good reason why ghosts, particularly female ghosts, could not be staged in the same style as other "supernatural" creatures or as mere objects of horror. The ghost had a special function: it allowed the exploration of a self in a sort of subjunctive mode because, disembodied, it was no longer subject to the strictures that governed bodies still enmeshed in everyday social networks, in the communities of the living. The ghost, in short, was interesting because it could be freed from the basic set of Confucian relationships (parent and child, lord and retainer, and so on) that were so important to both actual society and the kabuki plays based in conventional *sekai*.[44]

This is clear in the case of the female ghosts Nanboku brought to the stage, of which Oiwa was the prime example. In contrast to the heroes of earlier kabuki plays, these ghosts, almost without exception, were obsessed not with the survival of the basic socioeconomic unit of the household as "a corporate unit comprising ancestors, family members, and descendants," but with a grudge that might be described as private insofar as it was severed from the values of the community that defined the living.[45] In this sense, female ghosts can be viewed as figures for the articulation of an emerging early modern selfhood and, thus, from a larger historical perspective, as an occasion to reevaluate the conventional narrative of the emergence of subjectivity and interiority in Japan as a specifically modern phenomenon. Early modern treatments of the abject female body, and especially of female ghosts, should be seen, I argue, as a precursor to modern explorations of affect. In part, the concept of interiority came into being when private feelings that had been understood in the nineteenth century as the exclusive property of the female body—above all, negative feelings like resentment and jealousy—came to be seen as universal.

In the early nineteenth century, then, Edo kabuki was groping its way toward a dramatically new vision of the world. For most of their history, kabuki theaters had been transforming samurai culture and heritage into a local popular culture accessible to all. Nanboku found new commercial potential in a woman whose private resentments exiled her from the community that the stock male heroes had always struggled to preserve in conventional *sekai* and who was capable of creating intense drama without using grand historical narratives or samurai heritage.

It seems a bit of a stretch, however, to extrapolate from this that Nanboku was implicitly resisting authority or attempting to overturn the existing order, because he did not in fact completely abandon the *sekai* celebrating the shogunal lineage. Rather, I am highlighting the role female ghosts played both in a larger shift that was taking place in the conceptualization of the self and in the changes that took place in Edo kabuki as its audience gradually began losing its sense of the relevance of the samurai past. The concept of the *sekai* is complex and evolved a good deal over time, especially near the end of the nineteenth century as new plot paradigms emerged to replace older ones. Originally, though, the *sekai* were centered largely on the world of the samurai and functioned not just as sets of characters and relationships on which playwrights drew in creating plays but also as a crucial element in the structuring of the Edo kabuki calendar—that is, in the workings of Edo kabuki as a *process*. In this sense, the *sekai* as it had conventionally existed came to an end in the nineteenth century when both the existing *sekai* and the various conventions associated with them were modified or allowed to fall by the wayside. This book thus illuminates the transition of Edo kabuki from a theatrical form that created its present through historical samurai worlds to one represented by the vengeful female ghosts that broke down this communal vision.

EDO KABUKI AND THE CONSTRUCTION OF REGIONAL COMMUNITY

Another theme that figures in this book is the role that Edo kabuki played in the creation of a community in the city it entertained. I am not, however, making the case for the existence of a broad consciousness of Japan as a nation before the modern period. The rise of print has often been associated with the reorganization of societies, the construction of national communities and publics. Benedict Anderson's famous exploration of the nation-state as an imagined community posits a shared language and the wide circulation of texts and information as preconditions for the formation of a nation.[46] Several insightful studies then followed Anderson's lead in considering the impact of print and the circulation of information as a catalyst in the construction of Japan as a community. Susan L. Burns's *Before the Nation*, for instance, focuses on nativist studies (*kokugaku*) and the imagination of Japan as a community before the advent of modernity. Mary Elizabeth Berry's *Japan in Print* ties the emergence of information networks to a prenational consciousness of Japan as a community. Here I complement these perspectives by providing a way of thinking about the production of an ever-changing community that is regional rather than national. Kabuki was always site specific until drastic measures were taken in modern times to unify the different local traditions, so it provides excellent material for thinking about the creation of urban communities. Since I will be considering the case of Edo kabuki, my analyses will pertain most directly to the construction of community in Edo and to one particular element of that process. If the Tokugawa government played a crucial role in shaping the ideological premise and ethic of early modern society, the licensed theaters—driven largely by commercial motives that had very little in common with those of the authorities—contributed to the formation of an appealing popular culture capable of adapting to the needs and tastes of different audiences over time.

Historical developments and transitions do not take place at the same time or at the same pace in all regions or in all areas of cultural production. Theater is arguably more restricted to a given physical space than are many other narrative genres. Whereas books, prints, and other publications featuring depictions of actors circulated well beyond the confines of the cities in which the actors were based, kabuki tended to maintain a strong regional identity throughout the early modern period. Kyoto, Osaka, and Nagoya each had its own style, history, and tradition distinct from those of Edo. Over time, Edo kabuki fandom gradually extended its reach beyond the city as actor prints and books relating to the theater became popular "souvenirs of the East" (*azuma miyage*) and products such as towels and tobacco pouches marked with the crests and patterns associated with, for instance, the quintessential Edo actor Danjūrō found their way into the hands of residents in other areas of the country. But none of this weakened the association of Edo kabuki with the city that gave rise to it. Names such as Ichikawa Danjūrō and Matsumoto Kōshirō were symbolic of Edo, while even names that originated in Kamigata, such as Onoe Kikugorō and Iwai Hanshirō, acquired an Edo identity once they were transplanted to Edo. These actors' ties to the city followed them when they performed in Kyoto and Osaka. There, too, they were always marked as visitors from Edo and were routinely identified as such in actor critiques, playbills, and so on.[47] Even an actor like Danjūrō VII, who often traveled and spent many years in exile acting in theaters in Osaka, Kyoto, Nagoya, and even Nagasaki and Hakata, never lost his identity as an Edo actor. Nor could he, because that identity was part of his name.[48]

In short, even after woodblock printing permeated the country and information began circulating at an unprecedented pace, Edo kabuki continued as a theatrical form to be oriented toward its local community. The theaters created a space in which Edo could be linked to its "past"; they invented annual customs capable of serving as secular rituals, taking the place of the religious rituals that had shaped people's experience of the calendar in the medieval era.[49] Kabuki owed its ability to create a sense of community not only to the content of the plays and the theatrical calendar but also to the actors, whose lineages linked the present to the past, producing another basis for historical reflection specific to Edo. Perhaps we might say that all this happened because that was what the city itself required. Just as temples had to be built in Edo in accordance with the precedents set by the imperial capital of Kyoto, so too the residents of the new shogunal capital needed to produce a history and traditions of their own that could function on the most ordinary, everyday level as the city developed from a barren marshland into what was probably the largest metropolis in the world.

Kabuki retained its regional specificity in small theaters even during the Meiji period, when new Western-style theaters began participating in the construction of a new kind of theater that carried very different meanings. Eventually, though, kabuki did come to be mobilized in the creation of a national, rather than a regional, identity. When intellectuals began trying to find something in Japan that could stand as the Japanese national theatrical form, which they perceived as necessary and lacking, they selected the Edo style of kabuki as the best option. In order for Edo kabuki to be enjoyed by people from different parts of Japan, and even other countries that did not share the memories the form had generated and relied on in the early modern period, these intellectuals had to suppress the fluidity of its production style, in which old plays spawned new plays through a particular vision of history and regional tradition. In order to be universally embraced, Edo kabuki had to be tamed, to be funneled through the institution of literature, given the stability of a textual tradition. That is the point at which this study concludes.

THE STRUCTURE OF THIS BOOK

The first chapter, "Presenting the Past: Edo Kabuki and the Creation of Community," provides the backdrop against which the rest of this book is staged, by offering a new interpretation of kabuki's social and cultural position in the city of Edo. In this chapter, I conceptually reposition kabuki theater in Edo as both a performative practice and a virtual cultural space, showing how its constant representation of historical material, often related to samurai lineages, produced a new popular culture relevant across class divisions. Far from being an entertainment barely tolerated by disapproving officials, kabuki was actually privileged over other types of performance. The three great kabuki theaters were licensed and given land in a central location in the city, where they remained until they were relocated, near the end of the early modern period. I devote particular attention to the basic mechanism by which kabuki plays were produced, in which contemporary settings and characters were layered over fixed historical worlds often derived from medieval military chronicles.

The remaining chapters examine Tsuruya Nanboku's *Yotsuya kaidan*. For most of its history, *Yotsuya kaidan* was a fluid work transmitted not as a single, authentic, fixed text but through kabuki performances, popular fiction, actor prints and other theatrical ephemera, and the rare hand-copied script. As with any kabuki play from Edo, it took shape through a complex web of lineages and the reworking of earlier materials. Thus, rather than consider the first production in 1825 as a stable point of origin, in chapters 2, 3, and 4, I situate scenes and images from various productions of the play both synchronically and diachronically in larger contexts in order to interpret their meanings. I show how *Yotsuya kaidan*, and particularly the figure of the female ghost, drew on various histories. These include earlier kabuki productions and types of performance as well as religious, medical, and ideological discourses and practices stretching back into the seventeenth century and sometimes even earlier. At the same time, I consider the ways in which Nanboku mobilized the trope of the female ghost in the 1825 production as part of a broader effort to lead Edo kabuki in a new direction, now that it was no longer so necessary for it to perform its earlier social and cultural roles.

Chapter 2, "Overturning the World: *The Treasury of Loyal Retainers* and *Yotsuya kaidan*," initiates my exploration of the changing landscape of Edo kabuki in the early nineteenth century that will be the main concern of the central three chapters by analyzing the first production of *Yotsuya kaidan* in 1825 in a double bill with the acclaimed vendetta play *The Treasury of Loyal Retainers*, first staged in 1748. *The Treasury of Loyal Retainers*, which had long been famous in both Kamigata and Edo, explores the tension created by the pursuit of loyalty no matter what sacrifices it requires. *Yotsuya kaidan* stands in many ways as the antithesis of *The Treasury of Loyal Retainers*, both paralleling and disturbing the meanings of the public male vendetta through its mobilization of the trope of the female ghost. Tracing the reception of *The Treasury of Loyal Retainers* through ukiyo-e prints, illustrated booklets, and other ephemera, I show that the play was subject to constant reinterpretation on the kabuki stage during the seventy-seven years since it was first staged and that when Nanboku paired it with *Yotsuya kaidan* in 1825, he was drawing on changes that had occurred in earlier productions to displace its interest in a collective consciousness and shared mission. That is, he was trying to define an early modern subject that was to some extent removed from the dominance of the social unit of the household.

Chapter 3, "Shades of Jealousy: The Body of the Female Ghost," delves more deeply into the meaning of the trope of female ghost, especially vengeful female ghosts like Oiwa, in nineteenth-century kabuki. I begin by considering the gendering of ghosts in Japan as feminine through a long process of discursive framing rooted in Buddhist discourse about the female body. I then show how, near the end of the early modern period, the female ghost came to serve, in kabuki and other forms of popular culture, as a site for the exploration of private emotion, and thus for the creation of drama that moved beyond the conventional worldview based on the military *sekai*. I also address the significance of the male-role actor in establishing new possibilities for depicting the female body as grotesque and defiled rather than as alluring, as was the case with female-role actors' portrayal of women. By reorienting the gender of the *acted* ghost, I argue, and working with various new role types such as the *iroaku* (erotic rogue) and the *akuba* (chivalrous bad woman), Nanboku was able to displace the conventional male hero, an embodiment of military power who had stood at the heart of Edo kabuki, and thus to reimagine the theater for a new age.

Chapter 4, "The End of the World: Figures of the *Ubume* and the Breakdown of Theater Tradition," extends my earlier discussion of the female body and the revamping of kabuki as a cultural institution through another lens: the uses of female ghosts tied to childbirth in *Yotsuya kaidan*. The chapter opens with an analysis of a scene in the first production of *Yotsuya kaidan* in which Nanboku staged Oiwa as an *ubume*—the ghost of a woman who died during pregnancy or childbirth—who appears holding her baby and trying to revive it. After outlining the long, complex history of the *ubume* as a visual motif rooted in religious belief and medical discourse relating to the female body, I argue that *ubume* allowed female characters to assume for the first time a central role in conventional household-struggle and revenge plays by saving the heir to a household on the verge of collapse. I then show how, in *Yotsuya kaidan*'s first production, Nanboku defied the expectations established by earlier *ubume* characters by having the ghost of Oiwa destroy her husband's line, murdering her own son in a highly symbolic act. This is a crucial moment in the playwright's dismantling of the structure of the *sekai* and thus in his bid to make theater new again in the Edo context.

The final chapter, "Another History: *Yotsuya kaidan* on Stage and Page," takes the reader into the 1920s, decades after Edo became Tokyo and after later playwrights like Kawatake Mokuami (1816–1893) completely dispensed with conventional Edo-style playwriting. I show that in the 1920s, *Yotsuya kaidan* and Nanboku were given a second life, drastically different in significance from what had come before, through the construction of a new image of the author and his oeuvre as part of a nostalgic attempt to recover Edo and its past in the aftermath of the Great Kantō Earthquake. The most significant changes that the advent of modernity made to kabuki were not, I argue, those that occurred early in the Meiji period (such as the *katsureki* [living history] movement) but those prompted by the perceived need to preserve a memory of Edo kabuki as a historical artifact—above all, through the preparation of typeset editions of scripts. If Nanboku's mobilization of the female ghost to dismantle the conventional structure of the *sekai* brought about the first major rupture in theater history in which *Yotsuya kaidan* played a central role, this chapter explores the second: the construction of a new interpretive apparatus that detached kabuki from the historical perspective of the *sekai* and its Edo-specific social functions, both of which I discuss in chapter 1. Ironically, the modern rediscovery of kabuki, and particularly Nanboku's plays, clearly parallels the historical function of kabuki in Edo, creating a sense of shared history accessible to the city's population regardless of class, only here the notion of history is explicitly national rather than local and functions less through direct participation than through a discourse of inheritance.

The modern theater and literary critic, writer, and playwright Tsubouchi Shōyō (1859–1935) invoked the metaphor of the chimera—a beast in Greek mythology that was part lion, part goat, and part serpent—to distinguish, with a certain hint of pride, kabuki as an art form that was uniquely Japanese, unlike many other forms of cultural production.[50] Although he never says this explicitly, he was perhaps partly thinking of kabuki's evocation of a vast web of lineages and memories and its endless ability to proliferate. Kabuki flourished in both Edo and Kamigata, he writes, "growing in a messy sprawl over the course of three hundred years of change, developing from its beginnings as a wild, teeming art whose appearance recalled a clump of grass in the rainy season . . . into a great institution of entertainment suited to urban tastes."[51] The flames and dark smoke the chimera breathes blind the eyes, he continues, making it almost impossible for anyone to grasp its true form, even as one tries, in the modern fashion, to reform it. For a modern intellectual like Shōyō, who crossed the Tokugawa–Meiji divide and was able to witness and participate in kabuki's transformation, kabuki was a chimera that had to be tamed. This book is not an attempt to tame kabuki. Instead, I try to come to grips with its glorious monstrosity, to see it not as one thing with a stable identity but as a complex and shifting fusion of many different elements, whose form and meaning varied from city to city and over time.

PART I

The Birth of Edo Kabuki

[1]

PRESENTING THE PAST

Edo Kabuki and the Creation of Community

If one had to name the kabuki character who best represents the city of Edo, the title would probably go to a gallant, good-looking townsman named Sukeroku. Dashing, popular, and extremely bold, Sukeroku habitually tosses off lines like "Write my name three times on your palm and lick it! You'll never be dumped by a courtesan."[1] In one particularly famous scene that was incorporated into any number of plays throughout the early modern period, the commoner hero makes an ostentatious display of scorn for his rival, an important samurai named Ikyū, by offering to share a pipe lit by Agemaki—Sukeroku's lover, a courtesan of the highest rank in the Yoshiwara pleasure quarters—and then placing the pipe's stem between his toes and proffering it to Ikyū with his foot. To this day, Sukeroku's charisma and bravado are held up as embodying the ideal of the Edo townsman, an association made explicit in the title of one of the many plays featuring Sukeroku that is still performed: *Sukeroku: The Flower of Edo* (*Sukeroku yukari no Edozakura*).

Given Sukeroku's canonical status in Edo kabuki and his reputation as an embodiment of the Edo spirit, it might come as a surprise to learn that he first became familiar as a stage character in Kyoto in a number of plays based on the double suicide of a young man named Yorozuya Sukeroku and his lover Agemaki, a courtesan at an establishment in the Shimabara pleasure quarters.[2] Kabuki theaters in Edo transplanted Sukeroku to their own city, giving him a complete makeover not only as a "son of Edo" but also, and even more importantly, through the provision of what Barbara Thornbury called a "double identity" as a tough samurai in disguise, an addition necessitated by the Edo convention of basing even contemporary plays on historical frameworks known as *sekai* (worlds).[3] When Sukeroku first appeared on the Edo stage in a 1713 production called *House of Flowers: Aigo's Cherry Blossom* (*Hanayakata Aigo no sakura*), Ichikawa Danjūrō II gave him a secret identity as Daidōji Tabatanosuke, a character in the *Aigo no Waka sekai*, which centered around the tragic fate of a character who ultimately commits suicide. Three years later, in 1716, Danjūrō II once again starred as Sukeroku in a play called *Ceremonial Gentle Soga* (*Shikirei yawaragi Soga*), which for the first time situated him in the well-known tale of the Soga brothers' revenge. Sukeroku, handsomely decked out in an all-black kimono, was presented as the commoner identity of Soga Gorō. Ultimately derived from the fourteenth-century military chronicle *The Tale of the Soga Brothers* (*Soga monogatari*), plots in the Soga *sekai* follow two brothers—Soga Gorō and Soga Jūrō—who in 1193 broke into the camp of a chief adviser to Shogun Minamoto no Yoritomo to avenge their father's death.[4] After Danjūrō II's successful performance in *Ceremonial Gentle Soga*, Soga Gorō became Sukeroku's staple secret identity, an association that has endured until the present. Although this Edo-style Sukeroku frequented the Yoshiwara pleasure quarters, his indulgences there were merely a cover for the vendetta he was plotting as Soga Gorō.

The presentation of a contemporary Sukeroku/Soga Gorō in *Ceremonial Gentle Soga* was a mélange of past and present. It has become a commonplace that kabuki, and early modern cultural production in general, routinely disguised the present as the past as a means of evading censorship, making it possible to engage with current events despite governmental prohibitions against doing so. In fact, for reasons this chapter will explore, it is more accurate to say that kabuki brought the past into the present. *Ceremonial Gentle Soga*, for example, brought the Kamakura-period (1185–1333) samurai Soga Gorō back to life in the familiar context of Edo, effortlessly bridging a gap of centuries when he strode onto the stage dressed as a fashionable townsman. The same effect was repeated in *The Black Hand Gang and the Fight in the Pleasure Quarters* (*Kurotegumi kuruwa no tatehiki*), *Sukeroku: The Flower of Edo*, and countless other Sukeroku plays. In each instance, the famous figure of Soga Gorō was translated into the present. Despite the theater's reliance on historical worlds or frameworks, these plays were not focused on staging the "past" per se; Edo kabuki neither promoted nor invoked the sense of objective distance necessary to constitute the past as "history." Instead, the theater used the past to suit present needs as a means of constructing the present.

Unlike narrations of the past inflected by modern notions of history, early modern kabuki was free from the need to be faithful to documents, period dress, or time lines. Productions reinvented figures of the past without regard to linear notions of antecedence or "post-cedence." In a book of conversations with Bruno Latour, philosopher Michel Serres presents a view of time as a nonlinear phenomenon, a collection of moments that eddy and swirl in all directions: "time does not flow; it percolates."[5] He imagines drawing a circle on a handkerchief and then crumpling it up so that "two distant points [on the circle] are suddenly close, even superimposed."[6] Time, he says, is like the crumpled handkerchief. As an important element in the cultural landscape of Edo, kabuki was consciously engaged in producing precisely this sort of time—the creation of a cultural space in which the past, particularly the samurai past, could be infused into the present, instilling in audience members from all levels of society an awareness of that past as something that remained implicated in the here and now and in which they themselves in turn were implicated. To attend a kabuki performance and see characters and events of the past brought to life on stage was to take part in the percolation of time.

Edo kabuki's incessant invocation of the past was not just a response to government prohibitions, a mere attempt—and an extremely blatant one at that—to get around the rules. Instead, the theater actively created productions in which the past figured as a time coeval with the present. The act of literally *present-ing* figures and events of earlier ages was, indeed, central to the form. The particular content of the past that Edo kabuki presented to its audiences was largely derived from medieval military tales that had circulated both in textual form and through oral performances on city streets and private stages, and especially from historical material that the Tokugawa shogunate had used in constructing its own lineages.

Kabuki drew on these stories, and on images of samurai culture more broadly, to produce a new popular culture and new tastes that would be accessible to a wide swath of Edo's population. Not only was Sukeroku, "the flower of Edo," the contemporary alter ego of Soga Gorō, but his identity as a contemporary townsman was figured through associations with the ruling class. His characteristic all-black kimono (*kurohabutae*) was an unprecedented choice for a costume that drew on the everyday attire of the Tokugawa shogun and his daimyo. The extent to which kabuki succeeded in broadening the appeal of elite culture, instilling in ordinary Edoites a desire to see themselves in connection to it, is evident in the black kimono's spread from the stage to the wardrobes of prosperous commoners, who began dressing in black on their visits to the pleasure quarters.[7] This fostering of social cohesion through a sense of shared history, a shared knowledge of elite culture and plot patterns—and, of course, of actors and acting lineages—was necessary in Edo, a relatively young city that attracted newcomers from different backgrounds from all across the land and that was home to enormous numbers of samurai lords and their attendants. Edo kabuki helped bring these people together, producing a sense of community.

Edo kabuki's class-crossing crumpling of the handkerchief, its merging of samurai plots from the past with the commoner present, transformed the theater into a "chronotope"—a site where, to quote Mikhail Bakhtin's definition of the neologism, "time . . . thickens, takes on flesh, becomes artistically visible; likewise, space becomes charged and responsive to the movements of time, plot and history."[8] This chapter considers the question of what Edo kabuki was for most of its history, what position it occupied in the local culture, and what social function it served. I propose a new understanding of the form, showing how it produced a space—both physical, in the theaters themselves, and discursive—in which past and present fused and elements of samurai culture were incorporated into popular urban culture. To do this, I first consider the position that kabuki theaters were assigned in the city, by both the public and the government. I then show how deeply implicated in the construction of a unique sense of time and space Edo kabuki was, focusing on three topics: the concept of the *sekai*, the calendar, and the actors. A crucial point I hope to convey in this chapter and throughout this study as a whole is that Edo kabuki is best understood not as a corpus of plays but as an ongoing process by which certain views of the past were constantly mobilized and rewritten, production after production and year after year, in ways that profoundly affected how the inhabitants of Edo viewed themselves in the present.

THE HISTORY OF KABUKI AND
THE SPACE OF THE LICENSED THEATERS

As I noted earlier, it has become almost a cliché that kabuki and other related forms of early modern cultural production habitually disguised depictions of contemporary events, which the law forbade, by setting them in the distant past. This understanding goes hand in hand with the widely accepted notion that kabuki was a subversive form that the authorities frowned on. I think we need to move away from this view and to acquire a more nuanced understanding of the role that kabuki played in Edo. To do this, we must first reconsider the meaning of the government's licensing of kabuki theaters, which has almost always been discussed in terms of censorship and control and, by extension, the theater's relationship to authority and to the broader imagination of Edo as a city.

Theaters were more than just places; they were symbols of Edo and of what people wanted Edo to be. This special aura is well conveyed by one of the earliest pictorial representations of Edo, the lavish *Folding Screens of Famous Places in Edo* (*Edo meishozu byōbu*, artist and date unknown), which offers a vibrant portrait of the city in the early to mid-seventeenth century, including parades, temple performances, bustling commercial districts, the pleasure quarters, and, of course, the theaters (figure 1.1). One of the pair of screens depicts a thriving theater district near the water and accessible by boat, even though the playhouses were actually gathered in the center of the city, far from Edo Bay. Hattori Yukio has cited this image in arguing that the frequent inclusion of water in both visual and narrative representations of the theaters alludes to conventional images of utopias, which were typically reached via a journey across water: the kabuki theaters, too, were portrayed as utopian spaces.[9] At the same time, their proximity to water could also reflect earlier associations of performances with liminal spaces such as riverbanks, temples, and shrines, all of which served as gateways to the other world.[10] Either way, the depictions of Edo's playhouses in *Folding Screens of Famous Places in Edo* can be read as figures of the extraordinary, the non-everyday.

The utopian, nonordinary imagery associated with Edo's kabuki theaters and other spaces of performance in this scroll suggests a resemblance to the public theaters of Elizabethan England. In terms of

FIGURE 1.1 The theater district in Edo in the early seventeenth century (*bottom*), as illustrated in *Edo meishozu byōbu* (detail of one of two sets of eight-panel folding screens). (Courtesy of the Idemitsu Bijutsukan, Tokyo)

real-world urban topography, however, the location of the theaters in Edo and London, and the spatial rhetoric to which they were subject, could not have been more different. Steven Mullaney has discussed the marginality of public theaters in Shakespeare's London—their location in the transitional zone of the suburbs, licensed by the court but banned by the city—and has shown how this position helped frame them as a cultural domain of ideological ambivalence and dislocation from the existing social order.[11] Kabuki theaters, on the contrary, were not only licensed by the shogunal government but also given a place in the very heart of the city, where they remained until the 1840s.[12] Only then were

THE BIRTH OF EDO KABUKI

they banished outside the city limits, to Asakusa. This attitude toward the theaters stands in stark contrast to the authorities' treatment of the Yoshiwara pleasure quarters, which were relocated to Asakusa in 1657 after a calamitous fire essentially burned down all of Edo. Tellingly, while some expected that the kabuki theaters would be forced to move after they were destroyed by another fire in 1682, they were not.[13] Clearly, the government thought it was worth keeping the kabuki theaters where they were. Indeed, in the seventeenth century, kabuki enjoyed the patronage of the very highest ranks of government. Just a few years before the earlier fire, during the first four months of 1651, the third shogun, Tokugawa Iemitsu, and his son Ietsuna invited Nakamura Kanzaburō's troupe to Edo Castle no fewer than six times and rewarded the actors handsomely.[14]

My analysis of the cultural space kabuki occupied in Edo will be limited to the period beginning with kabuki's development into something like the form we know today—that is, after the emergence of what is known as "Genroku kabuki," a loosely defined efflorescence that generally includes the Genroku period (1688–1704) and the three periods before and after it: Jōkyō (1684–1688), Hōei (1704–1711), and Shōtoku (1711–1716).

In standard narratives, the origin of kabuki is traced to dances that a woman named Okuni is said to have performed on the dry riverbed of the Kamo River in Kyoto at the dawn of the early modern period. According to this story, Okuni's dances paved the way for other female performers and *yūjo* (courtesan) kabuki. Then, after the government banned female performers in an effort to cut down on prostitution, kabuki came to be performed by young men known as *wakashu*, who had not yet cut their bangs. Finally, after these young male performers were banned in their turn, troupes of older men (*yarō*) began staging productions, prompting a shift from erotically inflected dancing to narrative theater. This understanding of the linear development of early kabuki was essentially invented in the absence of sufficient documentation, especially in the case of *wakashu* and *yarō* kabuki; blank periods had to be filled in to produce a tidy story of progress and continuity. In any event, the earlier forms of kabuki were different enough from what followed that it makes sense to treat them as distinct. The essential characteristics that continued to define Edo kabuki throughout most of the early modern period began to coalesce during the Genroku period.

This was when the licensed kabuki theaters acquired a stable position in the Tokugawa government's urban planning, when the laws governing the theater were first established, when the system of acting lineages came into being, and when kabuki began to operate according to its own calendar.

It was also during the age of Genroku kabuki that the theaters in Edo and Kamigata gradually began catering to a broader segment of the public and pioneered the kind of theatrical experience that audiences in later periods would know and enjoy as kabuki. That is, kabuki progressed from being a mere prelude to prostitution or a series of simple, stand-alone skits centered on acrobatics and dancing to being an all-male form centered on narrative productions. These decades witnessed the creation of "multiact plays" (*tsuzuki kyōgen*), in which four or five acts united by an overarching plot and reliance on a certain *sekai* were staged under a single title, as well as the establishment of role types (*yakugara*) and the emergence of figures akin to playwrights.[15] The cumulative effect of all these changes was that writers, and presumably the theatergoing public at large, experienced Genroku kabuki as something altogether different and new rather than as just another stage in the theater's development.

Writing in the late seventeenth century, nearly a hundred years after the dances Okuni is said to have performed, the author of the actor critique *Adult Male Actor's Sumo* (*Yarō sekisumō*, 1693) commented in an explanation of the dominance of *yatsushi-goto* (acting that involves disguised identities) that, "of course, kabuki began fairly recently."[16] For him, kabuki referred specifically to *yatsushi-goto*, not to the various types of acting that preceded it. The author of *All About the Actors* (*Yakusha zensho*, 1774) also understood kabuki in a limited sense, distinguishing pre-Genroku kabuki, with its various types of troupes—some comprising both male and female dancers, some featuring young male acrobats, and some composed entirely of women and serving as hubs of prostitution—from the licensed productions of his day. Indeed, he writes that "the term kabuki [in its original sense] ceased to be used at this point" in the years leading up to the Genroku period. The author is perhaps referring here to a shift that was taking place in the orthography of the word *kabuki* as the character 妓, which had once been used for the *ki*, was gradually replaced by the homophonous 伎. Switching out the "woman" radical 女 for the gender-neutral "person" radical 亻 divested the word *kabuki* of its original meaning: "dances of courtesans and female entertainers." [17] *Homecoming Stories of Edo* (*Kokyōgaeri no Edobanashi*, 1687) also notes that the term "kabuki" died out after the government banned young male performers, explaining that it was replaced by "Shimabara" plays featuring affairs with courtesans played by male actors and eventually by performances that were "entirely dramatic" (*kyōgenzukushi*)—which is to say, theater centered on multiact plays rather than on dance.[18] Such statements suggest a history of early kabuki best conceived of as a series of ruptures rather than as a smooth, linear process of development.

Once the government had designated the licensed theaters, they were supervised as the only permissible venues for kabuki productions. In 1661, after the authorities banished courtesans from kabuki and then removed the Yoshiwara pleasure quarters from their original central location near the kabuki theaters to a remote area of the city, they restricted kabuki performances to three districts where the four kabuki theaters—the Nakamura, Morita, Ichimura, and Yamamura—were located.[19] These theaters were already competing with one another during the golden age of Genroku kabuki, and the four-theater structure survived until 1714.[20] After the Yamamura Theater closed in that year, the three remaining theaters continued to dominate Edo kabuki until the late eighteenth century, when the debt they had racked up made it difficult to go on producing plays in the same way. Productions in these licensed theaters were known as "major productions" (*ōshibai*), and the theaters were actually required to stage them throughout most of the year. Indeed, so firm was the government's position that "the show must go on" even when circumstances such as fire or excessive debt forced one or more of the licensed theaters to close its doors temporarily that three "subsidiary theaters" (*hikae yagura*) were established: the Miyako, Kiri, and Kawarasaki. Major productions stood in contrast to "temple and shrine productions" (*miyachi shibai*), conventional venues for theatrical productions, and other "small productions" (*koshibai*), permission for which had to be requested before each production. For these venues, permission would be granted for a maximum of one hundred days.[21] "Temple and shrine productions" and "small productions" thus were referred to as "hundred-day productions" (*hyakunichi*

PRESENTING THE PAST

shibai). Especially during the Genroku period, the major theaters often collaborated with temples during religious festivities, taking charge of the theatrical element—yet another indication of the theaters' new importance.[22]

The division between licensed and unlicensed theaters was mirrored by a clear social distinction between their performers. This was particularly true in Edo, where actors in the major theaters were, in principle, forbidden to perform outside the licensed theaters, while actors in the minor theaters were forbidden to perform in them.[23] The licensed theaters and their actors also were overseen by different offices of the government from the unlicensed theaters. Whereas the licensed theaters were directly administered through the Edo commissioner's office (*machi bugyōsho*), most other types of performers were grouped as "commoner street and temple performers" (*gōmune*) and placed under the control of the outcast leader Danzaemon.[24] Furthermore, in addition to the restrictions on the actors, kabuki performances were forbidden outside the major theaters. Temples had to register their productions as "gesture dancing" (*teodori*), indicating that they would not be staging kabuki plays or dances even when they were basing their acting on kabuki, and they were not allowed to use kabuki-style stage devices and costumes. In reality, however, during the late eighteenth and early nineteenth centuries, productions in temples sought ways to offer the public a cheaper alternative to those in the major theaters. At times, they even used rotating stages like those in the major theaters, although records indicate that these productions could be risky, since the individuals responsible were sometimes punished for having staged kabuki plays.

The fact that kabuki theaters and actors were elevated above temple and small productions and the actors who performed in them complicates our understanding of the position of kabuki in Edo society, especially the notion that the government found kabuki a nuisance and tried to repress it, which in turn suggests the need for a more refined sense of the manner in which the government regulated theaters. We might begin by looking more carefully at the theaters' legal status and the regulations governing their employment of actors. Governmental prohibitions in the seventeenth century, such as the banning first of female and then of young male troupes, have been interpreted as crucial steps in the development of *yarō* (adult male) kabuki, and thus in the history of kabuki as a whole. As Moriya Takeshi has noted, however, the regulations and bans that *followed* the rise of *yarō* kabuki have received considerably less attention, even though these later laws are much more important to understanding the legal structures that governed kabuki for most of the early modern period.

Legal developments after the emergence of *yarō* kabuki made it necessary for actors to enter into an annual contract with a single theater, giving rise to what Moriya called the "theater affiliation system" (*zakakae sei*). As part of the same process, theater managers were put in charge of overseeing both actors and productions.[25] Unlike most employment contracts during the early modern period, which began in the third month, kabuki contracts began in the eleventh month.[26] Each actor submitted a written pledge (*tegata*) to the manager of his theater for the next year, and a proof of affiliation was sent to the government office. A compilation of old customs, *Miscellany of Precious Things* (*Sunkin zattetsu*, early nineteenth century), by the author and scholar of "Dutch learning" Morishima Chūryō (1754–1810), includes a transcription of an eighteenth-century contract of affiliation (*yakusha ukejō*) between the actor Ikushima Koheiji and Nakamura Kanzaburō, the manager of the Nakamura Theater:

To Nakamura Kanzaburō,

Written pledge
I will be engaged in service [*hōkō*] as an actor at your theater from the first day of the eleventh month to the end of the tenth month the following year. We agreed on a salary of 13 *ryō*, of which 3 *ryō* and 2 *bu* was paid as an advance; I will receive the remainder, 9 *ryō* and 2 *bu*, at the time of payment, at the same time as the rest of the actors. If circumstances, such as my appearing in plays at other theaters or neglecting my service, should prevent me from fulfilling my duties, I will return my salary, and I will not be permitted to perform in theaters not only in Edo but also in Kyoto and Osaka for many years and must accept this condition without protest. I belong to the Nichiren Buddhist sect. I will remain faithful to these conditions and prohibitions. In the event that this contract is violated in any way, the surety must respond immediately. I will also obey all prohibitions from the government.

Eleventh month, 1703
Ikushima Koheiji, Takasago-chō
Surety Shirozaemon, Ōya Naraya Kihei store, Osaka[27]

This document indicates that actors came under the supervision of the theater managers. It also confirms that actors were obliged to work exclusively for a single theater and were prohibited from acting in any other. This prevented them, at least on paper, from traveling and performing at remote regional playhouses for extra cash.[28] The religious affiliation was listed so that the manager could trace the actor to his registry. By signing a new contract of this sort each year, actors secured a position in a theater and became subject to the legal structures and systems of Edo kabuki.

At the same time, the contract legally obliged the theater to pay its actors. Tensions emerged whenever actors requested more money or managers tried to cut their salaries. While the more or less unknown actor Ikushima Koheiji agreed in his contract to accept a payment of 13 *ryō*—a decent salary but modest in comparison with those of star actors—less than twenty years later, Yoshizawa Ayame and Ichikawa Danjūrō II each signed contracts for 1,000 *ryō*.[29] It is notoriously difficult to convert figures of this sort into modern currency, but this was certainly a very enviable salary. The fact that actors were able to demand so much indicates that the balance of power in the theaters was not as clear-cut as the contract just cited suggests in positioning Koheiji as the "servant" of the theater manager. The crucial point, however, is that the annual contract system divided the kabuki theater into two sides even as it bound those sides together, pitting the manager against the actors, setting the employer against his employees, and, to some extent, aligning the manager with the authorities. The kabuki theater itself thus comprised people with very different interests; it was not a unified institution with a single, uncomplicated relationship to the government. Indeed, when Koheiji swears to "obey all prohibitions from the government," he is still swearing to Nakamura Kanzaburō: here the manager stands as the government's representative.

The contract system itself reflects the position of the theater manager (*zamoto*) as an administrative functionary in Edo, further blurring the distinction between the kabuki theater and those who regulated it. In Edo, each theater manager was simultaneously the owner of a hereditary license to produce plays (*nadai*) and the owner of the theater itself (*shibainushi*), with its government-sanctioned *yagura* (turret). The concentration of both these roles in the theater manger was a unique feature of Edo kabuki; in Kyoto and Osaka, these privileges were often split between different individuals.[30] The supervision of a theater's employees and the responsibility for its productions came to be entrusted to its manager, who had to be in close communication with the city magistrate and would occasionally be called in for consultation on matters relating to the theater. In short, kabuki theaters in Edo were largely regulated from within. With the exception of a series of strict reforms promoted during the Kyōhō (1716–1736), Kansei (1789–1801), and Tenpō (1830–1844) periods, when regulations relating to various types of commerce were issued in an attempt to curb extravagance, theater managers were generally left to run their theaters as they saw fit.

The position of the licensed theaters and their managers was solidified in 1725 when all three theaters—by then, the Yamamura Theater had been stripped of its license—were asked to submit a lineage (*yuisho*) to the city magistrate. These documents retrospectively established the role that the theaters played in Edo. The text that Nakamura Kanzaburō prepared, for instance, included information concerning when and where the theater had been granted its official license, a history of its managers, and a list of rewards it had been given by the authorities and invitations it had received to perform at the shogun's castle and at the court in Kyoto.[31] All this served to emphasize the Nakamura Theater's prestige and gave those associated with the theater an opportunity to reflect on its significance to the city.[32] More broadly, the lineages illustrated the symbolic centrality of the three kabuki theaters, especially in relation to other, less prestigious, performing venues and troupes. As Furuido Hideo has observed, it is no coincidence that after they submitted these lineages, all three theaters began using the phrase *Edo ōshibai* in their playbills, exhibiting a new pride and an awareness of the tradition of "the great productions of Edo."[33]

The complexity of the kabuki theater's relationship to the authorities is evident also from the fact that the government consulted the three theater managers, as the holders of official licenses, with regard to certain decisions. The managers were called in, for example, along with city elders (*machidoshiyori*) and district elders (*machinanushi*), when edicts relating to the theater were under consideration.[34] In 1734, Kiri Ōkura, an actor and the manager of a troupe that claimed its lineage could be traced back to a group of female kabuki performers, asked to be licensed as a full-fledged kabuki theater with a *yagura*, providing the officials with a detailed history of his troupe and its productions. The three managers of the licensed theaters were consulted, and Morita Kan'ya of the Morita Theater submitted their recommendation to Ōoka Echizen:

> Kiri Ōkura writes that they have been performing in a theater the size of twelve *ken*, the same size as ours, and requests a kabuki license. We have heard nothing about this, so we consulted my seventy-year-old father, Kan'ya, of three generations before the present Matakurō, who has been in the theater business for seventy years, as well as another man of seventy years or so. They, however, have never heard of any theater of twelve to thirteen *maguchi* in size aside from my own and those of Yamamura Chōdayū, Ichimura Takenojō, and Nakamura Kanzaburō. . . . I find it difficult to accept because Kiri Ōkura has come asking for permission to produce kabuki citing his lineage [*yuishogaki*] of female kabuki productions. All small sideshows, plays by children, and magic tricks performed at temple and shrine sites and outdoor theaters are given permission to perform for only ten, twenty, fifty, or a hundred days. For this reason, I suggest that Ōkura not be granted permission to stage kabuki, that is, major productions [*kabuki ōshibai*].[35]

The following year, Edo Shichidayū, a manager of temple productions, also requested a kabuki license. This time, Nakamura Kanzaburō wrote to the city magistrate recommending that permission be denied because "temple productions are called 'leaf curtains,' subject to the outcast *gōmune*, and thus are terminated after a hundred days."[36] Again, Kanzaburō was marking the difference in status between kabuki at the licensed theaters and other types of productions. In both cases, the authorities heeded the theater managers' advice. These examples give a sense of the relative prestige that Edo's licensed theaters enjoyed and of the authority that the managers' position within the administrative bureaucracy gave them over matters related to kabuki.

In addition to being granted special privileges not afforded to other performance troupes, the licensed theaters received governmental assistance at critical junctures, such as when their finances had deteriorated to an unsupportable level. In the late eighteenth century, for example, all three licensed theaters accumulated so much debt that they were temporarily obliged to entrust their performance licenses to the subsidiary theaters. In one extreme instance in 1793, all three of the important "face-showing" productions that kicked off the kabuki new year had to be staged by the subsidiary theaters. The following year, the subsidiary theaters' managers submitted a proposal called "Document Requesting a Decision Regarding Regulation of the Three Kabuki Theaters" (Sanshibai kyōgenza torishimari hōgi sadame shōmon), in which they suggested that the government set 500 *ryō* as the upper limit for the top actors' salaries, except in cases when theater revenues exceeded a certain amount. Calling their proposal "Regulation for the Eternal Perpetuation of Kabuki" (Kabuki eizoku no shihō, 1794), they requested that they be allowed to let actors who had contracted with one theater appear in productions at the other two when financial difficulties prevented the first theater from holding its face-showing production.[37] The government responded favorably, setting an upper limit on actors' salaries and loosening the annual contract system to help stabilize the kabuki theaters' finances.[38] This response indicates the degree of the government's commitment to the theaters' preservation, even if it meant completely rewriting the rules that had governed their behavior.

The relationship between the theater managers and the government was complicated. Theater managers were responsible for their actors, so misconduct by an actor could result in the loss of a license. This is what happened to the Yamamura Theater, one of the original four licensed theaters in Edo, in the wake of what is known as the Ejima–Ikushima incident.[39] On the twelfth day of the first month of 1714, two groups of women from the shogun's inner quarters set off on a trip to the Zōjō and Kan'ei Temples on behalf of Gekkōin, the mother of the seventh shogun, Ietsugu. Motojima Chishin's (1697–1734) *Getsudō's Collection of Things Seen and Heard* (Getsudō kenmonshū, 1730s) relates that once the women arrived at the temples, they changed from castle attire into fashionable kimono.[40] They then quickly got their official duties out of the way and headed off to the Yamamura Theater, where an attractive lineup of stars—including Ikushima Shingorō, Ichikawa Danjūrō, and Yoshizawa Ayame—were performing. According to *The Inner Chambers of Edo Castle* (Chiyodajō ōoku, 1892) by Nagashima Imashiro and Ōta Yoshio, a Meiji-period work on customs, secrets, and incidents related to the shogun's inner chambers, the group consisted of 130 men and women, for whom roughly fifty *ken* (a space 295 feet long) of second-floor *sajiki* boxes were reserved and a hundred lunch boxes were ordered. They drank heavily and invited Ikushima Shingorō and other actors to their boxes, causing a commotion. At one point, someone spilled saké on a samurai who was watching the play with his wife in a first-floor box seat, and an attendant had to rush down to apologize.[41]

Disregarding entreaties that they return to the castle, the women proceeded from the theater to the private residence of the theater manager, Yamamura Chōdayū, and departed only in the evening.[42] The government conducted an investigation and discovered that the chief attendant from the shogun's inner quarters, a woman named Ejima, had been involved in a long-term affair with Ikushima Shingorō. A total of fifty-seven women were expelled from the castle, and some of the men were killed. Although Ejima's life was spared, she was banished from Edo; Ikushima, too, was exiled. The discovery that this was not an isolated incident but part of an ongoing affair, plus the resulting decision to issue punishments, had an impact on the entire theater industry, most notably in the revocation of Yamamura Chōdayū's performance license, which meant the end of the Yamamura Theater. The three remaining licensed theaters also were forced to suspended their activities for a few months, and nine temple productions were terminated.[43] Theater managers were responsible for overseeing their troupes and avoiding trouble in return for the protection the government granted to the licensed theaters. The penalties that followed the Ejima–Ikushima incident demonstrate the severity of the punishment that could befall a manager, and the industry as a whole, when a manager failed in his duty to oversee his actors.

The complex mixture of regulation and privilege to which Edo's kabuki theaters were subject was reflected, one might argue, in the physical structures of the playhouses themselves. Government-licensed venues for entertainment—including both the pleasure quarters and the kabuki theaters—bore architectural marks associated with the ruling class, being carefully modeled on daimyo castles and mansions.[44] In the case of the theaters, this is perhaps best suggested by the symbolic *yagura* (watch tower, turret) that crowned the building, which was a feature seen on the residences of prominent samurai. Shikitei Sanba (1776–1822), Katsukawa Shun'ei (1762–1819), and Utagawa Toyokuni I's (1769–1825) guide to kabuki, *The Illustrated Encyclopedia of Theater* (*Shibai kinmō zui*, 1803), contains a picture of the crowded Nakamura Theater, its *yagura* marked with the playhouse's octagonal ginkgo crest (*sumikiri ichō*) (figure 1.2).

The inclusion of a *yagura* in theater architecture was not a Tokugawa innovation, as similar structures had been erected over the stages used in medieval nō performances and temple productions, where they held a

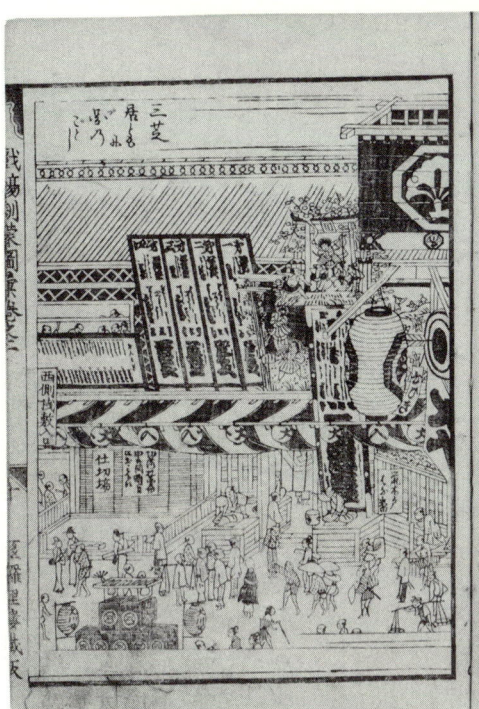

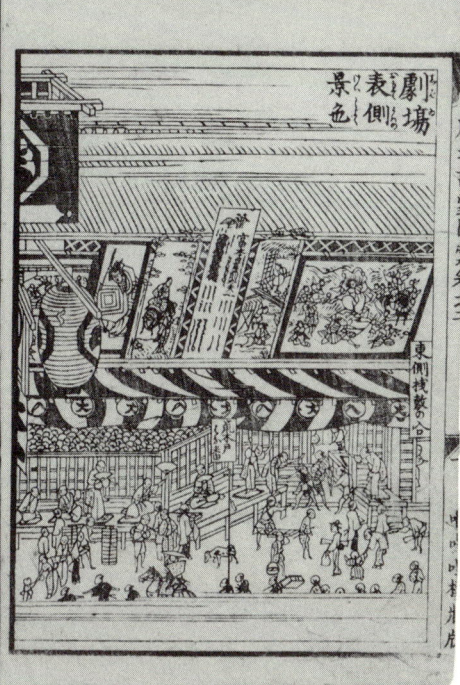

FIGURE 1.2 The outside of the Nakamura Theater, as illustrated in Shikitei Sanba (text), Katsukawa Shun'ei (pictures), and Utagawa Toyokuni I (pictures), *Shibai kinmō zui* (fascicle 2, 10 *ura*–11 *omote*). (Courtesy of the Art Research Center, Ritsumeikan University, Kyoto)

symbolic meaning as seating reserved for the gods. Suwa Haruo observed that in kabuki theaters, "the gods were finally chased out of the *yagura* and shut up in a small backstage altar. The exiled god's old place in the *yagura* came to be occupied instead by the early modern period's new god—the authority of the Tokugawa government, which granted permission to build the theater."[45] The *yagura* was a feature of official kabuki theaters, permitted only to the four and then three that were licensed by the government, and the word *yagura* came to be used synecdochically as a means of referencing this privilege. The managers of licensed theaters thus came to be known as "*yagura* owners" (*yagura nushi*) who paid "*yagura* fees" (*yagura sen*) to the government for their license, and the subsidiary theaters that took over productions when the main theaters had to close their doors were known as "backup *yagura*" (*hikae yagura*). In this way, the licensed theaters were visually associated with the authority of the ruling class. Playhouses were built with *yagura* from very early

PRESENTING THE PAST

on, if not from the very beginning, as their presence on the theaters depicted in *Folding Screens of Famous Places in Edo* suggests. When people entered a kabuki theater, they were stepping into a space that was regulated but at the same time sanctioned by the shogunal administration.

THE SAMURAI ROOTS OF EDO KABUKI

The general understanding of kabuki as a commoners' theater has obscured its deep affinity with the samurai, especially during the seventeenth century when they constituted its primary audience. Given the various ties that bound kabuki as an institution to the Tokugawa government, we should hardly be surprised that the samurai played an important role in the formation of Edo kabuki. Moreover, one of the most prominent characteristics of Edo kabuki, along with other early modern performance genres, was its heavy use of settings and themes derived from recent military history.

Throughout most of the seventeenth century, Edo was characterized by the size of its samurai population. When Tokugawa Ieyasu marched into the area in 1590, it was just a small fishing village, but after his arrival, and especially after he became shogun in 1603 and made Edo his new administrative capital, samurai of all ranks began streaming into the city to fill various bureaucratic posts. In the 1630s and 1640s, the shogunate institutionalized the system of "alternate attendance" (*sankin kōtai*), whereby all daimyo were required to maintain a permanent residence in Edo in addition to the one they had in their home domain, and to move back and forth between the two, leaving their wives and families in Edo. The need for samurai to manage the Edo residences led to a further swelling of the city's samurai population. Commoners began moving to the city to meet the needs of this large group, but even so, until their numbers finally caught up in the 1730s or so, the city was inhabited largely by young men of the samurai class.[46] Some sense of the samurai's prominence can be gleaned from the distribution of land in a Meiji-period survey, which shows that up to 69 percent of Edo was given over to samurai residences, compared with the 15 percent occupied by temples, shrines, and commoners.[47]

The audiences in seventeenth-century paintings of Edo's kabuki theaters invariably include members of diverse classes, from aristocrats and samurai to commoners and monks. This is the case in Hishikawa Moronobu's *Screen Depicting a Kabuki Performance* (*Kabuki-zu byōbu*, 1680s) (figure 1.3),

FIGURE 1.3 (*Above*) The audience watching a play at the Nakamura Theater, as illustrated in Hishikawa Moronobu, *Kabuki-zu byōbu*; (*below*) detail of the audience seats in the left and center panels. (Courtesy of Tokyo National Museum)

in which the socially varied crowd of theatergoers at the Nakamura Theater seems to symbolize the vibrancy of the urban space. Many samurai appear in this picture, including some who are mingling with commoners, hiding their faces with straw hats; others occupy special seating raised above the ground-level areas. Later portrayals of kabuki audiences, in paintings as well as in an entire genre of woodblock prints depicting the theaters, exhibit a similar social hybridity. Of course, there is always the question of how accurately such pictures represent reality. Tellingly, the scene unfolding on the stage in Moronobu's painting is not based on an actual production; instead, the artist seems to have intentionally offered a generic representation of a lavish finale in which all the actors come out on stage and dance at once.[48] Moronobu's crowd, too, could be more metonymic than mimetic. Still, there seems little doubt that kabuki audiences comprised people of all different classes, including a sizable number of samurai.

During the seventeenth century in particular—leading up to the time when Moronobu painted his screen depicting the Nakamura Theater—samurai formed the core of kabuki audiences. Early modern theater did not cater from the outset to a broad range of classes, and especially not to commoners. Indeed, it took quite a long time for performances to become centered on public theaters and for performers to reach the point that they could make a living solely by acting in productions at licensed theaters. Before the licensed theaters grew in importance, Edo offered entertainers a unique market with ample opportunities to perform both in conventional public venues, such as temples, and in private residences. Aristocrats' residences and the imperial court were important venues for kabuki performances in Kyoto, and samurai in Edo continued this conventional, medieval style of theatrical patronage at their own residences well into the middle and even later years of the early modern period. Relatively few materials survive from before the very end of the seventeenth century that show productions on dry riverbeds, at the theaters, or at other venues central to the commoner reception of Edo kabuki. By contrast, a relative abundance of military household (*buke*) records and other such resources give us a glimpse of kabuki performances at daimyo and military houses in Edo.[49] Productions of this type are known as "residential kabuki" (*zashiki shibai*).

In contrast to nō, which served as a more formal, official form of entertainment, kabuki constituted an important type of private entertainment even for upper-ranking samurai, particularly during the first century of the early modern period.[50] Taking place at the houses of samurai and wealthy merchants and even at the residences of daimyo, these productions gave actors a relatively stable income before it became possible for them to make a living from theater revenues in the late seventeenth century.[51] From the 1660s to the 1680s, the names of top actors appear in daimyo house records.[52] Takei Kyōzō has concluded from an inspection of such records that before the 1680s an average of six or seven kabuki and puppet-theater productions were staged each year in many daimyo residences in Edo.[53] Felicitous occasions both public and private called for such performances as part of the celebrations. Accompanied by meals and snacks, the entertainment would continue for at least half a day and sometimes all day long. In peak seasons, arrangements for these performances undoubtedly had to be made well in advance, as indicated by the rather humorous records of a daimyo struggling to book a kabuki troupe.[54]

From the somewhat limited sources available for study, it appears that kabuki and the culture that grew up around it retained their socially diverse nature throughout the early modern period. Beginning in the seventeenth century, audiences at the major theaters came to be divided into two groups. For instance, in his *Famous Sites of Edo* (*Edo meishoki*, 1662), the writer Asai Ryōi (1612–1691) distinguishes between "the ladies and gentlemen in the *sajiki* boxes" (*sajiki ni aru katagata*) and "the herd at the play" (*shibai no yakara*). The "ladies and gentlemen" were spectators from samurai households who sat in the best places, and the "herd" referred to the commoners in the cheaper areas. While the proportion of wealthy commoners increased over time and the demographics of the two seating areas changed, actor critiques, beginning with *The Actor's Vocal Shamisen* (*Yakusha kuchijamisen*, 1699), continued to make a similar distinction. According to Matsuzaki Hitoshi, based on a survey of documents from the early eighteenth to the early nineteenth century, "the spending capability of spectators in the *sajiki* boxes was in actuality at least a few dozen times [*sūjuttaiichi*] greater than that of the spectators in the ground seating [*doma*]."[55]

Edo kabuki is characterized as a genre by its inheritance of narratives and performance traditions cherished by the samurai class. In contrast to productions in Kyoto, which were supported from the beginning by court nobles and, more importantly, by rich and powerful merchant burghers (*machishū*) who exerted a considerable influence on culture, productions in seventeenth-century Edo were meant to appeal to the distinctly larger population of that city's samurai class. This sort of regional distinction in audience and thus in taste was not limited to kabuki, of course; such differences were the rule rather than the exception. The pleasure quarters in Edo, for instance, strove to create a much more familial atmosphere than those in other cities because they targeted the city's large population of single men, particularly the numerous young retainers who were required to remain in Edo, leaving their families behind in their home provinces. Courtesans in Edo were almost always accompanied by little apprentice girls (*kamuro*) who attended to the visitors and hovered around the couple like surrogate children—a practice unique to Yoshiwara and unknown in other parts of the country.[56] When a man became a regular visitor to a brothel, the establishment also began keeping a pair of chopsticks for his use, with his name inscribed on them. One can think of these conventions as a performative means of fostering a sense of pseudofamily, intended specifically to answer the needs and desires of Edo's samurai population.

One example of the influence that Edo's demographic characteristics exerted on the city's kabuki can be seen in the theaters' continued celebration and dissemination of the medieval story of the demon Shutendōji, which was treasured by the Tokugawa family and the inhabitants of Edo and had long been reworked in various narrative and performative genres, as well as in visual culture. The story features the Heian-period (794–1185) general Minamoto no Yorimitsu and his four guardians, who together defeat the gigantic demon (*oni*) of Mount Ōe in order to protect the imperial family and restore peace. The emergence during the Muromachi period (1336–1573) of tales about the heroism of the Minamoto guardians has been analyzed by scholars of medieval literature as a rewriting of conventional kingship myths, which had been centered on the emperor and court culture, in a manner calculated to appeal to members of the samurai class.[57] While the emperor retains an important position in this story as a symbolic figurehead, the samurai are the ones who actually restore peace. This narrative paradigm celebrated the Seiwa Genji lineage, which had been closely tied to that of the Tokugawa shogunate ever since Tokugawa Ieyasu, the first Tokugawa shogun, had essentially invented a lineage for himself after his victory in the battle of Sekigahara in 1600, tracing his ancestry to this particular branch of the Genji, founded by Nitta Yoshisada.[58] While plays featuring the Seiwa Genji line were popular in Kyoto and Osaka, it is striking how much narratives and plays of this type were privileged in Edo kabuki and, indeed, in earlier performance genres. Records of kabuki productions at samurai residences during the seventeenth century include many references to the demon Shutendōji, and the Nakamura Theater, the most prestigious of the licensed theaters, designated *The Demon Shutendōji* as its "house play," a special work that was staged on ceremonious occasions.[59]

Stories of the Minamoto guardians' military triumphs and their defeat of a demon formed the core of an early puppet genre called "Kinpira puppet plays" (*Kinpira jōruri*), which emerged in Edo during the 1650s.[60] The name of the genre derives from the protagonist Sakata Kinpira, a superhuman son born to a female demon (*yamanba*) and Sakata Kintoki, one of the original four guardians of Minamoto no Yorimitsu. Kinpira puppet plays proliferated remarkably, coming to include the first generation of guardian warriors; the second generation, which served Minamoto Raikō (Yorimitsu); and even the third, which was charged with protecting Yoriyoshi and Yoshiie. In a way, these plays can be understood as a samurai version of the classic "noble in exile" (*kishu ryūritan*) plot, a standard pattern in Heian-period court narratives in which an aristocratic hero endures exile and various other trials but eventually returns to power. In the aristocratic context, the hero generally regains his original position through supernatural assistance, but here the warriors exercise their own wit and force. Expanding from medieval plots focused on defeating the supernatural to include political struggles and transforming the medieval hero's private service into a larger, public mission, Kinpira puppet plays established a formula in which the Minamoto generals found their positions threatened, by either slander or a sudden rebellious uprising, and were saved when the four guardians united to fight on their behalf, clearing their names and allowing them to regain the imperial favor they had lost.[61] During the early modern period, a time of protracted peace, these plays served to affirm the rule of the samurai and to create a fantasy surrounding the splendor of their military tradition. Akimoto Suzushi has noted that although in their original Heian-period context, the four guardians were "merely heads of military clans serving a specific regent household," in Kinpira puppet plays "they are turned into warriors who protect the entire realm."[62]

In addition to celebrating the samurai, Kinpira plays specifically targeted the male demographic of Edo by responding to the city's seventeenth-century fascination with "tough and chivalrous men" (*otokodate*). *Homecoming Stories of Edo* has a famous description of Kinpira as Edo's new hero: "People said that Benkei, Tokimune, and Asaina couldn't even come close to matching the strength of just one of Kinpira's arms. Thus fools who love superhuman powers and supernatural creatures took delight in listening to stories of Kinpira being chanted at close quarters with their fists clenched, gritting their teeth."[63] The battle scenes, especially those featuring Sakata Kinpira, with his superhuman strength and penchant for violence, were the highlight of such plays. *Hot-Blooded Tales of the Kantō Region* (*Kantō kekki monogatari*, early to mid-eighteenth century), which introduces various rough men of Edo, both historical and contemporary, contains an entry on Tanba Izumidayū, a chanter of Kinpira puppet plays who was celebrated for his roughness and strength. His son Izumidayū II also was a forceful chanter who would even break the puppets he used.[64]

Genroku kabuki in Edo, too, was characterized by plots featuring the defeat of demons and other evil figures and the forcible restoration of peace to a broad territory—though it could also be just a single household—by a warrior or a supernatural god. The lead male actor would often appear as an embodiment of the Buddha or some other god who had come to kill an evil demon. According to Satō Eri, forty-three of the fifty-four surviving prompt books for Genroku plays staged in Edo conclude with the appearance of a superhuman figure or a god.[65] Plots of this sort, which generally climaxed in a display of military force, led to the development in Edo of rough *aragoto* characters (young heroes with tremendous strength) and the acting patterns used in playing them.[66] Typically, at the end of the play an unruly god or hero would stomp his feet, engage in a tug of war with his enemy, or sometimes push or engage in sword fighting with a demon, a ghost, or another enemy. While it is difficult to establish a direct link from Kinpira puppet plays to *aragoto* kabuki, both forms exhibit certain physical similarities, such as their use of forceful foot movements (*chikara ashi*) in which the hero subdues the enemy by stomping his feet.[67] In the case of *aragoto*, Ichikawa Danjūrō I (1660–1704), who is generally known as the style's preeminent practitioner, established it as an innocent, free expression of power "by imitating children of seven or eight."[68]

This military orientation was not limited to the seventeenth century but continued to distinguish Edo kabuki from kabuki in Kyoto and Osaka over the long term. We can see this in a passage in Nyūgatei Ganyū's (Namiki Shōza II) *Notes on Playmaking* (*Sakusha shikihō kezairoku*, 1801), a text about kabuki playmaking that sets out a stereotypical view of the inhabitants of each of the three major cities and the types of plays that succeeded in each as a result:

> People in Kyoto are mild by nature, and in accordance with their sensibilities, for a long time now, about 60 percent of their plays have been dedicated to love affairs; the plots are too mild and somewhat lacking in force. They are like beautiful women. If plays were people, they would be the skin.
>
> People in Edo are rough by nature, and in accordance with their sensibilities, for a long time now, their plays have been focused on grand historical drama, about 70 percent cutting down and throwing people—all very silly; the plots are rather stiff and do not appeal to women. They are like a samurai. If plays were people, they would be the bones.
>
> People in Osaka get hung up on logic, and in accordance with their sensibilities, for a long time now, about 80 percent of their plays have centered on *giri* [moral obligation]; the plots are often too forced and sometimes bore the audience. Osaka plays are like chivalrous commoners [*otokodate*]. If plays were people, they would be the flesh.[69]

Kyoto kabuki was characterized by the *wagoto* (gentle, delicate) style and by plots centering on love affairs between handsome young men and courtesans. Edo plays, which focused on drama in a masculine, samurai mold, were best represented by the *aragoto* style, which appeared in the late seventeenth century. Plays in Osaka tended to be most interested in commoner heroes who emerged in the eighteenth century, such as gallant townsmen, sword fighters, and sumo wrestlers.

The emphasis on the defeat of the enemy and *aragoto* performance was not simply a matter of taste but was deeply rooted in a cultural and historical perspective that was meaningful in Edo. This is clear when we compare Genroku kabuki in Edo with that in Kamigata, which came to be characterized by an almost exclusive reliance on "household disturbance" (*oie sōdō*) plots—relatively tightly structured social dramas with a contemporary rather than a historical orientation that began with a crisis threatening to bring down a daimyo household and ended with its resolution and the restoration of order. Often such plays would feature an irresponsible heir who ignores his duty to manage the household and instead spends all his time in the pleasure quarters, leaving his intelligent retainers to try to find a way to restore the household to its former glory. Plots of this sort reflected the early modern inheritance system and the nature of the household as an administrative unit.[70] Andrew Gerstle has proposed that we think of both the puppet theater and kabuki in Kamigata during the Genroku period in terms of a "cyclical imagination" in which "the end is actually a return—after a roundabout route—to the original point of departure."[71] Genroku kabuki in Edo also follows a cyclical structure, with the crucial difference being its incorporation of a romantic view of the samurai past. Edo kabuki had a much stronger mythical/historical thrust, in other words, and was concerned with restoring peace, through a display of superhuman military force, to a community larger than a single household or domain.[72]

A large majority of the evil spirits or demons that attempt to take over a samurai household or threaten an entire domain are not merely eliminated or tamed, but transformed into protective guardians. This is another element of the felicitous conclusion that Genroku kabuki in Edo incorporated into its portrayal of military force. Gunji Masakatsu sees in the early history of Edo kabuki a deep commitment to rewriting the medieval samurai notions of guardian spirits (*goryō shinkō*) and rough gods (*arahitogami*). These are the resentful spirits of noted public figures, always male, who die in vain and then return to visit mischief on a community but can be turned into guardians through pacification and deification.[73] This sense of lineage and protection is evident in the kabuki play *The Courtesan of Asama Mountain* (*Keisei Asamagatake*), a Kamigata play rewritten to suit the tastes of the Edo audience for the spring production at the Yamamura Theater in 1700. The thunder god Gorō—depicted in the prompt book for the play as a type of demon with horns—tortures Minamoto no Yoritomo. When the Minamoto clan gives Gorō a letter of pacification, he is transformed into a "rough god" who will serve from then on as the guardian of the Minamoto warriors' bows and arrows. In this way, Edo kabuki made the lineages of the ruling elite and popular stories of the military past into integral elements of its theatrical universe by rewriting them over and over, showing in play after play how a threat to the status quo was overcome and concluding every time with the promise of continued prosperity.

Eventually, as influences from Kyoto and Osaka continued to find their way into Edo in the early eighteenth century—notable examples being the contemporary household disturbance plot and especially the sophisticated plot structures typical of puppet plays—the mythical tales of evil demons that had stood at the core of the Edo kabuki repertoire were replaced by stories about evil aristocrats and samurai. The *aragoto* gods and their sacrifices also were supplanted by rough men and selfless attendants in daimyo households who gave their lives for the public good.

One of the clearest instances of the celebration of peace through the intervention of the samurai is found in a kabuki ritual unique to Edo. In the early eighteenth century, it became customary to incorporate *Wait a Minute!* (*Shibaraku*) into the very first act of the first play of the "face-showing production" (*kaomise kyōgen*) in the eleventh month—the start of the kabuki new year. Now regarded as a distinct play in its own right, and famous enough that it was canonized in the early nineteenth century as one of the eighteen classics of Edo kabuki, *Wait a Minute!* was originally more like a skit that could be inserted into whatever historical world had been settled on for the face-showing production. The skit featured a young man in the *aragoto* mold, always played by an actor in the Ichikawa line, who confronts an evil aristocrat intent on declaring himself the new emperor or shogun. Often the aristocrat, outraged that a princess he loves has rejected him, has taken the imperial family hostage and is on the verge of beheading them all. The *aragoto* hero comes to the rescue in the nick of time, running down the *hanamichi* dressed in red clothing with impossibly huge sleeves, his hair in an impressive coiffure, carrying giant swords, and calling out "Wait a minute, wait a minute!" (*Shibaraku, shibaraku!*). The identity of this young man would change, depending on the *sekai* that was being used in a given year. Most often he was Shinozuka Iganokami in *The Chronicles of Great Peace* (*Taiheiki*), Arajishi Otokonosuke in the Higashiyama *sekai* of the shogun Ashikaga Yoshimasa, or Watanabe Kisō in *The Tales of the Heike* (*Heike monogatari*), although each of these *sekai* provided other possibilities as well.[74] Essentially it did not matter who he was; he was simply a military figure whose job it was to return each year to the stage and restore order in a grand style, celebrating the peaceful rule of the samurai and creating a symbolic fantasy of power, allowing a popular audience to internalize a vision that was originally part of the heritage of the ruling class. The annual staging of *Wait a Minute!* continued well into the nineteenth century, maintaining kabuki's connection to one of the core cultural lineages of Edo kabuki, even as it continued to evolve in interesting ways—there were, for instance, versions featuring a female hero.

LAYERED TIME: *SEKAI* AND *SHUKŌ*

Early Edo kabuki focused on military plots celebrating the world of the samurai, but not in a way that emphasized the distinction between the samurai and the other classes. Instead, it consciously presented stories of the samurai past through the lens of the landscapes, customs, and conventions of early modern Edo in a manner calculated to appeal to a broad audience, across class demarcations. Military figures who had lived centuries earlier were presented in early modern commoner dress and would keep popping up in the pleasure quarters and neighborhoods of Edo, where they behaved in accordance with familiar early modern customs. Already in the age of Genroku kabuki, characters from the Heian and medieval periods—such as the four Minamoto guardians, the powerful Benkei, or gods such as Narukami and Fudō, who had never been associated with romantic themes—had been shown having affairs with women or men, falling in love, and burning with jealousy, often in an early modern setting. In *Kinpira's Visit to the Pleasure Quarters* (*Kinpira rokujōgayoi*, 1685), for instance, Ichikawa Danjūrō I turned Kinpira into an amorous man who heads to the Shimabara pleasure quarters in Kyoto. In the picture prompt book for *The Legend of Narukami from the Genpei War* (*Genpei Narukami denki*, 1698), a play set in the *sekai* of the four guardians, the thunder god Narukami not only fell madly in love but also appeared on stage in the distinctly contemporary attire of a low-class samurai attendant (*yakko*). Introducing stock mythical-historical characters such as Narukami and Kinpira into the urban present in this way must have been at least partly intended to surprise the audience by giving these characters contemporary associations. In this sense, the notion of *yatsushi* (dressing down)—a common theme in Kamigata kabuki that often involved an heir to a samurai household, played by a *wagoto* actor, who would indulge himself in the pleasure quarters in disguise while his household collapsed—can also be applied, albeit with slightly different connotations, to the *aragoto* heroes of Edo kabuki.

The melding of the past and the present retained its importance in eighteenth-century kabuki. For instance, Sukeroku, the Edo dandy introduced at the opening of this chapter, served as a contemporary, surrogate body for Soga Gorō in the often used *sekai* of the Soga brothers' revenge. The future shogun Minamoto no Yoritomo appears in the second part of Sakurada Jisuke's (1734–1806) play *Big Business on Leech Island* (*Ōakinai hiru ga kojima*, 1784) as a teacher in a village school for young girls. Looking on the surface like any other lighthearted young man, Yoritomo is patiently waiting for an opportunity to resurrect the Genji clan. Such scenarios stand in contrast to nō plays, which exhibit a clearer consciousness that a line separates the present moment from events that have receded into the space of memory as well as from the world of the spirits. Zeami's dream plays (*mugen nō*) staged visitations of dead warriors and other figures in order to recognize and hold on to scenes deeply lodged in public memory, not in order to rewrite them in a contemporary context. While a nō play might, for example, feature a fisherman who is oddly able to recount the details of an ancient battle to a traveling priest and who mysteriously vanishes, only to be replaced by the very warrior whose story he has told, the focus is always on the warrior as a figure of the past and of the other world, never on his ongoing, present existence in this world. The fisherman is simply there to tell the story.

Early modern theater was the first to introduce characters from *gunki* (military narratives) who had often been taken up in earlier periods into the contemporary urban landscape. In Edo, this incessant calling up of the past was so important that even the stories of contemporary figures—including double suicides like that of Osome and Hisamatsu or Ochiyo and Hanbei; the greengrocer's daughter Oshichi, who started a fire in Edo in the late seventeenth century; and Nuregami Chōgorō, a character based on a popular sumo wrestler who murdered a samurai—would be superimposed on characters from historical *sekai* such as the Soga brothers' revenge, *The Chronicles of Great Peace*, and the *Diary of Izu* (*Izu nikki*), which featured Minamoto no Yoritomo. This process of superimposition rendered communally accessible the narratives that had been the provenance of the ruling class. It, too, can be understood in terms of the mechanisms of *yatsushi* and *mitate* (seeing as) exploited in various early modern genres, from *haikai* (popular linked verse) to painting. In other genres, the hybridization often involved combining pictorial and poetic associations rooted in the culture of the Heian court with "vulgar" contemporary themes. In kabuki, military culture and the contemporary urban landscape formed the two axes.

The author of the actor critique *The Actors' Double Shamisen* (*Yakusha nichōjamisen*, 1702) summed this up when he wrote that Edo playmaking was about the "relocation of the past into the present."[75] Furuido Hideo coined the phrase "historical contemporaneity" (*jidai sewa*) to describe the same convention. Oscillating between the "historical" (*jidai*) and the "contemporary" (*sewa*), Edo kabuki allowed times and places that might from today's perspective seem distant from one another to meld in the minds of their early modern audience members.[76] At the same time, it also achieved a similar layering effect with respect to class, depicting samurai characters both high and low in a fashion that made them look, from the standpoint of non-samurai audience members, *just like us* and, in fact, as though they were *part of us*.

This doubling, which rendered porous the boundaries between the samurai past and a present shared by members of a diverse audience and between earlier warrior tales and contemporary urban lives, is the origin of the much discussed concepts of *sekai* and *shukō*. They served as a means of incorporating elements of history into the social landscape of contemporary Edo in a manner that transcended both time and class. As previous scholarship has discussed, the process of kabuki playwriting started with selecting a well-known *sekai*—one of the "worlds" in which kabuki plays were set—and introducing a fresh twist known as the *shukō* that made the old pattern new again. Nyūgatei Ganyū's *Notes on Playmaking* is frequently cited as offering an explanation of *sekai* and *shukō* as a playmaking principle:[77]

> The conventional *sekai* have been so overused that they contribute nothing to the plot of a play. Since plotlines are mixed, we talk of vertical plotlines [*tate*] and horizontal [*yoko*] plotlines.... The vertical plotline is the *sekai*; the horizontal plotline is the *shukō*. The first act is vertical. Combining plotlines all the way to the end contributes nothing. The horizontal will contribute even if it is brought out from the middle, showing the play in a new light—this is an important matter.[78]

Nyūgatei, or Namiki Shōza II, was a Kamigata playwright, and his perspective probably fits Kamigata kabuki playmaking better than Edo kabuki. Plays in Kamigata, where kabuki playwrights also wrote tightly structured puppet plays, tended to be more logically constructed and staged than in Edo, where plays had a looser structure and freely jumbled different *sekai*. Still, this passage shows that the *sekai* functioned as a shared archive of settings from which kabuki in all cities drew. The playwrights would start with the *sekai* and then incorporate new theatrical twists, or *shukō*.

As Katherine Saltzman-Li explained, "Along with the choice of a *sekai* that is based in past stories or events, the introduction of *shukō* into *sekai*, that is the present into the past, was the codified method to re-create in kabuki and other Tokugawa performing arts."[79] In short, the *sekai* was a setting based on communal historical memory, while the *shukō* served as the crux of playmaking, the element that bridged the gap between the present and the historical world, refashioning the latter into something contemporary. *Notes on Playmaking* gives as examples of an effective *shukō* twisting an older play by replacing an old male character with a female character or an idiot with a lead male, or by making a historical play contemporary.[80] As the Edo playwright in Gachikuken's *Sloppy Comic Sermon on Things Heard* (*Hetadangi chōmonshū*, 1754) explains, *shukō* specifically required "making the greengrocer Oshichi into a blood relative of Soga or having Yoritomo go off to Yoshiwara. You beat your brains out day and night to make the setting new. You make a play by incorporating the present way."[81] These two playmaking concepts were fairly fluid and were used in different ways at different periods and in the three major cities. In Edo, the workings of *sekai* and *shukō* tended to be more strongly aligned with modes of past and present, historical warrior tales and urban customs, samurai and commoner.

The importance of jumbling past and present in Edo kabuki led to the creation of manuals containing entries on all the theatrical *sekai* and their major characters. In 1791, the playwright Kanai Sanshō (1731–1797), under whom Tsuruya Nanboku IV apprenticed, compiled a manuscript called *The Handbook of Theatrical Worlds* (*Sekai kōmoku*) to transmit knowledge to his grandson about the *sekai* and their characters. This manuscript, which reflected the distinct character of Edo kabuki in its selection as well as in the expansive set of characters listed under the *sekai* of the Soga brothers' revenge, was then disseminated to other playwrights.[82] We know from the hand-copied versions of this manual possessed by Edo playwrights that it was consulted in the late eighteenth and early nineteenth centuries. Although no written records survive, it would not be surprising if earlier playwrights had similar manuals at hand. Just as *haikai* manuals and pictorial encyclopedias (*gafu*) were important to practitioners of *haikai* and painting, this guide to the *sekai* was central to kabuki playmaking. A large majority of the *sekai* it contained were military worlds that were listed in the first category, "*Sekai* for Kabuki History Plays" (Kabuki jidai kyōgen sekai no bu). The contemporary affairs of the *buke* (warrior houses) were placed under the heading "*Sekai* for Kabuki Household Disturbance Plays" (Kabuki o[ie] kyōgen sekai no bu), which included the subcategory "Revenge Plots (and Similar Types)" (Oie kyōgen no uchi katakiuchi no bu narabi ni rui).[83] Lists of relevant reference books, titles of associated music, and the roles pertinent to each heading appeared under nearly 150 fixed *sekai*, including *The Tale of Yoshitsune* (*Gikeiki*), *The Chronicles of Great Peace*, and *The Tales of the Heike*. As the practice of jumbling several worlds intensified during the nineteenth century, *The Handbook of Theatrical Worlds* became increasingly necessary if a playwright wanted to keep track of all the characters who might be incorporated into a given *sekai*.

Not all *sekai* were given the same importance. Edo playwrights were not particularly interested in the defeated Heike warriors from *The Tales of the Heike*, characterized by a coexistence of the legitimation of the Genji and the pacification of the Heike spirits. Instead, they highlighted narratives that concluded with the restoration of peace, especially through the triumphs of the Genji clan and their retainers. The most prominent examples of such *sekai* are *The Tale of Yoshitsune* and the *Diary of Izu*. The most frequently used *sekai* was the Soga brothers' revenge, which became a staple of the spring production that began in the first month. Originally staged in the seventeenth century during the festival of the dead (*bon*) in order to appease the souls of the two brothers, plays set in the Soga *sekai* came to be performed in the early eighteenth century as a celebratory event during the first month.[84] Since the Soga *sekai* was staged every year without fail, the number of Soga plays and contemporary plays created as extensions of the Soga *sekai* was considerably larger during the early modern period than the number of plays set in any other world. The Edo tradition of staging a Soga production in the spring was closely connected to the city's particular social landscape. It is telling that when the influential Kamigata playwright Namiki Gohei was contracted by the Miyako Theater and brought to

Edo in 1794, he reportedly had no idea that the spring production had to be centered on the Soga brothers' revenge, since this was not the practice in Kyoto and Osaka. According to Mimasuya Nisōji, the theater's sponsor (*kinshu*)—an investor who would fund an entire year's productions—had to step in and draft the playbills for him.[85]

There are many reasons why the Soga brothers' revenge had a special significance for Edo audiences. First, the characters and their settings were particularly relevant to the inhabitants of Edo, as many of the historical events had unfolded in the vicinity of the city. At the same time, stories about the Soga brothers were able to incorporate many prominent *sekai* that featured the Genji, such as *The Tales of the Heike*, the *Diary of Izu*, and *The Tale of Yoshitsune*. The Soga brothers' story also functioned as a celebration of the New Year (the ordinary New Year, not the kabuki new year) that united images of this special time of the year associated with the ordinary urban populace, on the one hand, and with the daimyo and the shogun, on the other. The first part of the production, staged during the first month, often included a scene known as "Oniō's Hovel" (Oniō hinka no ba). Since each production was different from every other, this could take various forms, but the general outline was more or less fixed. It centered on a loyal attendant of the Soga household named Oniō Shinzaemon and his family's struggles to make ends meet at the end of the year while desperately trying to help the Soga brothers in the short time remaining before the New Year celebrations at the shogun's palace. Oniō must raise funds to recover a suit of armor that the Soga brothers will present to the shogun, Minamoto no Yoritomo, or sometimes he must track down a missing sword. In some versions of the story, Oniō sacrifices his own daughter or commits murder to obtain the money. Although Soga plays are categorized as "history plays," "Oniō's Hovel" is oriented much more toward contemporary commoner life in Edo: Oniō is shown running around town, going from his family's residence to the pleasure quarters, trying to raise cash, searching for the missing sword, and so on.[86] Even though it focuses on the world of the samurai, the play incorporates the harried mood of the year's end, when people of all classes had to pay their debts and prepare for the New Year.

A second frequently staged scene depicted the New Year ceremony at the palace and then a ceremonious "meeting" (*taimen*) between the Soga brothers and a number of high-ranking samurai who ridicule the brothers' elaborate clothing as inappropriate to the occasion. Furuido Hideo has suggested that this scene operates on two levels, simultaneously contributing to the play's plot and allowing the audience to participate vicariously in the New Year's "face-showing" (*nenshi tōjō*) that took place at the shogun's palace, a ritualistic first meeting between the shogun and important daimyo. In fact, the costumes worn by the actors playing high-ranking samurai were based on the daimyo's and shogun's actual outfits, which accorded with the "ancient customs" (*yūsoku kojitsu*) of the imperial court.[87] The scene thus translated a ritual of the ruling class into a context that made it more broadly accessible. The Soga brothers' revenge was a ritualized *sekai* that, through its incorporation each year of new *shukō*, bridged past and present, high and low. Here, again, we see a "double vision" that allowed a wide segment of society to envision itself in connection to the narratives and culture of the ruling class.

CYCLIC TIME AND ENDLESS REWRITING

To understand the compositional principal of the *sekai* and the related notion of the *shukō*, it is helpful to see how neatly they fit into the larger system of early modern urban cultural production, including poetry, narrative, and the visual arts.[88] Early modern culture was characterized by an emphasis on sociality and communality in which shared traditions were mobilized as a platform for creation. This remained the dominant mode of production and circulation until the advent of notions of authorship and copyright. In fact, the terms "horizontal" and "vertical" used in *Notes on Playmaking* echo the language of *haikai* poetics, in which the vertical theme (*tate no dai*) refers to archetypal topics already established in earlier poetry and the horizontal theme (*yoko no dai*) refers to the new addition or twist.[89] The term *shukō* itself was often used in the context of poetic composition to refer to the innovation that a poet makes by simultaneously drawing on and departing from a classical poem (*honkadori*). While poetry dealt with the history of classical poetics and kabuki dealt with military history, both forms had a similar social function.[90] In each case, the technique of linking served to make the past newly relevant to the present—not to distance the present but to incorporate the past into the present.

Sekai in Edo, which returned incessantly to the celebration of military heritage, can be viewed as a kind of dialogue, a means of using the past to produce a shared cultural knowledge particular to the city during a long, potentially endless, string of productions. Kabuki scholar Hattori Yukio offered a useful version of this "dialogic" perspective on Edo kabuki, invoking the metaphor of linked poetry (*renga*) to describe what might be called the "fundamentally interperformative" nature of its plays:

> Linked poetry and linked verse freely develop their worlds through the repeated act of linking [*tsukeai*]. Linking is a form of dialogue, and this dialogue expands the possibilities as each successive poet adds a new verse that the preceding poet would never even have imagined.... The moment a poet adds his verse, it becomes subject to incompleteness. In linked verse, the author's pure creation is completed only after three verses have been composed: the first verse, his own verse, and the next verse. Linked verse is based on a communal structure in which one lives only by giving life to others, and others live only through one's own life.... Fundamentally, linked verse is supposed to repeat the process of linking [*tsukeku*]. Eternal incompleteness is the characteristic of linked poetry [*renga*] and linked verse [*renku*].... Kabuki clearly reflects this structure. The final act [*ōzume, ōgiri*] is but a temporary closure imposed by structural constraints. Its roots speak to what would be its eternal continuity if there were no restrictions placed on it by time and the actors' energies.[91]

This is an excellent metaphor for explaining the structure of Edo kabuki as a form that constantly continued to build on and transform elements inherited from the past. Each production—each new rendition of a particular *sekai*, each new manifestation of the endless drive to make the samurai past present and open to imaginative participation across class lines—advanced a theatrical dialogue in which the public was involved. This means both that each production represented a continuation of those that came before and that, in principle, no production should ever arrive at a definitive conclusion. Kabuki theater was characterized by its endless drive to recycle material from the past, on the one hand, and by its incomplete productions, which remained open to endless future rewriting, on the other. *Sekai* and *shukō* were important as the mechanisms that made this dialogue possible.

Over time, as kabuki continued to develop as a space of dialogue and endless rewriting, it came to be increasingly oriented toward the incomplete. Rather than actually representing the defeat of the enemy, kabuki came to prefer an open-ended structure in which closure was postponed. Characters transplanted from the past into the present generally would not succeed in achieving their revenge, or even in engaging their main enemy in battle. Rather, the moment of confrontation between good and evil was emphasized, and the play would end with a promise that the conflict would be settled on another day. Harmony was restored, but the threat of future disruption remained. The best example of this is undoubtedly *Wait a Minute!* While the minor characters are defeated, the self-proclaimed emperor simply vows to come back to fight another day and then leaves, putting off his final defeat for yet another year. In this sense, kabuki exhibited a strong tendency toward cyclicality.

This penchant for linking also was reflected in the production structures and the way that plays were advertised to the general public. In the age of Genroku kabuki, productions at the Nakamura and Ichimura Theaters had four parts (*yoban tsuzuki*), and those at the Morita and Yamamura Theaters were made up of five.[92] Each part was divided into between two and four acts, and since the audience changed after each part, each part had to be capable of standing on its own, accessible even to those who had not seen the rest of the play. By the mid-eighteenth century, after the government shut down the Yamamura Theater following the Ejima–Ikushima incident, productions at the three remaining theaters came to consist of essentially two parts. For most of the eighteenth and nineteenth centuries, though, playbills and other ephemera printed in connection with the face-showing and spring productions continued to advertise four parts with made-up roles for actors, even though theatergoers knew that in most cases only the opening two parts—the first oriented toward a "historical" setting and the second more casual and contemporary—would actually make it to the stage, and that much of the advertised content would not be performed.[93]

The fact that the two major productions of the Edo kabuki calendar, the face-showing and the spring productions, continued to be represented in print as though they would be made up of four parts and feature many more characters than would actually appear in the performance reveals a great deal about how people thought of kabuki plays and about how important the fluid, linked verse–like development of productions in Edo was. Theaters routinely made drastic changes to the content of productions when audiences began to dwindle, and in extreme cases, they might even cancel a production altogether. Conversely, if a production was a hit, it might be drawn out for months, with new acts based on the same *sekai* added over time.[94] Theaters were particularly hopeful that they would be able to extend the face-showing and, above all, the spring productions in this way, and the continued use of a four-part structure in advertisements for these productions was a reflection of this optimism. Even after audiences had come to recognize that productions usually had only two parts, the possibility always remained that additional parts would be staged.[95]

In a fundamental sense, then, the kabuki scripts we read today are a product of a very different understanding of kabuki that arose only after this production system—so typical of Edo—came to an end. The extent to which the system was characteristic of Edo kabuki is evident from contemporary comparisons of productions in Edo with those in Kamigata. *The Origins of Kabuki* (*Kabuki jishi*, 1762), a history issued by the Hachimojiya publishing house in Kyoto, addresses these differences explicitly:

> Kabuki productions in Kyoto and Osaka must show everything from the opening scene to the defeat of the villain; otherwise, the audience would be puzzled. It is a different story in Edo: there, a production can open with only the first part, and if there is enough of an audience on the first day, the second day, the third day, or even on the tenth or twentieth day, a theater will repeat just the first part. When the audience begins to dwindle, then it starts staging the remaining acts, one after the other.[96]

In Edo, productions were meant to be open-ended, and their conclusions were intentionally deferred in order to maintain the possibility of future linking.

The idiosyncratic nature of Edo kabuki also was evident in the organization of its calendar. By the eighteenth century, Edo's kabuki theaters were operating on a distinctive schedule that supplemented the sequence of annual festivities and rituals, centered on temples and shrines, that had traditionally served as the primary means of marking time throughout the year. Scholars have discussed early modern theaters and the pleasure quarters in this respect as topoi that achieved a "routinization of the festival atmosphere" (*hare no nichijōka*).[97]

Because the production calendar has been discussed in detail in previous scholarship, I will touch on it only briefly here. As Barbara Thornbury and Katherine Saltzman-Li have explained, the kabuki calendar was divided into between four and six seasons: the face-showing, spring, third-month, fifth-month, "summer"—which generally started in the sixth or seventh month and, in the latter case, was called the "festival of the dead" (*bon kyōgen*)—and ninth-month farewell productions.[98] The seasons were not necessarily associated with the start of a new production. More accurately, perhaps, they could be viewed as a commercial strategy that allowed a production that was already under way to be imbued with elements that kept it new and made it appropriate to the current time of year. In terms of the actual production schedule, the annual calendar of Edo kabuki was organized around two pillars: the face-showing production and the spring production.

The face-showing production, which was centered on the announcement of the new casts who would be performing at each theater throughout the upcoming theatrical year, including Edo stars as well as popular actors from Kyoto and Osaka, was a clever way of exploiting the annual contract system. That is, it made an event internal to the theater serve as a temporal marker for the city as a whole, much as festivals and the blossoming of certain flowering trees did. In the first half of the tenth month, at the beginning of the theatrical year, each theater would hang boards listing the new actors' names outside and publish a poster-size, illustrated "face-showing playbill" (*kaomise banzuke* or *yakusha-zuke*) portraying the actors arranged according to their position in the theater hierarchy.[99]

Figure 1.4 is an example of a face-showing playbill issued by the Nakamura Theater in 1822. The highest-ranked stars in the new troupe appear in the center. It is not clear how many face-showing playbills each theater printed, but the number must have been fairly large, as some records show that roughly one thousand copies would be reserved for the theater manager to distribute to officials in the commissioner's office (*machibugyōsho okakari yaku'ningata*), to town elders (*machidoshiyori*), to the guild association (*kumiai*), to the censor (*nanushi*), to the inspectors (*kimoiri*), and to the actors themselves.[100] The day after

FIGURE 1.1 The face-showing playbill for a production at the Nakamura Theater in 1822. (Courtesy of Tokyo University, Kokubungaku Kenkyūshitsu)

all these copies were sent around, the playbills would be offered for sale to the public.

Some sense of the enthusiasm and attention that the face-showing production generated is suggested by both the initial cost of the prints and the speed with which their value depreciated. Early in the tenth month, a freshly printed face-showing playbill might sell for 1 *bu*—equivalent to several hundred dollars in today's currency—only to have its price drop to nothing as soon as the information was widely known.[101] Patrons of particular actors would heap clothing and other offerings outside the theaters shortly after the new casts were announced, creating a magnificent and festive display. Then on the seventeenth of the tenth month, the actors would conduct a procession from the theater with which they had contracted during the previous year to their new theater, each accompanied by an attendant holding a lantern—an event known as "the first gathering" (*yorizome*). Although this does not appear to have been intended as an event for spectators, people still flocked to watch.[102]

The excitement generated by the announcement of the new cast would be heightened and given direction once fans learned which *sekai* would be used in the face-showing production. Information relating to the selection was jealously guarded until, toward the end of the tenth month, the main title of the production (*daimyōdai*) was written on a board and hung outside the theater.[103] Generally, knowledgeable kabuki-goers would be able to identify the *sekai* from the title, and once they knew what it was they could begin to imagine and discuss what the new group of actors might do in the face-showing production: which actors would play enemies and which would play lovers, and what sort of twists they would introduce into the familiar *sekai*. The posting of the title was another major event, for which "mountains of people, one upon the other" would gather, craning their necks to see.[104] The renewal of the theaters' casts thus launched the new year, creating a sense of anticipation that culminated in the first act of the face-showing production, which consisted of the ceremonial *Wait a Minute!*

If the face-showing production was meant to showcase the new cast and the playwright's choice of a *sekai*, the main interest of the spring production lay in the new twist it would introduce into the *sekai* of the Soga brothers' revenge, whose use was settled from the start. The Soga *sekai* thus was important in two ways: first, for the pleasure of seeing how it would be tweaked in a given year and, second, for the very fact of its repetition—the role it played in the kabuki calendar, in the construction of kabuki time. Over time, it came to be expected, or at least hoped, that the Soga-themed spring production would continue from the first month until the actual day of the brothers' revenge on the twenty-eighth of the fifth month. This tradition of devoting months to plots based on the Soga brothers' revenge initially seems to have originated in a single particularly successful production, but soon all three theaters adopted it.[105]

If a theater's spring production did indeed continue to attract audiences for as long as the manager and the actors hoped, they would keep adding new acts relating to the Soga world, trying to extend the run as long as possible, though they seldom managed to keep it going until the end of the fifth month. Theaters also began incorporating into the production a celebration of the Soga brothers' revenge on the twenty-eighth of the fifth month that had formerly been conducted backstage, using this event to appease the brothers' spirits and mark the official end of the spring production. By the An'ei period (1772–1781), this event had acquired the status of an annual festival that involved neighboring towns, people at the teahouses, parades, and flower dances by children, and it continued for days after the celebration on stage.[106] By the first week of the sixth month, even the most popular spring production would finally come to an end. The final day was celebrated as the "closing performance" (*senshūraku*) and was identified as such on a board hung outside the theater. The ideal of the long spring production remained a fixture of the kabuki calendar through most of the eighteenth century, even though most audiences would tire of the Soga *sekai* and the theaters would find it difficult to keep bringing in audiences for a full five months. When this happened, the production would be "crushed" or "terminated" (*tsubureta* or *tsubure*) and replaced by a new one.

The theaters managed to keep the Soga productions going for such a long time by changing the content over the months. As the days, and thus the performances, began getting longer in the second month, theaters would incorporate contemporary acts featuring characters who lived in Edo.[107] By the third month, the entire first part of the play, which had focused on the Soga brothers, would be replaced by new acts more loosely tied to the Soga world, which were presented as the second part.[108] As we saw at the beginning of this chapter, this was conventionally the time when plays featuring the Edo gallant Sukeroku could be staged, although they were not an annual occurrence like *Wait a Minute!* Generally, performances in the third month would involve a magnificent display of cherry blossoms in full bloom, timed to coincide with the cherry blossom season. In plays featuring Sukeroku, these displays specifically evoked the hundreds of cherry trees that were transplanted to the Yoshiwara pleasure quarters to celebrate the coming of spring, only to be dug up and removed as soon as they were past their prime.[109]

During the nineteenth century when the Soga production generally petered out fairly quickly, theaters would turn in the third month to plays centered on female characters. This was a commercial decision targeting the large number of ladies-in-waiting at daimyo houses, who were customarily given leave to stay with their families during this month. Plays of this sort included vendettas and household disturbance plots set in the female quarters of daimyo residences, such as *Mirror Mountain: A Woman's Treasury of Loyalty* (*Kagamiyama kokyō no nishikie*), familiar stories presented with female rather than male main characters, and plays that ordinarily featured a female character, such as those dealing with the priest Seigen and his obsessive love of Sakurahime. After this, the theater would hastily throw together a new production or two to fill whatever time remained before the Soga festival or the official last day of the spring production. These were called "overnight pickles" (*ichiyazuke*). According to Takamura Chikuri's *An Illustrated Mirror of the Theatrical Calendar* (*Ehon shibai nenjū kagami*, 1803), a work that consciously explicates Edo theatrical traditions not mentioned in Kamigata-based publications, "overnight pickles" included revenge plays, chivalrous commoner plays, and preexisting puppet plays.[110] Since the puppet-theater repertoire was relatively fixed and the texts used by the chanters could be staged with minimal rewriting, Edo playwrights from Nakamura Jūsuke II (1745–1803) to Mimasuya Nisōji took a very dim view of kabuki reworkings of puppet-theater material, regarding them as a dereliction of the playwright's responsibility to keep pushing in new directions the *sekai* and the dialogue they enabled.

As we have seen, the face-showing production and the spring production were the two most significant productions in the kabuki calendar; the other seasons were of secondary importance. After the long spring production, the major stars generally took long breaks, leaving the theaters in the hands of apprentice actors who would work to refine their talents.[111] By this time, the theater managers and playwrights would already be considering which actors they might try to contract for the following kabuki year. In the six month or during the "lingering heat" of the seventh month, the apprentices would stage a "summer" production (called *bon kyōgen* or *aki kyōgen* [autumn production] in the seventh month, depending on the source), and sometime in the eighth month the stars would return. The theatrical calendar came to a close as preparations got under way for the face-showing with a production in the ninth month featuring actors who would either be leaving for or returning to Kyoto and Osaka; this was known as the "farewell production" (*onagori kyōgen*).[112]

As this brief consideration of the calendar suggests, *sekai* and *shukō* were not simply playmaking principles that playwrights drew on to generate their scripts. Not only did they enable the creation of plays, they also, and perhaps more importantly, structured the annual calendar, enabling the continuation of kabuki as a process that translated stories focused on the samurai past into familiar, everyday contexts, thereby producing a new vision of the present that could be broadly shared by the population of Edo.

EMBODIED TIME: ACTORS AND THEIR LINEAGES

It goes without saying that kabuki actors also participated in the production of shared time and history in Edo. Over several decades, actor's bodies were gradually transformed into privileged sites for preserving memories of the theater. Each actor belonged to a particular acting lineage, defined by the inheritance of a stage name that carried its own associations and memories of earlier actors; his body was a literal instantiation of Bakhtin's phrase "Time . . . takes on flesh."[113] This desire to create a lineage was particularly pronounced in Edo kabuki, in contrast to kabuki in Kyoto and Osaka, where important names like Yoshizawa Ayame (1673–1729) and Sakata Tōjūrō (1647–1709) might be allowed to languish.

Actors' bodies mediated the presentation of the past. Sukeroku is a prime example of this. Ever since Danjūrō II first played him in 1716, his role has been inherited by—and the ability to play him has been transmitted through—successive actors in the Ichikawa Danjūrō line. For much longer than a century, members of this lineage were responsible for keeping Sukeroku's character, including his double identity as Soga Gorō, alive throughout the early modern period, by transferring memories of his performance from one body to the next. This process culminated in the mid-nineteenth century when Danjūrō VII designated *Sukeroku* as one of the eighteen kabuki classics (*kabuki jūhachiban*), canonizing it as the quintessential play in the Danjūrō repertoire and as the epitome of the spirit of Edo kabuki that his lineage represented. In this way, through a construction of the actor as a seemingly immortal body in which the theater, the actors themselves, publications related to the theater, and audiences all participated, Edo kabuki succeeded in constituting a communal present by means of a ceaseless cannibalization of the samurai past. Shared knowledge of generations of actors congealed into a sort of time line of the city's history. Like the theater itself, the actor's body became a vessel in which time percolated.

It would not be going too far to suggest that by the late eighteenth or early nineteenth century, on the popular level the kabuki theater and its actors had come, more than any formal list of era names or a historical chronology, to serve as a measuring stick by which the passage of time in Edo could be marked.

In a sense, kabuki actors were "ghosted"—to use Marvin Carlson's term—by earlier actors in their line: their bodies came to serve, as did the *sekai*, as archives of popular memory that could be passed down from one generation to the next by members of the Edo public. This ghosting was achieved not only on stage and through the audience's participation in the theatrical experience but also through a collaboration with popular print media, which circulated the images of actors even in their absence. But it began in the theater. Originally, actors who were also theater managers, such as Nakamura Kanzaburō of the Nakamura Theater and Morita Kan'ya of the Morita Theater, would pass on their names to their sons so that the sons could inherit the legal license necessary to produce plays—a process not unlike that in the houses of domain lords, who designated their heirs.[114] Sometime in the early eighteenth century, it became common practice for actors to progress through different names in the course of their careers, inheriting the reputation, roles, and acting styles that went with each one. Acting in a given role, they would simultaneously resurrect memories of the bodies of actors of previous generations and rewrite them with their own acting.

One early instance of this kind of inheritance occurred in the Ichikawa family: Ichikawa Danjūrō I's son Kuzō began appearing on stage as "the present Danjūrō" (*ima Danjūrō*) after his father was murdered on stage by a fellow actor. According to Tatekawa [Utei] Enba I's (1743–1822) *Edo in Bloom: A Kabuki Time Line* (*Hana no Edo kabuki nendaiki*, 1811–1815), Kuzō "took a leave until the sixth month, during the forty-nine days after his father's death. From the seventh month, at Yamamura Chōdayū Theater in Kobiki-chō, he changed his name to Ichikawa Danjūrō II and, after an introduction by Miyazaki Denkichi, gave a speech in memory of his father. Everyone in the audience, both high and low, wet their sleeves with tears."[115] The play *Moving the Capital to Heian* (*Heianjō miyako sadame*, 1704), in which Danjūrō II acted on this occasion, was essentially a string of highlights from his father's career.[116]

Danjūrō II kept repeating performances memorializing his father throughout his life until his own body came to be fully invested, in the eyes of his fans, with memories of his predecessor. At the same time, he also transformed certain roles, making them his own. Accordingly, we might think of his body as being subject to a double vision in which present and past overlap, and of his acting as being constructed as much by audiences' perception of him in connection to his father as by his performance on stage. As this mode of appreciation increasingly came to underwrite the audience's enjoyment of the theater, new requirements were placed on the actors. Each kabuki name came with a set of roles that had to be mastered, and the name was not necessarily inherited by the actor's actual son. When Matsumoto Kōshirō II became Danjūrō IV in 1754, he had to switch from being an "evil role" (*jitsuaku*) actor to being a lead-male-role (*tachiyaku*) actor in order to take on the characters that were associated with the Danjūrō name. In other words, kabuki actors were not regarded as ordinary people, living their lives from start to finish. Their bodies were invested with a particular sort of interbodily meaning that transformed them into the corporal equivalent of a chronotope—what we might perhaps term a "chronosome"—as vehicles for realizing a sense of time. Indeed, over the years, theatergoers' memories of actors also came to serve a function in marking the passage of time on a larger, generational scale. Among the many conversations about kabuki that take place in both the women's and the men's baths in Shikite Sanba's *The Bathhouse of the Floating World* (*Ukiyoburo*, 1809–1813), for instance, is one in which men of four different generations use kabuki to express their relationships to one another:

> KIMOEMON: You're a little younger than me, so you must not know Danjūrō II?
> FURUZAEMON: No, I remember him vaguely. KIMOEMON: Was it the final act of some play? All the actors stood on a platform that gradually rose up, and then Danjūrō II came up through an opening on stage in flaming *aragoto* style. He came up with a glare, holding a clenched fist to his chin, with a *shimadai* [decorative ornament representing an isle of eternal youth] hooked on the hilt of his huge sword. ABATAMI: No one would pay money to see a performance like that today! KIMOEMON: Oh, you guys are no good. Listen, that's what kabuki plays are supposed to be. That's where the difference between real life and plays lies.
> FURUZAEMON: That's right. I don't know that performance by Danjūrō II, but I do know the pattern. I saw Ichimura Uzaemon IX do it. He was such a master.

CHŪROKU: Oh, even we know him. Didn't he do the *Dance of Three Transformations* [*Mitsuningyō*]? ABATAMI: These days, that's done by Bandō Mitsugorō III. CHŪROKU: Yes, Mitsugorō is the son of Uzaemon.[117]

In order to understand this conversation, which is structured by the contrast between the relatively "true-to-life" style then in vogue and the more stylized acting that Kimoemon remembers from nearly half a century earlier, we should know that Ichikawa Danjūrō II passed on his acting techniques and styles to Ichimura Uzaemon IX (1725–1785), who—having made his own modifications to what he inherited—then passed them on to Bandō Mitsugorō III (1775–1831). Although the exact ages of the four men in this passage are not clear, Kimoemon and Furuemon obviously belong to a different generation than Abatami and Chūroku, and their understanding of the gap that separates them, and thus of their relationships to one another, is given shape by their knowledge of kabuki. This is a vivid illustration of the process by which kabuki came to serve as the ground on which the imagined community of Edo was constructed. It was not something forced on people from above; it was generated through the culture of the theater.

Earlier I discussed *Folding Screens of Famous Places in Edo*, a panoramic painting of the city that includes a depiction of the theater district, represented as if it were encircled by water even though it was actually in the heart of the city (see figure 1.1). This pictorial framing of the theater district as an isolated utopia, which recalls similar depictions of utopian spaces separated from the ordinary world by a body of water, does not alter the fact that in the painting as a whole, the theaters remain very much integrated into the cityscape: the screens offer the viewer an expansive, crowded vista of which the theater district is just a small part. The focus here is on the extent and the vibrancy of Edo itself, already on its way to becoming the largest city in the world.[118] Significantly, almost all seventeenth-century depictions of Edo's theaters are like this, appearing as part of a representation of the broader urban landscape.

Beginning in the middle of the eighteenth century, artists began producing prints and book illustrations of a very different sort. Known as "theater pictures" (*gekijōzu*), they showed the interiors rather than the exteriors of kabuki theaters.[119] A triptych by Utagawa Toyokuni I de-

FIGURE 1.5 The inside of the Morita Theater, as illustrated in a print by Utagawa Toyokuni I. (Courtesy of Waseda University, Tsubouchi Memorial Theater Museum, 1-1293, 94, 95)

picting the Morita Theater is typical, as only the inside of the theater is visible, as if the space were self-contained, completely cut off from the urban landscape outside (figure 1.5).

Theater comprises and creates a world of its own; it becomes a space, both physical and imagined, in which the people of Edo can reside. Around the same time, books thematizing theater interiors as a cultural space, as a separate country known as "Theaterland" (*kejōkoku*), began to appear. Examples are Hōseidō Kisanji (1735–1815) and Katsukawa Shundō's *An Illustrated Encyclopedia of the Three Stages of Edo* (*Ukan sandai zue*, 1791); *The Illustrated Encyclopedia of Theater*; and Kyokutei Bakin and Utagawa Toyokuni's *Famous Views of Actors* (*Yakusha meisho zue*, 1800). In *The Illustrated Encyclopedia of Theater*, for instance, we find each actor presented as a country titled after his poetry name—Ichikawa Danjūrō V is the Country of Hakuen (Hakuen-koku), Segawa Kikunojō III (1751–1810) is the Country of Rokō (Rokō-koku), and so on—in a manner that plays on the various depictions of "myriad lands" (*bankoku*) that began to circulate in popular publications after the Spanish and Portuguese introduced new maps and cartographical knowledge to Japan.[120] The powerful hold of the theater and its culture on much of the population of Edo as an autonomous space of the imagination was famously captured in a rueful comment made by Buyō

PRESENTING THE PAST

Inshi, a moralistic nineteenth-century samurai with a hearty dislike of the theater: "These days kabuki doesn't imitate the world; kabuki is the model and the world tries to imitate kabuki."[121]

CENSORSHIP AND THE AUDIENCE

The understanding of Edo kabuki that I have offered in this chapter, as an institution that gradually created a sense of time and space capable of being shared across classes, is somewhat at odds with the prevalent image of the position of kabuki in early modern society—above all, the widely accepted notion that it was a sort of oppositional theater of the common people that subverted the interests of the ruling class. This notion of kabuki as a site of popular resistance to shogunal authority is closely tied to the impression that it was heavily censored and that it was a theater patronized primarily by commoners. As we near the end of this chapters, we thus must reconsider the nature of government censorship and prohibitions as they relate to kabuki and its audience, both in the seventeenth century, before the annual contract system was established and the legal status of kabuki was settled, and throughout the rest of the early modern period.

I will begin my consideration of the Tokugawa government's relationship to kabuki by looking at a series of early laws pertaining to the kabuki theater. In the seventeenth century, the shogunate issued a series of bans on different kinds of performances. It is commonly understood that women were banned from acting in kabuki in 1629 and that the boy actors known as *wakashu* were banned in 1652, but the enforcement of these prohibitions seems to have taken place much more gradually and been subject to considerable regional variation. Historical records suggest that women actors were banned in 1622, 1629, and 1634, and that there were repeated prohibitions on productions featuring both men and women from 1603 to 1640 and, again, in 1645. Restrictions on *wakashu* kabuki were issued from 1651 to 1653 in conjunction with prohibitions on male and female prostitution both during and after this period.[122] These prohibitions have frequently been interpreted as a series of attempts by the government to suppress kabuki itself that were met by a corresponding series of responses by performers trying to evade the prohibitions. This process culminated in the emergence of *yarō* (adult male kabuki), which in turn developed into a new type of theater that the shogunate no longer tried to ban outright. By separating kabuki from prostitution and deemphasizing the beauty of the performers, the argument goes, this back-and-forth of suppression and resistance spurred the creation of the more content-driven theatrical form we know today, which the shogunate reluctantly allowed to survive, if only as a necessary evil. This theory is useful to some extent as an explanation of the emergence of narrative theater, but it leaves one wondering why, if the government was so intent on banning kabuki itself, it did not just ban all kabuki. Given that samurai were such an important segment of the audience for kabuki during the first part of the early modern period, it seems more plausible that the string of prohibitions, issued with regulations on prostitution, reflected a broader concern with samurai conduct and an attempt to curtail samurai involvement with kabuki. The various laws were meant less to restrict subversive activities by commoners, in other words, than to control indirectly the behavior of upper-class members of society—samurai, above all, but also aristocrats.

Since commoners were not a significant element of the audience for kabuki in Edo until the end of the seventeenth century, it seems only natural that regulations relating to kabuki were meant to target the samurai audience. It is still uncertain whether the ban on *wakashu* kabuki in Edo was enforced in Kyoto and Osaka as well, or how effective it was even in Edo, but this ban, as well as others prohibiting female kabuki troupes and performances featuring both male and female actors, represented an attempt to detach kabuki, as a form of entertainment specifically associated with the upper classes, from prostitution. First, the government tried to isolate female prostitution by moving prostitutes into the licensed quarters; then it tried to eliminate postproduction meetings with kabuki actors. In fact, the ban on *wakashu* kabuki was accompanied by a broader prohibition against anyone keeping young boys for business purposes, a ban that itself included *wakashu* actors.[123] These rather drastic measures to suppress prostitution at the theaters were followed by bans specifically prohibiting actors from visiting samurai residences, which were issued repeatedly over two decades beginning in 1655.[124] By working to regulate both the unruly proliferation of different types of performances and the theaters' postproduction business, the government in effect centralized kabuki in the licensed theaters. The intention was not to ban kabuki but to make the theaters take responsibility for supervising their actors. As many scholars have observed, over time these laws had a sanitizing effect on kabuki, shifting the focus of performances from dances that showcased the beauty of young female and male actors to the acting and the narrative content of the plays. This does not change the fact, however, that in an important sense, the real target of the laws was the primary audience for Edo kabuki at this time: the samurai.

As a result of the repeated prohibitions against visits by actors to samurai residences, the number of performances by major actors at daimyo houses decreased dramatically after the 1680s. Even so, the practice seems to have survived, carried on mainly by actors who were not affiliated with the licensed theaters. This is evident from the repeated appearance in the *Kanpō-Era Compilation of Legal Documents* (*Ofuregaki Kanpō shūsei*) of bans against visits by nonprofessional actors to daimyo residences.[125] At the Edo residence of the daimyo of Kaga, at least eighteen puppet plays and ten kabuki viewings were recorded between 1698 and 1727. These performances, attended by hundreds, were staged as private entertainments on occasions such as the visit of a married daughter or as a treat for household workers.[126]

The government also prohibited samurai from visiting the licensed theaters, though this appears to have been largely an empty gesture. Diary entries indicate that even in the eighteenth and nineteenth centuries, samurai and the occasional daimyo were still attending the theater, and visits of this sort appear in literary works and plays; kabuki playbills were also delivered to samurai residences.[127] And as I noted earlier, while actors at the major theaters were no longer able to perform freely at daimyo residences, from the eighteenth century onward theaters began staging plays that specifically appealed to the female attendants at daimyo houses in the third month of every year, when these women were given leave to visit their families. This kept the higher echelons of society connected to the culture of kabuki. Furthermore, the late eighteenth and early nineteenth centuries witnessed a proliferation of regulations prohibiting amateur performers, particularly women, from going to samurai residences. The fact that the government issued so many prohibitions during this period suggests that even after the seventeenth century, kabuki's popularity continued to extend beyond the licensed theaters and an audience of ordinary townspeople. The frequency of the edicts also indicates that they did not hold the same legal force as laws do today and that getting performers to obey them was not easy.

That said, the precise makeup of the audience for kabuki in the second half of the early modern period is difficult to pin down. In the late eighteenth and nineteenth centuries, theaters increased the number of expensive *sajiki* boxes and reduced the number of cheap areas, such as the "boxes at the back of the theater" (*mukō sajiki*) and the "leftovers" (*kiriotoshi*). The price for admission also rose during this period as the theaters tried to extricate themselves from financial difficulties.[128] Based on an investigation of depictions of kabuki audiences at late-eighteenth-century plays in Edo, Hattori Yukio speculated that a typical audience consisted largely of samurai and their guests and workers, wealthy merchants, upper-class store owners and their attendants and guests, intellectuals such as literati and monks, and courtesans and performers with their patrons.[129] At the same time, there are records of less affluent kabuki fans sneaking into the theaters. One of many examples is an incident in 1812, when four or five *tobi*—construction workers who also served as firefighters—were kicked out of the Nakamura Theater after they sneaked in without paying. The men returned in the evening with sixty of their fellows in the "Ha Group" (Ha-gumi), armed with bamboo arrows. During the fight, one of the *tobi* was killed, many were injured, and several hundred people fled in panic from the theater. A number of the *tobi* were arrested, but some returned the next day and disrupted the production once again.[130] These repeated fights involving thugs, as well as references to "cockroaches" (*aburamushi*) who slipped in without purchasing tickets, reveal that the temptation to try to see performances without paying the regular price of admission was strong.

Prices varied a good deal from one production to the next, as well as from season to season and according to a particular theater's position in the hierarchy. While the face-showing production was expensive, the cost of attending a summer production could be a fraction of its price. When Nanboku staged his extremely popular summer production of *Tokubei from India: A Tale from Foreign Lands* (*Tenjiku Tokubei ikoku banashi*) at the Kawarazaki Theater in 1804, the cheapest tickets sold for 64 *mon*, the equivalent of a few bowls of soba noodles, and audience members could sit in even the best areas of the theater for one-third the usual price.[131] Cheap seats seem to have been available at many or all performances during the nineteenth century, if only in reduced numbers, and there was also the option of paying to watch only a single act.[132] According to *Dustheap Stories* (*Chirizukadan*, 1814), the average price of watching a play from the edge of the stage was 100 or 130 *mon* per person when the price for a bowl of soba noodles, at least at one soba shop in Edo, ranged from 16 to 48 *mon* and a roasted eel cost from 170 to 200 *mon*. This seems like a fairly affordable price for a full day's entertainment.[133] Kabuki scholar Gunji Masakatsu (1913–1998) also suggested that the three theaters had a practice of admitting the audience for free on the opening day of each new production.[134] Depictions of ordinary commoners attending performances or talking about their experiences at the theater are, moreover, commonplace in various nineteenth-century genres of fiction.

In short, it is clear that kabuki was not always a theater for commoner classes throughout the early modern period and that the audience seemed to shift even as the theatrical culture continued to engage diverse groups of people. After the late eighteenth century, as Hattori Yukio suggested, the core audience for kabuki must have been made up of relatively well-off groups of people, and yet it also seems an exaggeration to say that kabuki became inaccessible to most. There are abundant descriptions of ordinary commoners going to the theaters and fairly great ranges in price, depending on the season of the production. Yet it is safe to say that kabuki was not accessible to all commoners, especially toward the end of the early modern period. The increasing number of poor laborers who streamed into Edo during the nineteenth century in search of jobs, only to find themselves just managing to scrape by, were certainly not part of the usual kabuki audience. If anything, they might have enjoyed the "temple productions" and "small productions" that flourished during the early nineteenth century as a sort of illicit kabuki, distinct from the "major productions" at the licensed theaters.[135] Performances of these types provided a cheap alternative for those who could not afford regular visits to the major theaters.

This brings us back to the issue of censorship, and in particular the assumption that the authorities routinely censored the content of kabuki productions because of the threat they seemed to pose to the social order. In 1644, the government issued a ban on the use of real or important last names in performance. But, generally speaking, censorship of content was rare because for most of the early modern period, there was no system in place to censor play scripts that were not published in print. On occasion, specific complaints from important families or institutions did result in changes to plays; the names of characters from *The Treasury of Loyal Retainers* had to be altered, for instance, because descendants of the participants in the original historical incident on which the play was based submitted a complaint to the Edo city commissioners.[136] Similarly, plays about the monk Shinran were repeatedly banned in Kyoto and Osaka as a result of objections from Higashi Honganji Temple.[137] Edicts prohibiting the staging of contemporary news items, including love suicides, also appeared from time to time.[138] From this perspective, the history of kabuki can undoubtedly be viewed as a struggle against government regulations that tried to restrict the staging of contemporary customs. A survey of the two volumes of *Collected Laws on Edo Kabuki* (*Edo kabuki hōrei shūsei* and *Zoku Edo kabuki hōrei shūsei*), however, reveals that surprisingly few plays were censored for their political content.

What sorts of prohibitions were issued, then? The truth is that most regulations pertaining to the theater were related to fire and sumptuary issues. The fear of fire is clear from the frequency with which edicts urging caution were issued and from the restrictions on theater architecture and the materials that could be used to build the theaters throughout the early modern period. From 1789 into the nineteenth century, for instance, numerous edicts were issued prohibiting the use of candles in the theaters and requiring that performances end by 5:00 P.M. Most of the other bans in the latter part of the early modern period tended to focus on sumptuary issues. There was a good reason for this: according to the official social hierarchy, actors were considered outcasts and were required to live in designated areas of the city; but in reality, many of the star actors lived almost as lavishly as daimyo, in sprawling mansions with attendants and servants even for their wives, mistresses, and children.[139] As a result, the shogunate viewed actors as subjects of inappropriate and unseemly extravagance whose free-spending ways might have a deleterious effect on the public. There was a particular concern with costumes, since the actors supplied their own. Such regulations were issued over and over again throughout the early modern period, and there are many instances of punishments meted out in response to infractions. In 1730, for example, Ichikawa Danjūrō II got into trouble for wearing silver clogs in the role of Watōnai in *The Battle of Coxinga*, and Segawa Kikunojō III was reprimanded in 1775 for using real gold in his costume. Compared with these specific concerns, which come up repeatedly, edicts relating to the content of plays are infrequent and seem to have been issued on an ad hoc basis, in response to particular incidents.

Censorship of kabuki also appears to have been less rigorously enforced than in other fields of cultural production. Throughout most of the early modern period, there were two forms of censorship: "preliminary inspection" (*shita-kenbun*) and "on-site inspection" (*hon-kenbun*).[140] An on-site inspection was conducted when someone from the city magistrate's office actually attended a play to check its content. On these occasions, the inspector would sit in a specially designated "official's box" (*yaku sajiki*) that the theater kept in one of the best areas of the house. Theaters were often aware in advance of the dates of on-site inspections, a situation that may indicate a degree of collusion between the theater and the censors. Onoe Kikugorō V (1844–1903), who was the manager of the Ichimura Theater at the end of the early modern period, describes this cozy relationship between the inspector and a special employee in the ticket office (*shikiriba*) known as the "official's handler" (*oyakugakari*):

> The *oyakugakari* developed an intimate relationship with the official. On the day of his visit, a cotton carpet or the like with a viewing hole would be hung in front of the box, but on other days the box would be sold for the personal profit of the official. The theater was cheated in this way. When the officials came to visit, the official's handler would provide meals. In addition, the theater manager would use bribery, asking the officials to go with him to [the famous restaurant] Yaozen about twice a year so that he could treat them to saké.[141]

This passage shows the rather murky state of on-site censorship, especially when we remember that the dates of the visit were known in advance. And preliminary inspections, which supposedly required the review of all scripts and costumes before the face-showing and spring productions—the two most important productions in the kabuki calendar, as we have seen—did not always have the desired effect. Legal records include cases in which a theater got into trouble for presenting a plain costume to the inspectors during the preliminary inspection and then switching to a much more elaborate one for the actual production.[142] In 1762, Segawa Kikunojō II (1741–1773) got into trouble for wearing a lavish costume made with the best white silk (*rinzu*), worn only by the highest of the samurai classes. The costume, which had been given to Kikunojō by a daimyo house, was seized by the city magistrate, but the magistrate later allowed the production to continue without punishment, after the daimyo house interceded.[143] In any case, the vast majority of the records pertaining to the censorship of kabuki are related to costumes. We must keep in mind that during most of the early modern period, there was no system in place for censoring manuscripts, a situation that contrasts with that for printed books. Officials seem to have begun asking to see scripts only after the Tenpō reforms (1841–1843).[144]

In short, it is time to move away from the notion that early modern kabuki was a subversive institution that allowed townspeople to express their opposition to the ruling class or fomented such opposition in its content or subject matter. From the late seventeenth century, Edo kabuki served to rewrite samurai history as a publicly shared present, forging a connection between elite and commoner culture. The theater gradually fashioned itself into a performative space capable of fostering a dynamic cultural imaginary specific to Edo. It was only around the nineteenth century, around the time that Tsuruya Nanboku was first elevated to the status of head playwright, that the theaters began doing away with the conventions that they had treasured for so long, causing a transformation of their culture. It is to this transitional moment, and in particular to the significant contribution made by Nanboku's female ghost plays, that I now turn.

PART II

The Beginning of the End of Edo Kabuki

Yotsuya kaidan in 1825

[2]

OVERTURNING THE WORLD

The Treasury of Loyal Retainers and *Yotsuya kaidan*

THE BEGINNING OF THE END OF EDO KABUKI

Tsuruya Nanboku IV began his celebrated career as a playwright during a time when Edo's kabuki theaters were in the midst of a radical transformation. In chapter 1, I traced the rise and development of Edo kabuki as a cultural form particular to that city, from its emergence near the end of the seventeenth century to its crystallization in the eighteenth century, and showed how it came to serve as a powerful vehicle for promoting a sense of community. By the time Nanboku started creating his plays, many of the characteristics that figured in this discussion—the theater-affiliation system, with its annual contracts tying the actors to a single theater; the practice of announcing newly contracted casts in the eleventh month; and, indeed, the entire kabuki calendar—were waning in importance. Even the formerly crucial practice of "presenting the past," fusing urban settings and characters with familiar stories derived from samurai history and doing so in a manner that allowed ordinary Edoites to feel connected to the shogunal lineage and the culture it spawned, was losing its significance. Nanboku's plays were both a product of their age and a force that pushed these transformations along. As such, they are the ideal material for exploring the process by which the traditions of Edo kabuki began to crumble in the early nineteenth century, giving rise to something altogether new and in some sense paving the way for the reinvention of kabuki as a national rather than a local form in the first decades of the twentieth century.

The nineteenth century was a difficult time for kabuki in Edo. By the 1790s, the Nakamura, Ichimura, and Morita Theaters, which for more than a century had been the city's three major venues for kabuki, could no longer sustain the enormous debts they had racked up by staging so many lavish productions over the years. In 1790, the Morita Theater had been compelled to entrust its performance license to the Kawarasaki Theater, its "backup turret," after a lengthy period during which its doors remained closed. In 1793, the Nakamura and Ichimura Theaters, both bankrupt, followed the Morita Theater's example and signed tentative five-year contracts that put their kabuki production rights in the hands of the Miyako and Kiri Theaters, respectively.[1] Thus in the eleventh month of 1793, for the first time in the long history of Edo kabuki, none of the major licensed theaters was able to stage its face-showing production. Clearly, the theaters could no longer go on operating as they had; something would have to change.

In the tenth month of 1794, the three backup theaters submitted to the city magistrate the "Document Requesting a Decision Regarding Regulation of the Three Kabuki Theaters" (Sanshibai kyōgenza torishimari hōgi sadame shōmon), in which they proposed a number of fundamental changes in the way the theaters operated, and whose stated goal was "regulation for the eternal perpetuation of kabuki" (*kabuki eizoku no shihō*). Among these changes were the capping of actors' salaries and the revision of the annual contract system, especially when no sponsors could be found for the face-showing production.[2] Specifically, the three theater managers asked that they be given the freedom to rotate actors among the theaters even within a given year, paying them by the performance rather than for an entire year's work. When these proposals were approved at the end of the year, they triggered a profound transformation in Edo kabuki: They made it easier for the theaters to stay in business, but at the same time they also undermined the characteristics that had made kabuki and its calendar so important to the city as a system, the object of a communal fantasy.

Predictably, the dissolution of the theater-affiliation system brought about a gradual decline in the importance of the face-showing production. After all, an actor could now appear in one theater in the morning and then perform with a different group of actors at a different venue in the afternoon. For more than a century, the face-showing production had helped the theaters cultivate a sense of anticipation and excitement about the coming kabuki year, so this was a significant change. Theaters gradually lost the function they had had as a cultural space in a government-regulated system, instead coming to resemble modern theaters that competed to hire freelance actors.[3] Despite the cap of 500 *ryō* that was placed on their annual salaries, popular actors appeared in many productions and started taking roles that fell outside their conventional specialties, with the result that their earnings actually ended up increasing, a situation reflected in the repeated issuance of regulations on salaries during the nineteenth century. A print sold in 1827 that ranked actors by their incomes indicates that six actors in Edo earned more than 1,000 *ryō* that year; Nakamura Utaemon III, who headed the list, raked in 1,400 *ryō*.[4] And at the same time that the theaters were trying to deal with these financial difficulties, repeated fires made it necessary to cancel productions while the theaters were being rebuilt and to temporarily entrust performance licenses to the backup theaters.[5] Overall, nineteenth-century kabuki is characterized by irregularly scheduled productions at unconventional venues and by an increasingly radical deviation from the conventional calendar.

The changes were not limited to salaries and the calendar; the content of productions also shifted. This is best symbolized by the decreasing importance of the *sekai*. Mimasuya Nisōji writes in *Collected Essays on Kabuki* (*Kabuki shūdan*, 1851) that the practice of meeting on the twelfth of the ninth month to decide on a world for the next year's face-showing production came to an end in the 1830s: "For the past twenty years," he explained, "there has been no *sekai*."[6] The symbolic inclusion of *Wait a Minute!* in the face-showing production and the spring production's invariable use of the military world of the Soga brothers seem to have lost something of their original meaning as the content of plays came to be dominated by other interests.[7] Simply put, Edo kabuki came to rely less on the framework of the *sekai* rooted in samurai narratives as it became more focused as a form on the presentation of recent events in the city and its environs. During the last decades of the early modern period, the historical military *sekai* was pushed into the background in a majority of plays, treated as a residue of Edo's past rather than as a necessary element of the present, until the use of a *sekai* itself came to be regarded as a *shukō*.

Nanboku's staging of *Yotsuya kaidan* in 1825 stands as a perfect encapsulation of the transformation that kabuki was undergoing during this time. He experimented in various ways in the new financial and social context in which he found himself, bringing in large audiences with sensational stage effects involving water, blood and gore, and depictions of lower-class urban spaces that had not formerly played a role in the theater. He succeeded particularly well with his repeated staging of ghosts, and especially female ghosts—a ubiquitous trope in popular literary and theatrical productions in early-nineteenth-century Edo. Using popular beliefs related to both the female body and female ghosts liberated from their bodies, Nanboku's plays broke away from the samurai worlds that had shaped Edo kabuki for more than a century to create an entirely new kind of theatrical experience.

In this and the next two chapters, I look at these issues—Nanboku's use of female characters both living and dead—in order to explore the profound changes that were taking place in nineteenth-century Edo kabuki. This chapter analyzes *Yotsuya kaidan* as a sort of gendered rebuttal of the famous revenge play *The Treasury of Loyal Retainers*, with which it was first staged in 1825 in a double bill. Before we turn to this production, I describe the ways in which the cultural system of Edo kabuki, discussed in chapter 1, was beginning to break down during the period when Nanboku was active.

GRAVITATING TOWARD THE LOW

Tsuruya Nanboku is probably the most famous early modern kabuki playwright and is certainly much better known than, for instance, Tsuuchi Jihei or Sakurada Jisuke. But there is something unusual, even paradoxical, about his celebrity. In contrast to Tsuuchi and Sakurada, each of whom is familiar to kabuki specialists as a representative playwright of one of the great golden ages of Edo kabuki—the early and late eighteenth century, respectively—Nanboku is regarded as an embodiment not of Edo kabuki at its height but of a particular mood or aesthetic that is thought to have infused early-nineteenth-century kabuki and that has been assigned a privileged position in the history of the theater for the manner in which it is said to have expressed the tensions that emerged in Japanese society as old feudal structures headed toward collapse. This rich and fascinating period is habitually described using the phrase "overripe and decadent" (*ranjuku taihai*), and Nanboku's *Yotsuya kaidan*, more than any other play, is seen as the most perfect instantiation of this mood or aesthetic. Indeed, it is not an exaggeration to say that twentieth-century interpretations of *Yotsuya kaidan* have formed the core of the popular image of this "overripe and decadent" time. To some extent, *Yotsuya kaidan* and the image of Nanboku as a playwright that the play's modern reception has promoted have come to be regarded on a popular level as capturing something essential to Edo kabuki, even to kabuki in general. In the eyes of many modern and contemporary critics, Nanboku and *Yotsuya kaidan* transformed the early nineteenth century into a sort of super golden age that surpasses even the conventional golden ages of Edo kabuki.

The situation looked rather different to Nanboku's contemporaries, however. From the perspective of playwrights active in the early nineteenth century—none of whom, I should note, could compete with Nanboku's fame—the time in which they lived was unambiguously a period of decline, and they looked back nostalgically to the mid- to late eighteenth century as an age of efflorescence. Nagashima Juami (1769–1848) spelled this out explicitly in his now lost *Notes by Juami* (*Juami hikki*): "Kabuki was all the rage from the Meiwa [1764–1772] to the Tenmei [1781–1789] period. Actor critiques thus appeared without interruption. Kabuki gradually went into a decline beginning in the Kansei period and hit absolute bottom during the Bunka, Bunsei, and Tenpō periods."[8]

Nanboku climbed to stardom during the periods when, according to Juami, kabuki "hit absolute bottom." Not surprisingly, given this context, his tastes and his style differed considerably from those of his predecessors, and he pursued them through somewhat unconventional means. Rather than concentrate his energies on lavish face-showing productions, which had originally been the high point of the kabuki calendar, Nanboku introduced various innovations in a series of summer horror plays (*kaidan kyōgen*) that showcased Onoe Matsusuke I and then Matsusuke's foster son Onoe Kikugorō III. As we saw in chapter 1, summer productions took place during the six and seventh months, when star actors generally took a long vacation to recuperate after the spring production, which in a good year would have kept them busy for five months in a row, beginning in the first month. When Nanboku was promoted to head playwright, he decided to change the schedule, and some actors proved willing to stay and work with Nanboku on summer productions full of entertainingly horrific spectacles that were produced on an unusually low budget. Some sources note that the actors were paid very little for these productions and that the theaters managed to sell tickets in even their most lucrative areas for a mere 15 *mon*, less than half the usual cost.[9] Previously, neither illustrated street playbills nor illustrated billboards had been created for summer productions, since they were so minor. Nanboku decided that the advertisement was necessary, but in order to reduce costs, he would sometimes have posters printed that showed only the names of cast members and then have the woodblock for the poster cut up and used to print a cast playbill.[10]

If Nanboku's new emphasis on summer productions represented a major innovation in the kabuki schedule, so too did the content of his plays. Perhaps most notable was his heavy reliance on stage effects. According to Furuido Hideo, water effects were a crucial element in Nanboku's early ghost plays, on which he collaborated with Onoe Matsusuke.[11] Matsusuke would splash into a big tank of water on stage and then, just moments later, emerge from another part of the stage in a different costume, playing another character, and completely dry. Matsusuke first introduced this effect in 1804 in *Tokubei from India: A Tale from Foreign Lands*, and the audience was stunned. According to *Edo in Bloom: A Kabuki Time Line*, "People raved about this effect because no one else was able to imitate it. The usually empty summer production was packed. Matsusuke is a true master of the art."[12]

The trick behind Matsusuke's quick change was never revealed, and the water effect remained one of the major highlights of Nanboku's ghost productions during the first few decades of his career as head playwright.[13] *What Really Happens Backstage* (*Okyōgen gakuya no honsetsu*, 1858–1859), a guide to kabuki special effects that includes numerous entries on ghosts, explains the mechanism of a related trick by which a ghost is able to appear from a pool of water. Basically, the actor enters a smaller pool at the back of the stage and moves from there into the main pool, out in front. The pool in the back is not visible to the audience because the stage covers it.[14] Once the actor reaches the main pool, he hides under a few conveniently placed lotus leaves, standing on a wooden platform that then lifts him out of the water, as we see in figure 2.1.[15]

Staging a scene like this required an incredible amount of work. First of all, a pool had to be constructed on stage. According to the Meiji-period actor Onoe Kikugorō V, "There were no water pipes in those

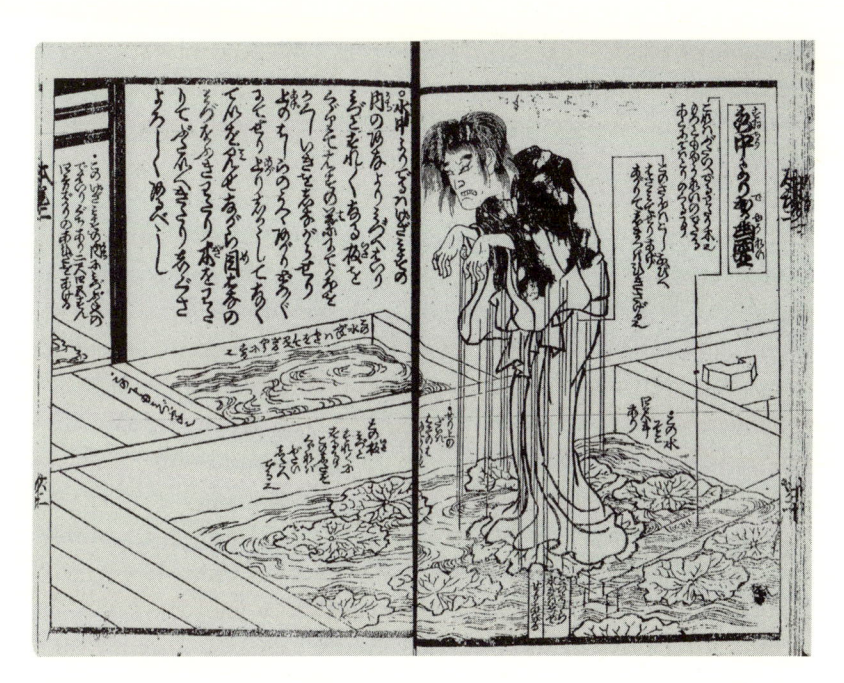

FIGURE 2.1 A ghost appearing from water, as illustrated in Santei Shunba (text) and Utagawa Kunitsuna (pictures), *Okyōgen gakuya no honsetsu* (fascicle 4, 22 *ura*–23 *omote*). (Courtesy of the Tokyo Metropolitan Library)

days, and since it would have been impossible to draw so much water from wells, the troupe scooped up water every night from the Sumida River."[16] Performing the scene was not easy for Matsusuke, either, as he was already too old to be jumping into cold water day after day, especially when a play was successful enough that it continued well into the autumn. In *Otogizōshi in Color* (*Iroeiri otogizōshi*, 1808), Matsusuke's foster son (Kikugorō III, though at this time he was still Eizaburō) had to take over the quick change in the water because the effect was too demanding for the aging actor.[17] The actor critique *An Actor's Book of Great Learning* (*Yakusha daigaku*, 1809) commented on Kikugorō III's successful takeover of the quick change: "Matsusuke injured himself during the quick change. This special effect is a secret of his acting house, so the part could not be taken over by other actors. The replacement was well done, well done indeed."[18]

Nanboku's frequent experimentation with special effects of this sort says a lot about kabuki in the particular age in which he lived. As a playwright active during a period when theaters were often in dire financial straits, his position was never stable, especially when he was in his twenties and thirties. Few materials have survived to document his life, but from what has remained, early in his career Nanboku seems to have supplemented his income by participating in regional plays and, most interestingly, in the tent shows known as *misemono*. One surviving record indicates that in his youth, Nanboku collaborated with the writers Hiraga Gennai (1726–1779) and Tatekawa [Utei] Enba on a tent show at Ekōin Temple in the Fukagawa District. Nanboku was not alone in his interest in these shows. The head stage-set builder Hasegawa Kanbei XI (1781–1841), with whom Nanboku worked on the special effects in *Yotsuya kaidan*, is also known to have been involved in creating tent shows, as was the wig maker Tomokurō, who is mentioned in Nanboku's plays and appears in backstage illustrations with Nanboku.[19]

Tent shows, which ranked much lower than kabuki in the hierarchy of performance genres, showcased all kinds of unusual spectacles and tricks. They were staged at temples, at shrines, and, most of all, in the area around Ryōgoku Bridge, and were all the rage from the early nineteenth century through the end of the early modern period. Unlike kabuki theaters, which had to pay star actors very large salaries, these spectacles could be cheaply put up, produced, and immediately torn down when they ceased to be profitable. According to Kawazoe Yū, a successful tent show could generate in a hundred days the equivalent in today's currency of a few million yen in profit, or tens of thousands of dollars.[20] It makes sense, therefore, that the business-savvy Nanboku would not only help stage tent shows but also incorporate into his plays stage effects similar to those used in tent shows. Indeed, many of his plays include scenes featuring snake charmers, giant female sumo wrestlers, and tightrope walking—all of which were familiar sights in tent shows.[21] To some extent, then, Nanboku's innovative approach to the content of summer productions—above all, his extensive use of special effects—can be interpreted as an attempt to give his plays a new excitement by drawing on a lower stratum of culture, hybridizing the traditions of Edo kabuki that he had inherited with less costly forms of entertainment that were flourishing at the same time.

This tendency to gravitate toward the low, including the tent shows, is apparent as well in Nanboku's choice of settings. Rather than set the events of a contemporary play in a conventional location, such as a merchant household, he would have them unfold in the seediest possible areas of Edo, including illegal prostitution shacks and the plazas off Ryōgoku Bridge, where so many of the tent shows took place. This was how he managed to work in the snake charmers and female sumo wrestlers. Spaces like these, which pulsated with the energies of the lower classes, had never before been invoked on the kabuki stage, and Nanboku's attention to them signaled the emergence of a sensibility so new that a fresh term was coined for plays in this style: in contrast to conventional "*sewa* plays," which took place in contemporary settings and often originated in Kyoto or Osaka, Nanboku's plays came to be described as *kizewa*, which might be translated as "true *sewa*," "live *sewa*," or "raw *sewa*."

Nanboku had excelled in eccentric and surprising showmanship even before he became a head playwright late in life. Based on a survey of many of Nanboku's plays, including productions from before his promotion, Gunji Masakatsu concluded that from early on, Nanboku specialized in humor (*okashimi*) and incorporated startling spectacles into his plays. One often cited reference to a special effect that Nanboku created early in his career occurs in Tamenaga Shunsui's *The Iwai Bathhouse: Umbrella in a Light Rain* (*Iwaiburo shigure no karakasa*, 1838). In the scene that Shunsui describes, which is known as the "whale pantomime" (*kujira no danmari*), the curtain was drawn to reveal nothing but a perpendicular expanse of black paper that blocked the audience's view of the stage and was meant to represent the massive belly of a whale that a fishermen had caught and brought ashore. A bandit dressed in lavish clothing then jumped out of the belly, breaking the paper and bringing with him the treasures of Emperor Antoku, who had famously died as an infant when his grandmother, the Nun of the Second Rank, leaped into the ocean cradling him in her arms during the Heike warriors' decisive defeat at the naval battle of Dan-no-ura. The startling notion that Emperor Antoku had been eaten by a whale must have delighted the audience, but the visual composition of the scene was even more creative. As Shunsui noted, "Nanboku's brilliance lies in the eccentricity and freedom with which he composes his plays, and his ability to surprise the audience, never boring them."[22] Whales were among the earliest subjects of the Ryōgoku Bridge tent shows, so it is easy to guess where Nanboku got the idea.[23]

THE DECLINE OF THE FACE-SHOWING PRODUCTION

The innovations that Nanboku introduced into the summer productions gained in importance as he gradually began incorporating them and their novel sensibility into the two major productions of the year: the face-showing and spring productions. It is important to realize, however, that the changes he pioneered did not immediately overturn earlier conventions. Nanboku continued to use well-known *sekai* even in his most radically contemporary productions, though he often altered their meaning by jumbling together a number of different *sekai* in a somewhat haphazard manner. The early nineteenth century thus was an age of transformation built on the fundamental paradigms that had been established in the eighteenth century. Even as various new effects and themes were brought to the stage, the plays continued to draw on classic *sekai* such as the four Minamoto guardians or, in the case of face-showing productions, the *Pre-Chronicle of Great Peace* (*Zentaiheiki*). In fact, these *sekai* saw something of a resurgence at this time, which suggests that playwrights were consciously borrowing from older conventions.[24]

One of the best examples of Nanboku's innovative approach to playmaking is *The Four Guardians: A New Splash at Tamagawa River* (*Shitennō ubuyu no Tamagawa*), a face-showing production staged at the Tamagawa Theater in 1818 that featured stars such as Ichikawa Danjūrō VII (1791–1859), Matsumoto Kōshirō V, Iwai Hanshirō V (1776–1847), and Segawa Kikunojō V (1802–1832).[25] Set in the conventional world of the four guardians, the production's style was nonetheless quite unconventional, reflecting Nanboku's taste for horror and low-brow entertainment. It opened with a scene in which the dead son of the Heian-period rebel Taira no Masakado comes back to life in order to destroy the Genji clan and proceeds to offer the audience both a spectacular presentation of the four guardians' defeat of a gigantic spider on Mount Katsuragi and a ghastly vision of the ghost of a mountain hag (*yamauba*). The popular story about how Yorimitsu and his guardians saved the imperial family by defeating the demon of Mount Ōe was translated rather hilariously into a commoner setting in which the guardians set up a tent show as a way of making money off the demon.[26] Nanboku also included a scene depicting a vender selling playbills for the production as a way of celebrating the opening of the new

Tamagawa Theater, which is also alluded to in the "new splash"—or, more literally, the "birthing bath" (*ubuyu*)—in the title.

The most unconventional element of the play was the excision of *Wait a Minute!*, which had long been a staple in face-showing productions. In fact, Nanboku did not delete it altogether but moved it from the opening of the first "historical" part, where it conventionally belonged, to the second "contemporary" part. He staged it as a play within a play as a way of poking fun at the venerable but now largely meaningless Edo convention of returning endlessly to the same sequence, with its celebration of samurai force and their pacification of the realm. The second part of *The Four Guardians: A New Splash at Tamagawa River* is still set in the world of the four guardians, but it takes place in the theater district just as the actors are celebrating the upcoming face-showing production. The act opens with actors, decked out in congratulatory gifts from patrons, coming to pay their respects at Danjūrō's house. Danjūrō VII plays the role of Danjūrō VII. Early in the act, he makes a ceremonious speech (*kōjō*)—another staple element of the face-showing production—and reads a sutra to memorialize the thirteenth year of his father's death.

Then, in a startling turn of events, a Ming princess named Shōkajo walks in bearing such treasures as a tiger skin, coral trees, and a Chinese harp. She explains that she has come to Japan as the Chinese emperor's envoy to Minamoto no Yorimitsu—the Heian-period general in whose service the four guardians were engaged—and, on her way back, has dropped by Danjūrō's house to meet the famous actor. This jumbling of past and present is, of course, typical of Edo kabuki. Disappointed by Danjūrō's unimpressive appearance, since he is wearing neither his costume nor his makeup, Shōkajo questions his identity. She takes out an actor print by Utagawa Toyokuni I that shows Danjūrō in *Wait a Minute!* Speaking through an interpreter, she says: "Danjūrō is famous even in China. Look at this print—prints depicting his face are imported even there. Now who in the world are you? You look completely different from this image. Although your eyes are similar to his, you don't even have broad, red strokes on your face. Such a miserable looking man can't be Danjūrō of Japan. Even China has better stars."[27]

In the end, Danjūrō decides that an unimpressive Danjūrō is "an embarrassment to Edo, and an embarrassment to Japan."[28] And so, right there in front of the audience, he sets about putting on his costume and makeup for *Wait a Minute!* Shōkajo, disappointed by what she calls the deceptive fame of Yorimitsu and even Danjūrō, is on the verge of tearing up her Toyokuni print when, in a play on the climactic moment of the act as it was conventionally performed, Danjūrō rushes out and stops her, shouting "Wait a minute, wait a minute!" He is now acting the role of Usui no Sadamitsu, a character from the world of the four guardians. A hilarious metaplay ensues in which other people are startled by the sudden, inappropriate appearance of the exaggeratedly made-up samurai character from the historical *Wait a Minute!* in the middle of the "contemporary part" (*sewa-ba*) of the face-showing production. In the end, Matsumoto Kōshirō V is forced to play the character often called Monk Catfish (Namazu Bōzu)—a minor role whose identity differs depending on the world being used and whose name derived from the long, braided sideburns that descended from his otherwise bald head, suggesting the whiskers of a catfish. Monk Catfish was almost never assigned to a major actor like Kōshirō, since his sole function was to offer his opponent an opportunity to demonstrate his strength, and he is defeated almost immediately. Nevertheless, Kōshirō, who is playing a minor actor, takes the strings from the Chinese harp to use for whiskers and chips in to complete this ludicrous, diminished version of *Wait a Minute!* His comments must have delighted the audience: "They assign me an unexpected role in this face-showing production. Of all things, for me to be performing the Catfish Monk! The now deceased Danjūrō could never have imagined it."[29] The scene is depicted in a picture-book playbill and an actor print (figures 2.2 and 2.3).

In the end, we learn in a farcical manner that all the characters have double identities. Shōkajo turns out to be an ordinary lady from a daimyo house, a crazy fan who disguised herself as a Ming princess in order to get close to Danjūrō; the low-ranking actor whom Kōshirō plays turns out to be the historical rebel Iga Jutarō. Having removed his *Wait a Minute!* costume and makeup, Danjūrō reveals that the kabuki actors were in fact protecting the heir to the Genji clan from his enemies, disguising him as a new female-role actor. By the conclusion of the play, everyone but Danjūrō has assumed his historical identity, and the play ends with Danjūrō refusing to cooperate when Kōshirō demands that he reveal who he is: "I'm one of the Edo-based Ichikawa line. Danjūrō is my stage name, but I am in truth Danjūrō, after all. . . . What stupid

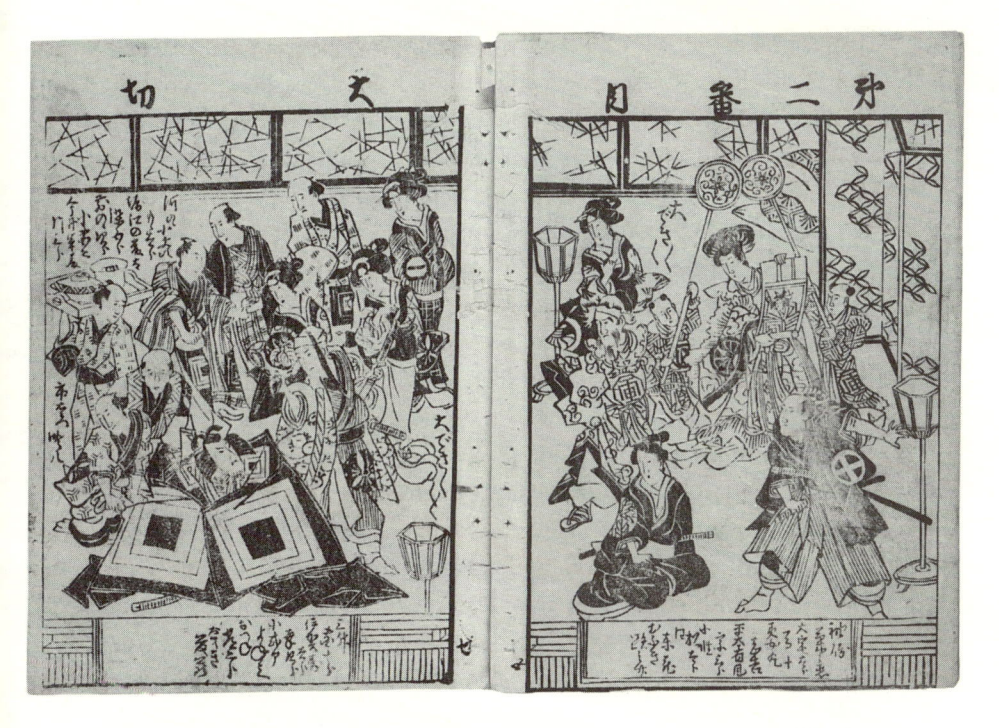

FIGURE 2.2 Danjūrō turning into the *Shibaraku* hero (*left*) and Shōkajo from China (*right*) in the picture-book playbill for the production of *Shitennō ubuyu no Tamagawa* at the Tamagawa Theater in 1818 (6 *ura*–7 *omote*). (Courtesy of Waseda University, Tsubouchi Memorial Theater Museum, *ro*-23-1-454)

FIGURE 2.3 Ichikawa Danjūrō VII as Danjūrō (*left*), Matsumoto Kōshirō V as Namazu Bōzu (*center*), and Segawa Kikunojō V as Shōkajo (*right*) in Utagawa Kunisada's triptych for the production of *Shitennō ubuyu no Tamagawa*. (Courtesy of Waseda University, Tsubouchi Memorial Theater Museum, 2-1541, 0027, 0994)

reason can there possibly be for Sanshō [Danjūrō's poetry name], whose line has continued for seven generations, to have a *real* name? Who the hell do you think I am! What a dumb question."[30] Even as it gestures toward the world of the four guardians, this production concludes in the present. *The Four Guardians: A New Splash at Tamagawa River* is a celebration not of the shared historical *sekai* but of the audience's shared knowledge of Edo actors.

In this play, we witness the hollowing out of the long-standing ritual of the face-showing production, which had continued for so long in order to pay homage to the social structure of Edo through its glorification of the samurai who saves the day, continuing year after year to free the imperial hostages from demons, evil aristocrats, or fake emperors. The once special *Wait a Minute!* has been relegated to the status of just another familiar story that can be adapted and changed for fun, and the larger ritualistic meaning of its depiction of the restoration of peace has been diminished, used as an occasion to showcase Danjūrō and his many faces. Indeed, Danjūrō's proud refusal at the end of *The Four Guardians: A New Splash at Tamagawa River* to join the other characters in their halfhearted return to the world in which the play should conventionally have been set illustrates the nature of the shift that has taken place. Even though the old *sekai* and their sets of characters from the past were inherited by nineteenth-century Edo kabuki, their meaning is no longer the same. One mode of imaginary that had been sustained through a constant process of dissolving the historical into the present—of presenting the past—is replaced by a completely different mode in which the present itself is the focus, unmediated by the depth of a historical framework.

As I mentioned earlier, at the same time that this transformation was taking place on the level of content, the face-showing production itself also was losing its conventional meaning as the moment when each theater announced the cast it had contracted for the upcoming theatrical year—a change that had taken place much earlier in Kyoto and Osaka. For example, Iwai Hanshirō V, a star who appeared in *The Four Guardians: A New Splash at Tamagawa River*, was simultaneously performing in the evening segment of the face-showing production at the Nakamura Theater, which was called *The Ise Taira Clan: The Divine Wind of the Devotees* (*Ise Heiji hiiki no kamikaze*, 1818). According to the actor critique *A Dream Team of Actors* (*Yakusha yume awase*, 1819), "He was employed at both the Nakamura and the Tamagawa Theaters for the face-showing, as both were short on female-role actors."[31] Hanshirō was given a particularly prominent role in the first part of *The Four Guardians: A New Splash at Tamagawa River* in order to make up for his absence later in the play.[32] In earlier periods, his simultaneous appearance in productions at two separate theaters would have been unthinkable and, in fact, would have violated his contract. This is another example of the breakdown of the conventions that sustained Edo kabuki as a cultural imaginary.

During the nineteenth century, kabuki playwrights in Edo became less fixated on fashioning a shared culture based on stories and sets of samurai characters derived from historical *sekai* and instead started to pour their energies into creating productions that continually reinvented the present through repeated depictions of the lives of lower-class Edoites.[33] After the government finally forced the theaters to relocate from their former central locations to the peripheral area of Asakusa in the 1840s, the conventionally central *sekai* was reduced to a mere decorative twist, a structure of obligations that often do not bind the characters. This is particularly evident in the works of Kawatake Mokuami, who began crafting plays with a largely domestic focus. Favoring characters who are orphans and emphasizing filial bonds among bandits unaffiliated to any social group such as a household (*ie*) or clan, Mokuami finally brought about the end of the conventional *sekai*—the end of the world as Edo had known it—making it possible for popular contemporary narratives to take their place. In his plays, conventional *sekai* and samurai lineages are less important than bonds of friendship or are useful only as a way for commoners to fake their identity.[34] As a result, the contemporary frameworks that he repeatedly drew on were eventually elevated to new *sekai*.

YOTSUYA KAIDAN AND THE TREASURY OF LOYAL RETAINERS

The production of *The Four Guardians: A New Splash at Tamagawa River* in 1818 illustrates how Nanboku was starting to dismantle the structure of Edo kabuki and its calendar. Seven years later, the first production of *Yotsuya kaidan*—which became Nanboku's representative work and the preeminent ghost play in the entire kabuki repertoire—took another step in a new direction, moving away from an interest in characters defined vis-à-vis their sociocultural community and toward a notion of selfhood largely deprived of such context. As I noted earlier, *Yotsuya kaidan* was first staged at the Nakamura Theater in 1825 as part of a double feature with a kabuki version of *The Treasury of Loyal Retainers*, a vendetta play that had remained extremely popular throughout the early modern period, ever since it was first staged as a work for the puppet theater in 1748. Nanboku's dual presentation of *Yotsuya kaidan* and *The Treasury of Loyal Retainers* stands as a clear instance of the dismantling of the legacy of earlier Edo kabuki: it departed from the "cyclic imagination" in which revenge was achieved, a household was restored, or the peaceful perpetuation of a domain was assured, and instead enacted a hollowing out of these values. In this particular production, as we will see, this dismantling was carried out in gendered terms.

The concluding lines of the text that Nanboku prepared for the street playbill advertising the first production of *Yotsuya kaidan*—a familiar element of such playbills that is known as the *katari* (address [to the public])—state explicitly that the play was created with the intention of questioning the logic of *The Treasury of Loyal Retainers* and imply that it will accomplish this through the depiction of a female vendetta: "A farewell letter at the time of the divorce, written in a woman's hand—it's a woman's *kana* practice, a brutal protest against Takeda Izumo's still-popular play. The new performance, a flowering example of kabuki!"[35] The references to "a woman's [calligraphic] hand" and "a woman's *kana* practice" play on the *kanadehon* (a *kana* primer) that appears in the older play's full title, and they frame *Yotsuya kaidan* literally as a gendered rewriting of *The Treasury of Loyal Retainers*. Rather than concentrate on male samurai and their demonstration of their samurai morality through a communal, public mission to avenge the death of their lord, Nanboku tells potential theatergoers, this play will turn its attention to the female characters—the women whose bodies are often at the disposal of their fathers and husbands in conventional plays based on military *sekai*, of which *The Treasury of Loyal Retainers* is a representative example. Indeed, *Yotsuya kaidan* does not simply focus on female characters but also borrows more specifically from images and beliefs associated with the female body and with the possibilities unleashed when women die and become ghosts—powers of the disembodied that are socially inscribed in the female body, as I show in chapter 3.

This shift in interest from male to female, from the social community of the household to smaller-scale marital relationships, and from living to dead was part of the process by which Edo kabuki reoriented itself to meet the needs and tastes of its urban audience during the nineteenth century. As we will see, its effects are evident in the new play *Yotsuya kaidan* as well as in the transformation it occasions in the meaning of *The Treasury of Loyal Retainers* itself. The double production of these two plays in 1825 offers us an unusually clear vision of these changes and can be understood on the most basic level as an attempt to rewrite the cyclic structure that had governed Edo kabuki productions for so long.

The initial production of *The Treasury of Loyal Retainers* in 1748 was a puppet-play retelling of the so-called Akō incident (*Akō jiken*) in which the events were transplanted into the *sekai* of *The Chronicles of Great Peace*. The Akō incident, which unfolded in Edo between 1701 and 1703, was essentially a revenge killing: forty-seven former retainers of Lord Asano Naganori plotted to kill Kira Yoshinaka, the man responsible for their lord's death, and then, after successfully completing their mission, committed ritual suicide.[36] As Henry D. Smith II showed so well in his essay "The Capacity of Chūshingura," the historical Akō incident has been subject to a tremendous number of rewritings and reimaginings for diverse audiences and in various different media.[37] Among these different media, theatrical adaptations played a particularly significant role in shaping the reception of the story, and while numerous plays for both the puppet theater and the kabuki stage had dealt with the incident before *The Treasury of Loyal Retainers*, this version was by far the most successful. Indeed, before long it came to supplant the incident itself in terms of its importance in the popular imagination.[38]

Basically, *The Treasury of Loyal Retainers* offers a romanticized portrayal of the suffering of Lord Enya's retainers, of their loyalty, and of the personal sacrifices they make in order to participate in the vendetta. The tragedy is precipitated when Kōno Moronao, the shogun's grand master of ceremonies, tries to act on the lust he feels for Lord Enya's wife, Kaoyo. Moronao bullies Lord Enya to the point that he can no longer tolerate it and, in act 3, draws his sword against Moronao at court. This grave violation of protocol costs Lord Enya his life, and his suicide results in the fall of the Enya house and the dispersal of all his retainers, depicted in act 4. Ōboshi Yuranosuke, Lord Enya's closest attendant, secretly starts plotting a spectacular revenge while pretending to have abandoned his samurai status and given himself over to drink and debauchery.

The ensuing acts present a number of episodes involving individual retainers. For example, one episode that was extremely popular in Edo concerns a retainer named Hayano Kanpei, who had been unable to prevent Lord Enya from drawing his sword because he was outside flirting with his lover, Okaru. Kanpei, overcome with remorse and hoping to get his revenge, follows Okaru to her parents' home in rural Yamazaki. Acts 5 and 6 focus on him and a disloyal former retainer, Ono Sadakurō. Figure 2.4 shows the picture-book playbill depiction of acts 5 and 6 in the double production with *Yotsuya kaidan*. The upper part of the

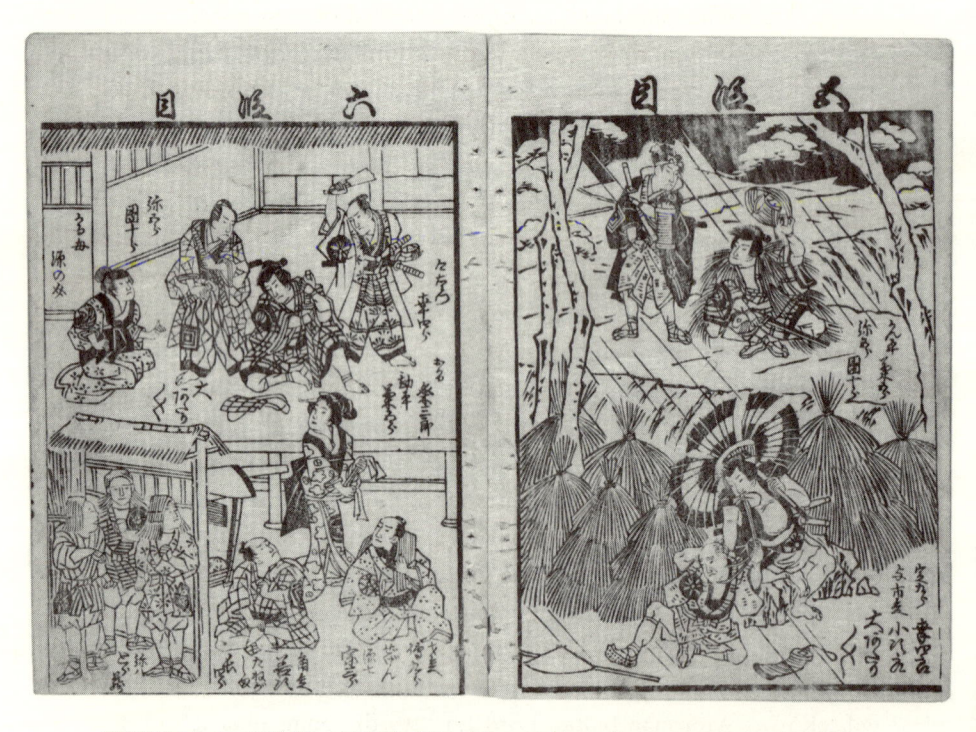

FIGURE 2.4 Acts 5 (*right*) and 6 (*left*) of *Kanadehon chūshingura* in the picture-book playbill for the double production with *Yotsuya kaidan* at the Nakamura Theater in 1825 (3 *ura*–4 *omote*). (Courtesy of Waseda University, Tsubouchi Memorial Theater Museum, *ro* 23-1-533)

THE BEGINNING OF THE END OF EDO KABUKI

half representing act 5 shows Kanpei, played by Onoe Kikugorō III—dressed in hunting clothes and carrying a gun with which he hopes to shoot a boar—encountering another retainer named Senzaki Yagorō, from whom Kanpei learns of the secret revenge plot. The lower part of the image shows Sadakurō, played by Matsumoto Kōshirō V, stabbing Okaru's father, Yoichibei, and stealing a pouch of money from him. Yoichibei had earned this money by agreeing to sell Okaru to a teahouse in the Gion pleasure quarter in Kyoto; he had hoped that by sacrificing Okaru into prostitution, he could enable Kanpei to help fund the revenge. Immediately after Sadakurō murders Yoichibei, he himself dies, having accidentally been hit by a bullet that Kanpei shot at a boar. In the darkness, Kanpei realizes that he has shot someone without knowing who it is and finds the pouch of money. He takes it, feeling guilty about what he has done, and prays for the unfortunate man.

The lower part of the picture representing act 6 shows Okaru on the verge of being taken from Kanpei by men from the pleasure quarter. When Kanpei returns and learns that the men from the pleasure quarter had given Yoichibei a pouch of money, he mistakenly assumes that he has unwittingly killed his own father-in-law. Kanpei and Okaru are married by this time and Okaru leaves Kanpei in tears. Afterward, when Yoichibei's body is carried into the house, everyone, including two samurai who have come to give Kanpei the good news that he has been admitted to the conspiracy, believes that Kanpei has killed his father-in-law and stolen the pouch from him, so he is forbidden to join the plot after all. In his grief, Kanpei confesses what happened and commits *seppuku* (see figure 2.4, *left*). Just as he is breathing his last, one of the retainers notices that Yoichibei's wound is not from a bullet and Kanpei's name is cleared. Kanpei dies without being able to participate in the revenge, still angry at himself for having failed to be in attendance on his lord at a critical moment. Ensuing acts continue to show other dramatic incidents involving various retainers and their families until the play concludes with the final, thrilling, revenge scene.

In the production in 1825, *Yotsuya kaidan* and *The Treasury of Loyal Retainers* were presented as related plays whose plots were to some extent woven together: *Yotsuya kaidan* was a sort of side story that inherited the basic setting of *The Treasury of Loyal Retainers*. The same set of actors appeared first in *The Treasury of Loyal Retainers*, which constituted the historical part of the production, and then took to the stage again in the contemporary part to act in *Yotsuya kaidan*. Since the rest of this book centers on *Yotsuya kaidan*, I first will outline the basic trajectory of the play as it is represented in illustrated digests and surviving scripts.

Yotsuya kaidan begins after Lord Enya has been forced to commit ritual suicide for injuring Kōno Moronao at court, leading to the collapse of Enya's house and the dispersal of his retainers. In contrast to *The Treasury of Loyal Retainers*, which depicts the enormous lengths to which the former retainers go as they try to find a way to avenge their master's death, *Yotsuya kaidan* turns its attention to the seedy areas of Edo where a number of the former retainers are hiding with their wives. Act 1 opens with a lively festival at the Asakusa Shrine at which we are introduced to many of the former retainers. Yotsuya Samon, who is one of these men, has two daughters: Oiwa, who later appears in the typical guise of a street prostitute, and Osode, who works at a toothpick store but also takes customers at night. Samon has demanded that Oiwa separate from her husband—Tamiya Iemon, another of Enya's former retainers—because he suspects that Iemon stole money from the Enya house in the chaos following its collapse. Osode is married to yet another former retainer, Satō Yomoshichi, from whom she, too, is temporarily estranged.

In the latter half of act 1, the scene shifts to the house of a masseur that also serves as a venue for prostitution. Naosuke, who was formerly a low-ranking samurai of the Enya house but now works as a medicine peddler, has arranged to buy Osode for the night, only to have her snatched away from him when her husband, Yomoshichi, turns up. Naosuke, who is madly in love with Osode, resents Yomoshichi's interference and follows him out into the dark of night. He then proceeds to murder Yomoshichi—or so he thinks, except that without Naosuke's realizing it, Yomoshichi has switched clothing with Naosuke's master, Okuda Shōzaburō, in order to carry out a secret mission. Meanwhile, Iemon, furious at his father-in-law for refusing to allow him to be reunited with Oiwa, kills Samon in the woods, in the very same area where Naosuke has killed Shōzaburō. The two cold-blooded murderers peel off the faces of the bodies so that they will be unrecognizable. Just then, Oiwa and Osode come along the path looking for Yomoshichi and Samon and discover the two bodies, whom they recognize by their clothing. While they are grieving, Iemon and Naosuke, who have concealed themselves nearby, return and promise to find and kill the murderers. Little realizing that Iemon and Naosuke themselves are the guilty parties, Oiwa and Osode consent to be reunited with them.

Act 2 centers on Iemon and Oiwa's household. Oiwa has given birth to a son and is suffering a severe "disorder of the blood" (*chi no michi*)—some type of postpregnancy sickness—and Iemon has been treating her very cruelly. Soon their neighbor Itō Kihei, a retainer of Moronao's who is secretly scheming to separate Oiwa from Iemon and have his granddaughter Oume marry him instead, sends over what he says is a packet of medicine, though in reality it is a potent poison intended to disfigure Oiwa horribly. Oiwa takes the "medicine" while Iemon is next door being showered with money by the wealthy Kihei. As she writhes in pain, Iemon ends up betraying her, agreeing to marry Oume. When she learns what happened, Oiwa is enraged. She inadvertently disfigures herself further while putting on makeup, saying that she must thank Kihei for his generosity, and then suddenly dies, accidentally cutting her throat on a sword stuck in a post. Returning to find her dead, Iemon decides to make it appear as though she had been having an affair with Kohei, a servant whom he and his friends had locked up in a closet for stealing a special medicine. Iemon kills Kohei and nails the two bodies on either side of a door, which he has his friends toss into a river. That very night, Iemon marries Oume. But, possessed by the ghosts of Oiwa and Kohei, he ends up murdering both his new wife and his father-in-law. From here on, Oiwa's ghost continues to seek revenge on Iemon and his friends and family.

Act 3 depicts an encounter that Iemon has with the ghosts of Oiwa and Kohei when he happens to catch sight of the door drifting down the river and hoists it up to have a look. Act 4 presents episodes involving two different sets of characters: one recounting Osode's life with Naosuke and the other showing Kohei's devotion, even in death, to his sick master, the former Enya retainer Oshioda Matanojō. Although she married Naosuke in the hope that he would avenge her husband's death, Osode has insisted on keeping her chastity. Only when she learns of Oiwa's death does she finally decide to become Naosuke's official wife, thinking that this will obligate him to avenge the deaths of her loved ones. No sooner have they consecrated their marriage, however, than Yomoshichi, whom Osode had believed to be dead, appears. Unable to forgive herself for unknowingly betraying her true husband, she tricks

OVERTURNING THE WORLD

each man into thinking he will be killing the other in the dark when in fact they will be killing her instead. She leaves a note for Naosuke before she dies. When he reads it, he discovers that she was only adopted by Samon and was actually the daughter of Motomiya Sandayū, who is Naosuke's father. Realizing that he has committed incest and learning that the man he murdered thinking that he was Yomoshichi was actually his former master, Naosuke immediately kills himself.

Meanwhile, at Kohei's house, Matanojō, Kohei's true master, lies in bed unable to walk because of his sickness. In a clear parallel with the scene leading up to Kanpei's death in *The Treasury of Loyal Retainers*, a messenger comes to inform him of the date on which the former Enya retainers have decided to carry out their vendetta. But at the same time, he tells Matanojō that he will not be allowed to participate because he has come under suspicion of having stolen goods from a pawnbroker, which could bring disgrace on the rest of the group. Matanojō eventually realizes that Kohei's ghost committed the theft for his sake and, touched, decides to take Iemon's medicine, which Kohei's ghost delivers. Having recovered completely from his illness, he regains his place as a member of the vendetta.

In the final act, Iemon dreams that he is having an affair with a beautiful girl in the country, who turns out to be Oiwa's ghost. He wakes up from this awful nightmare at a temple, where he has been hiding, trying to escape Oiwa. Despite the pacifying rituals that the priests have been performing for him, Oiwa's ghost returns and murders his friends, his mother, and, indirectly, his father. As the play draws to a close, Oiwa's ghost disappears from the stage, but Yomoshichi, Osode's former husband, comes to kill Iemon, as Osode wished.

After the first production, *Yotsuya kaidan* took on a life of its own as a popular ghost play, entirely independent of *The Treasury of Loyal Retainers*, and the fact that it had first been staged as part of a double bill was all but forgotten. In considering the initial production, however, it is important to remember that Nanboku's ghost play used the basic dramatic environment of *The Treasury of Loyal Retainers*—though as even my brief summary of the play shows, it is structured so as to evoke a very different moral universe. *The Treasury of Loyal Retainers* portrays a world in which men engage in extreme sacrifices to demonstrate their loyalty to their dead master, whereas *Yotsuya kaidan* revels in betrayal, murder, and torture, and features a private revenge by a woman who has turned her back on the values held up by the community to which she once belonged.

COMPLICATING THE COMPARATIVE APPROACH

Yotsuya kaidan tends to be characterized as a parody of *The Treasury of Loyal Retainers* or as a work that challenges the worldview of *The Treasury of Loyal Retainers*.[39] The two plays have also been interpreted as representing different historical epochs: *The Treasury of Loyal Retainers*, it is said, reflects the optimism and ideals of the first half of the early modern period, while *Yotsuya kaidan* represents the chaotic mood and the repressed desires of Edo in the period's later decades.[40] These arguments and analyses are often astute and are persuasive as far as they go, but they have tended to be developed and supported through a comparison of the two plays and largely with reference to scripts.

In considering the double production itself, we need to supplement this basic approach, considering the two plays not merely as seemingly static texts—as a new play paired with an older one, since the notion that the plays belong to different eras is itself rooted in a textual understanding—but as a new play paired with an old play that was made new again amid the ongoing process of Edo kabuki each time it was performed. The kabuki version of *The Treasury of Loyal Retainers* had been performed differently on each occasion that it was staged in the seventy-seven years since it débuted, and *Yotsuya kaidan* was interacting not with the 1748 version but with the 1825 version. Thus in order to understand the double production, we must adopt a diachronic perspective on *The Treasury of Loyal Retainers*, taking into account its evolution over time, and recognize that even *Yotsuya kaidan* might not have been staged in the form in which we now know it. We need, in short, to begin our analysis of the two plays by considering the various types of fluidity that characterize early modern kabuki and that make purely textual comparisons of *Yotsuya kaidan* and *The Treasury of Loyal Retainers* insufficient.

In the introduction, I noted that two separate street playbills for the double production were issued in advance of its opening: one for the "first day" and one for the "later day." As a result, it has long been believed that the theater first staged six acts of *The Treasury of Loyal Retainers*, followed by two or possibly three acts of *Yotsuya kaidan*.

The "later day" may have begun with a repetition of act 3, followed by acts 7, 9, and 10 of *The Treasury of Loyal Retainers*; the last two acts of *Yotsuya kaidan*; and, finally, the climactic vendetta scene from *The Treasury of Loyal Retainers*.[41] This assumption makes a good deal of sense, but since kabuki productions in Edo were always very malleable and theaters were very responsive to their audiences, there is no way of knowing how long the various acts were staged or the precise manner in which new acts were added, adjusted, or switched. The program for the first day was most likely kept as long as there was an audience for it. As I also noted in the introduction, Akama Ryō has suggested that one of the later acts of *Yotsuya kaidan* that appears in modern texts might not have been performed at all.

The extreme fluidity of kabuki productions is revealed most starkly by a unique collection of 388 playbills dating from 1841 to 1867 that have been preserved at the Waseda University Tsubouchi Memorial Theater Museum, each of which has been annotated in red ink. The annotations, most likely by an artist named Kiyokawa Shigeharu (dates unknown), who himself worked on theater-related publications, record the opening and closing dates of productions, their composition, the actors who were on leave, the occurrence of fires, and political incidents that affected productions.[42] They reveal in concrete terms how different a kabuki production might be from its advertised content and how changeable: new acts might be added or removed, the content might be revised, or an unpopular production might be terminated before it reached what was originally supposed to be its scheduled "closing performance."

Consider, for instance, a double bill at the Kawarasaki Theater of *Yotsuya kaidan* and *Nightingale Tomb: An Old Tale of a Spear* (*Uguisuzuka nagara no furugoto*) that opened in the fifth month of 1851. The production, which was meant to mark the third anniversary of the death of Onoe Kikugorō III, who had played Oiwa in the original staging of *Yotsuya kaidan*, was advertised as being divided into a first and a second part, just as the production in 1825 had been. Ihara Seisei'en's monumental *Kabuki Chronology* (*Kabuki nenpyō*, 1956–1963)—the most reliable reference work on Edo-period kabuki productions in both Edo and Kamigata—states simply that the two plays were staged together beginning on the twenty-seventh of the fifth month, that *Nightingale Tomb* turned out to be unpopular, and that the production was terminated and replaced by a new play called *The Rise and Fall of the Heike and Genji: A Beginner's Version* (*Hiragana seisuiki*, 1739). This was an "overnight pickle," adapted from a puppet play, which began on the fifth of the sixth month.⁴³ Kiyokawa's notes tell a different story, however. He explains that the opening of the double production was delayed for three days and that when it finally got under way, the first act of *Yotsuya kaidan* was drastically abbreviated, leaving out many of the most important roles. Although the production was supposed to switch at a certain point from the first to the second part of each play, the theater ended up continuing to stage the first part day after day, ostensibly reserving the second part for a later occasion.⁴⁴ By the eighth of the sixth month, the unpopular *Nightingale Tomb* was completely dropped, and in its place, *Yotsuya kaidan* was staged in its entirety. At the same time, *The Rise and Fall of the Heike and Genji* was inserted into the middle of the production in order to fill up time.⁴⁵ And contrary to the explanation in the *Kabuki Chronology*, the theater seems to have made all these changes *without* terminating the production. This complex history highlights how little we know about how the first production of *Yotsuya kaidan* and *The Treasury of Loyal Retainers* might have unfolded, since no notes like Kiyokawa's have survived from the early nineteenth century.

I stated earlier that kabuki plays were also subject to enormous change. In fact, popular plays evolved so much during successive productions that each staging should be thought of less as a particular interpretation of a text than as part of larger work whose contours were defined and redefined over time by countless performative variations. *The Treasury of Loyal Retainers* offers a particularly good example of this type of fluidity, in part because it was among the most frequently staged plays in the entire kabuki repertoire. In *Edo in Bloom: A Kabuki Time Line*, Tatekawa [Utei] Enba comments that "*The Treasury of Loyal Retainers* has become kabuki's 'miraculous reviving medicine.'"⁴⁶ The "miraculous reviving medicine" (*dokujintō*) was a rare and expensive Chinese medicine made from a type of ginseng that was effective in the case of severe illness. Whenever a theater found itself in financial difficulties, it would stage *The Treasury of Loyal Retainers*, assured that it would attract a crowd. In fact, the kabuki version of *The Treasury of Loyal Retainers* was staged at least 233 times between the initial production in 1748 and the close of the early modern period.⁴⁷ Moreover, even this astonishing figure does not include radically new takes on the story with different titles, sequels, and other types of adaptations.⁴⁸

Because *The Treasury of Loyal Retainers* was staged again and again over many decades, the original puppet-theater script was extensively reworked, and the actors introduced a great variety of new performance styles. The effect of this proliferation of versions on how the play was conceived of as a work is captured by a passage from *Jinrikisha Days in Japan*, a memoir by the American journalist Eliza Scidmore, who visited Japan in the 1880s:

> I once asked a great star who had written his play.
>
> "I do not understand," said the tragedian; and a bystander explained that the manager had cut reports of a theft, a murder, and a shipwreck from a newspaper, and, discussing them with the star, evolved the outlines of a connected play and decided on the principal scenes and effects. A hack writer was then called in, who, under dictation, shaped the plot and divided it into scenes. The managerial council elaborated it further, allotting the parts, and the star then composed his lines to suit himself. In rehearsal the play was rounded, the diction altered, and each actor directed to write out his own part, after which a full transcript was made for the prompter.
>
> As to the authorship of the play of the "Forty-Seven Ronins," he said: "That is our country's history. We all know the story of their lives and glorious deaths, and many novelists and poets have written of them."
>
> "But who made it into a drama?"
>
> "Oh, every theater has its own way of representing the different scenes, although the great facts are historical and cannot be misrepresented, now that the Tokugawa's ban against the play is removed. Danjiro [Danjūrō] plays it in one way, and other actors have their versions, but none of them play it the same at every engagement, nor repeat just the same acts on every day of an engagement."[49]

Clearly, Scidmore was struck by the collaborative manner in which kabuki plays were "authored"—her interlocutor does not even understand what she means when she asks who wrote the play—and by the lack of authority placed in the text, represented by the fact that different actors might stage the same play using entirely different acting styles. The actor's emphasis on historical accuracy is characteristic of the Meiji period, but the relative lack of importance he placed on the script and his different understanding of authorship reflect the theatrical norms that kabuki had inherited from the early modern period.

Scidmore's question about the identity of the author and the response she got, which essentially attributed authorship to the theater and the actors, bear closely on our understanding of plays. When *The Treasury of Loyal Retainers* is staged today, the play the audience sees is not simply a kabuki version of Takeda Izumo and Namiki Senryū's puppet play; it is a fascinating patchwork of performance styles developed by numerous actors and playwrights over more than two and a half centuries. The "grand opening" (*daijo*)—the chanting of the actors' names by a puppet before the opening of the first act—was introduced in a production at the Ichimura Theater in 1773. The dance sequence during Okaru and Kanpei's journey scene (*michiyuki*), known by the title "The Traveling Groom Michiyuki" (Michiyuki tabiji no hanamuko), was created in 1833 by Mimasuya Nisōji.[50] We see, in particular, the considerable influence of the Meiji-period "living history" (*katsureki*) movement and of the great Meiji-period actor Ichikawa Danjūrō IX (1838–1903), who introduced radically new acting styles to kabuki. The battle sequences in the plays, choreographed with more than two hundred patterns of sword movements, are likewise derived from modern performance practice. This is especially true of the last *chanbara*-style battle scene at Moronao's residence, which consists of a mixture of sword-fighting movements from modern stagings by Kawatake Mokuami and by Kawatake Shinshichi III (1842–1901).[51] The style used in acting the part of Ono Sadakurō borrows from performances by Ichikawa Danzō IV (1745–1808), Nakamura Nakazō I (1736–1790), and Ichikawa Danjūrō VII; the style used in playing Hayano Kanpei comes mostly from Onoe Kikugorō III and the Meiji actor Kikugorō V. Of course, all these features represent only the successful, lasting innovations; innumerable other variations must have been tried but then vanished, so they are no longer performed.

I have been discussing the various ways in which kabuki is characterized by fluidity, and I should emphasize that even the scripts we rely on when we read *Yotsuya kaidan* and *The Treasury of Loyal Retainers* are a product of this fluidity. In fact, most of the surviving scripts of *The Treasury of Loyal Retainers* do not date back all that far—while the original *bunraku* script of *The Treasury of Loyal Retainers* has survived, those for the early kabuki performances have not. This is only to be expected, considering the play's long history and the tangential role that scripts played in kabuki in Edo. Since scripts were revised or entirely rewritten for each new production, the more often a play was staged, the more revisions it was subject to. Lines might simply be crossed out or replaced by a strip of text pasted over the old line, or an entire scene might be rewritten. For a popular play like *The Treasury of Loyal Retainers*, the incredible proliferation of versions makes it impossible to reconstruct much of the content of the play as it was performed early on. Furthermore, even though *The Treasury of Loyal Retainers* is much older than *Yotsuya kaidan*, critical editions of the former have generally been based on a number of hand-written scripts that date from much later in the early modern period than the staging with *Yotsuya kaidan* in 1825. Some such editions are based on still later texts, from the Meiji or Taishō period, some of which were printed only in order to be presented to the theater censors.[52]

One thing we can say for sure about the "original" kabuki productions of *The Treasury of Loyal Retainers*—if we can even speak in such terms about a work that existed from the first in so many different forms—is that they must have been considerably different from both the modern performances and the scripts as they appear in modern critical editions. The puppet-theater production of *The Treasury of Loyal Retainers* opened in Osaka in 1748, and kabuki theaters in Edo staged their own adaptations in the following year. All three of the major Edo theaters tried their hands at the play, and even though the performances were derived from the same source, each actor had his own interpretation of the role he was performing.

According to *Critique of The Treasury of Loyal Retainers Old and New* (*Kokon iroha hyōrin*, 1785), a work that outlines the history of actors and their performance styles in productions of *The Treasury of Loyal Retainers* between 1748 and 1785, in the Morita Theater's first production the female-role actor Arashi Koroku I (1710–1786), who played Kanpei, "did a back flip as he plunged a dagger into his stomach to commit *seppuku*, and the audience loved it."[53] For some time after Ichikawa Danjūrō II first played one of the retainers, Ōwashi Bungo, at the Nakamura Theater in 1749, the role was presented in an *aragoto* style: the character had bold, energetic stripes of red makeup (*kumadori*) on his face, marking the passionate throbbing of his veins, and carried a huge ax in his hand.[54] An actor print published in 1859 showing Kawarasaki Gonjūrō I (later Danjūrō IX) holding a huge mallet in this role retains traces of the acting style that Danjūrō II created (figure 2.5). Since the Meiji period, however, the revenge scene has been

FIGURE 2.5 Kawarasaki Gonjūrō I (later Ichikawa Danjūrō IX) as Ōwashi Bungo in Utagawa Kunisada's print for the production of *Kanadehon chūshingura* at the Ichimura Theater in 1859. (Courtesy of the Museum of Fine Arts, Boston)

staged using realistic sword fighting, and the *aragoto* style has diminished in importance. These are just a few of the many important ways in which earlier presentations of *The Treasury of Loyal Retainers* differed from both contemporary texts and contemporary performance.

The very idea of "*The Treasury of Loyal Retainers*" is loaded with meaning, as both performances and texts are conditioned simultaneously by the play's reception and production history. By the time the story found its way into Nanboku's hands so that he could pair it with *Yotsuya kaidan*, it was not the same play that it had been when it was first adapted for the kabuki stage in 1748. His version of *The Treasury of Loyal Retainers* had a new edge and was performed by a new troupe of actors: Onoe Kikugorō III, Matsumoto Kōshirō V, and Ichikawa Danjūrō VII, men who had made their names playing ghosts, evil figures, and erotic heroes. Thus the double staging of *Yotsuya kaidan* and *The Treasury of Loyal Retainers* in 1825 should be interpreted not only in light of a juxtaposition of the plays as they are now found in seemingly complete texts—be they hand-written manuscripts, critical editions, or even video or DVD recordings of modern performances—but also in light of the deeper structures and lineages that defined the plays and their relationship to each other in the late summer of 1825.

UNDERCUTTING THE LOYAL RETAINERS, RELATIVIZING THE HEROIC VENDETTA

Yotsuya kaidan represents a clear structural break from the worldview of *The Treasury of Loyal Retainers* and, by extension, most early modern plays that fall under the loosely defined structure of the "household-disturbance plot" (*oie sōdō mono*) and "revenge play" (*katakiuchi-mono*). *Yotsuya kaidan* relativizes these basic frameworks, which center on heroic sacrifices intended to keep a household or daimyo domain afloat, or on the successful completion of a vendetta on behalf of one's lord or father. It focuses on characters who are often excluded from directly participating in a public crusade and presents a revenge plot with a whole new meaning. Accordingly, the "brutal protest" that *Yotsuya kaidan* offers is leveled not only at *The Treasury of Loyal Retainers* but, more profoundly, at one of the plot structures most central to conventional Edo kabuki.

In early modern Japan, blood revenge was supported under appropriate conditions by a formal bureaucratic procedure as an action that accorded with the moral foundation of Tokugawa society.[55] To understand the significance of the vendetta in early modern literature, David Atherton looked at the relational constitution of early modern selfhood in the context of the household (*ie*). The socially sanctioned act of the vendetta for one's father or someone else in a position of authority within the family was, Atherton argues, not personally motivated but understood in the context of hierarchical social relations and duty, an auspicious act of social affirmation.[56] In the early modern period, individuals belonged to the household; beyond serving as their residence, the household gave its members social standing and defined their obligations. For the samurai, the household was a corporate entity to which each member contributed in order to guarantee its perpetual prosperity. Revenge in fiction, therefore, carried a moral implication that symbolized the subject's selfhood as a member of a certain community and in the broader social order.

Kabuki exhibited a particular concern with structures that tested characters' moral devotion to the perpetuation of the social order. In kabuki, revenge plays are classified as a subcategory of the dominant structure of the household-disturbance plot, which centers on the inheritance and perpetuation of the household and whose dramatic potential was actively mined in Kamigata during the Genroku period as theaters began developing sequential kabuki and puppet plays. Over time, plots in the household-disturbance mold became a staple of Edo kabuki as well, and the paradigm remained among the most important in both puppet and kabuki theater well into the nineteenth century.[57] Kabuki scholar Kawatake Shigetoshi summarized its basic elements:

> The play opens with a scheme to take over the house, and the house collapses after the loss of treasure, which leads to the lord's suicide. Attempts are made to poison the young heir, or an evil lord is tempted into drunkenness and debauchery. These events are followed by hardships and selfless sacrifices by former retainers and by strong, loyal female characters. Eventually, the evil plot against the house is exposed; there are punishments and confrontations; and finally the evildoers are crushed, the house is restored, and peace and unity are recovered.[58]

The revenge play is essentially a variation on this theme in which a household's retainers turn to revenge to appease the spirit of their lord and regain their moral standing in the community when it is no longer possible for their lord to recover his former social status or to restore his house, as is common in other types of household-disturbance plots. Revenge plays begin with an unfortunate and unjust death, then depict the hardships and sacrifices undergone by surrogates of the deceased—the loyal former retainers, usually under the lead of a clear-headed, middle-aged samurai—as they plot their revenge, and conclude when the vendetta has succeeded.[59] *The Treasury of Loyal Retainers* fits neatly into this paradigm, featuring the wise, experienced Ōboshi Yuranosuke as its central figure.

Revenge plays and household-disturbance plots more broadly exhibit considerable variety in their finer points, of course, and shifts in emphasis can be observed from city to city and over the decades. Mid-eighteenth-century Osaka witnessed a surge in the popularity of evil characters and large-scale disturbances, for instance. Still, the process leading to the revenge or the restoration of the household produces a time-space in which characters are detached from their ordinary social position and must stand strong in the face of a moral dilemma, demonstrating their participation in and loyalty to their community by sacrificing members of their immediate family or their personal well-being. Atherton calls this period in the revenge narrative "avenger time" and describes it as a period of existential struggle when "the social self becomes uncertain, endangered" and the individual strives to reintegrate himself into the everyday social structure.[60]

A similar dynamic is at work in the household-disturbance plot. Note, too, that in addition to enabling the dramatic depiction of a moral struggle, the time of uncertainty these narratives explored had the effect of overlaying the world of the samurai onto that of the commoner as samurai characters disguised themselves and traveled in different social spaces. The drama of early modern kabuki was deeply rooted in the struggle engendered by the requirement to privilege the collective ethics of samurai loyalty and notions of household honor. If the characters had a subjectivity, it was made visible in the struggle to maintain the status quo. In this sense, household-disturbance and revenge plots can be conceived of as sites for the relational construction of the characters' selfhood.

Yotsuya kaidan relentlessly undermines both the presentation of loyalty in *The Treasury of Loyal Retainers* and the language it uses to valorize loyal characters. *Gishi* (loyal retainer) was the privileged label used to describe the heroes of *The Treasury of Loyal Retainers* and was featured in the vast majority of plays based on the Akō incident. In contrast, *Yotsuya kaidan* turns the adoration of the *gishi* on its head, by both emptying the word itself of its meaning and portraying the loyal retainers in an unflattering manner while presenting their disloyal counterparts, the *fugishi*, in a style calculated to make them attractive despite their evilness. Nanboku begins his attack on the idea of selfless devotion to a vanished social unit and the idea of "loyalty" associated with such devotion by hollowing out the concept of the *gishi*, detaching the word from the actions that give it meaning. At its most basic level, *The Treasury of Loyal Retainers* presents a long series of ordeals that enable the retainers to prove that they are indeed true *gishi*—to live up to the expectations placed on members of their class and to show their loyalty by their suffering, determination, and ultimate success in carrying out their vendetta. The former retainers in *Yotsuya kaidan*, by contrast, refer to themselves as *gishi* and describe their secret notes as "oaths sworn by *gishi* in the name of the gods" even before they have indicated that they intend to carry out their revenge.[61] In Nanboku's play, the masterless samurai's status as a *gishi* is settled from the start; it is a matter of labeling, not content.

As it is evoked in *Yotsuya kaidan*, early-nineteenth-century Edo had no community in which the masterless samurai could symbolically take part in order to establish their heroic image. Instead, the loyal former retainers of Lord Enya—including Oiwa's father and Kohei's master, Oshioda Matanojō, who tries to endure the same struggles as the characters in *The Treasury of Loyal Retainers*—are portrayed as hapless, impoverished losers who do not seem to be doing much of anything but nevertheless persist in clinging to their anachronistic samurai values. In *The Treasury of Loyal Retainers*, the retainers' loyalty becomes deeper and more remarkable as they continue to hold fast to their values, despite everything. By contrast, in *Yotsuya kaidan*, the more tightly the loyal figures cling to the values of the vanished community, the more extreme their poverty becomes, and the more definitively they are excluded from the society around them.

The effectiveness of this unflattering portrayal of the loyal figures is heightened by Nanboku's juxtaposition of them with their disloyal counterparts, whom he presents as attractive, even alluring, figures. Iemon, for instance, who is the most disloyal of all Lord Enya's former retainers, was created in the mold of a new character type that began to emerge during the late eighteenth and early nineteenth centuies. This is the "erotic rogue" (*iroaku*), who is identified by the telltale combination of evil actions and the white-painted skin that had conventionally been associated with handsome, good, and often aristocratic characters. The use of this physical code encourages audiences to regard Iemon as an attractive character, making him much more than an unsympathetic evil figure. Nanboku further accentuates Iemon's charisma, and that of the other disloyal former retainers, by drawing attention to the men who play them. After Iemon kicks Oyumi, Oume's mother, into the lake in act 3, for instance, Iemon and Naosuke engage in a comic give-and-take that clearly alludes to the relationship between Matsumoto Kōshirō V, who played Naosuke, and Ichikawa Danjūrō VII, who played Iemon and had been taught to act certain evil roles by Kōshirō. Kōshirō-as-Naosuke comments, "Hmm, you are mighty evil," and Danjūrō-as-Iemon responds, "Yeah, I take after you." Inspired by this dialogue, subsequent performances have tried to accomplish a similar effect by using different inside jokes.[62]

At the same time that Nanboku undermines the appeal of the "good guys," he also presents the disloyal figures as much more clever characters. Again and again, Iemon and his fellows manipulate and deceive the loyal figures by appealing to the samurai code of honor. The attendant Kohei becomes incapable of protecting himself from Iemon, for example, when Iemon reminds the unfortunate young man that he had been in Iemon's service, if only temporarily. Similar things happen to the women as well: Oiwa and Osode cannot follow their father and husband in death because Iemon and Naosuke persuade them that doing so would violate the moral code that binds the daughters of samurai. In *Yotsuya kaidan*, the concept of loyalty itself becomes a weapon that the disloyal turn against their enemies.

We have seen that in *Yotsuya kaidan*, the clear-cut binary that *The Treasury of Loyal Retainers* establishes between good *gishi* and disloyal *fugishi* ceases to have any validity: Nanboku turns the disloyal retainers into attractive antiheroes and the loyal retainers into pathetic victims of their own outdated moral code. This undermining of the notion of loyalty and the loyal characters as they are presented in *The Treasury of Loyal Retainers* takes place through the manipulation of words, images, and events in the play. At the same time, *Yotsuya kaidan* questions the notion of revenge in the older play through its focus on a female character. Most household-disturbance and revenge plots relied on a clearly gendered division of labor: the feudal hero who led the revenge or played the key role in bringing a household's troubles to a happy resolution was invariably an experienced, middle-aged samurai. For the most part, female characters, especially wives and daughters, could prove their devotion to their community and its moral code only through the disposal of their bodies in a manner decided by their husbands, fathers, and male siblings. Female bodies were always available for use; women could be killed, sold into prostitution to raise funds, or sacrificed in any other way that the relevant male characters deemed appropriate, as long as it made for affecting drama. The case of Okaru in *The Treasury of Loyal Retainers* is a perfect example. Not only is she sold by her father to a teahouse to raise the money that her husband, Kanpei, needs in order to join the vendetta, but she comes close to being murdered by her own brother after she happens to catch sight of a letter that lists the names of the loyal retainers. The situation was similar in regard to children, whose bodies could be disposed of by their mothers and fathers, sacrificed instead of the lord's son in order to preserve the household.

In *Yotsuya kaidan*, Nanboku makes Oiwa the focus of the drama, privileging a character whose sacrifice could have been only a side story in *The Treasury of Loyal Retainers*. He also strips the original meaning from the dedication of the female body to the father, husband, and older brother by having Oiwa and her sister, both of whom belong to the samurai class, find themselves compelled to marry or remarry the very men who killed Samon and Yomoshichi, precisely because these men promise to avenge the deaths. Here, the women's exclusion from directly participating in a vendetta ends up leading them to join forces inadvertently with their enemies. Ironically, the sacrifice they make lies in their marrying these men, not in being abandoned by them. In other words, Oiwa's desire for revenge, and her preoccupation with her samurai status, at least early on in the play, only increase her suffering. There is never any hope that she might restore her family's fortunes or regain the status she considers as hers, because her family is already gone and there is no community around her capable of acknowledging the value of her loyalty. Nanboku uses Oiwa to question the current relevance of the central idea that sustained the romantic vision of the samurai in *The Treasury of Loyal Retainers*—the notion that carrying out a revenge killing could demonstrate the *gishi*'s loyalty and thus reaffirm his position in the social order. This particular sense of community and communal values that was integral to the definition of early modern selfhood is largely missing in *Yotsuya kaidan*.

Once Nanboku has highlighted this contradiction, he focuses on those characters who are marginalized and sacrificed in conventional revenge plays, creating an entirely new type of vendetta with Oiwa, a woman, as its subject and overturning all the essential elements of the standard household-disturbance plot. Conventional household-disturbance plots were framed as the characters' struggle to prove themselves as loyal samurai and to live up to samurai notions of honor. *Yotsuya kaidan* dispenses with that basic structure altogether. At the beginning of the play, Oiwa returns to Iemon only because he promises to avenge her father's death, but after she is transformed into a ghost, she forgets her filial responsibility, concentrating her vindictive energies on Iemon, the members of the Itō family, and various others who either wronged her personally or are associated with those who did. In short, unlike conventional household-disturbance plots, which represent the tensions inherent in collective missions with a public meaning in the feudal context, Oiwa's revenge is purely private and personal. And while the conventional household-disturbance plot moves toward a resolution that brings a world out of order back to its original state or witnesses the restoration of honor of a samurai who died wrongfully, *Yotsuya kaidan* ultimately does not return to the status quo. Oiwa's revenge is not intended to set things right; it is destructive rather than regenerative. It is telling, in this respect, that her ghost does not attain enlightenment at the conclusion of the play. Considered from this vantage point, *Yotsuya kaidan* represents a striking, fundamental departure from the conventional household-disturbance plot or the conventional revenge play because it abandons the "cyclical imagination." At the same time, it also abandons the deferral of closure that had characterized kabuki for so long and that made it possible for the form to continue endlessly presenting the past.

We have seen how *Yotsuya kaidan* carried out its attack on *The Treasury of Loyal Retainers* and on the worldview inherent in the dominant theatrical frameworks. At this point, it will be helpful to reflect briefly on what made it possible for the play to accomplish so much—that is, the figure of the vengeful female ghost. One might argue that the most significant change that Nanboku introduced into the revenge play was his transformation of the subject of the vendetta from a group of *living* male samurai who act as surrogates for their wronged master to a single *dead* woman who acts on her own behalf. It is only in the latter half of the play, after all, after Oiwa's death and her subsequent "rebirth" as a ghost, that she is able to exact her revenge. Death allows Oiwa to break out of the desire to cling to a lost social imaginary, to her vision of herself as a samurai woman. At the same time, death also makes it impossible for Oiwa to achieve closure, the way the loyal retainers do in *The Treasury of Loyal Retainers* by living just long enough to symbolically recover the honor of their lord.

Earlier, I discussed Nanboku's undermining of the concept of the *gishi*. Oiwa's revenge does even more to confuse the distinction between loyal and disloyal, good and bad, and the subject and object of a vendetta. Oiwa's vengeance is incredibly chaotic and grotesque: she causes the deaths even of those unrelated to the plot against her, and the deaths occur with a spectacular violence that easily overwhelms the structured, righteous, socially sanctioned violence of the vendetta in *The Treasury of Loyal Retainers*. At the core, however, we find a certain twisted logic. Oiwa marries Iemon in the hope that he will avenge her father's death, not realizing that he is actually her father's murderer. Later, in carrying out her revenge on the Itō family, she leads Iemon to do most of the dirty work by causing her own face and Kohei's to appear in place of those of Itō Kihei and his granddaughter, prompting the terrified Iemon to behead them. When Oiwa's face appears in place of Oume's and Kohei's appears in place of Kihei's, we witness a literal reversal of roles, which leads to a further inversion in which Iemon unwittingly ends up fulfilling his promise to carry out Oiwa's revenge. Not only does the victim herself become the avenger, but she causes the aggressor to act on her behalf and against himself. The clear distinction between good and evil found in *The Treasury of Loyal Retainers* has been completely undone, and we are left in a world in which the very possibility of such stable roles seems, at best, questionable.

THEATRICAL FRAMEWORKS: THE HISTORICAL AND THE CONTEMPORARY

This analysis shows the various ways in which *Yotsuya kaidan* can be read as a critique of *The Treasury of Loyal Retainers* on both a micro and a macro level. It also can be understood as an elaboration of Nanboku's concise description of *Yotsuya kaidan* as a "brutal attack" on the famous revenge play. In the rest of this chapter, I complicate this understanding of the relationship between the two plays by moving from a mode of analysis focused mainly on their scripts to one that takes into account the double production of 1825 itself. I consider this production first as part of the development of the structure of the Edo kabuki production and then in the context of the history of productions of *The Treasury of Loyal Retainers*.

Text-based comparison like that in the previous section reveals a lot about the two plays and the nature of *Yotsuya kaidan*'s critique of *The Treasury of Loyal Retainers*. That said, this approach is slightly misleading: *The Treasury of Loyal Retainers* and *Yotsuya kaidan* exist as separate texts, and each can be treated as a discrete play; but in considering them in this way, we obscure a crucial complexity or ambiguity in the plays' status as two parts of a single production, one historical and the other contemporary. In an important sense, *Yotsuya kaidan* and *The Treasury of Loyal Retainers* were not really independent plays at all, so it is more accurate to conceive of the double production itself—the entire thing, not just the contemporary part—as a reworking of the conventional view of the loyal retainers and as part of a broader movement toward dismantling the long-standing structures of Edo kabuki. All this can be recognized, however, only if one understands how kabuki productions were conventionally structured in Edo and how this was changing in the early nineteenth century.

It was customary in Edo for kabuki productions to couple a historical "first part" (*ichibanme*) with a contemporary "second part" (*nibanme*) that shared the same *sekai*; this was part of the process I have described as "presenting the past." This two-part structure came into being in the early eighteenth century.[63] The interconnected nature of the two parts of an Edo kabuki production, which was an effect of both the fluid manner in which productions evolved and the crucial role of the *sekai* as the glue that held everything together, is related to the notion of "historical" and "contemporary" in Edo kabuki. Even though an awareness of a distinction between the historical part, which was based on an established *sekai*, and a contemporary part, which transplanted the same *sekai* into the present, has become commonplace in modern scholarship—and, indeed, people often speak of historical and contemporary *plays* rather than parts—the categories of historical and contemporary, *jidai* and *sewa*, were not clearly established from the beginning in Edo. Rather, they entered people's consciousness gradually as the two-part structure took shape. Once the notion of a contemporary part featuring recent incidents and customs took root, the conventional part that drew on established settings and characters came to be understood retroactively as historical.

According to Gunji Masakatsu, the term "contemporary play" (*sewa kyōgen*) made its first appearance in the actor critique *The Three Acting Houses* (*Yakusha mitokoro setai*, 1700).[64] For more than a century after this, however, Edo kabuki continued to rely heavily on the *sekai* in all the parts of each production, and playwrights showed no interest in developing contemporary plays independently from these worlds. Indeed, in the early nineteenth century, playwrights and, in particular, Nanboku, began collapsing several different *sekai* into a single play and incorporating ever more contemporary elements. In his treatise *Strange Transmissions on Composing Plays* (*Denki sakusho*, 1843–1851), Nishizawa Ippō praised Nanboku for this ability to "weave various familiar plots together and make them fresh."[65] Nanboku carried this tendency to greater and greater extremes in his later works, as we can see in one of his last, *Maples and Deer: The Long Sleeves of the Soga Brothers* (*Momiji ni shika furisode Soga*, 1829). In this, even the shortest act includes at least four *sekai*. If anything, the historical and contemporary parts of Edo kabuki productions became even more mixed up over time than they had been at first.

This general trend was challenged at one point in the late eighteenth century, however, when the Osaka playwright Namiki Gohei I introduced a Kamigata style of production to Edo. In 1795, Gohei put on a production that combined two separate plays: *The Gilded and Auspicious Soga in Edo* (*Edo sunago kichirei Soga*), which drew on the *sekai* of the Soga brothers, and *Five Powers That Secure Love* (*Godairiki koi no fūjime*), a domestic play based on the recent murder of five people in Osaka that had nothing to do with the Soga *sekai* and involved none of the characters from *The Gilded and Auspicious Soga in Edo*.[66] This two-play—as opposed to two-part—production was a great success, and Gohei went on to stage other productions in which the contemporary play stood apart from the historical framework of the historical play. Furuido Hideo has pointed out that plays such as *Five Powers That Secure Love* that did not draw on any of the historical plots that were conventional in Edo "represent the birth of the plot anyone could understand, even someone outside the communal imagination of Edo."[67]

Nanboku was working as a low-ranking playwright in the same theater when Gohei introduced the Kamigata two-play style to Edo, so he probably had an opportunity to study Gohei's process of composition.[68] While as an Edo playwright, Nanboku continued to use the classical Edo-style of playwriting that he had learned from his local predecessors—playwrights such as Kanai Sanshō and Sakurada Jisuke I—the new style did, to a certain degree, affect his playwriting. Nanboku's staging of *Yotsuya kaidan* with *The Treasury of Loyal Retainers* is a case in point. It represents a fusion of the Edo-based tradition of "jumbling" in which the first and second parts of a production, one historical and one contemporary, remain closely joined with the two-play structure that Gohei imported from Kamigata. Thus although *Yotsuya kaidan* works with the world of *The Treasury of Loyal Retainers* in the conventional Edo manner, Nanboku followed Gohei in giving *Yotsuya kaidan* a separate title instead of subsuming it completely within the former play.

Yotsuya kaidan is often spoken of as the representative "raw *sewa*," or *kizewa*, play because of its highly contemporary nature and its focus on the lives of poor Edoites. But until the final decades of the early modern period, even *kizewa* plays were hardly ever staged as independent stories, unrelated to the historical frame in which they were situated. *Kizewa* is frequently understood as denoting a high degree of realism. In fact, though, it refers to the emergence of plays that depicted the contemporary urban culture of Edo, including the lives of people living in wretched, slum-like areas, as opposed to earlier contemporary plays that might nominally be situated in Edo or Kamakura but were based on works first staged in Kyoto and Osaka.[69]

When viewed in the context of the historical development of the structure of the Edo kabuki program, we realize that Nanboku's double production of *The Treasury of Loyal Retainers* and *Yotsuya kai-*

dan was in fact doing something quite innovative. In *Yotsuya kaidan*, Nanboku created a work that functioned as a contemporary side story within the larger historical *sekai* of *The Treasury of Loyal Retainers*— as the contemporary part of a conventional two-part program—and yet also stood to a certain extent on its own, as an independent *kizewa* play. *The Treasury of Loyal Retainers* and *Yotsuya kaidan* together formed an odd pair that could be considered as either a single play or two closely connected plays. Either way, the situation was more complex than you might realize if you simply lined up the scripts of the two plays, treating each one as a discrete unit. Consequently, rather than describe *Yotsuya kaidan* as an attack on *The Treasury of Loyal Retainers*, it is more accurate to say that as a whole, the double production itself constituted a critique of *The Treasury of Loyal Retainers*— and *The Treasury of Loyal Retainers* not as a play, but as a work that existed as the sum of a long lineage of different productions. In the double production of 1825, in other words, *The Treasury of Loyal Retainers* itself became part of a critique of *The Treasury of Loyal Retainers*. Over time, the celebrated play began evolving to the point that it was ripe for reinterpretation, and the particular thrust of the reinterpretation that Nanboku gave it.

THE TREASURY OF LOYAL RETAINERS EVOLVES

Nanboku's transformation of *The Treasury of Loyal Retainers* through the vehicle of the double production did not come out of the blue. In various ways, *The Treasury of Loyal Retainers* had already begun heading toward *Yotsuya kaidan* when Nanboku took it up, spawning new meanings quite far removed from the play's reception in its original mid-eighteenth-century context. We see this even outside the theater, in fiction and other popular publications. Shikitei Sanba's *The Bathhouse of the Floating World* includes an amusing scene in which a number of women at a public bath chat about *The Treasury of Loyal Retainers*, offering a novel interpretation focused more on lust than on loyalty: "Take *The Treasury of Loyal Retainers*, where did all that trouble come from? It all starts when Moronao falls in love with Kaoyo.... And how about that Kanpei? He accompanied his lord, but lost his head over his affair with Okaru and was unable to prevent the incident. All the troubles can be traced back to affairs with women."[70] Similarly playful treatments of the play's characters had appeared three decades earlier in *Evaluating The Treasury of Loyal Retainers' Characters* (*Chūshingura jinbutsu hyōron*, 1781), published by Hatanaka Kansai (1752–1801) under the pen name Grumpy Hermit (Henkutsu Dōjin).

Not surprisingly, significant changes were taking place in *The Treasury of Loyal Retainers* on the level of performance, as well. By the end of the eighteenth century, evil and disloyal characters had achieved a new prominence in both Kamigata and Edo, which resulted in a shift in the emphasis given to different figures in the play. We see this, for instance, in the staging of Ono Sadakurō, the man who kills Yoichibei in act 5 and then dies after Kanpei, out in the dark hunting wild boar, accidentally shoots him. Originally, the part of Sadakurō was not played by a first-rate actor, since he did very little apart from die and was dressed in the typically disheveled, rather unattractive clothing of a mountain bandit: he wore a wide-sleeved striped, padded robe and a straw hat.[71] An illustrated play summary (*kyōgen ezukushi*) for the production at the Morita Theater in 1779 recycles an old-style image of Sadakurō, who is depicted in simply patterned clothing, with a mussed, cropped head of hair and an overgrown beard—hardly the way a former samurai ought to look (figure 2.6).[72] *Critique of the Treasury of Loyal Retainers Old and New* captures the sense that this role is ill-suited to showcasing a major star's talents: "There is not much of a scene for Sadakurō in act 4; the mugging in act 5 is accompanied by *jōruri* chanting, but it is not very important . . . as I mentioned earlier, in the beginning

FIGURE 2.6 Ono Sadakurō murdering Yoichibei (*bottom*) in the illustrated play summary for the production of *Kanadehon chūshingura* at the Morita Theater in 1779 (5 omote). (Courtesy of the Nihon Daigaku Sōgō Gakujutsu Jōhō Sentā, Tokyo)

Sadakurō is a mere thief wearing a padded kimono with bold stripes that look like a nightgown."[73]

All this began to change around 1766, when Nakamura Nakazō I boldly invented a new style for presenting Sadakurō, now dressed in a manner more typical of a masterless samurai, in a series of productions of *The Treasury of Loyal Retainers*. We see this in an actor print created by Katsukawa Shunshō (1726–1792) for a production in 1783 at the Ichimura Theater (figure 2.7). Nakazō decided to dress in a single-layered kimono of black silk and had his face and body painted white—a combination that conventionally signified a particularly handsome hero. He wore an unshaven-samurai wig (*sakaguma*), rolled up the sleeves of his kimono and tucked up the hem to expose his thighs, and carried a broken umbrella in his hand. He also poured water over himself just before he walked out on stage, to indicate that he had come through the rain and as a means of highlighting the erotic charge of the evil Sadakurō. Having just committed a brutal murder, he pauses nonchalantly to wring out his kimono and wipe the raindrops from his hair, all the while giving the audience a good look at his dripping body. According to *Singing My Own Praises* (*Temae miso*, 1850s–1880s)—a history of the Nakazō actors by Nakazō I's grandson, Nakamura Nakazō III (1809–1886)—the playwright

FIGURE 2.7 Nakamura Nakazō I as Sadakurō in Katsukawa Shunshō's print for the production of *Kanadehon chūshingura* at the Ichimura Theater in 1783. (Courtesy of the Museum of Fine Arts, Boston)

Kanai Sanshō gave Nakazō I this small part in order to embarrass him, only to have Nakazō transform it into a spectacular highlight of the play that was inherited by later kabuki and even puppet-theater productions of *The Treasury of Loyal Retainers* right up to the present day.[74] Indeed, Nakazō's creation of this new Sadakurō eventually gave rise to a whole new role type that was neither simply handsome nor simply bad: the *iroaku*, an "erotically evil" male character who could best be performed by a first-tier actor with an important position in the troupe.[75]

Nakazō's reinvention of Sadakurō led to further experiments with the role. Originally, Sadakurō made his appearance from the *hanamichi*, chasing Yoichibei, whom he then stabbed. Ichikawa Danzō IV came up with the idea of having his arm emerge suddenly from a bale of hay on the main stage. Then, having killed Yoichibei, Sadakurō would pull him into the hay before stepping out onto stage himself. This allowed Danzō to play both Sadakurō and Yoichibei in a seamless "quick change" (*hayagawari*). A print by Utagawa Toyokuni I shows the actor being dressed as Sadakurō behind the scenes by his assistant and the wig attendant while half his body is still performing Yoichibei (figure 2.8). We are even given a glimpse of the audience beyond the stage. Danzō's Sadakurō is depicted in this print in bandit clothing, but his unexpected appearance from the hay suited the mysterious, alluring figure that Nakazō had developed, and in later performances the two innovations were combined.

Nanboku, too, made brilliant use of this popular "erotically evil" character type, the *iroaku*. In the double production with *Yotsuya kaidan*, Matsumoto Kōshirō V—affectionately known as "high-nosed Kōshirō" (*hanataka Kōshirō*) and famous for having a glare so fierce that children in the theater often cried when they saw him—took on the role of Sadakurō. Kōshirō respected Nakamura Nakazō's acting and had, in fact, learned from him how to play evil roles.[76] Nanboku had the role of Iemon in *Yotsuya kaidan* serve as a counterpart to that of Sadakurō by dressing him in a similar black kimono and having him, like Sadakurō, kill an old man, Oiwa's father. The metatheatrical exchange from *Yotsuya kaidan* quoted earlier, in which Iemon makes a sly remark about how he learned to be evil from Naosuke, can thus be interpreted as referring not only to kabuki acting lineages but also to the particular acting patterns of the characters they play. Danjūrō VII learned how to play evil roles from Kōshirō, of course, but the role of Iemon itself was also derived from Nakazo's new interpretation of Sadakurō, which

FIGURE 2.8 Ichikawa Danzō IV as both Sadakurō and Yoichibei in Utagawa Toyokuni's print *Ichikawa Danzō hayagawari* for the production of *Kanadehon chūshingura* at the Nakamura Theater in 1801. (Courtesy of Waseda University, Tsubouchi Memorial Theater Museum, 100-0389)

Kōshirō magnificently reenacted and brought back to life in 1825 in the double staging.

The Treasury of Loyal Retainers had become firmly established as a theatrical paradigm long before the nineteenth century. This meant that the play, conceived of as a system, could tolerate even the most subversive rewritings: it had achieved a combination of fluidity and resilience that encouraged any number of bold rewritings. Nanboku himself rewrote or substantially invoked *The Treasury of Loyal Retainers* in at least four plays, including *Yotsuya kaidan* and two *gōkan*. One of these *gōkan*, *A Woman's Fan: The Essence of Loyalty* (*Onna ōgi chū-shin kaname*, 1826), offers a female reinterpretation of *The Treasury of Loyal Retainers* set after the loyal former retainers have carried out their revenge and killed themselves. In the play *The Chrysanthemum Bond: Bandit on a Moonlit Night* (*Kiku no en tsuki no shiranami*), produced at the Kawarasaki Theater in 1821, the villain Sadakurō, played by Kikugorō III, strives to restore the Enya household after the death of the forty-seven retainers. *The Chrysanthemum Bond* offers a jumble of characters from *The Treasury of Loyal Retainers* whose genders and roles have been reversed. Act 7, for instance, plays cleverly on Sadakurō's death in act 5 of *The Treasury of Loyal Retainers*: Sadakurō appears in the same black silk kimono that Nakazō had pioneered for the role, dripping wet, the hem of his kimono tucked up, and wearing the same wig.[77] He discovers his dead wife, Kakogawa, floating in the Sumida River (in *The Treasury of Loyal Retainers*, Kakogawa is a male attendant who has nothing to do with Sadakurō), and then her ghost appears before him. Instead of a boar, a festive dancing lion passes by, and then there is the sound of a gunshot. At this point, of course, the audience expects Sadakurō to die, since they have in mind the scene from *The Treasury of Loyal Retainers*, but instead they hear a voice offstage cry "Tamaya!" (There's a shot!); a thin curtain behind Sadakurō falls; and they see fireworks rising from boats floating in the Sumida River, lighting up the night.[78] The picture-book playbill for the production offers a wonderful portrayal of this scene: Kakogawa's ghost is shown once to Sadakurō's right from the viewer's perspective and then again to his left, when she appears dressed in ordinary human clothes, after the fireworks (figure 2.9).

The actor critique *A Fast-Food Take on the Actors* (*Yakusha sokuseki ryōri*, 1822) includes a dialogue on this scene. After someone called "an old man" describes the effect, he comments, "This is playing on act 5 of

The Treasury of Loyal Retainers. I wish there were more straightforward drama." Another theatergoer defends Nanboku and his second playwright, admitting, "You're right, but it's the playwrights' trick to hit on the right note and do something fresh."[79] It is easy to dismiss something like this as a silly parody, as the first theatergoer does, but the second commentator is surely right to regard this as a more sophisticated sort of nonsense: it is made possible, after all, only by Nanboku's skillful manipulation of the audience's horizon of expectations.

In *On Drama: Boundaries of Genre, Borders of the Self*, Michael Goldman observes that it is crucial to maintaining a genre that "certain things apparently destructive to the performance actually get included as we go along."[80] *The Treasury of Loyal Retainers*, which was almost like a genre in how it was incessantly repeated and rebelled against, continued to function as a basic framework precisely because it was constantly violated and thus renewed and made contemporary. From the late eighteenth to the early nineteenth century, the values that had previously been so important to *The Treasury of Loyal Retainers* were being turned inside out, and as a result, the play was moving closer to *Yotsuya kaidan*.[81]

FIGURE 2.9 The picture-book playbill for the production of *Kiku no en tsuki no shiranami* at the Kawarasaki Theater in 1821 (5 omote). (Courtesy of Waseda University, Tsubouchi Memorial Theater Museum, ro-23-1-478)

THE TREASURY OF LOYAL RETAINERS AS A GHOST PLAY

I have been considering various ways in which situating the double production of *Yotsuya kaidan* and *The Treasury of Loyal Retainers* in the context of the changes taking place in the structure of kabuki productions in early-nineteenth-century Edo, on the one hand, and in the manner in which *The Treasury of Loyal Retainers* itself was staged, on the other, offers new possibilities for thinking about the meaning of the double bill. Next I address the question of what it actually meant—of how, specifically, the double production transformed *The Treasury of Loyal Retainers*.

As I mentioned earlier, female characters in kabuki were generally excluded from the main action of household-disturbance plots, with the exception of a relatively small number of plays that focused on political fighting in the female quarters, such as *Mirror Mountain: A Treasury of Woman's Loyalty*. In most cases, all a woman could do to help out was sell herself to raise money for her father and husband, sacrifice herself, have her earnest prayers answered by the gods, or cause a miracle. *Yotsuya kaidan* allows Oiwa to escape this peripheral position because as a ghost she is able to stand outside social norms—and outside the household-disturbance plot's focus on the preservation of the house—and concentrate all her energies on her own personal resentments. Yet at the same time, the figure of Oiwa is an extension, on a very basic level, of the tradition that sustained the conventional household-disturbance structure. Like Lord Enya, who is mercilessly bullied by Kōno Moronao until he is no longer able to endure it, Oiwa is goaded toward her awful transformation and her accidental death by her husband's cruel abuse. There is a critical difference between the two figures, however. Whereas Oiwa must act on her own, male figures like Lord Enya are avenged by other men who come to act as their surrogates. Ōboshi Yuranosuke, for instance, appears on stage in the scene of Lord Enya's ritual suicide, where he receives the blade supposedly drenched in his lord's blood. Kikugorō III's grandfather, Kikugorō I, devised a method later in his career of playing Yuranosuke in which he took the blade away with him and, alone, smeared the blood that covered it over his hands and then licked the blood from his skin.[82] This gripping scene constituted a visual representation of the transfer of Lord Enya's resentment to his surrogate. This transfer, which we might think of as a sort of possession of Yuranosuke by Lord Enya, is the reason why Lord Enya has no need to wander as a ghost, as does Oiwa.

Kanpei's suicide, which became a crucial scene in kabuki stagings of the play, is even more revealing of the way in which male surrogates or avengers obviate the need for a character to become a ghost in a conventional household-disturbance or revenge plot. Feeling unbearably guilty for having gone off to flirt with Okaru in the hour of his lord's greatest need and convinced that he murdered his father-in-law, Kanpei kills himself. As he dies, he speaks lines that resonate with Oiwa's chilling "As if I would just let this grudge slide!" After two of Lord Enya's former retainers encourage Kanpei to attain Buddhahood, Kanpei feebly replies, "Ah, it is repulsive to me to think of Buddhahood. I will not die, I will not go. My spirit [*konpaku*] will remain on this soil, and I will definitely follow you to carry out our revenge."[83] The line "my spirit will remain on this soil" (*konpaku kono do ni todomatte*) is one of a number of phrases describing spirits who wander in this world that are frequently used in plays and prose fictions featuring ghosts. Kanpei invokes language that has been spoken by many who turned into ghosts, and the reason for this overlapping is clear: we see where Kanpei is heading.

And yet Kanpei manages to die in peace. This is because the men present at his death accept his emotions as their own and proceed to act as his surrogates. In order to show that they have inherited his desire to participate in the vendetta, they allow Kanpei to stamp the petition for permission to join the group with his blood. Kanpei, having cut open his stomach, wrenches out his intestines—the location of the spirit or mind—and presses them against the document. This action completes the transfer of Kanpei's spirit and brings his life in this world, as both a human and potentially a ghost, to a terrible but peaceful end. The former retainers then take the pouch containing Kanpei's money—described as "a wallet that contains Kanpei's spirit"—to the scene of their collective revenge and burn incense before it after the revenge has been achieved.

The presence of surrogates and the exchanges that take place at the scenes of both Lord Enya's and Kanpei's deaths contrast with the dark, deeply introspective scene in which Oiwa undergoes her transformation—a scene that is centered, tellingly, on monologue rather than dialogue. In this climactic scene, Nanboku created a moment of piercing solitude: Oiwa further disfigures herself, sunk in a state of utter isolation emphasized by the gloomy chanting (*meriyasu*) of the main singer, a musical effect generally used in tearful or sentimental situations.[84] Rather than pass a knife dripping with blood over to trustworthy surrogates or wrench out her guts and press them onto a petition, Oiwa, completely invested in her grudge and all alone, pulls out her hair and squeezes blood from it, letting it splash across a wooden divider as she swears never to let go of her rage. Oiwa derives much of her power as a character from this brilliant, spine-chilling sequence.

In the 1825 performance, the power of this scene and, in particular, its effectiveness as a means of transforming *The Treasury of Loyal Retainers* were further heightened by the fact that all the roles of the four victims in the two plays, Lord Enya and Kanpei in *The Treasury of Loyal Retainers* and Oiwa and Kohei in *Yotsuya kaidan*, were performed by Onoe Kikugorō III. Imagine Kikugorō killing himself twice as Lord Enya and Kanpei, then dying twice more as Oiwa and Kohei in *Yotsuya kaidan*—presumably all in the same day! Both the parallels and the differences between the deaths would have been unmistakable.

Defined by their social role—their position in the household—most characters assigned to lead-male-role actors are unable to linger on in the world as ghosts for entirely personal reasons, as do Oiwa and other female ghosts. The only exceptions to this rule were socially feminized characters of relatively low status who were not well integrated into the surrounding community, such as fallen monks, actors, peasants, and servants. The actor Kohada Koheiji and the monk Seigen are two famous examples. In a sense, then, focusing on female characters allowed Nanboku and other playwrights to develop avenues of expression that would have been impossible in more conventional plays. Of course, there were other ways in which a military man could allow his "soul to remain on this soil" if it were tied to a public purpose. For example, in *The Mountain Witch with a Child* (*Komochi yamanba*, 1712), a man named Tokiyuki who failed to carry out a revenge killed himself in order to free his spirit so that it could enter his wife's womb: "I will cut up my belly so that my spirit can fly into yours, to turn into a boy powerful and worthy of a thousand men and destroy our enemy."[85] Visual representations of this scene present Tokiyuki in the form common to ghosts (figure 2.10).

The decision to have Tokiyuki kill himself, only to be reborn as a boy, approximates what happens to Lord Enya's and Kanpei's spirits: we do not actually see them flying out of their bodies and lingering on as ghosts in the way that Oiwa does, but they are not entirely absent from the stage either. Even when plays privilege the selfless pursuit of honor or community over an individual's life and attachment to family, they repeatedly stage moments of anger, resentment, and other violent affects that prevent characters from resting in peace, scenes that push

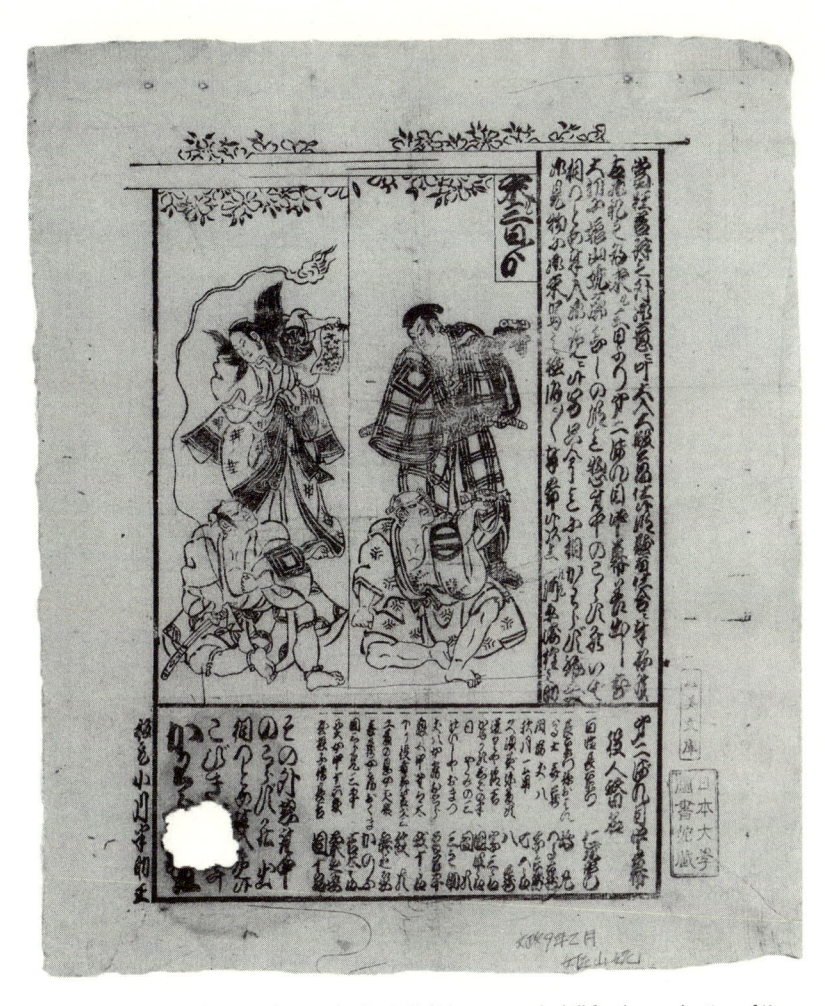

FIGURE 2.10 Tokiyuki's spirit leaving his body (*left*) in a street playbill for the production of *Komochi yamanba* at the Kawarasaki Theater in 1826. (Courtesy of the Nihon Daigaku Sōgō Gakujutsu Jōhō Sentā, Tokyo)

characters almost to the point where they would linger on as ghosts. This, perhaps, is the core of transformation that the double production of *Yotsuya kaidan* and *The Treasury of Loyal Retainers* realized: it revealed *The Treasury of Loyal Retainers* in a new light, as a male ghost play based on a worldview profoundly different from that which inspired the creation of Oiwa in *Yotsuya kaidan*, making visible a latent rhetoric that had in fact long haunted plays centered on romantic views of social reintegration. It took a disfigured woman to finally reveal the potential of these works as male ghost plays and thus to make them fresh to their nineteenth-century audience.

POSTSCRIPT

A production staged at the Nakamura Theater in 1827, just two years after the double bill with *Yotsuya kaidan*, actually presented *The Treasury of Loyal Retainers* as a ghost play. This lends credence to the notion that *Yotsuya kaidan* had unlocked the hidden potential of *The Treasury of Loyal Retainers* as a play centered on a kind of possession in which the living become surrogates for the dead. I began my analysis of *Yotsuya kaidan* by offering a reading of *Yotsuya kaidan* in relation to *The Treasury of Loyal Retainers* that was based largely on their scripts. My subsequent unpacking of the double production uncovered even richer and more complex resonances between the plays as they were actually performed.

Yotsuya kaidan was written nearly a century after *The Treasury of Loyal Retainers* and a century and a quarter after the historical Akō incident. It was a product of a time when Edo was witnessing the decline of the samurai and their traditions, experiencing an influx of poor day laborers and an expansion of the boundaries of the city. When Nanboku shifted his focus to the vibrant marginal spaces of the city in *Yotsuya kaidan*, and when he concocted the idea of a double staging with *The Treasury of Loyal Retainers*, he was mirroring in microcosm the unpredictably changing social order and existential meaning of class and community that constituted the self outside the theater.[86] He was forging a new path forward in an age when the long-standing conventions of Edo kabuki—above all, the largely samurai values embodied in the *sekai*—were rapidly coming to seem less relevant.

Yotsuya kaidan and *The Treasury of Loyal Retainers* were performed together only once in the early modern period, in 1825; after this, they were staged separately. *Yotsuya kaidan* went on to be appreciated as a ghost play in its own right, entirely independent of its original framing in the world of *The Treasury of Loyal Retainers* and apart from the older play's historical framework. For its part, *The Treasury of Loyal Retainers* ceased to be seen as having anything to do with ghosts and is certainly not considered a ghost play today. If *Yotsuya kaidan* had continued to be presented with *The Treasury of Loyal Retainers*, might it have altered popular views of the vendetta play as it gradually came to be internalized as a national epic during the twentieth century? Could it have fully transformed *The Treasury of Loyal Retainers* into something different, and if so, how would this have affected the play's subsequent canonization? There is, of course, no way to answer such counterfactual questions.

The Treasury of Loyal Retainers always consisted of an accumulation of different versions of itself, each version updated for a new audience and infused with new life by the actors who played in it and created new acting patterns to pass on. Tsuruya Nanboku's pairing of *Yotsuya kaidan* with *The Treasury of Loyal Retainers* in the double staging created a ripple in this early modern performance history. The double production offers us a glimpse of the new meanings that Edo kabuki was striving to find in an age when the fantasies that Edo kabuki had been perpetuating had begun to lose their luster, and when the practice of "presenting the past" no longer served the purpose it once had. In 1825, Edo kabuki was groping its way toward a future in which the conventional *sekai* and its social meanings would no longer be necessary for the construction of the present and the early modern subject who inhabited it.

[3]

SHADES OF JEALOUSY

The Body of the Female Ghost

In the double staging of *The Treasury of Loyal Retainers* and *Yotsuya kaidan* in 1825, *Yotsuya kaidan* presented a chaotic revenge by a female ghost who completely disregards the ethics of the society to which she belongs: the basic human relationships defined in Confucian teachings, including filial piety and loyalty, that helped ensure the perpetuation of the household and formed the basis of the dramatic tension in *The Treasury of Loyal Retainers*. Premodern literature and theater often depicted the resentful spirits of figures such as Sugawara no Michizane and Emperor Sutoku, men who, having suffered disastrous political defeats during their lives, returned to the capital after they died as what were known as *onryō* (resentful spirits) and caused fires and other calamities as a means of venting their resentments. Even in death, these male spirits were public creatures. By contrast, the female ghosts, who suddenly became popular in the early modern period and are best remembered today through the example of Oiwa, tended overwhelmingly to be in the thrall of *private* resentments inspired by a lover's betrayal or the pain of unrequited love. In this sense, the female ghost was a natural choice for Tsuruya Nanboku IV in planning a production centered on a figure unbound by ordinary social mores.

The depiction of Oiwa's ghost in the first scene of *Yotsuya kaidan*'s last act, commonly known as the "dream scene" (*yume no ba*), is emblematic of the early modern understanding of the female ghost and reveals how feelings of anger, resentment, and jealousy inspired by a betrayal in love were central to the ghost's construction as a trope and to the early modern understanding of the female body more broadly. The dream scene takes place around the time of the Star Festival (Tanabata), which is on the seventh day of the seventh month, and shows Tamiya Iemon wandering into the countryside and falling in love with a girl who—from the audience's perspective at least—looks exactly like Oiwa. Bamboo branches festooned with colorful strips of paper for the festival and pretty hanging lanterns decorate the girl's house, which stands at the center of the stage. Iemon appears on the *hanamichi* holding an attractive paper lantern printed with morning glories. He has been out hunting and was led to this place by his hawk, which flew off and finally landed on one of the hut's lanterns. Iemon and the girl notice each other, and their eyes meet while he is still walking along the *hanamichi* and she is standing near the center of the main stage. They freeze, adopting a dynamic pose. For a moment, they stand there without moving, in different parts of the theatrical space, like Altair and the Weaving Maid—the two stars whose reunion the Star Festival celebrates.

In this lovely scene, Iemon is no longer the cruel, impoverished man whom the audience met earlier in the play. Now he is stylishly dressed, and the first words he utters are a poem on the topic of the Star Festival inspired by one in the *Collection of Old and New Japanese Poems* (*Kokin wakashū*, 905). Iemon instantly falls in love with the girl and reaches for her obi in order to loosen it, undoing her kimono. She rests her head on his shoulder, and the bamboo blinds hanging from the eaves of the hut slowly descend, by themselves, to hide the lovers in their intimacy. Before long, Iemon's attendant, Akiyama Chōbei, arrives and peeps into the hut to see what is happening inside, and his horror allows the audience to discern the true identity of the girl, if it is not already clear: she is not some rustic maiden, she is Oiwa's ghost. Chōbei flees in terror, leaving the unsuspecting Iemon alone with the apparition.[1]

In the following scene, presumably after Iemon and the maiden have been united, Iemon begins to speak bitterly of Oiwa. This finally causes her to break into a ferocious rage, revealing her true identity. All at once, the beautiful dream turns into a nightmare:

OIWA: How dare you, Iemon.
IEMON: What is this?

Iemon leaps away from her. The hawk perched on his fist turns into a rat and attacks him. Dark clouds cover the shining moon. A black screen falls at the rear of the stage, and there is an eerie drumming sound. The stage suddenly goes dark. Kikugorō takes off the top layer of his kimono in an onstage costume change [hikinuki] and instantly changes into Oiwa. The drumming intensifies, and the two glare at each other.

IEMON: So it's Oiwa, her undying resentment, bringing rats to interfere.
OIWA: I'll drag you down to hell with me. Come, Iemon!
IEMON: How stupid. Go away.

Iemon draws his sword and tries to kill her. The drumming intensifies. Several shōchūbi [flames made by burning alcohol-soaked cotton] emerge. Iemon slashes at the soul flames [shinka] one by one and then becomes exhausted. At just the right moment, the spinning wheel catches on fire and the "one-wheel cart" spins, enveloped in flame. Oiwa pulls Iemon toward her in a renribiki *[pull of affection] movement and freezes in a pose. To the sound of the drumming, the two disappear from sight as that part of the stage is lowered [seri sage].*[2]

Although the scene begins on a dreamy autumn evening in the countryside, by the end Iemon is standing at the verge of hell itself while Oiwa, posed in front of the burning wheel, evokes a cart rolled by demon messengers. The key to this drastic shift in mood—and, indeed, to the entire scene—is Oiwa's use of the force known as *renribiki*, which literally means "pulling of linked branches" but suggests the "pull of affection" and refers simultaneously to the mutation of a once romantic love into feelings of rage and resentment, to the power by which the ghost works her will on her victim, and to the victim's helpless capitulation to the ghost. Shikitei Sanba, Katsukawa Shun'ei, and Utagawa Toyokuni I's *The Illustrated Encyclopedia of Theater* includes a depiction of a ghost exercising this power (figure 3.1). The ghost, presented here under the heading "All-Consuming Obsession" (Mōshū no ichinen), can be seen at the right of the page, standing on a device used to raise her into the air (*tsuriage* or *mokkō*); she extends her hand, loosely clenched into a fist, toward the object of her former affection and current resentment.

The term *renri* (linked branches) that appears in *renribiki* is originally from the famous Tang-dynasty poem "Song of Lasting Pain" (Chang

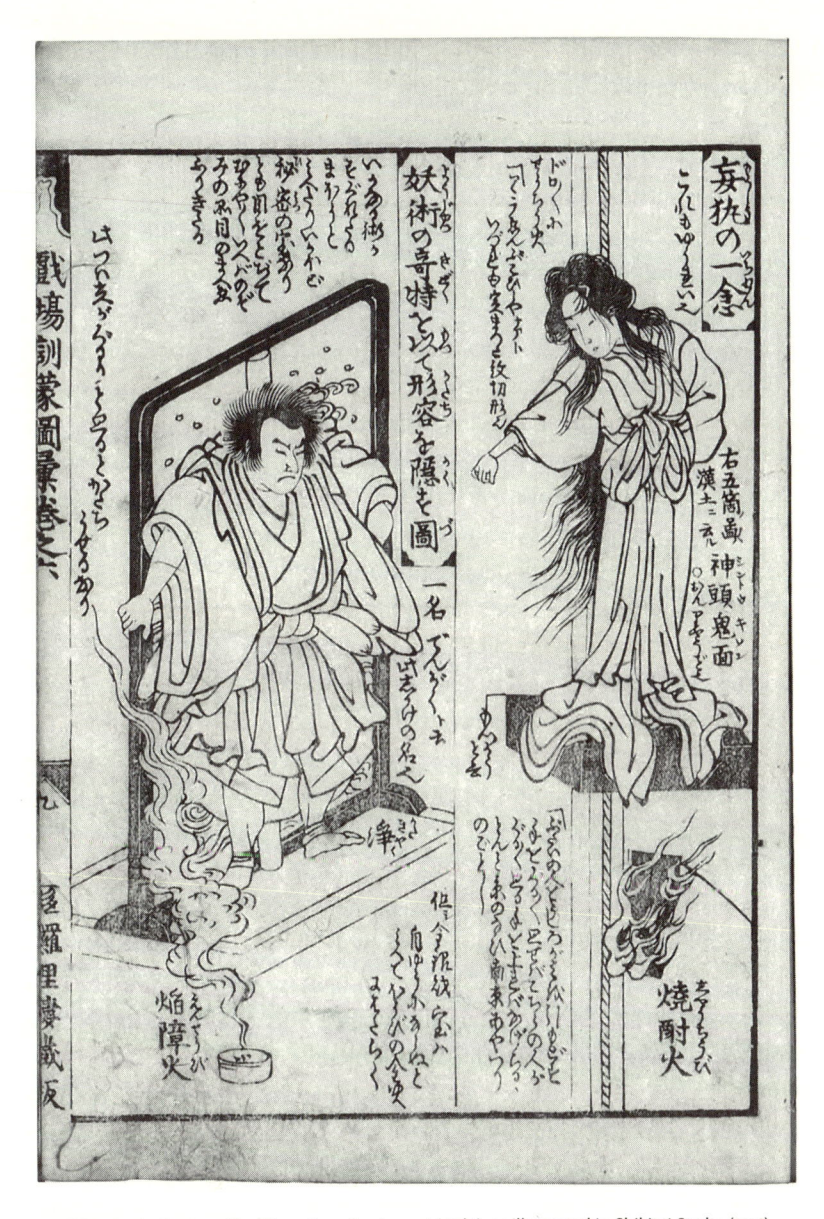

FIGURE 3.1 A ghost and her lingering attachment (*right*), as illustrated in Shikitei Sanba (text), Katsukawa Shun'ei (pictures), and Utagawa Toyokuni I (pictures), *Shibai kinmō zui* (fascicle 6, 9 *omote*). (Courtesy of the Art Research Center, Ritsumeikan University, Kyoto)

hen ge, 806) by Bai Juyi (772–846), in which Emperor Xuanzong and his consort, Yanguifei, swear eternal love:

> if in Heaven, may we become
> those birds that fly on shared wing;
> or on Earth, then may we become
> branches that twine together.[3]

The phrase *renri* is an abbreviation of *hiyoku renri* (shared wings and linked branches) and is the Japanese reading of the relevant line of the poem, which for almost a millennium had been circulating in Japanese as an allusion. It refers to the powerful bond between a man and a woman in love. The power of the "*renri* pull" and of the female ghost who exercises it can thus be understood as an inversion of the love that she once felt for a man who has betrayed her.

Vengeful female ghosts are defined by this inversion on the most basic level, as a sort of disembodied embodiment of betrayed or unrequited love. Generally, early modern female ghosts can be understood only in the context of their relationships with men and, more specifically, in the context of their *failed* relationships, whose failure inspires a resentment that women can act on only in death. The frail wavering of the ghost's hand as she practices her "pull of love" is thus a powerful weapon, having the strength not merely of the dead but of the jealous dead. The wavering fist is an icon of the betrayed, the wronged, its pull impossible for any man to resist, no matter how physically strong he may be.

The recognition that jealousy, love, and resentment are core elements in the construction of the female ghost helps elucidate the resonances of this early modern trope. To clarify still further the meanings that Oiwa and other characters like her evoke, we must trace the origins of their jealousies, their loves, and their resentments in the larger history of the discursive construction of the female body and sex in premodern Japan.

Why did early modern ghosts tend overwhelmingly to be gendered as female in both the theater and literature, a characteristic that contrasts sharply, for example, with a corpus of medieval nō plays that incessantly brought back the spirits of male warriors? Why was it more fitting for a woman, rather than a male samurai, to be the subject of *Yotsuya kaidan*—the figure who, by dying, breaks free from the constraints that bound her in life and engages in a solitary revenge so chaotic and spectacular that it overshadows the communal vendetta of *The Treasury of Loyal Retainers*? And how did female ghosts come to be associated with jealousy? To answer these questions, we must explore the ways in which the female body was discursively constructed in premodern, and specifically early modern, fiction and theater. As we will see, female ghosts were tied to what is often referred to as "serpentine feeling" (*jashin*) or jealousy (*toshin* or *shitto*), a range of emotions that in the Meiji period and afterward came to be seen as universal, not associated with any particular class or gender. In addition to tracing the origins of the new experiments that Nanboku and some of his fellow playwrights were carrying out with female characters, and the reasons why female characters were the preferred site for such experimentation, this exploration of the trope of the female ghost will illuminate early modern conceptions of the body, the ways in which affect was tied to body and gender, and, finally, the web of relationships through which the self was defined in early modern Japan.

THE FEMALE BODY AND THE FIGURATION OF DANGEROUS AFFECT

In premodern Japan, what we understand today as "emotions" were often understood as a material, bodily reality. Affect was generated by the body. In particular, jealousy, a dangerous and disruptive feeling that accompanied the end of an amorous relationship, was predominantly a property of the female body. Oiwa's transformation into a vengeful ghost in *Yotsuya kaidan* is best viewed through the lens of this historical discourse that framed the female body as abject, an instance of what Barbara Creed calls the "monstrous-feminine."[4] Nearly every element in the scene of Oiwa's transformation is encoded as feminine, and even everyday feminine practices—sitting in front of a mirror, applying makeup, combing hair—have grotesque, uncanny resonances. When act 2 opens, Oiwa is suffering from a "disorder of the blood" (*chi no michi*), a catch-all term for specifically female conditions relating to menstruation and pregnancy. In this case, the problem is a sort of postpregnancy lassitude. The medicine that Oiwa and Iemon's neighbor Itō Kihei sends over is referred to as a "wondrous medicine for the disorders of the blood" (*chi no michi no myōyaku*), though in reality it is a disfiguring poison that makes a boil-like bulge erupt over one of Oiwa's eyes and causes her hair to start falling out.

The centerpiece of the scene is a long sequence in which Oiwa, after discovering her disfigurement in the mirror, sits down to "beautify" herself so that she can, as she says, go to thank her neighbor for what he has done. She begins by blackening her teeth, as was customary for certain classes of women in premodern Japan, only to smear the black dye across her lips and around her mouth, making it look grotesquely wide. The audience must have felt an acute sense of discomfort watching this scene, imaging the metallic taste of the dye spreading throughout Oiwa's mouth, especially since new mothers were forbidden to blacken their teeth. Their discomfort would have intensified as Oiwa began combing her hair to the accompaniment of dark, eerie music, only to have big clumps come out in her hands, further revealing the swelling on her scalp. This awful image of Oiwa pulling out her hair is the core of this scene, and it culminates when, in a moment of rage, she squeezes the tangle of hair in her hands, causing bright red blood to stream through her fingers and splash across a standing screen.

The importance of this gruesome display centered on hair and blood is suggested by the care and inventiveness that went into staging it, which in turn is suggested by the explanation of the trick behind it in *What Really Happens Backstage* (figure 3.2). On the right-hand page, we see the actor playing Oiwa combing his wig, and the left-hand page shows a dressing stand with a mirror and the implements used to blacken teeth resting on a bowl of water beside it. The text explains how the actor made it look as though Oiwa's hair were coming out and the technique that produced the spurt of blood at the climactic moment:

> To make it appear as if Oiwa is pulling out her hair as she combs it, the actor has a stagehand pass him extra hair from below. The exchange takes place behind the dressing mirror so the audience is unable to see this. In any case, the theater must be dark. The blood that runs from Oiwa's hair comes from a pouch concealed within the hair that is filled with water in which a blowfish has been boiled with *suō* flower. After combing the hair, the actor squeezes the liquid from it.[5]

This explanation leaves out a crucial detail, however: the scene took advantage of a new type of wig that Tomokurō, a wigmaker with whom Nanboku often worked, had only recently invented. Known as a *habutae*, the wig simulated a natural hairline and thus made it possible to show the hairline receding as hair was pulled out.

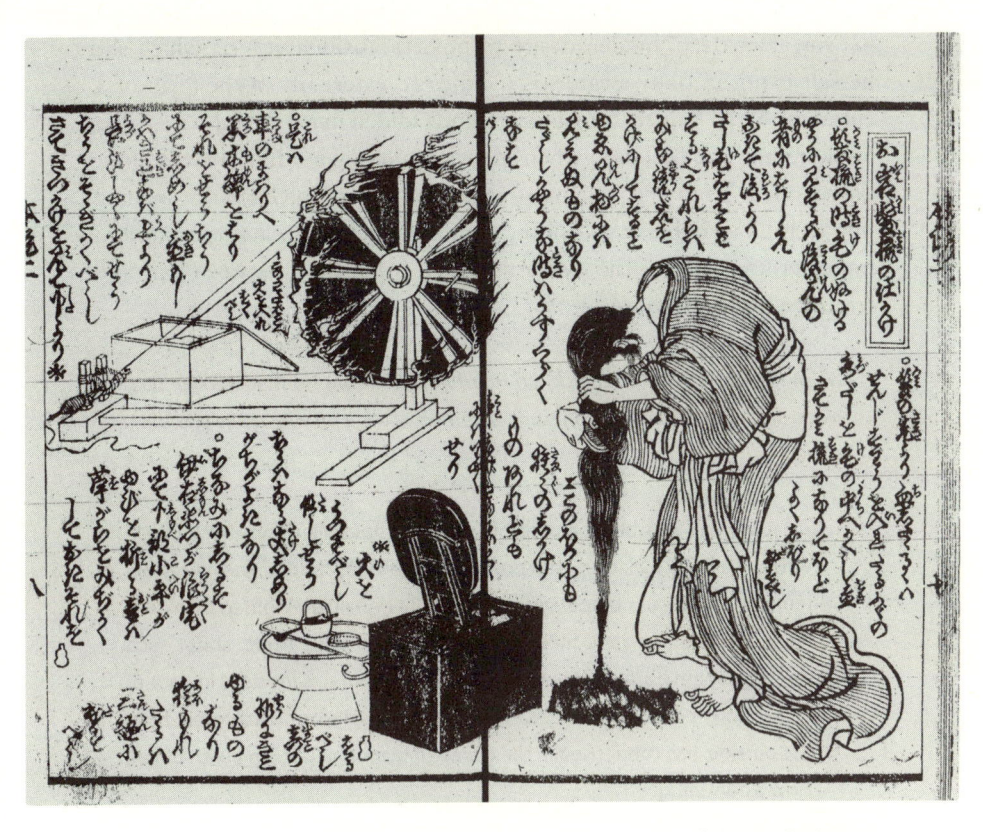

FIGURE 3.2 Oiwa's transformation, as illustrated in Santei Shunba (text) and Utagawa Kunitsuna (pictures), *Okyōgen gakuya no honsetsu* (fascicle 3, *1 omote–8 ura*). (Courtesy of the Tokyo Metropolitan Library, Kaga Bunko Collection)

Hair and blood were not given such prominence in this scene simply to showcase these special effects, however, or to create a generic atmosphere of horror. Rather, they gave Oiwa's transformation a particular significance by evoking a long line of premodern representations of the monstrous-feminine that centered on hair and blood. One especially clear presentation of the meaning that hair and blood had acquired can be found in the play *The Great Favorite Subscription List* (*Gohīki kanjinchō*), which was first staged in 1773 as a face-showing production at the Nakamura Theater. In the second part of the play, Shinobu no Mae, the young daughter of a warrior, is burning with jealousy, having learned that the Kamakura-period warrior Minamoto no Yoshitsune, whom she loves, is married to Princess Iwate, who has given birth to his son. Her deep, hidden desire to possess Yoshitsune—of which she herself is not initially aware—is manifested externally in the form of a clump of black hair that Yoshitsune finds folded in a piece of paper that Shinobu no Mae had used when she was combing her hair. Hot, jealous blood oozes from the hair as soon as Yoshitsune picks it up, leading him to the inevitable conclusion that it must belong to a woman and to interpret it in light of the well-established connection between hair and feminine lust and jealousy:

When Kōshirō [Yoshitsune] picks up Hanshirō's [Shinobu no Mae's] fallen hair, blood drips onto his knees. Yoshitsune, surprised, wipes it off with tissue and takes a look:

YOSHITSUNE: Can this be? A clump of black hair has fallen from thick paper. When I casually pick it up, see how the blood drips from it. The hair is the remains of woman's blood and represents her qualities. Women by nature fixate on love and thus their jealousy is deep. I have heard about such strange supernatural incidents before. Considering this incident in light of those, how frightening a woman's heart is! Her mind, unperceivable from the outside, has condensed in the clump of black hair dripping with blood. How astonishing![6]

The association between hair and jealousy would have been as obvious to the audience as it was to Yoshitsune. Jealousy was lodged deep within the female body and made itself felt by others, no matter how hard the subject of the emotion tried to contain it. When Shinobu no Mae learns about Yoshitsune's discovery of the hair and realizes that it belongs to her, she too interprets it as a sign that she has unknowingly been consumed by jealousy, and she is overcome with shame. From this point on, her body becomes increasingly unruly. In fact, she gets so out of control that her father, a loyal retainer of Yoshitsune's, has no choice but to tie her to a plum tree to keep her from trying to separate Yoshitsune and Princess Iwate. At this point, Shinobu no Mae starts replicating the actions of the heroine in *Dōjōji* (*Dōjō Temple*), whose lust for a young priest turns her into a serpent.[7] Shinobu no Mae also tries to strike the "bell of hell" (*muken no kane*), much like Umegae in *The Rise and Fall of the Heike and Genji: A Beginner's Version* (*Hiragana seisuiki*), who strikes a water basin in place of the bell, praying that her hopes will be fulfilled even if she is consigned to hell as a consequence.[8] Shinobu no Mae's deranged desire is appeased only when her father takes her life. The emotions overflowing on stage were echoed by the overflowing audiences that came to see this enormously successful play. The theater was sold out three or four days before the opening, and some audience members ended up being pushed up onto the stage to watch. Evidently, the theater stopped selling tickets only when it was absolutely impossible to squeeze in another person.[9]

In its presentation of the connection of hair, blood, and female jealousy, *The Great Favorite Subscription List* reveals the extent to which jealousy was understood in early modern Japan as a specifically female emotion, as a "female malady" latent in every woman's blood, capable of consuming even the most faithful wife or lover without her even being aware of it. In performance, the invisible motions of jealousy, gushing in the female blood, are manifested through the hair, which is an extension of the blood. This is precisely what happens in the scene in *Yotsuya kaidan* in which Oiwa pulls out her hair and then wrings blood from it: she is slowly being overcome by jealous rage. The accompanying music, which consists of a single musician chanting over the plucking of a shamisen, emphasizes this in the lyrics of the piece, called "The Sparkle of Glass" (Ruri no tsuya), which speak of the intimacy between two lovers.[10] In fact, because scenes in which a woman combs her lover's hair had conventionally come to signify either the lovers' intimacy (*nureba*) or the pain of their imminent separation (*shūtanba*), the mere depiction of a woman combing her own hair already evoked a certain ominous atmosphere, since the act recalled memories of her former closeness with a lover, only to intensify her current loneliness, jealousy, and resentment.[11] Scenes of this sort were often staged using intimate, amorous music such as "Black Hair" (Kurokami). In them, the woman who sits alone in front of the mirror becomes an uncanny presence marked by the absence of her lover, teetering on the verge of some sort of transformation. In *Yotsuya kaidan*, the long scene in which Oiwa puts on her makeup and combs her hair, which is represented in many modern editions by a single line of text, can be read as an extended, gradually escalating evocation of jealous fury that draws on an archive of performance memory. Here, jealousy is figured as something that happens to the female body and, in particular, to her hair.

At the same time, one might say that by the time the "hair-combing scene" (*kamisuki*), as it is called, reaches its natural conclusion—when

Oiwa almost haphazardly slits her throat on a short sword that has gotten stuck in a post, falls down dead, and then reappears as a ghost—the crucial transformation has already taken place. What matters most is Oiwa's recognition, through her discovery of her disfigurement and her combing of her hair, that despite her intention to remain a loyal, patient samurai wife, she is incapable of stopping the jealousy that is already lodged in her body, that is gradually possessing her and pushing her toward her deranged revenge. That is, the crucial change takes place before her death.

From a modern perspective, it is interesting that for both Oiwa and Shinobu no Mae, emotions do not take place in what we might think of as a psychological space. In the premodern context, jealousy does not make itself felt by a subject who then expresses her feelings in words or actions. Instead, it is a physiological experience that transforms the subject externally and, only then, when the outward traces have been recognized, comes to be felt as reality. Another good example of this occurs in the *otogizōshi* work *Isozaki*, which describes what happens to a woman who puts on a demon mask to spy on her husband's mistress: the mask sticks to her face, so she becomes what it represents.[12]

This understanding of affect is the opposite of what came to dominate as modern notions of psychology and interiority took hold. In Oiwa's case, she is the very last person on stage to recognize her physical transformation, realizing what has happened much later than the audience, the masseur Takuetsu, and her husband, Iemon, do. As long as she remains ignorant, she is defined by her position in the community: she holds fast to her duties as the daughter and the wife of samurai. When she first catches sight of her disfigured face in the mirror, she reacts with fright and horror at the monstrous foreign object that has suddenly appeared before her. Only by repeatedly gazing into the mirror and touching her face with her hand does she gradually come to recognize that this reflected abject Other is an image of herself. Only then does she realize that she has been wronged. When Takuetsu explains Itō Kihei's scheme to disfigure her, her face "reveals her intensifying anger, and she peers intently into the mirror."[13]

Oiwa continues to think of herself as a member of the samurai class even after Lord Enya's forced suicide leaves her father and husband adrift without a master and makes it necessary for her to work temporarily as a street prostitute (*tsujigimi*).[14] The abject figure she sees in the mirror is what finally destroys her seamless image of the world and her position in it, transforming her into an embodiment of jealousy and a desire for vengeance even before her death. In contrast to Jacques Lacan's notion of the mirror stage as representing the subject's social formation, Oiwa's gazing into the mirror is the undoing and breaking apart of a self that has been defined in a larger communal context.[15]

In this sense, the mirror is the catalyst for her change. But what exactly does Oiwa see reflected in it? Or, rather, what does she *recognize* there? It is not merely a deformed image of herself that she discovers, but an image of the female body as it is constituted by the discourse to which Yoshitsune refers ("I have heard about such strange supernatural incidents before") when he finds the bloody clump of Shinobu no Mae's hair. In the mirror, we might say, Oiwa comes to see herself for the first time as part of a long history of feminine transformations that had been described in anecdotes, tales, and various types of theatrical works. These stories staged the consequences of a failure to tame the female body and represented the alienation from family and community that women suffered when their bodies got the better of them. Oiwa sees herself becoming one of those women.

In early modern Japan, the figure of the female ghost, particularly as it was represented on stage, was one of the most extreme instantiations of the female abject, of the discourses that preceded and formed the female sex and body. These discourses circulated in popular Buddhism, in works of Confucian metaphysics, in medical treatises, in women's educational texts, in popular fiction, and in the broad range of female roles represented on stage through the vehicle of the actor's body.

Consider a passage from "The Blue Hood" (Aozukin), a story in Ueda Akinari's (1734–1809) famous collection of ghost tales *Tales of Moonlight and Rain* (*Ugetsu monogatari*, 1776), about an amorous relationship between two men, in which a Zen monk named Kaian expresses astonishment on being told the story of a priest who, having indulged his love for a boy and eaten the boy's flesh after he died, turned into a demon:

> Among those who have been born as humans but end their days in foolishness and perversity, because they know not the greatness of the teachings of the buddhas and bodhisattvas, there are countless examples, from the past down to the present, of those who, led astray by the karmic obstacles of lust

and wrong thoughts, reveal their original forms and give vent to their resentments, or turn into demons or serpents to take retribution. There have also been people who turned into demons while they were still alive.... But these stories are all of women; I have never heard of a man. It is, after all, because of their perverse nature that women turn into shameless demons.[16]

The passage could hardly be more explicit in its articulation of the powerful association between supernatural transformation and the female sex in early modern Japan. Kaian had never heard of a man being transformed in this way, and from his perspective, this is only logical, since Buddhist doctrine often linked femininity to karmic obstacles, lust, and a perverse nature. Buddhist terms such as *aiyoku janen* (sexual desire and evil thoughts) and *goshō* (five karmic obstacles) were often invoked in describing the feminine, and women's possession of these characteristics made it much more likely that they would undergo supernatural transformations than that men would. According to *Fallen Leaves of Precept Ceremonies* (*Kaie rakusōdan*, 1804), a Sōtō Zen text that discusses women's condemnation to the gender specific Blood Pool Hell (*chi no ike jigoku*), "Those born as women have little inclination toward enlightenment in the next world, but deep reserves of jealousy and evil sexual desires. Their sins gather to become menstrual blood, flowing from their bodies month after month, disgracing not only the god of earth but all gods, and so after death they are condemned to hell where they must suffer limitless torments."[17] Here, members of the female sex are subject to what we might think of as a sort of physiological impediment: drawing on the stigma that during the late medieval era became increasingly attached to menstrual blood, the text describes the blood itself as an accumulation of jealousy and desire.

In the premodern context, gender was not inextricably linked to the physical body; rather, the female body was viewed as a state from which one could be mentally freed in order to achieve salvation. As Carolyn Hirasawa observed in her discussion of sixteenth- and seventeenth-century images of hell, the female body "insinuated shortcomings, impurities, and sin," and "salvation for women often involved a trading up of the female body for a male body."[18] Documentary evidence of the negative associations of the female body survives from as early as the tenth century, when references to the need for abstinence due to taboos and impurities related to female bodily functions, including pregnancy and menstruation, appear in court legal codes meant to protect the sacred imperial space.[19] By the late Heian period, the notion that women possessed innate physical impediments to salvation, known as the five karmic obstacles, had taken root.[20] That said, court ritual was relevant to only a small group of aristocrats, and there was considerable variety within Buddhist doctrine and among different types of discourses relating to women—ideological, institutional, and popular. This makes it difficult to determine just how widely these negative views of the female body circulated. In addition, the monks' interpretations of the five obstacles and those of the women searching for salvation were quite different.[21] As Lori Meeks demonstrated in her study of the medieval female monastic orders of Hokkeiji, until the late fourteenth century, discourses disparaging the female body were not necessarily applied systematically to women engaged in religious practices.[22] The notion that women and their bodies were intrinsically sinful and incapable of redemption came to have a powerful hold only during the Muromachi period with the creation of the concept of blood defilement.[23]

SERPENTINE IMAGERY AND THE CONSTRUCTION OF THE FEMALE BODY

In the passage from "The Blue Hood," the monk Kaian is surprised to hear that a male priest had turned into a *demon*, because the subject of every story of such a transformation that he knows was a woman. At first glance, this discussion of demons might seem to have little bearing on the figure of the vengeful female ghost. Early modern female ghosts (*yūrei*) are typically depicted in the form of a hazy figure that fades into nothing below the waist, as in a famous painting by Maruyama Ōkyo (figure 3.3). Oiwa and the other female ghosts who populated Nanboku's kabuki plays during the nineteenth century assumed a similar visual form: the actor wore a long robe that trailed off at the bottom, suggesting a spirit that had risen from its body. The specificity of this representation, which was developed through repeated visual depictions of ghosts, above all in print, has created the impression that the *yūrei* constitutes a category of its own, distinct from earlier types of female transformation such as serpents and demons.[24]

Suwa Haruo's historical treatment of the *yūrei* in *Japanese Ghosts* (*Nihon no yūrei*, 1988) is a case in point. In this study, he traces representations of the hazy spirits of the dead back in time, constructing a history of the development of the trope of the *yūrei* as "ghost."[25] Although his temporal extension of the category of *yūrei* allows him to discover similar representations that predate the early modern period, it obscures the gendered metaphysics that have underwritten different types of transformation throughout history. Rather than start from a definition of the "ghost" as a fixed visual category and extend it across time, we should view the hazy figure of the *yūrei*—which was, as a rule, gendered feminine—as a specific, early modern iteration of a broader range of representations of female transformation. "Female ghosts" are described by discourses different from those that gave meaning to male spirits and consonant with the discourses that framed earlier female metamorphoses. When Kaian identifies women's "perverse nature" as the cause for their tendency toward demonic transformation, he is also identifying the source of the power of Oiwa's "*renri* pull" and of the change she discovered by gazing at her transformed self in the mirror. When *Fallen Leaves of Precept Ceremonies* observes that the sins of "jealousy and evil sexual desires . . . gather to become menstrual blood," it paves the way for Yoshitsune's comment on finding the bloody clump of Shinobu no Mae's hair in *The Great Favorite Subscription List*, that "the hair is the remains of woman's blood and represents her qualities. Women by nature fixate on love and thus their jealousy is deep." In premodern Japan, representations of various instances of female transformation, including demons and snakes as well as ghosts, were framed by discourses surrounding the female body.

FIGURE 3.3 A female ghost in Maruyama Ōkyo's hanging scroll *Yūrei-zu* (1760s or 1770s). (Courtesy of the Zenshōan Temple, Tokyo)

The paradigmatic visual representation of the female body as an obstacle could be the image of a woman turning into a serpent—a distant predecessor of the early modern vengeful female ghost. Although in history, serpents had been assigned various roles, including as sacred beings in ancient mythology, Buddhist tales tended to invoke them in androcentric contexts as a metaphor for sexual desire.[26] As an example, Bernard Faure cited the following warning against women, which was versified to make it easier to memorize:

> A serpent full of venom
> Can still be seized with the hand;
> The woman who deceives men
> Must not be touched.
> The man who has knowledge
> Must not look at her;
> Or, if he is forced to see her,
> He will treat her as his mother or sister.
> Looking at her objectively,
> He will hold the woman
> As a heap of impurities.
> Not to reject the fire of lust
> Is to [condemn oneself] to
> Perish from its burn.[27]

Here, women are more poisonous even than serpents, as they can arouse sexual desires in men and corrupt them. According to Tanaka Takako, "The view of the serpent as a figure of women's evil nature was occasioned by the development of notions of female defilement and Buddhist sin from the end of the Heian period to the Kamakura period."[28] The corpus of works relating to *Dōjōji*, which focuses on a woman who becomes obsessed with a monk, turns into a snake, and forces herself into a temple in pursuit of him, is an example of this trend. This tale was first included in *Japanese Miracles of the Lotus Sutra* (*Dai Nihon hokke genki*, 1040–1043) and was subsequently retold in the thirteenth-century *Collections of Tales Old and New* (*Kokon chomonjū*, 1254) and many later texts. In these early iterations, the tale represents the invasion of a temple's sacred precincts by a woman who, by turning into a serpent, has exposed the dangerous qualities believed to lodge in her body. The tale concludes when the merits of Buddhist practice finally allow the priests to pacify the serpent.[29] Late medieval fiction and performance genres, including *otogizōshi* and *sekkyō*, and early modern *kojōruri* include many works featuring such tales of female transformation and Buddhist redemption. During the early modern period, however, redemptive stories of this type were gradually displaced by more sensational works, interested solely in the violent eruption of a woman's physical nature, that dropped the section exploring female salvation or demonstrating the power of Buddhist pacification.[30]

By the medieval period, the association of inherently feminine jealousy and attachment to the things of the world with serpentine qualities was deeply embedded in Japanese culture. A good example of this occurs in nō plays, in which vengeful female figures, dead or alive, were always staged using one of the demon masks known by the names *hannya*, *chūnari*, and *namanari*. For instance, Lady Rokujō in *Lady Aoi* (*Aoi no ue*) wears *hannya*—a mask with two horns and wide mouth—when she comes to attack Lady Aoi. This performance convention reflects a characteristically medieval perspective, according to which a person overcome with intense rage or resentment finally becomes incapable of remaining human and changes into a demon. According to Baba Akiko, all these various masks were associated with snakes, each one representing a different degree of serpentine nature.[31] *Hannya* is "half snake" (*hanja*), while the mask *honnari* (full transformation), which is used in the play *Dōjōji* to represent the woman's final state, represents a complete transformation into a serpent. Thus the image of the serpent is deeply embedded in, or coincides with, the cultural imagination of the demon as a representation of a deranged woman.

Serpent imagery found a place as well in the visualization of popular hells for women that began to appear during the Muromachi period—which is to say, in representations of what happened to women after death. By the late Muromachi period, in various newly created types of mandalas such as the *Mandala of the Heart and Ten Worlds of Kumano* (*Kumano kanjin jikkai mandara*) and *Mandala of Tateyama* (*Tateyama mandara*), three hells specifically related to women's lives became part of the popular imagination: Blood Pool Hell for the sin of shedding blood, Two-Women Hell (*futame jigoku* or *futamegurui jigoku*) for jealous women, and the Hell for Childless Women (*umazume jigoku*) (figure 3.4). These hells were represented using images of women drowning in pools of blood, some in the form of serpents;

FIGURE 3.4 *(opposite page, above) Kumano kanjin jikkai mandara; (below)* detail of Two-Women Hell *(left)* and Blood Pool Hell *(right)*. (Courtesy of the Hyōgo Kenritsu Rekishi Hakubutsukan)

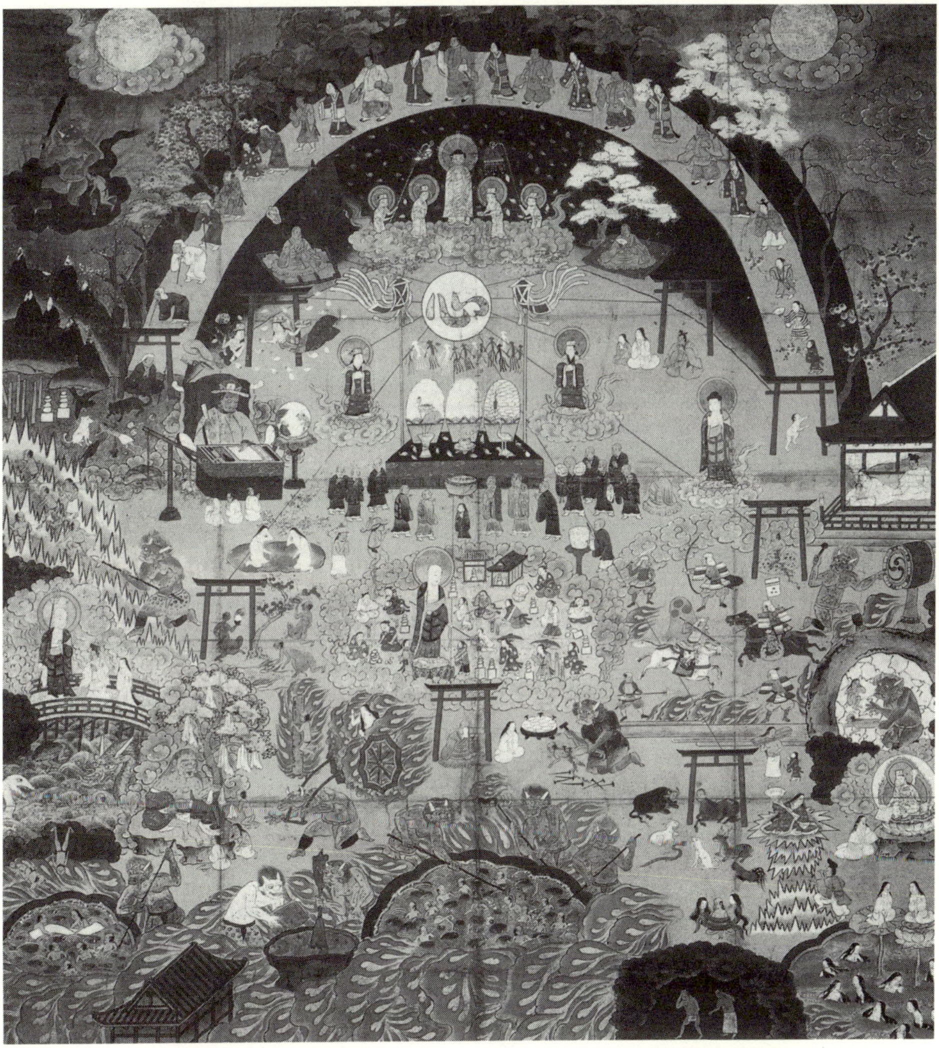

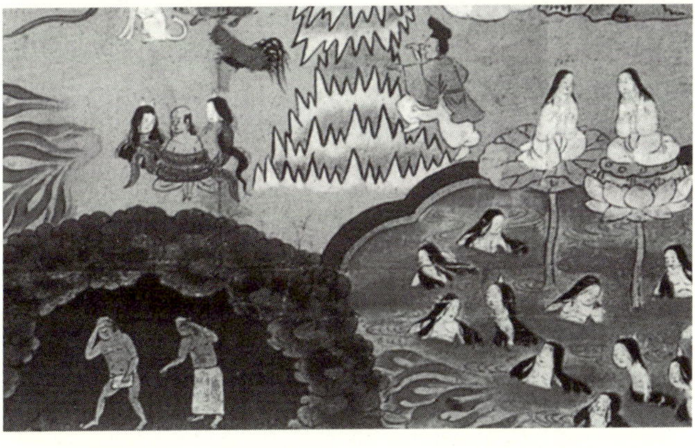

women who have turned into jealous snakes; and women crying as they attempt to dig up bamboo shoots (*takenoko*; literally, "the children of bamboo") with lamp wicks, a symbolic act suggesting failed attempts to have a child.[32] Two-Women Hell was visualized as two serpent women coiling their bodies around one man, with whom they had become involved in a triangular relationship.

These hells for women were popularized by traveling nuns known as *Kumano bikuni* and by Buddhist temples that published stories about female ghosts who required particular funerary practices in order to be saved from these hells. One frequently cited work in the seventeenth-century genre known as "fictions of the floating world" (*ukiyozōshi*), *The Basket's Ears* (*Kago mimi*, 1687), dismisses the nun's preaching as a commercial business targeting women: a nun would collect money from a group of women who had asked her to speak about the three hells for women. Thus, as a religious teaching and even as a commercial activity later in the early modern period, the notion of the three hells and their connection to serpent imagery continued to spread.

In early modern times, the connotations of serpentine imagery gradually shifted from a general stigmatization of the female body toward a more specific condemnation of lustfulness, jealousy, and resentment—all gendered specifically as female—that found its way into various genres of popular literature and theater. The entry for the word "serpent" in *Accompanying Boat* (*Haikai ruisenshū*, 1676), a handbook of "associated words" used in *haikai*, includes links such as "death," "the other world" (*higan*), and "lingering resentment" (*shūnen*). The notes add that "they say that a living spirit always turns into a snake and travels."[33] Another clear indication of the depth and ubiquity of the early modern association between serpents and jealousy appears in a print in Katsushika Hokusai's series *One Hundred Ghost Stories* (*Hyakumonogatari*, ca. 1831) that bears the title "Lingering Resentment" (*Shūnen*).[34] Here, the enduring grudge is represented simply as a snake coiling around a wooden mortuary tablet, a bowl of tea, and a tall tray containing an offering of sweets. The image has no description or explanation beyond the title, but none is needed. The long history of the serpent as one of the forms that a jealous woman might assume, and the abundance of tales concerning a jealous first wife and her ghostly revenge on a mistress or later wife that circulated during the early modern period, almost automatically evoked a domestic narrative of betrayal and resentment.

RIVALRY AMONG WOMEN: JEALOUSY IN EARLY MODERN SOCIOCULTURAL CONTEXTS

Whereas in earlier periods snakes tended to be invoked as a comparatively abstract symbol of feminine proclivities that became impediments to salvation, in early modern literature and theater the image came to be increasingly associated with eruptions of jealousy in a rivalry between two women. Instructional literature intended for women, such as *The Cultivation of Ladies* (*Fujin yashinaigusa*, 1689), an illustrated work in the "*kana* booklet" (*kanazōshi*) genre, adapted conventional representations of Two-Women Hell to illustrate the unintentional revelation of the jealousy that women supposedly harbored inside themselves, often without even realizing it. The text contains a picture of a scene in which a wife and a mistress, who outwardly seem to be on good terms, fall asleep, and their hair turns into two snakes that begin fighting (figure 3.5). This situation was based on a popular tale with Buddhist inspirations, *Monk Karukaya* (*Karukaya dōshin*), in which jealousy and rivalry also were visualized through an evocation of the image of Two-Women Hell. A similar scene was featured in the puppet play *Monk Karukaya, Souvenirs from Tsukushi* (*Karukaya dōshin Tsukushi no iezuto*, 1735), which was staged at the Toyotake Theater in Osaka.

The familiar *Dōjōji* narrative, which originally focused on the lustful woman's transformation into a serpent, itself underwent a significant and parallel transformation during the early modern period. In the seventeenth century, the emphasis of the narrative shifted away from the inherently lustful nature of the female body to the theme of jealousy, which was highlighted by the introduction into the story of a second woman. This tendency was particularly evident in seventeenth-century plays, which often featured a scene in which a woman's jealousy turns her into a serpent that then dives into the water and swims away.[35] Later examples of plays based on similar reinterpretations of the *Dōjōji* plot include Chikamatsu Monzaemon's (1653–1724) puppet play *Emperor Yōmei and the Mirror of Craftsmen* (*Yōmei tennō shokunin kagami*, 1705) and Asada Itchō and Namiki Sōsuke's puppet play *The Scales of Dōjōji, a Modern Adaptation* (*Dōjōji genzai uroko*, 1742). In all these versions, a woman becomes jealous of another woman, a trope that reflects a new interest in triangular relationships.

FIGURE 3.5 The moment two women fall asleep with their heads resting on a go board, their hair turns into snakes that start to fight, as illustrated in Baiu Sanjin, *Fujin yashinaigusa* (fascicle 4 *ge*, 29 *omote*). (Hirosaki Ichiritsu Hiromae Toshokan. Courtesy of the National Institute of Japanese Literature, Tokyo)

Even Ueda Akinari's well-known "A Serpent's Lust" (Jasei no in), another story from *Tales of Moonlight and Rain*, reworked the traditional *Dōjōji* paradigm in the same way. In this case, though, the reworking was complicated by the fact that "A Serpent's Lust," about a man haunted by an amorous, jealous serpent-woman named Manago, is actually a Japanese-language rewriting of a work in vernacular Chinese: Feng Menglong's (1574–1645) "Madam White Eternally Subjugated Under the Leifeng Pagoda" (Bainiangzi yongzheng Leifengta), which was included in *Warning Words to Penetrate the Age* (*Jingshi tongyan*, 1624) and was based on the familiar legend of the White Snake who lived in the West Lake. Feng Menglong's story focuses straightforwardly on a serpent woman who falls deeply in love with a man, whereas Akinari's rewriting foregrounds the theme of jealousy by introducing a second woman toward the end of the tale and allowing her to usurp Manago's place as the man's wife. Akinari creates an association with the *Dōjōji* plot and its various early modern renditions by bringing in a monk from Dōjō Temple to pacify Manago, but clearly the emphasis in this tale is quite different from that in earlier versions of the story.

The image of two women fighting over one man became prevalent in the early modern context because to a large extent, it reflected domestic life in an age when perpetuating the household was of the utmost importance. During the medieval period, the uxorilocal marriage system, which had been widely practiced during the Heian period, in which the man became part of the woman's family, gradually gave way to the virilocal *yomeiri-kon* system, in which the woman was incorporated into the man's family.[36] Wakita Haruko has shown that by the end of the fifteenth century, women of the samurai class had lost their inheritance rights and their interests had been subjugated to those of the family unit.[37] The woman's role in marriage became increasingly domestic in the higher echelons of society, and the wife's responsibility to produce an heir who could carry on the family line came to be paramount, especially in warrior households.[38] Although polygamy was technically illegal in the early modern period, mistresses (*shō*, *kakena*, or *mekake*) became important members of samurai households, so if a wife failed to produce an heir, a mistress would be found who could do so instead.

According to cultural historian Mitamura Engyo, in samurai households not only was the wife supposed to advise her husband to take a mistress but she herself was in charge of selecting and recommending the proper candidate.[39] Readers' and theatergoers' voyeuristic fascination with such complicated areas of domestic life resulted in numerous tales about this. Ihara Saikaku's *The Life of a Sensuous Woman* (*Kōshiku ichidai onna*, 1686) even includes a depiction of a "jealousy gathering" (*rinkikō*), in which women get together to give vent to their jealousy, cursing their husbands and their husbands' lovers. The rivalry between a first wife and a mistress who was brought into the household later was one of the most common causes of jealousy in ghost stories and inspired countless bloody tales of torture and murder, especially in nineteenth-century fiction from Edo. Santō Kyōden's (1761–1816) *Plum Flower and the Cracking of Ice* (*Baika hyōretsu*, 1807), a work in the "reading book" (*yomihon*) genre, is just one example. It features a good-hearted samurai wife who, incapable of bearing an heir, asks her husband to employ a mistress. Eventually, though, the wife is overcome with jealousy, and unable to control the resentment that wells up from her body, she brutally kills her rival.

Toward the end of the early modern period, commoners began imitating the samurai practice of bringing in a mistress when a wife failed to produce an heir. This probably contributed to the remarkable surge in representations of jealous and vengeful wives in nineteenth-century popular fiction. Mistresses were paid salaries at all levels of society, and their position in the household or in the place where they lived depended on the man's status. During the first half of the early modern period, the shogun, daimyo, and high-ranking samurai kept their mistresses in the same houses as their wives, while wealthy merchants who were able to afford mistresses kept them in separate lodgings.[40] Mitamura Engyo traced the commoner practice of maintaining a second house for this purpose back to monks who could not officially have wives and to popular kabuki female-role actors like Segawa Rokō I (1693–1749), who had to keep his off-stage life as a male concealed and thus visited his lover in a room he kept for her on the second floor of a teahouse.[41] Later, the mistress system spread to the lower classes, and even to servants and apprentices who could not afford a separate lodging but simply commuted to the woman's house in a practice referred to as *hangakoi* (half keeping" a woman). Another approach was to share a mistress with friends, which was known as *yasugakoi* (keeping on the cheap). In *Records of a Flourishing Edo* (*Edo hanjōki*, 1832–1836), Terakado Seiken (1796–

1868) tells a farcical story about men taking turns seeing their shared mistress, and examples of women making their living as mistresses appear quite often in works of "sentimental fiction" (*ninjōbon*).[42] These are still underexplored areas of the early modern marriage system—or, rather, of the unofficial, unwritten conventions that lay just outside the marital system—and further research would no doubt deepen our understanding of the sociocultural roots of the patterns that emerged in relationships between women in early modern theater and fiction.

Warnings against jealousy (commonly denoted by the words *rinki*, *shitto*, and, more specifically, *uwanari netami*, which refers to a wife's jealousy of a mistress or another woman) were a frequent feature of women's educational texts, which essentially updated the age-old stigma attached to the female body by adapting it to the context of the household. These warnings appear in both the instructional books that were known as *ōraimono*, which targeted adult women, and the moral guides for girls that were called *jokun*, both of which were widely published in the mid-eighteenth century. Late medieval Buddhist anecdotes about jealous women were sometimes cited in these texts as cautionary tales. Asai Ryōi's *Models of Women from Japan* (*Honchō jokan*, 1661), for example, states that "a jealous woman destroys the house" and cites the example of a wife in China who murdered the baby of her husband's second wife, thereby extinguishing the family line.[43] Similarly, the widely circulated *The Treasure Box of Women's Learnings* (*Onna daigaku takarabako*, 1716) lists jealousy as one of the seven reasons for husbands to divorce their wives (*shichikyo*).[44] Warnings against jealousy are repeated even in popular literary texts such as Miyako no Nishiki's *The Contemporary Mirror of Wisdom* (*Tōsei chie kagami*, 1712), which explains that "jealousy [*rinki*] is a threefold poison of the serpentine mind and the most serious fault of women. Because it is more harmful than poison, causing women to lose their minds and to torture and murder others, it is called the poison of jealousy."[45]

In this manner, the centuries-old association of women with lustfulness and jealousy, which originated in Buddhist discourse, was reapplied in the early modern period to regulate women in secular contexts. Representations of female transformation in the theater and literature explored those situations in which women's efforts to tame and control themselves failed. The reality of early modern women's lives was assuredly much more dynamic and varied than these educational and popular texts fusing Buddhist views with Confucian morals suggest, and, of course, much depended on a woman's class and specific situation. In discourse, however, the constant circulation of injunctions against jealousy in forms that overlapped with much older notions about the female body helped promote a broad, popular interest in female jealousy and the wild transformations it was said to trigger.

THE SERPENT AND THE GHOST

In early modern popular literature and theater, the long history of representations of women who assumed serpentine form gradually began to shift in another direction. That is, women in the thrall of extreme emotions came to be shown undergoing a different kind of transformation—dying and reappearing as ghosts. Here the ghost, conceived of not as a radical departure from the realm of the human but as a continuation of human life, was an embodiment of recent attempts to rationally understand the body and the spirit and the relationship between the two. At the same time, early modern representations of female ghosts often retained clear traces of earlier serpentine and demonic imagery. In cultural products ranging from seventeenth-century theater and *kana* booklets to nineteenth-century reading books, the symbolic resonances that had long been associated with snakes and serpentine transformation were transferred to the increasingly prevalent motif of the ghost in a white kimono, giving it deeper, older layers of meaning than it might otherwise have had. Or to put it in another way, the earlier connotations of the serpentine transformation were gradually absorbed into the image of the ghost.

Many female ghosts are depicted with serpentine patterns on their clothing. In the kabuki play *Three Generations of Dōjōji* (*Sanze Dōjōji*, 1701), an adaptation of the *Dōjōji* plot published as an illustrated prompt book (*eiri kyōgenbon*), an actor is shown having removed his arms from his kimono sleeves, revealing an underrobe decorated with a motif of small triangles known as a "scale pattern" (*uroko-moyō*), which is specifically associated with snakes. The scale pattern had long been used in nō costumes worn by jealous women, such as the *shite* (literally, the "doer," the main actor in a nō play) in *Dōjōji* and *Kanawa*, and Lady Rokujō, the *shite* in *Lady Aoi*. The scale pattern functioned as a symbolic evocation of burning jealousy even when a woman had not undergone a true physical transformation. Indeed, in most early modern plays, especially in kabuki, the use of the scale pattern took the place of an actual physical metamorphosis.[46] Here the serpentine nature of the female sex was manifested as a sort of residue of earlier beliefs, not in the transformation of the body itself, but on the surface of the body.

In Genroku kabuki, male spirits were generally depicted with horns, in the form of demons. Likewise, the scale pattern, serpentine bodies, and demon horns were used to visualize female "ghosts" in the theatrical genre known as *onryōgoto* (performances of resentful spirits).[47] This use of serpentine coding continued throughout the early modern period. At the same time, as I have noted, the hazy figure of the ghost with her disheveled hair also came to function as a stand-in for the serpent. Indeed, serpentine connotations could be evoked even by such a seemingly ordinary action as the touching or the combing of hair, as in the scene in *Yotsuya kaidan* in which Oiwa undergoes her own grotesque transformation. This is reflected in the fact that in kabuki, an actor would always untie the hair on his wig when he was portraying a woman consumed by jealousy—a hairstyle known as "disheveled hair" (*sabaki-gami*). In illustrations, the hair is shown rising into the air like snakes, as in the picture from *The Cultivation of Ladies* (see figure 3.5). Over time, allusions to serpentine transformation and the connotations associated with it became more abstract and fragmented, so that even the sudden movement of the obi in an illustration by Katsushika Hokusai for Ryūtei Tanehiko's *A Modern Ghost Story on a Starry Night* (*Kinsei kaidan shimoyo no hoshi*, 1806), for instance, could suggest the invisible presence of Osawa, the counterpart of Oiwa in this rewriting of *Yotsuya kaidan*.[48]

The gendered trope of the female ghost/serpentine figure therefore became a discursive site for exploring a newly emerging notion of an inner space that could be read through the body's surface: a juxtaposition of interior and exterior. Tsutsumi Kunihiko found that during the first decades of the early modern period, the conventional use of the serpent in Buddhist contexts as a symbol of feminine sinfulness gradually gave way to invocations of serpentine iconography in popular culture—including works without overtly religious overtones—as a symbolic evocation of the inner turmoil experienced by jealous wives and mistresses. Tsutsumi calls this the "discovery of the inner serpent lurking in the darkness of everyday life."[49] Stories of jealous women who undergo an actual physical transformation into a snake appear in medieval *setsuwa* (anecdotes or tales) and *otogizōshi*, but in the early modern period, this literal use of serpentine imagery gave way to a new metaphoric use whose purpose was the probing of inner space. In other words, rather than being used to represent women who leave their human bodies behind, snakes increasingly came to be invoked as figures for something that existed *within* the human body—for what we might now describe as a subconscious desire. Needless to say, the type of exploration the serpent allowed was quite different from what we see in modern novels, for instance, and is not "psychological" in the usual sense of the word. Nevertheless, the invocation of serpentine imagery—and, therefore, of the trope of the female ghost that inherited its symbolism—can be understood as an early modern counterpart to modern attempts to explore "interiority." In both the theater and literature, certain types of emotion almost always were manifested in this way on the body's surface and often did so before the subject of the emotion realized that she was feeling it.

The shift in emphasis from the serpentine to the ghostly in popular depictions of women in states of extreme emotional turmoil is linked to the rise, in the seventeenth century, of an early modern "enlightened" understanding of the body that had been formulated in scholarly treatments of death and the afterlife and that affected the interpretation and representations of supernatural creatures, including ghosts. This was part of a attempt by some early modern intellectuals, long before the so-called Meiji enlightenment, to offer rational explanations of various natural phenomena. As Kondō Mizuki has observed, Confucian scholars did not deny the existence of strange things (*kaii*) but "rationalized them in order to deny the mysterious and transcendental status of such phenomena."[50] We see this, for instance, in Hayashi Razan's (1583–1657) *On Ghosts* (*Yūrei no koto*, ca. 1645–1672), one of the first early modern translations of Chinese ghost stories, both old and new. After introducing the classical Chinese tale "The Peony Lantern" (Mudan dengji) from Qu You's *New Tales Under the Lamplight* (*Jiandeng xinhua*, 1378), Razan offers his explanation of *yūrei*:

> *Yūrei* are what remains of the *konpaku* [*kon* and *haku*] after a person's death. People never revive once they have died, just as flowers never bloom again on the branch after they scatter. This year's flowers are not last year's flowers—like the water that keeps flowing, they are always new. Today's waves are not the same as yesterday's waves. If there is *qi* [life force] in the roots, flowers will

bloom every spring and scatter again every autumn. If water keeps rising from its source, the stream will flow without cease, day and night. The birth of a human is just the same. And yet smoke remains after the flame is extinguished, and the heat of the *qi* is still felt as though it lingered. Even though the body dies, it is only logical that the spirit [*tamashii*] accord with this natural principle. Thus a person whose spirit is alive may well be invisible at certain times and visible at others. Eventually the spirit will disappear and return to its origin. To know its beginning and end is to know the mechanism of life and death. This work captures the in-between state—the *yūrei*.[51]

The *yūrei* in Razan's definition is gender neutral and universalized as a component of all bodies. During the early modern period, and certainly by the nineteenth century, popular literature and the theater placed greater emphasis on the notion of the ghost as a spirit (*konpaku*) freed from the flesh than on the vision of people suffering in various different hells—a motif that was common, as we have seen, in medieval contexts.

Satō Hiroo has pointed out that the early modern period witnessed a rise in the prevalence of family graves and the practice of engraving personal names on memorial tablets. He argues that this reflected a change in the understanding of the position that dead spirits were thought to occupy in the world: now part of the spirit remained with the buried bones, and the descendants of the deceased had to visit the grave to make sure that the spirit rested in peace.[52] This does not mean that the living and the dead were thought to belong equally to this world, as the ancients believed. Rather, in the early modern period, the realms of the dead and the living were considered to be separate but to exist in a rather alarmingly closer relationship than they had in the medieval period.[53] This led, naturally enough, to the depiction of ghosts who retained the form, if not the body, they had possessed while they were alive. Unlike the male spirits in Zeami's dream plays, though, their otherworldliness was clearly marked by their death robes, their semitransparent bodies, or the way their kimono faded toward their feet, and they tended to appear in the environments they had inhabited before they died. At the same time, the fusion of the new understanding of the body and its relationship to the spirit with the older, specifically gendered discourses about the female body that I discussed earlier led to a clear gendering of the ghost and the rise, in particular, of the vengeful female ghost.

The proximity of the dead to the living enabled ghosts to straddle the two realms and to appear in literature and on stage as creatures who, liberated from their mortal bodies, were nonetheless obsessed by memories and grudges from when they were alive that they felt compelled to act on. Even though ghosts were dead, they were still bound up in the lives they were supposed to have left behind. And herein lies the crucial difference between the symbolic meaning of the snake and that of the ghost. On the visual level, female characters of earlier periods who had changed into snakes or demons were passing into another, nonhuman form of existence, whereas in the early modern period, those who lingered in the world as indistinct apparitions of their previous selves remained more visibly connected to the human world, even as they evoked the specific symbolic values of the ghost and carried with them their memories of life even after their transformation.

This realization allows us to reconsider the concept of body and soul glimpsed in the Star Festival scene that I discussed earlier, in which Iemon makes love to a woman who turns out to be Oiwa. The scene is framed as an illusion or a mere figment of Iemon's imagination. It is, to a degree, simultaneously both a dream and an actual, physical experience. At the very beginning of this scene and again at the end, a panel cut in the form of the Sino-Japanese character *kokoro* (心; heart, soul) is lowered onto the stage. A picture of this panel appears with a brief explanation in *What Really Happens Backstage* (figure 3.6). The cardboard cutout was lowered on a string and later pulled out of view by means of another string that dangled from

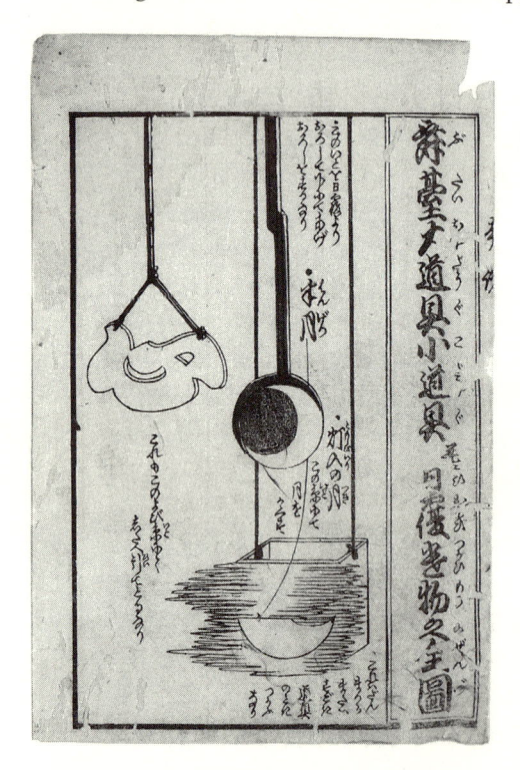

FIGURE 3.6 Panel showing the *kokoro* (*left*), as illustrated in Santei Shunba (text), Utagawa Kunisada (pictures), and Utagawa Yoshitsuya (pictures), *Okyōgen gakuya no honsetsu* (fascicle 1, 8 *ura*). (Courtesy of the Art Research Center, Ritsumeikan University, Kyoto)

the bottom. Kamakura Keiko has discussed the use of this visual device, which originated in early *jōruri* (*kojōruri*) productions as far back as the first half of the seventeenth century, to stage the dreams that ghosts, tormented by either jealousy or an inability to conquer fierce emotional attachments, would impose on their former lovers.[54] Furuido Hideo analyzed this dream scene and showed that it functioned as a symbolic alternative to a more direct visualization of human souls or spirits (*konpaku*) that had drifted away from their bodies as ghosts (*yūrei*) or living spirits (*ikiryō*).[55] During the early modern period, dreams were attributed to the fatigue of the "five organs" (*gozō no tsukare*), a situation that either made it possible for one's spirit to slip out of one's body or made it impossible to prevent another spirit from entering it. The *kokoro* panel thus suggests that Iemon's spirit is drifting out of his body to meet the girl's or, more likely still, that her spirit has entered his. In a sense, the ambiguity of this scene, which can be interpreted as a representation of either a dream or a spirit possession, reveals the fuzziness of the boundary between the ghostly and the worldly.

Hōseidō Kisanji's (1735–1813) *An Illustrated Encyclopedia of the Three Stages of Edo* (*Ukan sandai zue*, 1791)—an encyclopedia of stage devices modeled, with a number of playful twists, on Terajima Ryōan's *Collected Illustrations of the Three Realms, Japanese and Chinese* (*Wakan sansai zue*, 1712)—depicts some of the different ways in which specific ghosts and spirits were represented on the kabuki stage.[56] In the entry on *konpaku*, reproduced in figure 3.7, we

FIGURE 3.7 Spirits on the kabuki stage, as illustrated in Hōseidō Kisanji (text) and Katsukawa Shundō (pictures), *Ukan sandai zue* (22 ura). (Courtesy of the National Diet Library, Tokyo)

find this description: "The *konpaku* gleams like polished brass; the word *kokoro* [soul, heart] is inscribed on it in red. This red part lights up like a lantern . . . when this happens, the sound of a flute is heard, and then the spirit [*tamashii*] of the resentful ghost appears. The *konpaku* soars upward and then falls straight to the ground, and from the earth the deceased spirit [*bōkon*] appears."[57]

Not all *konpaku* have the word *kokoro* written on them, but it is worth noting that when this wandering spirit finally materializes, it is as a ghost. Kisanji explains further that "*bōkon* [deceased spirits], *yūkon* [hazy spirits], *yūrei* [ghosts; literally, "hazy spirits"], and *reikon* [spirits] all are the same thing. Each of these terms refers to the appearance of a spirit in the specific physical form that he or she assumed while alive."[58] All visual representations of ghosts are thus representations of the materialization of the *konpaku*. In this sense, it might not even be accurate to think of ghosts in the early modern Japanese context as "revenants," figures who have "come back" from the dead. They are, instead, figures who have never left, who have simply entered another stage of life; and in this sense, they are not all that different, functionally speaking, from spirits that leave a living body. In fact, at the bottom of the very same page from *An Illustrated Encyclopedia of the Three Stages of Edo*, Kisanji depicts living spirits that leave their bodies and assume the form of butterflies and sparrows (see figure 3.7).

Thus the vengeful female ghost who became such a fixture in nineteenth-century popular culture continued to evoke the rich connotations of earlier depictions of serpentine transformation, above all lustfulness and jealousy, even as it enabled writers and playwrights to explore these emotions in an entirely new way. The notion of "enlightenment" is associated with the Meiji period, of course, but the early modern period had a sort of enlightenment of its own.[59] The new metaphysical understanding of the body and the soul, the emergence of new burial customs, and a new perception of the afterlife all fed into the representation of ghosts in popular literature and the theater in a manner that kept them within the realm of the human, while simultaneously drawing on the long history of serpentine representations. The early modern trope of the female ghost is, in this sense, a much more hybrid creature than has conventionally been recognized.

THE ORIGINS OF KABUKI REPRESENTATIONS OF
THE VENGEFUL FEMALE GHOST

In an argument centered on a metaphorical reading of Oiwa's emergence from a burning lantern in some productions of *Yotsuya kaidan*, kabuki scholar Hattori Yukio proposed that the figure of the vengeful female ghost that is so prominent in early modern kabuki can be interpreted as an embodiment of the subversive potential of inversion. He traced the origin of this trope back to early kabuki stagings of jealousy (*rinkigoto*) in *onryōgoto* from the late seventeenth century, and argued that these depictions reveal the power inherent in the presentation of women's strong emotions—feelings of the sort described in Chikamatsu's puppet play *Emperor Yōmei and the Mirror of Craftsmen* as "resentment bred of longing, an all-consuming passion" (*renbo no urami shūnen no ichinen*)—to topple existing structures. Being consumed by an intense emotional state, Hattori maintained, allowed otherwise frail female characters to gain access to deep reservoirs of strength:

> The performance of jealousy [*rinkigoto*] expresses the inner strength and the violent eruption of emotion that lies behind a woman's tender feelings and love for her man. The acting must be distinguished from the more sedate expression of the strength and ferociousness of female warriors [*onna budō*]. The expression of jealousy is closer to the enactment of derangement [*kuruigoto*]. The reversal of values and meaning happens only in a possessed or deranged state. Women can, then, have strength equal to that of men, or even an unconquerable power that transcends that of men. This is the discovery of the power of inversion.[60]

To Hattori, jealousy, conceived of as something like a state of derangement, catapulted female characters out of their everyday lives and thus enabled them to overturn priorities and alter power structures, breaking free, if only temporarily, from the feudal mission that served as the core structuring element of the plays in which they appeared. This is precisely the sort of power we see Oiwa exercising in the scene discussed earlier, in which she performs her "*renri* pull."

Hattori's work frames Nanboku and his plays as a vibrant example of what he considers to be the subversive popular culture of the end of the early modern period.[61] Regardless of the validity of this position,

Hattori's emphasis on gender and the notion of a lineage of female characters that extends from early *onryōgoto* all the way to Nanboku's nineteenth-century vengeful female ghosts provides a useful framework for considering the functions that different types of characters performed in early modern kabuki. His focus on female characters needs to be complicated, however, through attention not just to the female gender of women deranged or otherwise transformed by jealousy but also to what I call the "stage gender" of the actors playing these women. For the first century and a half of kabuki's history, female characters were played exclusively by female-role actors, and the vengeful female ghosts popular during Nanboku's time were performed by male-role actors. To understand the power of the female characters, particularly of the vengeful female ghost, of which Oiwa is the prime example, we must consider the history of their presentation on stage.

In the age of Genroku kabuki, *onryōgoto* developed as a type of performance for female-role actors in which they portrayed characters transformed, by the depth of their jealousy and resentment, into spirits or serpents and other animals. Indeed, mastery of *onryōgoto* performance was a central element in the expertise of the female-role actor, along with the type of dance known as *shosagoto* or *maigoto*.[62] Performances in the *onryōgoto* mold clearly inherited conventional notions of female transformation from medieval plays and tales, and the "performance of resentful spirits" in kabuki was closely tied to the "performance of jealousy" (*rinkigoto*). In contrast to earlier presentations of violent jealousy and the transformation of women into serpents or demons, however, *onryōgoto* did not stress female abjection or defilement.

Female-role actors' performance in *onryōgoto* concentrated heavily on acrobatics (*karuwazagoto*), which were used to represent characters in a state of derangement (*kuruigoto*). In Chikamatsu Monzaemon's *The Courtesan and the Great Buddhist Service at Mibu* (*Keisei Mibu dainenbutsu*, 1702), for example, the jealous ghost of Omiyo, played by Arashi Kiyosaburō I (d. 1713), climbed onto her lover's shoulder and stood upside down.[63] Although the character is descending into jealous rage, the use of stunts had the effect of presenting this not as a scene of horror but as a lighthearted, pleasing spectacle. At the same time, however, the conventional association between jealousy and the female sex and body remained as strong as ever, as demonstrated by a male-role actor who ended up playing a jealous character. In a widely acclaimed production of *The Sought-After Grave* (*Keisei motomezuka*, 1706), Sakakiyama Koshirō I (1671–1747) played a man possessed by the ghost of Ōhashi, a jealous courtesan. Koshirō was a male-role actor for most of his career, and he also was known for his acrobatic skills. Part of his performance in this play involved the sudden adoption of a feminine manner as his body was being taken over by Ōhashi, who then made him walk on his hands, upside down, across the top of a folding screen (figure 3.8).[64] The actor critique *An Actors' Dancing Fan* (*Yakusha mai ōgi*, 1704), published two years earlier, commented on Koshirō's skills: "See how light he is. He is a master of acrobatics."[65] Even this instance of a male-role actor portraying jealousy incorporated the standard combination of female jealousy, the ghost, and acrobatics.

The gendered nature not of jealousy itself but of the *performance* of jealousy in *onryōgoto* is in fact more complex than it appears at first, however, because the acrobatic stunts used to present the emotion as specifically feminine actually had their origins in productions by young male kabuki troupes, rather than in kabuki dances performed by female troupes.[66] These male troupes were known for "spider stunts" (*kumomai*), which included tightrope walking, tree climbing, and hoop jumping.[67] According to *The Amorous Origins of the Various Pleasure Quarters* (*Shokoku yūri kōshoku yuraizoroe*), "[kumomai troupes] make a spider web in the air and perform tricks such as walking easily from eave to eave; this is why people call it a 'spider performance.'"[68]

Records of performances of this type appear from the Muromachi period to the middle of the early modern period.[69] The mid- to late-seventeenth-century *Screen Painting of the Shijō Riverbank District* (*Shijō kawara yūrakuzu byōbu*) shows a troupe performing spider stunts on a riverbank—a man does a handstand on a tall pole connected to a tightrope while another man slides down the rope—along with various sideshows and performances along the river (figure 3.9). Originally presented as part of temple festivities, spider stunts spread to the provinces and came to be associated with religious rituals. Meanwhile, troupes performing in urban centers like this one at the Shijō riverbank were gradually absorbed into kabuki productions as performers of "light

FIGURE 3.8 Sakakiyama Koshirō I doing a handstand on a screen (*lower right*) in the illustrated prompt book for the production of *Keisei motomezuka* at the Hayakumo Theater in 1706 (6 *ura*). (Courtesy of the Tenri University Library, Nara)

FIGURE 3.9 Acrobats performing the spider stunt, as seen in *Shijō kawara yūrakuzu byōbu* (detail of one panel of a six-panel folding screen). (Courtesy of the Museum of Fine Arts, Boston)

stunts" (*karuwaza*). Especially in the early years of kabuki's history, theaters hired various traveling performers, acrobats as well as "magic performers" known as *hōka*.[70] Originally, these stunts and tricks were inserted as filler during intermissions, but by the late seventeenth century they had become part of the main play.

Gunji Masakatsu writes that over time, acrobatics derived from spider stunts became a specialty of female-role actors because their bodies were light and flexible. At the same time, the notion that the female body inherently tended toward jealousy and derangement offered a convenient reason on the level of plot for incorporating acrobatics into plays.[71] The same was true of dances, which gradually came to take the place of more flashy stunts. The New Year performance of *The Courtesan of Asama Mountain* in 1698 at the Hayakumo Theater in Kyoto—the first of a long series of "Asama plays" (*Asama-mono*) that were staged in both Kyoto and Edo, eventually developing into a one-scene dance that continued to be performed into the early years of the Meiji period—featured a relatively subdued depiction of a living

SHADES OF JEALOUSY

spirit and her jealousy. The spirit of the courtesan Ōshū appears from the smoke of a brazier into which her lover Tomoenojō, forced to betray her by his fiancée Otowa no Mae, has just tossed a pledge and an amulet that Ōshū had given him. Ōshū then expresses her resentment in the form of a dance.[72] An illustration for a work published in conjunction with the first production shows Iwai Sagenta, the actor who played Ōshū, emerging from the brazier's flames, suggesting a parallel between her suffering from jealousy and the flames of hell (figure 3.10). Otowa no Mae and her attendants have fainted, leaving the stage to Ōshū and her dance.[73] (The text at the top of the page praises Iwai Sagenta for his performance and notes that the appearance of his character was a major highlight of the play.) Ōshū's hair is undone—a subtle allusion, as I explained earlier, to the long history of serpentine transformation that visually marked her abnormal state of mind.[74] Her plain kimono evokes the white robe (*kyōkatabira*) in which the dead were buried, and the speech in which she expresses her emotions draws on images of hellish suffering:

FIGURE 3.10 Ōshū emerging from the brazier's flames (*left*) in a production of *Keisei asamagatake* at the Hayakumo Theater in 1698 (9 *omote*). (Tokyo Geijutsu University Library. Courtesy of the National Institute of Japanese Literature, Tokyo)

THE BEGINNING OF THE END OF EDO KABUKI

No resentment or love remains. But to prove that my heart remained unchanged, I wrote a pledge. Why would you turn it into smoke? How spiteful of you. My heart blazes for you three times a night, and I long for you three times a day. Compare this smoke with that at Mount Asama. Go look closely at Mount Asama. The evil demon of lust tortures me. I can see my lover at the top of a mountain of swords. Joyfully, I try to climb the mountain. My longing for you crushes my heart—how terrible it is.[75]

The reference to the "demon of lust" is a clear allusion to hell, as is the image of Ōshū climbing a mountain of swords, a common conflation of the Mountain of Swords (*tsurugidake*), where demons chase sinners, and Sword-Leaf Hell (*tōyōrin jigoku*), where male sinners climb a tree with razor-sharp leaves, driven by lust for the women at the top. Presumably, this is an intentional play on the male gender of the sufferers in Sword-Leaf Hell, with Ōshū superimposing her own desires on those of the lustful men.[76] Although Ōshū is still a living spirit, both her appearance and her speech evoke images of the afterlife, as if she were a ghost speaking of her agonies in hell. It is no surprise that in later stagings of her story, Ōshū was turned into a ghost.

Jealous women like Ōshū frequently appeared to express their anger in historical plays, if only in a subplot. The performance of these roles often seems to have involved indications of a suppressed nature, especially involving the eyes—an allusion, perhaps, to nō demon masks, whose eyes are colored gold. This is clear from actor critiques such as Ejima Kiseki's (1666–1736) *A Secret Letter About the Actors* (*Yakusha yatsushijō*, 1701), which lavishes praise on Tamagawa Sennojō (active ca. 1650–1670), who specialized in young women's roles. According to Kiseki, Sennojō was beautiful but also excelled at using his eyes to portray a woman's resentment: "His performances of ghosts and spirits are splendid. Above all, his glares are so fierce they give you the chills. He is slim and too beautiful for evil stepmother roles."[77] The actor critiques also reflect the idea in the first part of the early modern period that since jealousy had to be concealed, its portrayal should not be exaggerated or overdone. Accordingly, Arashi Kiyosaburō was praised for the great subtlety of his expression: "He takes on a contemplative look without seeming to be jealous, but his eyes express jealousy. This was exceptionally well done."[78]

A famed female-role actor who specialized in both stunts and acrobatic dances depicting jealous women was Mizuki Tatsunosuke (1673–1745), a contemporary of the great female-role actor Yoshizawa Ayame.[79] In *A Modern Genji in Sixty Chapters* (*Ima Genji rokujūjō*, 1695), Mizuki expressed unrequited love and jealousy through an acrobatic dance that represented his character being transformed into a cat. Over time, physically demanding performances of this sort came to be replaced by more elegant dances, which were presented between acts as an emotional highlight.[80] This transition took place during the eighteenth century as female-role acting matured, opening up new possibilities for more sophisticated performances of femininity.

Even as this shift from strenuous acrobatics to restrained dance was taking place, playwrights active in the latter half of the eighteenth century began exploring female jealousy in a more visceral way, finding inspiration in an emotion that had long been condemned in religious discourse and educational books. The blood of a jealous woman, in particular, came to be invested with magical powers capable of bringing the usual struggles in a household disturbance to a happy conclusion. For example, it might be used to subdue villains, as in *Mount Imo and Mount Se: An Exemplary Tale of Womanly Virtue* (*Imoseyama onna teikin*, 1771), a play originally performed in the puppet theater. In this work, a commoner named Omiwa becomes romantically involved with the noble Motome at a time when he is concealing his true identity. Omiwa already is upset when she learns that her lover will be marrying another woman, and when her rival's attendants humiliate her by promising to let her see Motome if she dances for them and then ridiculing and abusing her when she does, she undoes her hair (*sabaki*) and twists her face into an expression of jealousy and rage (*gichaku no sō*). Before Omiwa can act on her anger, however, she is killed by Fukashichi, one of the retainers, so her blood can be used to disarm the evil Soga no Iruka. Learning on the verge of death that her lover was actually of high birth and that she will be able to help restore his clan, Omiwa dies content.[81]

The jealousy and rage exhibited by characters like Omiwa make them somewhat reminiscent of Oiwa and other vengeful female ghosts who appear in the nineteenth century. In regard to performance, however, there is very little resemblance. This is because every one of the earlier female characters was assigned to a female-role actor, and female-role actors would avoid doing anything that detracted from their looks. As a result, throughout most of kabuki's early modern history, rather than present the bodies of jealous women as ugly and abject, actors marked their suffering through changes of hairstyle and costume and through dances that were as lighthearted and visually pleasing as the earlier acrobatics. Nanboku's plays were able to depart from this convention and thus to realize the power of inversion that Hattori Yukio identified, only because he assigned his jealous women to male-role actors: first Onoe Matsusuke I and then Onoe Kikugorō III, both of whom were male-role actors who also had training in playing female parts.

Because of the particular acting lineage to which they belonged, Matsusuke and Kikugorō inherited the ability to perform quick changes in which they switched rapidly between playing male and female characters. Matsusuke tweaked this talent by incorporating female ghosts into the mix, and Kikugorō, who played Oiwa in the first production of *Yotsuya kaidan*, inherited this from him. This made it even easier for Kikugorō to play Oiwa in a grotesque manner, because she was only one of three roles he took on—he also played Kohei and Yomoshichi.[82] Indeed, part of the excitement of *Yotsuya kaidan* lay in seeing the handsome actor Kikugorō appear as Oiwa in a horribly disfigured form and then emerge seconds later as his usual comely self.

The shift from the use of female-role actors to portray ghosts to the use of male-role actors had other consequences as well. While the ghosts who appeared in Genroku kabuki were generally high-ranking courtesans or women of the samurai class, those in Nanboku's so-called horror plays (*kaidan kyōgen*) tended to be slightly older, more grotesque, much more violent in their pursuit of vengeance, and—significantly, especially in relation to Hattori's thesis—of lower status. The Onoe line of actors, which came to consider the acting of ghosts as one of its specialties, began portraying non-samurai or former samurai women who had lost their *buke* status as ghosts. Oiwa is a good example of this kind of character. At the same time, the focus in these later plays shifted from Buddhist salvation—the need of the jealous woman to be placated and released from her jealousy—to the resentment itself and how the woman acted on it. In some ways, the participation of male-role actors made it possible to present a female body subject to the horror of the jealous woman's transformation. Precisely because they were mediated by the bodies of male-role actors, nineteenth-century female ghosts on the kabuki stage were able to represent in its most extreme form the age-old stigma associated with the female body.

UNGENDERING JEALOUSY

In this chapter, I traced the long history of representations of female transformation and showed how closely connected serpentine and ghostly imagery were in early modern kabuki. We have seen how the particular meanings inscribed on the female body made it an appropriate vehicle for exploring private sentiment and for portraying the pursuit of private interests. This history is, in a sense, what Oiwa saw when she looked in the mirror: she saw herself assuming a form that had already been prepared for her by centuries of discursive construction of the female body, a form that would make it impossible for her to remain bound by her former class or her position as a woman. She recognized in the flat surface of the mirror a representation of an inner space of which she herself had been unaware. This inner space, defined in terms of the notion of women's inherently jealous nature, was what enabled Oiwa and other characters like her to assume a position at the very center of nineteenth-century literature and theater. Oiwa's female body—stained from the start by a history of blood—was the perfect counterpart to the *sekai* centered on the preservation of feudal order and male honor; her body was capable of serving as a structuring principle in an age when conventional *sekai* no longer meant what they once had.

Interestingly, in the rare cases in which male characters were placed in situations similar to Oiwa's in nineteenth-century kabuki, they, too, turned into serpents or ghosts, harking back to gendered visual codes tied to the female body.[83] Examples are Kohada Koheiji, an actor who is murdered by his wife; Seigen, a corrupt monk who is consumed by lust; and monks who are infatuated with their young male lovers. In all these characters, the emotions of jealousy and lust, which are typically associated with women, are invoked to depict men who are, on some level, feminized within the social structures that surround them. Tellingly, male transformations of this sort happen exclusively to non-samurai figures such as monks, actors, and beggars who stand outside the four-class system and the norms that apply to those within it. The ghost of Kohei in *Yotsuya kaidan*, whose character is based on that of the actor Kohada Koheiji—really a whole line of jealous male ghosts known by this name—is a representative case.[84] Kohei did not end up being depicted as a figure who is betrayed in love, but even so his association with serpents—his fingers turn into snakes several times during the play—is suggestive of his link to the jealous Koheiji, which in turn echoes the longer history of transformation of jealous women's body parts, or their whole bodies, into snakes.

I would like to conclude this chapter with a brief look at the modern afterlife of jealousy and female transformation. Subtly gendered portrayals of strong emotion through transformation or, more specifically, in a mode influenced by the early modern conception of the connectedness of the body and the soul, lingered for quite a while in modern times. Sanyūtei Enchō's (1839–1900) *The True View at Kasane Marsh* (*Shinkei Kasane ga fuchi*), a rewritten *rakugo* (oral storytelling) piece featuring the ghost Kasane that Enchō had written near the end of the early modern period under a different title, was transcribed in shorthand by Koai Eitarō and serialized in *Yamato shinbun* from 1887 to 1888, and had its theatrical premiere at the Masago Theater (Masago-za) in 1898. In one scene, a middle-aged female shamisen master is overcome with jealousy at the sight of her young lover becoming intimate with one of her students:

> When the master sees the two of them exchanging smiles, she appears calm but is suspicious of their relationship and secretly feels jealous. Hiding inner jealousy is extremely bad for the body, because you're always burning with anger and there's no time for the flame in your heart to die down. She develops headaches and female disorders [*chi no michi*] because her blood is boiling.... The master boils with anger, and the flame of jealousy is unyielding. Her blood boils and a strange growth appears under her eye. When the growth swells, it turns a reddish purple, it starts to droop down and pus starts oozing out.... Her hair is naturally thin and the edge of her forehead has swollen up, so she looks just like Kasane and Oiwa from kabuki plays.[85]

We might view this as a direct descendant of earlier discourses about female transformation, replete with obvious echoes of Oiwa's transformation. Enchō's version of this scene, however, reverses the direction of the transformation. Whereas Oiwa's physical transformation precedes her realization of the cause, or even her knowledge of Iemon's betrayal, the shamisen master's physical ailments are framed as the *consequence* of the jealousy she feels.

So pervasive and deeply rooted were the discourses surrounding the female body that writers in the Meiji period and beyond continued to draw on them in subtle ways, even as they attempted to establish a new, modern sort of interiority through explorations of the translated concept of "love," often as it was felt by young male protagonists. Many examples could be given, but perhaps the best appears in Futabatei Shimei's (1864–1909) *Drifting Clouds* (*Ukigumo*, 1887–1889), a work that has often been described as "Japan's first modern novel." The narrative concerns a student named Bunzō who is always in agony over his love for Osei, his landlady's daughter. One day, after having been humiliated by his rival, Bunzō is overcome by anger: "Bunzō felt so frustrated and disappointed and beaten down that he could hardly stand it. He forcefully held back the sudden, intense explosion of rage that erupted within him, so that it failed to burst forth and instead turned inward, gathering, growing until it filled him. His chest was sundered and his intestines split."[86] If this novel had been written a few decades earlier, Bunzō would have changed at this moment into some other sort of being, or his spirit would have erupted from his body. There is a tension in this scene between that conventional form of expression, which is realized only in its failure—his rage "failed to burst forth"—and the modern urge to keep the emotional force contained inside oneself. The description of Bunzō's resentment continues for several pages until he finds himself clenching his teeth and glaring at a police officer. Only then does he finally return to normal, feeling "as if he were waking from a dream" and looking around to see where he is.[87]

Futabatei's depiction of Bunzō's struggles suggests that the elaboration of a concept of love in modern fiction, or, indeed, of a broader notion of "interiority," should be regarded not simply as an importation of Western concepts but as a sort of translation relying on metaphors rooted in very old discourses surrounding the female body. Bunzō's internal agony is figured, in other words, as a brief but violent derangement that comes perilously close to assuming a grotesque physical form and strongly echoes scenes of demonic and serpentine transformation. Or it could recall Iemon's encounter in the last scene of *Yotsuya kaidan* with a lovely country girl who turns out to be Oiwa, bracketed by the appearance of a cardboard cutout reading *kokoro*, which ends as Iemon awakes, as Bunzō does, to the reality of his surroundings. From a certain perspective, modern literature's "discovery" of interiority was initially little more than a change in nomenclature. Modern authors described as internal what their early modern counterparts had depicted externally. Which is merely another way of saying that Tsuruya Nanboku and his contemporaries were already engaging in this kind of experiment when they invoked age-old discourses about the female body, using them to explore new possibilities that did not sit well with the conventional *sekai* or with the conventional early modern understanding of the self.

[4]

THE END OF THE WORLD

Figures of the *Ubume* and the
Breakdown of Theater Tradition

In the first production of Tsuruya Nanboku IV's *Yotsuya kaidan*, the ghost of Oiwa, played by Onoe Kikugorō III, appeared in act 5 by emerging from a consecration cloth with an infant cradled in her arms. Oiwa was thus figured as an *ubume* (literally, "a woman giving birth"), a particular type of ghost associated with pregnancy and childbirth that would have had deep psychological resonances for the audience of Nanboku's day. Nanboku had employed the *ubume* in a number of earlier productions, and it appears in almost all his major ghost plays. *Ubume* were ubiquitous in the theater and literature of this period, appearing again and again not only in Nanboku's works but also in the fiction of major writers such as Shikitei Sanba, Santō Kyōden, and Kyokutei Bakin. Our interpretation of the meaning of this scene in *Yotsuya kaidan* must thus be tied to a larger understanding of Nanboku's and the kabuki theater's mobilization of the *ubume* as a dramatic trope and of the roles the *ubume* played in the broader context of nineteenth-century cultural production. In other words, we must complement my examination in chapter 3 of the long history of representations of female transformation, and of the layered meanings of the female ghost, by asking why ghosts in the theater and literature of the early nineteenth century were associated so pervasively with pregnancy and why the *ubume* became so popular as a motif, particularly in the first three decades of the century.

The Flowers of Kikugorō's Farewell Performance: Ghost Stories at Yotsuya (*Nagori no hana Yotsuya kaidan*, 1826), an illustrated digest of

FIGURE 4.1 Onoe Kikugorō III as Oiwa (*left*) and Ichikawa Danjūrō VII as Tamiya Iemon (*right*), as illustrated in Hanagasa Bunkyō I (text) and Keisai Eisen (pictures), *Nagori no hana Yotsuya kaidan* (fascicle 2, 26 *ura*–27 *omote*). (Private collection)

the play published by Hanagasa Bunkyō I (1785–1860) and Keisai Eisen (1790–1848) immediately after the production, hints at how the scene in act 5 may have looked (figure 4.1). On the right, we see Ichikawa Danjūrō VII as Iemon, coming through a temple gate to pour water on a consecration cloth hung between four bamboo poles—an object known by the name of the ritual in which it is used: literally, "flowing consecration" (*nagare kanjō*). Iemon is offering a prayer for the repose of the spirits of Oiwa and their son even as he shudders with fear at the prospect of his dead wife's revenge. The water in the ladle has turned into fire, a "soul flame," a common visual representation of a spirit that either accompanies or stands in for the ghost itself. On the left-hand page, Oiwa's ghost rises from the cloth, hugging the baby to her breast.

Although *Yotsuya kaidan* was staged approximately twenty times during the last forty years of the early modern period in both Edo and

Osaka, the scene in which Oiwa emerges from the consecration cloth was dropped after the first production in 1825, and except for a few modern revivals, it played no part in the play's subsequent performative or cinematic reception. The meaning of the *ubume* and the *nagare kanjō* was so particular to its time that there was no reason to revert to the original staging, especially since, as I demonstrate in this chapter, Nanboku essentially used Oiwa to strip the *ubume* of its conventional associations.

In texts of *Yotsuya kaidan*, however, the scene has remained important. Gunji Masakatsu's edition of the script, generally acknowledged as the best attempt to reconstruct the text of the first performance, includes the following exchange between Iemon and the ghost:

> *Iemon picks up the ladle in the bucket and approaches [the nagare kanjō]. Then a ghost flute [netori] is played with the low beating of the drum [usu dorodoro], and there is the solemn sound of a small gong. Iemon pours water on the cloth. The water turns into a soul flame as it touches the cloth. The eerie sound of the drumming picks up its pace, growing more intense. Snow falls harder.*[1] *Oiwa appears from the cloth in the guise of an ubume; her lower body is drenched in blood, and she cradles her baby in her arms. Suddenly catching sight of her, Iemon steps back, startled. They change positions, and Oiwa proceeds to stage left, leaving red footprints on the white snow. Iemon edges back into the house, and Oiwa follows him. Torn pieces of paper are scattered throughout the house; Oiwa walks across them, leaving bloody stains.*

> IEMON: Hmm. What a spiteful woman. I know you're a ghost, but do listen to what I have to say. I married Kihei's daughter in the hope of sneaking into Kōno's residence and directing the other loyal retainers. Disloyal in appearance, I'm actually loyal at heart. And now everything has been ruined—all on account of a woman's stupid grudge! You made me kill my father-in-law and bride. Kihei's daughter and nurse drowned as a result of your ghostly curse! And on top of that, you cruelly murdered our newborn boy! Is this your curse, dead woman, to discontinue my line? What a frightening woman.

> *(Iemon shows emotion.)*

> *Iemon snaps at Oiwa. Oiwa in turn shows him the baby cradled in her arms. (Iemon shows emotion.)*

THE BEGINNING OF THE END OF EDO KABUKI

IEMON: Can it be! The dead woman appears to have raised the boy! (*Iemon shows emotion.*)

Iemon joyfully takes the baby in his arms.

IEMON: Despite all that came between us, you're still my wife. Well done, well done. If those are your true feelings, depart in peace. Hail Buddha, hail Buddha.

Iemon cradles the baby and chants Buddhist prayers. Oiwa covers her ears with both hands, blocking out Iemon's prayers.[2]

A moment later, Oiwa suddenly disappears. In his shock, Iemon drops the baby, who instantly turns into a stone statue of the Bodhisattva Jizō.

This is an incredible scene for a number of reasons. First, the stage effects must have been dazzling: imagine the bloody footprints and the spectacular sight of the ghost rising over the water and then being lifted into the air by a rope suspended from the ceiling, most likely with her lower body enveloped in flames. Although none of this is spelled out in the script, the effect is described in the guide to kabuki special effects *What Really Happens Backstage*, in an entry titled "Ghosts That Burn Like a Morning Glory" (Asagao-bi no yūrei)—a name that presumably derives from the shape of the ghost's burning robe (figure 4.2). The presence of a *nagare kanjō* in the illustration suggests that the effect would also have been

FIGURE 4.2 The special effect "Asagao-bi no yūrei," as illustrated in Santei Shunba (text) and Utagawa Kunitsuna (pictures), *Okyōgen gakuya no honsetsu* (fascicle 3, 16 *ura*). (Hōsa Bunko, Nagoya. Courtesy of the National Institute of Japanese Literature, Tokyo)

THE END OF THE WORLD

used in *Yotsuya kaidan*. As *What Really Happens Backstage* explains: "Ghosts that burn like a morning glory: the actor puts on a long robe that tapers below the waist. This is then saturated with *shōchū* [an alcoholic beverage]. When the ghost is hoisted up from above, the tip of the robe is lit on fire and the kimono burns below the waist. This is known as the 'morning glory.'"[3]

The second brilliant aspect of this scene is Nanboku's unconventional use of the *ubume* trope. These female ghosts, who generally appear holding babies, embody both the suffering of women who died during pregnancy or childbirth and their love and concern for the babies they left behind or took with them. Oiwa, however, is responsible for her son's death. In fact, he is her very first victim: the rats that act as her agents throughout the play drag the infant to her immediately after she dies in act 2. On the face of it, then, there is no reason at all for Oiwa to be appearing as an *ubume*. So why did Nanboku invoke this trope? What, exactly, is going on in this scene? The answer has significance for more than our understanding of this one play.

Previous scholarship on the *ubume* has concentrated on medieval and early modern forms of Buddhism and the gendered practices and beliefs associated with them.[4] Research on early-nineteenth-century literature and theater has continued this line of investigation, treating *ubume* in these contexts as a reflection of religious and medical discourses.[5] In this chapter, I am concerned with *ubume* less as a site for the preservation of religious and folk meaning than as a figure whose significance was constructed through its representation in kabuki, specifically in Nanboku's popular ghost plays. I will examine the complicated, layered meanings that *ubume* evoke and then explore how they were mobilized in kabuki plays and prose fiction by Nanboku and his contemporaries. I will show that Nanboku, especially, made these ghostly figures increasingly central to his plays and ultimately used them to move away from kabuki's conventional reliance on historical *sekai* and the drama of struggle and sacrifice in a world in which people are defined by their participation in a household and its ethical values.

Beginning in the seventeenth century, female ghosts were routinely woven into plays in order to add a touch of spectacle. These included works in various *sekai*, among them plays categorized as household-disturbance plots and revenge plots. Over time, Nanboku moved beyond these relatively peripheral invocations of the female ghost, gradually bringing them to the center of his plays as a means of reworking or even dismantling the *sekai* and, by extension, the long-established communal memory they embodied. In chapter 3, I noted the crucial innovation that Nanboku made in assigning the roles of female ghosts to male-role actors, specifically to *tachiyaku* or lead male actors. In contrast to earlier performances, in which female ghosts were the exclusive domain of female-role actors and remained largely confined to subplots, Nanboku's female ghosts managed to supplant the conventional male heroes and came to play the central role in entire plays, and thus in the history of kabuki itself. Focusing on the particular type of female ghost known as the *ubume*, this chapter shows that a highly self-conscious reworking of kabuki convention had already begun in the early nineteenth century, decades before the beginning of the Meiji era and its elite movements to reform the legal and social meaning of kabuki theater.

THE ORIGINS OF THE *UBUME* IMAGE

The association of ghosts with death during pregnancy or childbirth can be traced back a very long way. Pregnancy and childbirth could be a matter of life and death in early modern Japan. Complications from pregnancy and childbirth carry real risks, and the fear that they might lead to death inspired numerous tales in a wide variety of genres. The earliest account of a dead woman who appears as a ghost holding her baby in her arms—a distant ancestor of Nanboku's *ubume*—occurs in the early-twelfth-century collection *Tales of Times Now Past* (*Konjaku monogatarishū*), in the story "How Yorimitsu's Attendant Taira no Suetake Encountered a Woman Who Had Given Birth" (Yorimitsu no rōdō Taira no Suetake ubume ni au koto).[6] In this tale, a group of men are standing around and discussing a certain frightening *ubume* who has been appearing in a place called Watari. One of the men, Taira no Suetake, goes off on a dare to cross the river at Watari. As he makes his way across, a strange woman appears and asks him to hold her crying infant. The woman is not described in visual terms: her words are simply overheard by three of the other men from the group who were brave enough to follow Suetake and hide behind a bush as he crossed the river, and we are told that her appearance was accompanied by a terrible stench. The narrative concludes with an extremely ambiguous note by the compiler: "Some people say this *ubume* was a fox playing a trick on a human;

others say it was a woman who turned into a spirit [*ryō*] when she died before being able to give birth to her baby girl. That, they say, is the story that has been passed down."[7]

The image of the *ubume* had been fixed much more clearly in the popular imagination by the middle of the early modern period, when a revealing rewriting of the story appeared in *Emended Tales of Times Now Past* (*Kōtei konjaku monogatari*), the first widely circulated, woodblock-printed edition of stories from the Heian collection, compiled by the Shinto scholar Izawa Banryō (Nagahide, 1668–1730).[8] Banryō, who based *Emended Tales of Times Now Past* on a manuscript he that had discovered, included only stories in the Japanese section (which he called *wachō*), adapting them in a relatively easy-to-understand style that mixed kanji and hiragana. He published his collection in thirty volumes, the first half appearing in 1720 and the second in 1722, with illustrations by an unidentified artist.

Banryō's edition has been much criticized for its cavalier treatment of the original.[9] Banryō himself explains in his preface (*hanrei*) that because the manuscript from which he was working was old and contained numerous mistakes, he "made corrections by consulting old journals and records"; omitted episodes found in other anthologies, such as *A Collection of Tales from Uji* (*Uji shūi monogatari*, ca. 1180–1220), *A Miscellany of Ten Maxims* (*Jikkin shō*, 1252), and *Collections of Tales Old and New* (*Kokon chomonjū*); and corrected errors in the stated sources of stories.[10] In short, Banryō seems to have been most interested in preparing a readable, enjoyable text. He felt free to change the order of the anecdotes, to edit their content, to fill in segments missing from his source manuscripts, and even to include interesting stories from his own time period.

Viewed from the perspective of a specialist on *Tales of Times Now Past*, Banryō's reworking of the "original" diminishes its value, making it little more than a corrupt variant of the twelfth-century collection. Katayose Masayoshi, for example, takes issue with it as "a total rewriting in which the body of the text has been changed and reorganized and sections have been inserted and discarded as the editor saw fit." While he allows that "it may have had the positive effect of making the anecdotes in *Tales of Times Now Past* known to the public," he takes a dismissive attitude toward the edition itself, stating that "in terms of its value as a text and its success in transmitting the true form of *Tales of Times Now Past*, it is a poor edition."[11] For the vast majority of Tokugawa readers, however, apart from a select group of intellectuals who themselves had access to manuscript editions of the collection, *Emended Tales of Times Now Past* was the only available text of *Tales of Times Now Past*. It is clear that Banryō's edition was read by, and served as source material for, early modern authors of historical fiction, particularly *yomihon*, such as Tsuga Teishō (1718–ca. 1794) and Kyokutei Bakin.[12] In this regard, Banryō's editing and rewriting was a successful attempt to incorporate *Tales of Times Now Past* into the literature of his age and to make it resonate with early modern sensibilities.

The *ubume* anecdote from *Tales of Times Now Past* appears in volume 13 of *Emended Tales of Times Now Past* under the title "Taira no Suetake Meets an *Ubume*" (Taira no Suetake ubume ni au hanashi). While the general contours of the story remain the same, Banryō rewrote it to heighten the drama and made three significant alterations. First, he wrote the word *ubume* not as 産女 (woman who gives birth), but as 姑獲鳥, a combination that can also be read as *kokakuchō*, the Japanese pronunciation of the name of a large supernatural bird in Chinese legend, the *guhuoniao*. Second, he deleted the two explanations of the woman's nature that are offered at the conclusion of the Heian-period text. Clearly, by the middle of the early modern period, it was no longer even necessary to ask whether the figure was a mother or a fox, because the existence of the *ubume* was now widely accepted. Finally, as an indication that the figure of the *ubume* had by this time been defined in visual terms as well, the woman (who in the original is only heard by the men behind the bush) is shown in the illustration passing her infant to Suetake (figure 4.3). She has long hair; her lower body is drenched in blood, evoking the blood that she shed during her miscarriage and suggesting that she is suffering in Blood Pool Hell; and her body fades away, ghost-like, toward the bottom.

The Night Parade of a Hundred Monsters, Illustrated (*Gazu hyakki yagyō*, 1776) by Toriyama Sekien (1712–1788) offers a similar portrayal of this type of ghost.[13] Published fifty years after the first fifteen booklets of *Emended Tales of Times Now Past*, Sekien's work of fantastic creatures, many of which had not until then acquired an established pictorial form, had a huge influence on subsequent depictions of the beings it includes, especially in book illustrations. The entry on the *ubume* uses the same kanji for the name as Banryō's work does, alluding to the legendary bird. The picture shows a woman holding the baby she lost, whom she hopes to entrust to someone still alive and thus restore to life (figure 4.4).

FIGURE 4.3 The *ubume* in the tale "Taira no Suetake ubume ni au hanashi," as illustrated in Izawa Banryō, *Kōtei konjaku monogatari* (fascicle 13, 19 *omote*). (Courtesy of the National Institute of Japanese Literature, Tokyo)

FIGURE 4.4 An *ubume*, as illustrated in Toriyama Sekien, *Gazu hyakki yagyō* (fascicle 2, unpaginated). (Courtesy of the Tōkyō Geijutsu Daigaku Fuzoku Toshokan, Tokyo)

As in the illustration in *Emended Tales of Times Now Past*, her robe, which fades into thin air before it reaches the ground, is stained with blood—here, again, an indication that she is suffering in Blood Pool Hell.

The *nagare kanjō* that is visible in the background was typically erected in running water, along with a wooden stupa, for use in a Buddhist ritual intended to free the souls of women who died during pregnancy or childbirth from the agonies of Blood Pool Hell. The ritual took various forms but most often involved passersby chanting a prayer and pouring a ladle of water over the cloth. People would continue doing this until the words that had been written on the cloth (or sometimes the red with which the cloth had been dyed) were completely washed away.[14] The things we see here—the consecration cloth, stupa, and running water, as well as the ghostly mother cradling her baby in her arms—are precisely those that appeared in the first production of *Yotsuya kaidan*. Nanboku was drawing on an image of the *ubume* that had been firmly established by the eighteenth century.

The *Ubume*: Religious Beliefs and Medical Practice

As I noted, the kanji with which Banryō and Sekien chose to write the word *ubume* (姑獲鳥) evoked both the image of a dead woman holding the child she hoped to revive somehow and that of the legendary bird known in Chinese as the *guhuoniao*. This semantic duality was characteristic of the early modern reception of *ubume*, and the two seemingly different associations were in fact often loosely connected in contemporary writings.

To a large extent, the potency of the *ubume* as a symbol of death during pregnancy or childbirth derived from the conception of Blood Pool Hell and the religious and medical practices that emerged from this belief. Since the ninth century, both pregnancy and menstruation had been viewed in the context of *onmyōdō* (literally, "the way of yin and yang") as a source of female defilement, and women's connection to these conditions came to be seen as a reason to exclude them from Shinto rituals.[15] Then, as the blood taboo spread among aristocrats and even beyond, the notion of defilement was gradually reinforced at different levels through Buddhist androcentric discourses. By the Muromachi period, as the concept of Blood Pool Hell gained currency, death during pregnancy or childbirth came to be regarded as a great sin.

By this time, as discussed in chapter 3, pictorial depictions circulated visions of various new types of hell reserved specifically for women: Two-Women Hell, where jealous women were turned into serpents; Hell for Childless Women, for those who were barren; and Blood Pool Hell, for the sins of menstruation and the shedding of blood during childbirth. The fact that these hells were related to the major states that defined women's lives—love, marriage, and childbirth—gave them a particular immediacy. Already by the late medieval period, the existence of Blood Pool Hell was commonly accepted.[16]

The emergence of the belief in Blood Pool Hell has been linked to the importation from China, sometime in the medieval period, of a short Buddhist scripture known as the Blood Bowl Sutra (Ketsubonkyō). An apocryphal sutra that was first circulated by the members of local religions of China in the tenth century, the Blood Bowl Sutra came to be widely used over time by various Buddhist sects and laywomen as a central vehicle for women to attain Buddhist salvation.[17] In most texts, Mokuren Sonja, a disciple of Shakyamuni Buddha, visits Blood Pool Hell and sees the immense suffering that women are undergoing as punishment for the blood they shed during childbirth and menstruation, blood that pollutes drinking water and defiles the earth gods. For the sake of his mother, the disciple asks to be taught some means of obtaining salvation for women. He is told that women can be saved by attending or holding ceremonies at which a monk recites this very sutra.

The Blood Bowl Sutra and the hells associated with it were promulgated in the late medieval period by traveling nuns from Kumano. As Hank Glassman pointed out, Blood Pool Hell "only became a real place, capturing the imagination, when collectively recreated through public storytelling." The nuns' performances established a common vision of the topography of this hell and helped generate various redemptive practices.[18] Monks of the Jōdo sect actively preached the salvation of women in the first part of the early modern period, and then from the middle to the end of this period, Sōtō Zen monks became the sutra's most active proponents.[19] Throughout these years, the redemptive power of the sutra and, by extension, of the religious establishment offered a remedy for women's pollution at the same time that public storytelling and visual depiction reinforced it.[20]

As the view that it was deeply sinful for a woman to die with an unborn baby in her womb took hold, techniques were developed for freeing women from this sin, and thus from the fate that awaited them in Blood Pool Hell. The *nagare kanjō* was one such ritual. Special burial practices were also developed for pregnant women who had the misfortune to die before giving birth. The fear that the baby might still be alive in the dead woman's womb led to the practice of separating the mother and baby, either physically or symbolically. By the early modern period, if not earlier, it was common for the fetus to be surgically removed from the dead mother's body before burial.[21] Instances of the folk practice of surgically separating fetuses from their dead mothers are recorded in the *Compilation of Birth-Related Practices in Japan* (*Nihon san'iku shūzoku shiryō shūsei*, 1975), originally begun in the 1930s by the folklorist Yanagita Kunio (1875–1962).[22] The section on rituals and beliefs pertaining to the death of pregnant women reveals that separative surgery was practiced throughout Japan even after the Meiji Restoration of 1868.[23] Many of the materials presented in the section stress the importance of this surgery for preventing the mother's return as a ghost—that is, as an *ubume*.

For its part, the Buddhist clergy actively promoted paths to salvation that could replace the surgical practice by separating the fetus from the mother's corpse in symbolic ways. Tsutsumi Kunihiko described one procedure developed by the Sōtō Zen sect in which the monk would place a charm, often an inscription of a section of the Blood Bowl Sutra, in the dead woman's mouth and chant a prayer over her, thereby freeing her soul from the *ubume* fate.[24] The symbolic Buddhist ritual did not replace the surgery entirely, however, as seen in the persistence of the latter procedure into the nineteenth century and beyond. *Illustrated Explanation of Childbirth* (*Tassei zusetsu*, 1858)—a book on obstetrical nursing that consists primarily of a transcription by Kondō Kenzan (1814–1861) of the teachings of Kondō Naoyoshi (dates unknown), a doctor from Echizen Province—details the proper procedure for the separative surgery and argues that Buddhist practices are ineffective, serving only to alleviate people's fears.[25] Clearly, both practices coexisted throughout the early modern period.

Numerous fictional tales suggest just how prevalent was the fear of death during pregnancy. *The Tale of Kōya* (*Kōya monogatari*, Muromachi period), a collection of stories told by monks about the reasons why they took the tonsure, includes a revealing episode. In it, the narrator recounts the story of his pregnant mistress, who, in his absence, is brutally murdered and buried by his jealous wife. The mistress's ghost entrusts a monk with her bloodstained sleeve and a message written in blood, hoping that her lover will realize what happened and find her and separate the fetus from her body: "For a woman to die while pregnant is a terrible sin. Please swiftly dig me out of my grave and take out the infant inside me. And then please pray for me."[26] In the song "Japan: The Island of Women" (Nihon nyōgo no shima, 1692), a pregnant woman threatened with death pleads for her life: "I'm terrified of the Buddhist punishment that is bound to descend on me if I die with an infant inside me!"[27]

These beliefs and practices reflect changes that took place at the beginning of the early modern period in the way infants were regarded. In earlier times, children who died before they reached the age of seven did not have to be buried because they were not entirely "human"; they were considered closer to deities or to the other world. Only during the late Muromachi period and the beginning of the early modern period did children really come to be viewed as human, as we can see from the appearance in illustrated hell scrolls of the images of children suffering in a dry riverbed in the other world, a type of hell or limbo specifically for small children that was known as *sai no kawara*.[28] Infants and children were gradually incorporated into pacification rituals, as we see in *Stories Heard and Written Down About the Salvation of Dead Spirits* (*Shiryō gedatsu monogatari kikigaki*, first published 1690, first illustrated edition 1712). In this Buddhist tale, which illustrates the priest Yūten's holy powers and features his exorcism of the famous ghost Kasane, Yūten gives a Buddhist name to the spirit of a six-year-old boy who was drowned in a lake by his parents.[29]

Women had long been afraid of dying during pregnancy or childbirth; over time, they themselves gradually became subject to a new fear, nourished by a web of beliefs reinforced by Buddhist institutions and the popular circulation of Buddhist discourses. This new fear was centered on the dead woman who lingered in this world as a ghost trying to revive her child. Indeed, as time passed, the figure of the *ubume* seems to have changed from being an object of sympathy to being primarily an object of fear.[30] Yasui Manami has suggested that practices and beliefs originally intended to save women from suffering in hell gradually came to focus less on the woman herself than on those who survived her. Consequently, it became necessary to separate the deceased from her child and to perform rituals of pacification so that the woman would not appear as a ghost in an attempt to revive her baby.[31] This fearsome early modern image of the *ubume*, with her bloody robes and her baby in her arms, ultimately found its way into Nanboku's oeuvre, in which—even as it retained its potential to evoke the horrors and pain associated with Blood Pool Hell and separative surgery—he put it to a dramatically different use.

The *Ubume* as a Bird

As I noted earlier, the term *ubume* also referred to a legendary bird. The second meaning, superimposed on the image of the ghost of a woman who died in childbirth or pregnancy, appears in *An Analysis of a Hundred Ghost Stories Old and New* (*Kokon hyaku monogatari hyōban*, 1686). This *kanazōshi*, based on a manuscript by Yamaoka Genrin (1631–1672), offers a Neo-Confucian interpretation of the *ubume* as a hybrid image of a bird and a pregnant woman. A disciple asks his teacher about the familiar ghost: "Stories have been told that when a woman dies during pregnancy, her attachment [*shūshin*] takes the form of this ghost [the *ubume*]. Typically, her lower body is drenched in blood." The teacher replies:

> In China, the *ubume* is called *guhuoniao* or *yexing younü* [J. *yakō yūjo*; literally, "night-wandering woman"].[32] The *Record of Mysterious Creatures* (*Xuanzhong ji*) says that this bird is a type of evil deity. When it puts on feathers, it turns into a bird; when it takes off the feathers, it turns into a woman. This is what happens after the death of women in childbirth. For this reason, this bird has breasts and takes pleasure in snatching people's children and making them its own. You should never hang children's clothes outside because then this bird will drop blood on one of them as a mark, and the child will develop convulsions. This bird is often seen in Jingzhou Province. In addition, the *Compendium of Materia Medica* (*Bencao gangmu*) says that there are no male *ubume* and that it often appears at night in the seventh or eighth month to inflict harm. . . . Originally this creature must have emerged spontaneously from the corpse of a pregnant woman, and then later others of the same sort were born. Since it originated from the *qi* [energy] of the pregnant woman, it acts on that nature.[33]

The text continues with a general explanation of ghosts and spirits as the *qi* of people who harbor grudges and remain in this world after they die. Even though an illustration of a woman drenched in blood accompanies the text, the text clearly associates her with the form of a bird.

The idea of the *ubume* as a bird occurs frequently in early modern natural-science dictionaries and in the personal journals of literati, who had wide access to Chinese texts. Similar accounts of the *ubume* appear in *Questioning the Rare Things of Heaven and Earth* (*Tenchi waku monchin*, 1710), the encyclopedia *Collected Illustrations of the Three Realms, Japanese and Chinese* (*Wakan sansai zue*, 1712) by Terajima Ryōan (dates unknown), and *Journal of Matsuya* (*Matsuya hikki*, early nineteenth century), among other works. In these sources, the image of the bird was meant to inspire a view of the *ubume* as a rather aggressive and harmful ghost. As the passage from *An Analysis of a Hundred Ghost Stories Old and New* shows, this aspect of *ubume* belief drew heavily on the imported legend of the Chinese bird while also fusing it with older folk conceptions of the *ubume* as the ghost of a woman who had died in pregnancy or childbirth. The Chinese legend, however, had a completely different origin. Yamada Keiji has demonstrated that the *guhuoniao* came from old medical beliefs concerning malicious spirits that fly into a child's body, displacing the child's spirit and causing convulsions, as described in the earliest extant Chinese pharmacological work, *Prescriptions for Fifty-Two Ailments* (*Wushier bing fang*, ca. third century).[34] Old legends of the *guhuoniao* harming children gradually fused with another about women who could put on feathers and turn into birds, which then led to stories about pregnant women who coveted other people's children. Originally, then, the *guhuoniao* was a sort of metaphor-turned-folktale of a dangerous flying creature, a bird that pursued young children.

The coincidental development of this trope into a female bird connected with pregnancy was given another life in Japan. At some point, the Chinese characters for the bird acquired the Japanese reading *ubume*, expanding the term's semantic range. One early instance of the conjunction of the two images appears in *Collection of the Way of the Gods* (*Shintōshū*, fourteenth century), an anthology of shrine and temple foundation stories by an author from the Agui School of the Tendai Buddhist sect. In one story, a woman claims that if she is murdered before giving birth, she will turn into an *ubumedori* (written here with yet another set of kanji indicating a type of bird) and steal other people's babies in her next life.[35]

THE END OF THE WORLD

FIGURE 4.5 An *ubume* as a bird, as illustrated in a frontispiece to Kyokutei Bakin (text) and Katsushika Hokusai (pictures), *Bei Bei kyōdan* (fascicle 1, 7 *ura*). (Tosa Yamauchi Family Treasury and Archives, Kōchi. Courtesy of the National Institute of Japanese Literature, Tokyo)

Toward the end of the early modern period, the image of the *ubume* as a bird became more and more explicitly embedded in both theater and fiction. A frontispiece (*shūzō*) by Katsushika Hokusai for Bakin's *A Country Tale of Two Sisters* (*Bei Bei kyōdan*, 1815) depicts an avian *ubume* (figure 4.5). In the story, the ghost is not a bird but a woman who asks a man to hold her baby. Bakin may have been drawing on the scene in *Emended Tales of Times Now Past*. Here, in a perfect visual fusion of the two currents, the depiction of the *ubume* as a bird functions as a symbolic representation of the ghost.

The coexistence of the two conceptions of the *ubume* enriches the image of the ghost of the mourning mother, giving it a certain aggressive potential that Nanboku uses in *Yotsuya kaidan*. We see this, for instance, in a street playbill (figure 4.6) and an early actor print created for the first production of *Yotsuya kaidan* in 1825 (see figure I.1). Each reflects early preproduction ideas for the play that never made it to the stage. In both prints, we see Oiwa flying in the air with a baby—probably her sister's—in one hand and reaching out to seize her sister with the other. Although the choice of compositions may have been coincidental, the prints do seem to evoke the image of the *ubume* as a malicious bird. As I pointed out in chapter 3, the theme of jealousy between two women, especially a wife and a mistress, frequently appears in early modern literature and theater, as do women who are jealous of other women's babies or who even inflict violence on a pregnant second wife, as in *The Tale of Kōya*.

THE BEGINNING OF THE END OF EDO KABUKI

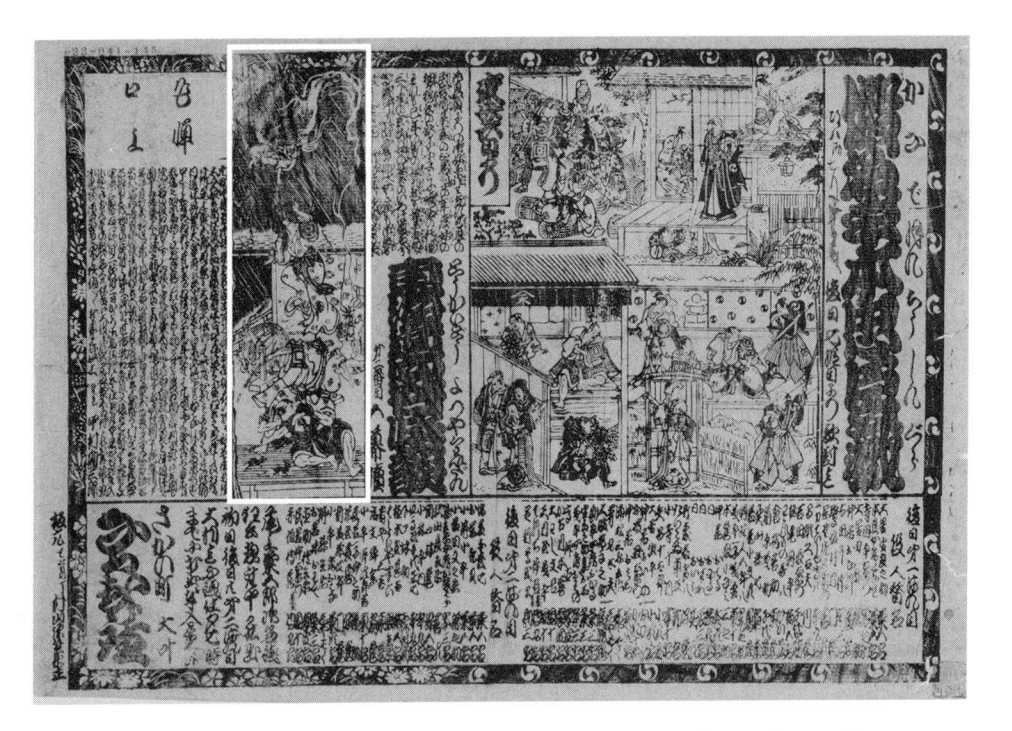

FIGURE 4.6 Oiwa flies through the air (*left*) in a street playbill for the production of *Yotsuya kaidan* and *Kanadehon chūshingura* at the Nakamura Theater in 1825. (Courtesy of Waseda University, Tsubouchi Memorial Theater Museum, ro 23-41-145)

The bird aspect of the *ubume* belief, circulated chiefly through the writings of literati who had firsthand access to Chinese texts, made the ghost even more frightening than it had been previously and expanded the possibilities for its use as a plot device. When Nanboku decided to have the ghost of Oiwa appear as an *ubume* in act 5 of *Yotsuya kaidan*, he was exploiting these possibilities to the fullest.

The *Ubume* in the Theater

In contrast to the many "contemporary plays" (*sewa mono*) that are staged in today's kabuki theaters, for most of its history kabuki in Edo typically based new scenes and plots in a production on established historical *sekai* and used their associated characters. This mechanism, which I have described as "presenting the past," was prevalent throughout most of the early modern period. Plays were usually

THE END OF THE WORLD

structured around the concerns of daimyo households, as the famous contemporary chronicler Kitagawa Morisada noted in *Morisada's Miscellaneous Notes* (*Morisada mankō*, 1837–1853): "In all three cities [Edo, Kyoto, Osaka], the 'first play' or the 'first number' is always a historical play. Historical plays focus on military households and so on, whether they are based on old military tales or draw on material from recent times."[36]

Kabuki frequently incorporated the folk, surgical, and religious practices surrounding a failed pregnancy, as well as the various meanings and images of the *ubume*, into plays about succession troubles and power struggles in daimyo domains. The household-disturbance plot drove the development of kabuki from one-act plays originating in seventeenth-century Kyoto and Osaka to increasingly fuller productions. Plays in this mold open with the fall of the daimyo house and conclude with the restoration of order, which is, of course, achieved by the lead male-role actor.[37] Children, babies, and even fetuses still in the womb serve a central purpose as keys to preserving a household or clan, in much in the same way that treasured objects such as swords, seals, and hand scrolls that have been bestowed on the household by the emperor or the shogunate functioned as emblems and guarantees of the household's status. When a woman pregnant with the future heir to a household is murdered—or, in an even more extreme version, the baby is stolen from the mother's womb—the ghost of the would-be-mother ultimately returns to try to deliver the son to the household's loyal retainers.

The play *The Reins of Yosaku of Tanba Province* (*Tanba Yosaku tazuna obi*, late seventeenth century, Kyoto) by Tominaga Heibei (dates unknown), for example, features the pregnant mistress of the daimyo of Tanba Province (disguised as Yosaku) who is unable to give birth for three years as the result of a curse put on her by the daimyo's mother-in-law to prevent her from producing an heir. After the mistress is murdered, the baby, protected by the Jizō of Koyasu Shrine, is born from a wound in her neck. The mistress then appears as a ghost to nurture the boy and ultimately deliver him to the daimyo as an heir.[38]

An even closer link between performance and folk practice can be seen in the puppet play *The Battle of Coxinga* by Chikamatsu Monzaemon, which was immediately adapted for the kabuki stage. Go Sankei separates a fetus from the imperial consort's corpse in order to keep alive the baby, the rightful heir to the throne. Go Sankei then kills his

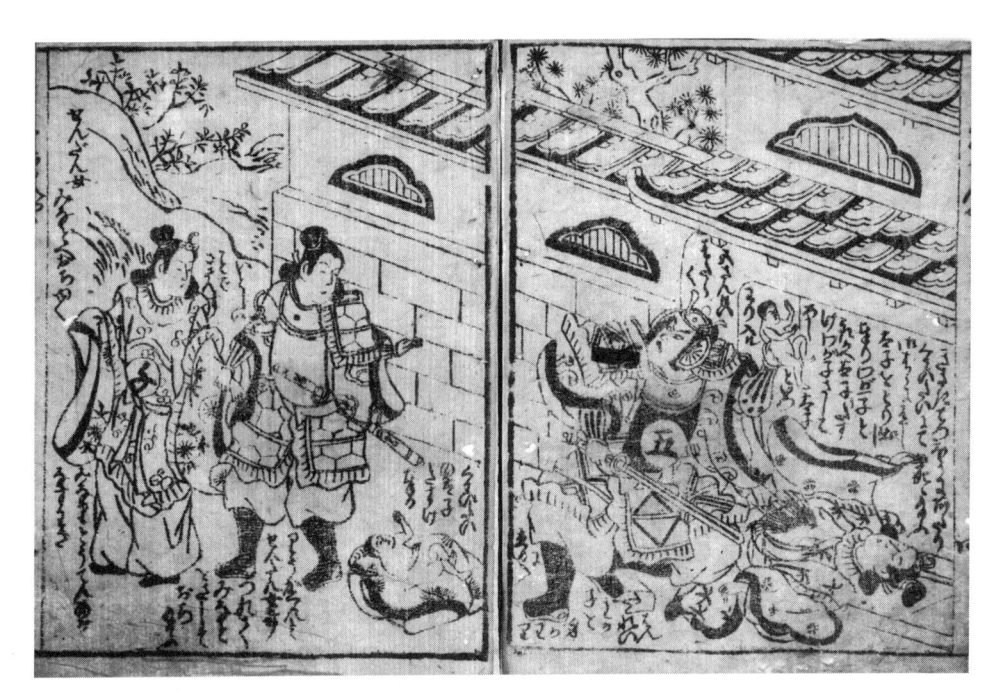

FIGURE 4.7 Go Sankei separating a fetus from the imperial consort (*right*), as illustrated in Torii Kiyonobu II (pictures), *Kokusen'ya kassen* (fascicle 1, 4 ura–5 omote). (Courtesy of Waseda University Library, Tokyo)

own infant son and inserts him into the consort's womb to fool the enemy.[39] Torii Kiyonobu II (active 1720s–1763) depicted the scene in his *kurohon* (black cover) digest *Kokusen'ya kassen* (before 1756), which recounts the first five acts of the puppet play largely through illustrations. Neither the puppet play nor the kabuki script explicitly mentions *ubume*, but the gruesome extraction of the infant from the mother's womb (figure 4.7) clearly places the folk practice of separative surgery in the framework of the theater.

During the late eighteenth century, especially after the publication of Sekien's encyclopedia of monsters, *ubume* were staged as they appeared in book illustrations. One of the first explicit theatrical references to an *ubume* is in *It Looks Like Flowers: The Deep Snows of Yoshino* (*Hana to mimasu Yoshino no miyuki*) by Fukumori Kyūsuke (1767–1818), staged in Edo in 1798[40] and set in the world of *The Chronicles of Great Peace*. The final act featured a dance by Kureha no Mae, played by Iwai Hanshirō IV (1747–1800), to a *tokiwazu*-style chanting of "Crane at

THE END OF THE WORLD

Night, the Fur in the Snow" (Yoru no tsuru yuki kegoromo), also known as "The *Ubume*'s Separation from Her Child" (Ubume no kowakare). She is accompanied by the usual music for ghosts (*yūrei sanjū*), which is also used in staging Oiwa's *ubume* scene: the eerie strains of the flute (*netori*) and a low, intermittent drumming representing the sound of wind (*usu dorodoro*).

After being murdered, Kureha no Mae returns as an *ubume*, cradling her baby in her arms as she walks through the snow to entrust her son to his father. As visualized in Tatekawa [Utei] Enba I's *Edo in Bloom: A Kabuki Time Line*, she emerges, holding the baby, from a little bird standing in the snow, possibly a prop and a visual evocation of the avian meaning of the word *ubume* (figure 4.8). The chanting explains: "I was killed and left this world. Hoping to entrust this child to his father, though I no longer exist among mortals, I've been wandering in Chūu [the intermediate existence between death and the next life]."[41]

FIGURE 4.8 Kureha no Mae as an *ubume*, as illustrated in Tatekawa [Utei] Enba I (text) and Katsukawa Shuntei (pictures), *Hana no Edo kabuki nendaiki* (fascicle 16, 35 ura). (Courtesy of Waseda University Library, Tokyo)

The figure of Kureha no Mae embodies both the mother's concern for her child's well-being and desire to preserve the household's heir and her mission to recover an important treasure, also necessary for the household's survival. "How sad that I'm going to the realm of the dead," Kureha no Mae says, expressing her torment at being deprived of her baby. "Once we are separated, I will never again see my son until the end of time. The attendants of Enma [the king of hell] are watching carefully, and I must depart. How I yearn to stay. How dear to me you are!"[42] According to the script and secondary sources published in connection with a contemporary revival of this dance, Kureha no Mae does a quick costume change called "turning-inside-out" (*bukkaeri*), in which the upper half of her white death robe drops away to expose a colorful red kimono as she picks up an iron rod decorated with flowers—a dazzling image appropriate to the final scene of the play. Kureha no Mae returns the baby to his father, retrieves the house treasure from the enemy, and passes it on to the loyal retainers, even as she is being tortured by the flames of hell.[43]

The association in kabuki of the *ubume* with both motherly sorrow and loyalty and the restoration of order is closely connected to the prevalence in Edo theater of the historical *sekai*. As we saw in chapter 2, according to the general kabuki conventions prevalent in the three major cities, a full day of performances opened with a historical play, called the *ichibanme* (first play), followed by a second story about contemporary situations (although in actuality it was not uncommon for productions to consist of only the "first" play). In Edo, however, for reasons that I explained in the introduction, it was customary to stay with the historical framework even for the second part. This was true even after Namiki Gohei I brought Kyoto- and Osaka-style kabuki to Edo in the 1790s, loosening the rigorous Edo-style adherence to the historical *sekai*.[44]

In the first decades of the nineteenth century, Nanboku both inherited and reinvented the uses of the child and the *ubume*. Nanboku's three representative ghost plays before *Yotsuya kaidan*—*Tokubei from India: A Tale from Foreign Lands*, *Otogizōshi in Color*, and *Lady Okuni's Makeup Mirror* (*Okuni gozen keshō no sugatami*, 1809)—all include female ghosts who exemplify the standard image of the *ubume* as defined in Sekien's *The Night Parade of a Hundred Monsters, Illustrated*, and, before that, in Banryō's *Emended Tales of Times Now Past*, but with two innovations.[45] The first was that Nanboku wrote almost all his ghost roles for male leads, specifically Onoe Matsusuke I and Onoe Kikugorō III, thus increasing the possibilities for the performance of the female ghost. As we saw in chapter 3, all the parts for female ghosts—including Kureha no Mae, who was explicitly designated as an *ubume*—had been written for and performed by female-role actors, who avoided scenes that detracted from their looks. These earlier ghosts provided excitement and action, creating visually arresting scenes as they presented their grief or longing for a lover through dances and acrobatic performances, but they usually were confined to subplots. Then, in a radical departure from this performance history, Nanboku's ghosts injected a note of dramatic, horrific spectacle, giving male-role actors a chance to perform as female characters who dive into water and erupt into the air, disfigure or wreak revenge on those who caused them to suffer, or vanish only to reappear (after a stunning quick change by the actor) as another, male character. In other words, Nanboku's female ghosts took over elements of kabuki performance—the settling of a household struggle or the perpetration of a revenge—that had previously been reserved for the male roles.

The representation of the character Kōzaki as an *ubume* in a street playbill for *Otogizōshi in Color* (figure 4.9), for example, indicates that the scene in which she appeared was one of the play's major highlights. Kōzaki, originally played by Onoe Matsusuke I, is the nursemaid of Lord Kikuchi's grandson. As a nurse, Kōzaki's mission is to protect the baby boy. On the verge of death after being gruesomely tortured, she nonetheless jumps into a river to rescue him when an enemy throws him into the water. When she surfaces, she has changed costumes, assuming the guise of an *ubume*: "Kōzaki emerges from the water as a ghost. There is a soul flame burning and she is carrying the baby.... Cradling the infant in her arms, Kōzaki walks over to the reeds and takes up the seal she had buried there earlier. She holds the seal between her lips when the baby cries; she pats the baby and lets it urinate. Then, peering at the baby's face, she bursts into tears as she stands among the reeds."[46] Kōzaki's tender treatment of the little boy and her sentimental reaction, even as a ghost, gives her ghastly figure a certain motherly warmth. The seal she digs up is the "seal of the female dragon" (*meryū no in*), one of two treasures that the Kikuchi household needs in order to continue to exist. Kōzaki later appears in the same *ubume* guise to hand over the baby and the seal to the baby's mother. No sooner has Kōzaki fulfilled her mission than she leaves. "I'm happy now," she says. "Having safely given the boy to you, I have no regrets."[47] The heroism of her act contains the conventional overtones of *ubume* sorrow.

Here Nanboku evokes the familiar cultural icon of the *ubume* as a nurturer, even as he translates it into a different context by focusing on the social mission of these women. The loss of the seal precipitated the Kikuchi clan's downfall, which provides the play's basic framework. Thus we see the combination of private, solicitous grief and a heroic,

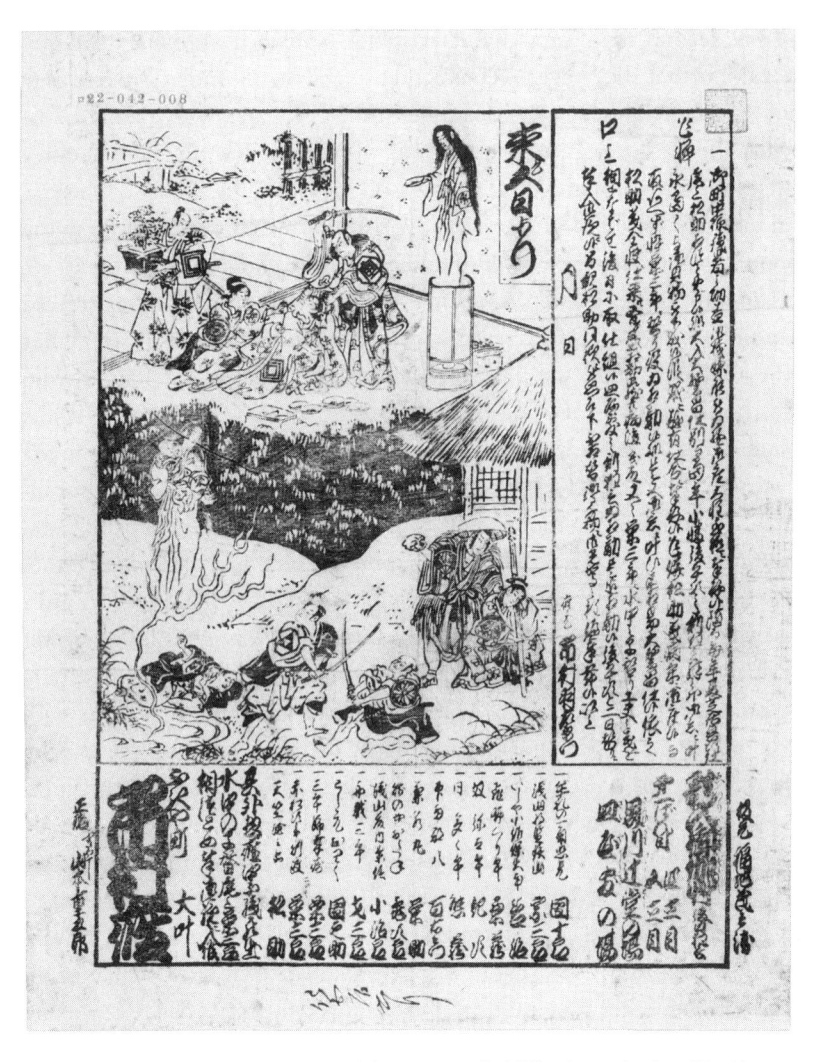

FIGURE 4.9 Kōzaki as an *ubume* (*bottom left*) in a street playbill for the production of *Iroeiri otogizōshi* at the Ichimura Theater in 1808. (Courtesy of Waseda University, Tsubouchi Memorial Theater Museum, *ro* 22-42-8)

social act by a secondary female character. This act also brings closure to the play, ending the struggle that gave it meaning and tying together the scenes that served as its highlights. The power that Kōzaki and characters like her exhibit even after death allows them not only to occupy the stage in climactic moments but also to rework the larger, overarching frame stories by taking the place of the male hero.

THE END OF THE WORLD

The second significant characteristic of Nanboku's *ubume*, including Kōzaki, is that they have no connection to childbirth. Indeed, in one play he even staged a male ghost emerging from the water with a baby. In essence, the motherly ghost was a distant vision that Nanboku consciously tried to evoke through visual and sensory associations, a sort of theatrical montage based on images of a type of ghost that resided deep in the popular imagination of his Edo audience. It is telling that Nanboku set his *ubume* scenes near water, often on riverbanks, since water offered a point of access to the other world, and running water in particular was associated with the pacification of ghosts. Except for Iohata, who was newly created for *Tokubei from India: A Tale from Foreign Lands*, Nanboku's *ubume*—Kōzaki, Kasane, and even the male Koheiji—all are based on historical and legendary figures related to water. Kōzaki, for instance, is modeled on the servant from the familiar legends of "the plate-counting mansion" (*sara yashiki*). In different versions, the servant either is killed or drowns herself in a well after breaking a plate in her lord's favorite set. Koheiji is murdered in a swamp, and Kasane is killed by her husband on a riverbank. The ghosts' connection with water naturally linked them to the *ubume*. When Nanboku staged these characters with a baby, he was superimposing the images of the *ubume* on them, using the trope to add layers of meaning to the spectacle unfolding on the stage.

By drawing on these distant images while linking the *ubume* to female characters who no longer had the conventional association with pregnancy, Nanboku summoned into the theater world ghosts that evoked deep fear but remained engaged with the world, carrying out a private mission even in death. This new type of female character, which originated in an earlier type motivated by an overwhelming desire to ensure the continuation of the community to which she belonged, ultimately enabled Nanboku to turn away from the strictures that had bound these women and had governed kabuki playwriting in Edo, as he did so spectacularly in *Yotsuya kaidan*.

The *Ubume* in Nineteenth-Century Literature: Jealousy and Private Interests

Nanboku's *ubume* also have to be situated in the larger context of early-nineteenth-century cultural production—above all, popular fiction (*gesaku*) in the *gōkan* (combined booklets) and *yomihon* genres, in which these female ghosts suddenly became ubiquitous. Here *ubume* were presented not as anonymous monsters, as was frequently the case in the earlier genre of *kibyōshi* (yellow covers), but as women with particular histories who played significant roles in narratives focused on revenge or household disturbances.

To a certain extent, plays and popular fiction belonged to different realms of cultural production, but the boundary between the two became increasingly blurred, particularly during the nineteenth century, when after the Kansei reforms (1787–1793), both *gōkan* and *yomihon* began to incorporate theatrical frameworks, characters, and plots. There are more concrete links as well: Gunji Masakatsu has pointed out that Nanboku and Kyōden consulted each other's materials,[48] especially works dealing with ghosts and supernatural figures using similar plots, scenes, and frameworks, including those of Tokubei from India, Koheiji, Kasane, and Sakurahime. Many of Nanboku's most spectacular scenes—involving, for instance, women's disfiguration, representations of *ubume*, ghostly hands emerging from death robes, and women's hair turning into serpents—have counterparts in the illustrations for Kyōden's *gōkan* and *yomihon*.[49] Kyōden's fiction resembled Nanboku's plays in their interest in mobilizing the uncontrollable private emotions inherent in the female body to break free from the frameworks that had oppressed characters by privileging the interest of the community. But Kyōden also used images of pregnancy and death for a very different purpose, especially in the works he published during the first decade of the nineteenth century.

The sudden popularity of *ubume* in popular fiction is comically captured in a fairly late *kibyōshi* work, *What Goes On in Shikitei Sanba's Mind: A Gesaku Sourcebook* (*Hara no uchi gesaku no tanehon*, 1811) by Shikitei Sanba. In this work, a humorous depiction of the technique by which writers produce *gesaku*, popular types of fictional characters are shown hanging out in Sanba's stomach (where the soul was believed to be located), like actors waiting backstage for their cues (figure 4.10). On the right-hand page, we see a selection of stock kabuki character types, including a look-alike of Matsumoto Kōshirō V in an "evil-character" (*kataki-yaku*) role at the upper left, a bandit resembling Nakamura Nakazō I on the right, a handsome man seeking revenge who appears with the obligatory straw hat and a raincoat at the lower right, and a tough, chivalrous commoner (*otokodate*) at the top. On the left-hand page, we see a courtesan drawn in the style of the artist

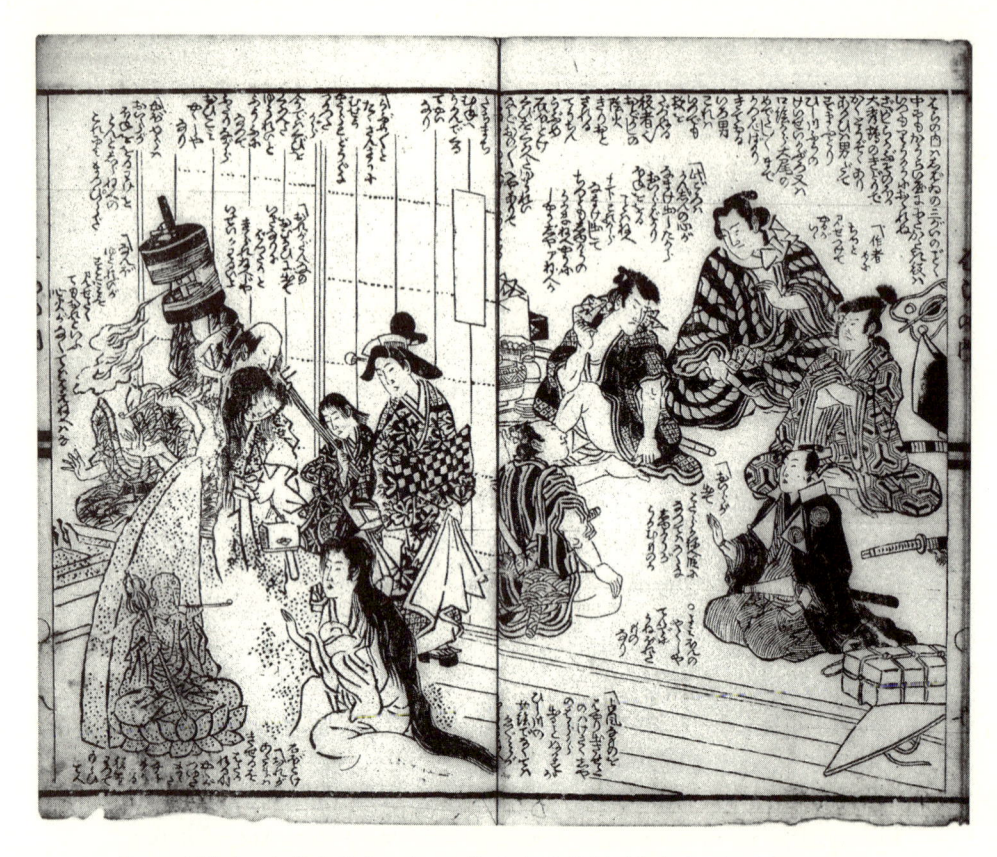

FIGURE 4.10 A cast of kabuki characters, as illustrated in Shikitei Sanba (text) and Ogawa Yoshimaru (pictures), *Hara no uchi gesaku no tanehon* (7 ura–8 omote). (Courtesy of the National Diet Library, Tokyo)

Hishikawa Moronobu (1618–1694).[50] Also on the left-hand page are two stars among the low-ranking "actors herded into a single dressing room" (*oikomi yakusha*): an *ubume* and a male ghost gnawing on a woman's head—an allusion to the ghost of Koheiji, who by then had been popularized in Nanboku's play *Otogizōshi in Color*, in illustrations by Hokusai and Utagawa Kunisada, and in Kyōden's narratives.

Needless to say, Sanba is poking fun at the overuse of these popular character types: "Writers have been strewing *ubume* everywhere, quite carelessly, using them as tools, and so now she's married the ghost gnawing on a head and they've joined the troupe as low-ranking actors."[51] Sanba even has the *ubume*'s husband criticize her for trying to be the center of attention: "You! You're just a female ghost, but you're an incredibly immodest one! You've been popping up totally randomly

THE BEGINNING OF THE END OF EDO KABUKI

in both *yomihon* and *gōkan*, and as a result no one takes us ghosts seriously anymore. You're a disgrace to me, your husband, as well!"⁵² *What Goes On in Shikitei Sanba's Mind* indicates just how popular the figure of the *ubume* had become—so popular that Sanba predicted that overuse would soon lead them to go out of fashion. In fact, though, *ubume* and other ghosts remained a popular trope in later years as well, although not to the extent that they had been in the first decade of the nineteenth century.

Sanba also playfully draws our attention to the fact that what we now think of as "literary" production was in fact closely and self-consciously bound up with the theater. The text envisions the characters as actors backstage in a kabuki theater and opens with a long metaphorical comparison of the process of writing popular fiction with that of mounting a puppet-theater production. Most important, the character types that Sanba introduces reflect the nineteenth-century interest in vengeance plots and household crises. Although different in format, presentation, and narrative interest, both *yomihon* and *gōkan* drew on common story paradigms that had been circulating in the theater. Something of this intergeneric fluidity is suggested by the promise made by the courtesan and the handsome man in the raincoat: "Even if we are used in *gōkan* and then transplanted into *yomihon*, eventually to find a home in a wastebasket, we'll still be man and wife."⁵³

This theatricalization of prose narrative is attributed to the Kansei reforms, which led writers to move away from witty depictions of the extravagance of the pleasure quarters. *Sharebon* (books of wit and fashion) disappeared; *kibyōshi* began to focus more on sober revenge plots and grew longer, evolving into the new genre of the *gōkan*; and *yomihon* began to experiment with different plot patterns and formats that incorporated theatrical frameworks.⁵⁴ In the case of *gōkan*, the relatively simple vengeance tales popular in the *kibyōshi* and early *gōkan* developed over time into the more complex plot type of the household disturbance, which were based heavily on motifs from kabuki.⁵⁵ This, in part, was what allowed a playwright like Nanboku to participate in the genre through a number of theater-inspired *gōkan*. His *Vengeance: This Is Takasago* (*Katakiuchi kokoro wa Takasago* or *Katakiuchi tokoro wa Takasago*, 1809), for example, was a *gōkan* rewriting of Chikamatsu's puppet play *Kako no Kyōshin Makes the Rounds of Seven Graves* (*Kako no Kyōshin nanahaka meguri*, ca. 1696).⁵⁶ In the play, Sono'o no Mae, the pregnant wife of the household heir, returns after her murder to nurture her son. Whereas in Chikamatsu's script her presence is indicated by only a blue soul flame, in the illustration for his version Nanboku had Kunisada depict the spirit in the typical guise of the *ubume* (figure 4.11), turning the ghost of the nurturing mother into a spectacle that clearly reflected his nineteenth-century sensibility.[57] In a rather startling twist, Sono'o no Mae's spirit possesses a male corpse and returns to the world as a male ghost breast-feeding an infant in order to deliver him to the house to which he is heir (see figure 4.11).

In his discussion of Edo-based *yomihon* of the nineteenth century, Takagi Gen observed that the *yomihon*'s temporal setting, place, and characters were subject to a specific structure: "the principle of the *sekai*, a traditional framework that was cultivated in the theater."[58] Even as writers constantly invented plot devices and scenes, *sekai*, which served as a communal imagination of historical worlds and as story paradigms, remained important elements of both *yomihon* and *gōkan*. Using the established theatrical *sekai* to hold their long narratives together, authors were able to work against these frameworks by concentrating on themes of prophecy, women's revenge, and karmic retribution (*inga ōhō*).[59]

FIGURE 4.11 Sono'o no Mae as an *ubume*, as illustrated in Uba Jōsuke (Tsuruya Nanboku IV) (text) and Utagawa Kunisada (pictures), *Katakiuchi kokoro wa Takasago* (2 *ura*). (Hōsa Bunko, Nagoya. Courtesy of the National Institute of Japanese Literature, Tokyo)

Kyōden, too, was deeply influenced by kabuki and attuned to the popular sensibilities of his fellow Edoites. Prophecies and grudges harbored by women played an important role in his iterations of the household-disturbance plot. In this perspective, Kyōden's narrative focus—particularly in his *yomihon*—on pregnancy, ghosts, and the figure of the jealous woman represents a significant experiment that differs markedly from Nanboku's early use of the *ubume* in similar stories. Kyōden was particularly fascinated by the conflict between a childless wife and a pregnant mistress and by the mistress's resentment after the wife murders her. The mistress returns not as a motherly *ubume* attempting to preserve her child for the sake of the house but as a ghost with a private grudge against the woman responsible for her death. This is seen, for instance, in *The Book of Dawn: The Whole Story of Princess Sakura (Sakurahime zenden akebonozōshi,* 1805) and *Plum Flower and the Cracking of Ice*, which are roughly contemporaneous with Nanboku's early *ubume* ghost plays.[60]

The Book of Dawn: The Whole Story of Princess Sakura opens as a typical household disturbance but soon shifts to a private struggle between Nowaki no Kata, who is unable to bear her husband a son, and Tamakoto, her husband's mistress, who lives in a separate residence and has been brought in specifically to give birth to a male heir.[61] Nowaki no Kata has a servant capture Tamakoto and torture her in her presence. Tamakoto begs Nowaki no Kata to let her live at least until the baby is born, but to no avail. Tamakoto's resentment and her attachment to her unborn baby are so intense that her hair turns into snakes as she dies. After her corpse is abandoned, a wild dog drags Tamakoto's baby out of a wound inflicted by the torture, and "a burning soul flame flies out of the wound" to revive the infant (figure 4.12). This infant turns out to be the monk Seigen, who later falls madly in love with Sakurahime. In Kyōden's version, Sakurahime is none other than the daughter to whom Nowaki no Kata gives birth in later years, adding a further twist to the popular story paradigm. Tamakoto's malevolent spirit continues to appear throughout the text, haunting Sakurahime in revenge for her mother's wrongdoings even after the household crisis is resolved, the point at which an ordinary play or story would have ended.

Kyōden's focus, then, is on using the female body to explore personal grudges and private spaces, not on the tragedies that arise from efforts to preserve the basic social unit of the household that governed early modern life. At the same time that Nanboku was both working within and reinventing the framework of the household disturbance,

FIGURE 4.12 Tamakoto's baby is revived, as illustrated in Santō Kyōden (text) and Utagawa Toyokuni (pictures), *Sakurahime zenden akebonozōshi* (fascicle 2, 2 *ura*–3 *omote*). (Courtesy of Waseda University Library, Tokyo)

Kyōden—through his interest in the themes of jealousy, pregnancy, and death as played out in the private struggles between two women—was moving away from these same theatrical frameworks, which had been transported to fiction in the late eighteenth century.

OIWA AS AN *UBUME*

Finally, having worked through the complex tangle of meanings and traced the various lineages of the *ubume*, we can return to *Yotsuya kaidan*. By situating Oiwa as an *ubume* in a story not about a household crisis but about personal revenge, much as Kyōden had done with his female ghosts, Nanboku dissociated her from the commitment to communal duties that his previous *ubume* had embodied. Oiwa overturns the trope of the *ubume* itself: although herself a mother, she appears as an *ubume* only to flaunt in front of her husband her total lack of concern for her son, and to do so, again, in a manner similar to that of Kyōden's mothers. Oiwa retains her own resentments and determination to extinguish, instead of to preserve, her husband's family line. We see this, for example, in the scene of her death, in which her attention suddenly shifts away from the child—who would have stood at the center of the plot in the typical household-disturbance play—and is concentrated instead on private, personal matters. Oiwa tears out her hair in a rage and then, as blood drips from the tangled clump in her hands, she cries out in fury: "How can I rest until I've carried out my will!"[62] It is this inward turn—the violent break with the community, above all the household, and a new focus on her descent into a ferocious, jealous rage—that Nanboku had Kikugorō III express through the character of Oiwa.

This shift becomes even more interesting when we consider *Yotsuya kaidan* in relation to the popular image of Oiwa that Nanboku took from the various versions of her story that preceded the play. According to manuscript texts of *Collections of Rumors in Yotsuya* (*Yotsuya zōdanshū*) that circulated through lending libraries as "true accounts" and served as source material for both *gōkan* and *yomihon*, Oiwa marries Iemon only to have him fall in love with the pregnant mistress of another man.[63] Oiwa flies into a rage when she finds out, haunts Iemon and the woman's children, and years later, as a ghost, successfully terminates his family line by killing the woman, now married to Iemon and again pregnant. The crucial point is that in these earlier representations, Oiwa is jealous of another woman, who has a child while she does not. The relationship between the two women is the same as that in Kyōden's tales. When we bear in mind Nanboku's reversal of the original story of Oiwa's life, the names of the two women in *Yotsuya kaidan*, Oiwa and Oume, take on a horrible irony. In Japanese literature, the name Iwa, written with the character for "stone," hints at sterility, whereas *ume*—literally "sour plum," a food that pregnant women were said to crave—is associated with pregnancy.[64]

By making Oiwa a mother who later appears as an *ubume*, Nanboku was invoking the various resonances that the *ubume* had acquired over its long history, only to obliterate that conventional image. Here, the ghost with the baby is at odds with its complex lineage of meanings, as a sign of motherly sorrow and a paragon of dutiful concern for the preservation of a household. Thus Nanboku used Oiwa to overturn the fundamental dramatic structure of early modern kabuki, countervening the notion that characters could be defined only in terms of their participation in a larger community, even if this required the most unimaginable sacrifices. Oiwa is an ironic *ubume*, for instead of trying to preserve the heir's life, she has sworn to destroy Iemon's family line. Indeed, the baby turns into a stone statue of the Bodhisattva Jizō the moment she hands it to Iemon—another cruelly ironic twist, since Jizō is considered the savior of parentless children in hell.[65]

In Oiwa, Nanboku discovered a means to turn away from the larger communal interests of the conventional *sekai* and their plot types and instead explore deeply personal emotions. He found a way, in other words, to begin dismantling the kabuki tradition. The onset of modernity is often portrayed in terms of transition, change, and new beginnings brought on, especially in Japan, by external influences. At the same time, however, we might interpret it as an internally motivated process of destruction, iconoclasm, and loss. This was one way in which kabuki gradually began to shed some of its most basic conventions, traditions that had retained their symbolic significance for more than a century. The *sekai* had served not only as a basic plot-structuring device but also—through the mechanism I have described as "presenting the past"—as an important conduit of communal history and as a socially unifying force in the relatively new, bureaucratic city of Edo. But it increasingly fell apart as conventional divisions between female and male roles were abandoned and new types of plots emerged.

The loss of interest in the conventional *sekai* is obvious in the work of playwrights who followed Nanboku, including Segawa Jokō III (1806–1881) and Kawatake Mokuami. Mokuami's plays, in particular, tend to feature characters without military bonds or blood ties, including non-samurai figures or abandoned children whose affiliation with a particular household was either unknown or of secondary importance. This, of course, would have been an impossibility in the vengeance or household-disturbance plot. Tellingly, the ritual of "deciding on the *sekai*" (*sekai sadame*), in which the theater community gathered before the start of the kabuki new year to decide which of the established *sekai* would be used in the first production, had by the 1830s already come to an end.[66] We could say that the contemporary worlds that Mokuami brought to stage again and again constituted a renewal and an expansion of the meaning of the *sekai*, but this does not change the fact that the *sekai* had ceased to serve as a function in the way it had in Edo kabuki. The loss that this shift entailed for kabuki in the theater's social function in Edo, even as it revitalized the plays themselves, is tragically symbolized by the forced relocation of Edo's kabuki theaters in 1842 and 1843 to the then-rural part of Asakusa that came to be known as Saruwaka-machi. This happened as part of the Tenpō reforms, after a fire that burned down two theaters, the Nakamura and the Ichimura, located in Sakai-cho and Fukiya-chō, respectively.

Nanboku wrote in a period of intense cultural, social, and political transformation. Early on, his *ubume*, staged as female figures deeply implicated in a complex layering of everyday fears and beliefs, participated in the fantasies rooted in the established feudal *sekai* by taking over roles conventionally reserved for male heroes. Then one of his female ghosts buried those shared traditions altogether. Oiwa is probably the first Japanese ghost, at least in the history of kabuki, who did not quickly attain salvation after accomplishing her purpose. Instead, her relentless resentment has lingered, hovering over stage after stage and even moving beyond theater walls into literature and other artistic realms. Still, there is something special about her appearance as an *ubume* in the production of 1825. As a fleeting performative moment that occurred in the very early history of *Yotsuya kaidan*, never to be staged again until modern times, it marks the loss of a certain cultural form—the beginning of the end of early modern Edo kabuki as it had been known. Perhaps we might even see the image of Oiwa as an *ubume* bent not on saving her son but on destroying him and the particular future and structure he represents, as a symbolic, metatheatrical representation of the playwright Tsuruya Nanboku himself, casting aside the treasures he had inherited so that the theater could be new again.

PART III

The Modern Rebirth of Kabuki

[5]

ANOTHER HISTORY

Yotsuya kaidan on Stage and Page

In the decades after Edo was renamed Tokyo in 1868, the city experienced demographic shifts on a vast scale as new residents, including many elites—from the emperor himself to aspiring young intellectuals—streamed in from all across the country. The changes in the face of the city and the nation as a whole transformed theater culture, and kabuki, which had already undergone a revolution of sorts during the first half of the nineteenth century, found itself in another period of sudden, dramatic transition.

This book began with an exploration of Edo kabuki as it developed through an intricate, constantly evolving dialogue with past productions in which canonical paradigms from samurai pasts—the *sekai*—were invoked again and again as a means of constructing a shared history and a communal sense of the present. By the time Tsuruya Nanboku IV's *Yotsuya kaidan* was first staged in 1825, the sociocultural function of "presenting the past" was no longer necessary; the grand tradition of Edo kabuki was starting to lose its relevance and so had begun morphing into something new. Concentrating on the figure of the female ghost who began appearing in horror ghost plays staged in the formerly slow summer months, I examined the process by which, in the early nineteenth century, kabuki began to relinquish the cultural heritage that had once been so important to it and to Edo, the city that gave rise to it. In this concluding chapter, I move forward into the modern period and show how kabuki began heading in a new direction suited to the needs of a Tokyo audience: how intellectuals, who had, in a sense, come to see kabuki as a means not of "presenting" but of "representing" the past, began to promote a textual, literary understanding of kabuki and of Nanboku's work in particular.

In 1924, the renowned theater scholar and critic Ihara Seisei'en published *From the Sajiki to the Study* (*Sajiki kara shosai e*), a collection of essays that had first appeared during the second decade of the twentieth century. The enormity of the gap between the understanding of kabuki embodied in this book and the early modern view is clear from its title, which advocates a move away from the theater's very best seats—two levels of balcony seating on each side of the theater that are known as the *sajiki*—to the private space of the study. The study is a metonym for the practice of reading, of course, and *From the Sajiki to the Study* includes reviews of kabuki productions in Tokyo from 1914 to 1917 that treat them specifically in terms of their relationship to the "original" (*gensaku*) or the "script" (*kyakuhon*). In Seisei'en's writings, the constantly evolving, performative dialogue that characterized Edo kabuki gives way to the flat, settled surface of the script; by devaluing the actors and the shared, historical memory inscribed on their bodies, which had long stood at the core of theatrical reception, Seisei'en proposes a new privileging of the text as the location of authority. Moreover, he maintains that the solitary act of reading, rather than the communal experience of theatergoing, allows the most direct access to both the play and its author. Written just a few decades after the death of the playwright Kawatake Mokuami and a decade after the deaths of star actors Ichikawa Danjūrō IX and Onoe Kikugorō V, whose careers had straddled the divide between early modern and modern, Seisei'en's book is an attempt to construct a new interpretive apparatus for Japanese theater and marks the next major rupture in the history of Edo kabuki after the conventional style of playmaking was dismantled during the final fifty years of the early modern period.

For Seisei'en, kabuki was no longer a form of popular theater associated with the particular local community that supported it. Rather, it was part of a consolidated national tradition, a history that he, an intellectual who was born in Shimane Prefecture, far from Tokyo, saw as his own. This is made abundantly clear in a letter that Seisei'en included as a sort of preface at the beginning of *From the Sajiki to the Study*. In it, he responds with embarrassment to an innocent comment made by a foreign woman identified only as "Mrs. P":

"Every Japanese tells me that this play [*Kanjinchō*] was first performed by Ichikawa Danjūrō VII, but no one seems to be concerned about who wrote the script, who composed the music, and who choreographed the play. That seems so strange to us foreigners."

When you told me this, if I may be honest with you, I blushed. You are absolutely right. I blushed because I was embarrassed that as you suspected, the Japanese view of drama and the script completely misses the point.

In fact, Japanese theater has been overly centered on actors and remains so even now. This is because the Japanese view of art is infantile and superficial. Most people who gather at the theater are fixated on the actors' art—or, more likely, on the actors themselves—but have no interest in the script or the music. They immediately applaud the actor, oblivious to the fact that he speaks sophisticated lines only because they are written down in the script. . . .

I am embarrassed to have this contradiction pointed out by a foreign lady like you, but I feel in all earnestness that your words offer us Japanese a truthful lesson. I sincerely hope that you will continue to give me such painful advice. And while you point out to us the faults of Japanese theater, there would be no greater joy for me than if you could introduce to your people its virtues—as no doubt, you are someone who understands them, too.[1]

The letter offers little information about Mrs. P, indicating only that she was a kabuki enthusiast: she had attended a lecture by Seisei'en and joined him for a performance at the Kabuki Theater in 1914. In researching the archive of Seisei'en's letters at Waseda University, however, I found nine letters from Zoë Kincaid Penlington, an American woman who, writing as Zoë Kincaid, published the first extensive study of kabuki, *Kabuki: The Popular Stage of Japan*. Some letters are signed "Zoë Kincaid Penlington," others just "Zoë Penlington." Penlington lived in Japan for many years with her husband, the British journalist John N. Penlington, founder of the journal *Far East: An Illustrated Weekly Journal*. The nine letters, written from 1915 to 1925, give a clear sense of the friendly relationship she had developed with Seisei'en, much like that between a student and a mentor. We learn, for instance, that he had sent her one of his books on Japanese theater, and she had someone translate several chapters.[2] In three letters from 1917, she asks Seisei'en to help her obtain a book about Danjūrō IX from the Horikoshi house—Horikoshi was the Danjūrō surname—and then thanks him for his assistance.[3] In *Kabuki*, Penlington also expresses her profound gratitude to Seisei'en for having shared his deep knowledge and for having been such a wonderful friend.[4]

Seisei'en's semianonymous address to Mrs. P functions, in the context of the collection, as a framing device whose effects are more complex than they might at first appear. Most obviously, it allows him to introduce a foreign perspective to the book, questioning the current state of kabuki by invoking Western theater. The early modern mode of appreciating kabuki, centered on the art of the actors—an approach that still dominated Meiji and Taishō reception on the popular level—is reduced in Seisei'en's words to an "infantile and superficial" form of nonappreciation vis-à-vis the more prestigious foreign tradition. The tidy binary between "Japanese" and "foreign" modes of appreciation is complicated, however, when we reach the last pages of the collection. Opening with the letter to Mrs. P, the book ends with a second letter to an anonymous friend, unidentified even by an initial, who lives outside the city that is now Seisei'en's home: "I'm counting the days until your outstanding figure will set foot on the broad platform of Tokyo station. And I am looking forward to taking you directly to see the performances I love so much."[5] Here Seisei'en is expressing his desire to welcome into the world of kabuki a friend who lives outside Tokyo, someone who, like Seisei'en himself, has no direct experience of Edo kabuki—who has, that is, no experience of kabuki as a theater enjoyed by a local audience with a common historical memory and a firsthand knowledge of actors' lineages. Thus the exterior gaze that defines kabuki in *From the Sajiki to the Study* is foreign in more than just national terms. Seisei'en is writing for a new audience of *readers* coming to Tokyo from various locations both inside and outside Japan. Indeed, the parallel placement of the two letters at the beginning and the end of the book has the effect of uniting the two perspectives, situating Japanese readers in the externalized position of foreigners trying to understand an unfamiliar tradition that they are, simultaneously, being encouraged to claim as their own.

The expansion of the kabuki audience to include people who previously would not have been part of its sphere, especially intellectuals from other parts of Japan, was clearly connected to the new importance placed on the script and the reconceptualization of kabuki through the lens of a sort of translational awareness—a "hypothetical equivalence," to use Lydia Liu's term, between Japanese and Western theatrical traditions. Not surprisingly, these tendencies also characterized the early-twentieth-century reception of *Yotsuya kaidan*. Over time, the "essence" of the play came increasingly to be seen as a property of the script, and performances began to be both conceived and understood in terms of a correspondence with an imagined "original." Seisei'en expresses unambiguously this privileging of script over performance in his review of a production of *Yotsuya kaidan* mounted in 1918 at the Imperial Theater: "Whenever I see old plays like this brought to the stage, I find the experience of reading the original script [*gensaku no daihon*] much more enjoyable and striking than seeing it on stage."[6] The well-known historian of early modern customs Mitamura Engyo took this implicitly literary approach still further in an essay tellingly titled "Is *Yotsuya kaidan* Just a Ghost Play?" (*Yotsuya kaidan* wa obake shibai ka, 1925): "[Nanboku] portrayed the very worst sides of life in the Bunka and Bunsei periods. His depictions are a good deal more detailed even than those in Russian novels."[7] This equation of Nanboku's portrayal of the lives of the poor with similar depictions in novels—and in translated Russian novels, no less—represents a completely new understanding of *Yotsuya kaidan* and kabuki more broadly.

The 1910s and 1920s saw a burgeoning of interest in kabuki plays as reading material, and scholars and critics began collecting and editing scripts for various works, including *Yotsuya kaidan*, with the explicit goal of establishing a text that best represented the playwright's original intentions. Initially appreciated and discussed as a play showcasing the acting abilities of Onoe Kikugorō III and his successors, *Yotsuya kaidan* was thus subjugated to a new discourse bound up with the circulation of typeset, sometimes annotated, editions that were created and marketed specifically to be read, and to be read as a product of Nanboku's imagination. It is a fascinating paradox that while *Yotsuya kaidan* is one of the most visually oriented plays in the entire kabuki repertoire, its surviving manuscripts have also been more extensively studied, compared, edited, and published in book form than those of any other kabuki play.

The readers of such texts are aware, of course, that the drama takes place somewhere else, not on the page they are reading, and thus that the printed transcription of the script is not the "final product." Nevertheless, as I will demonstrate, these texts came to be viewed to a large extent as the primary vehicle for the play's meaning. This is a somewhat unexpected change, considering how averse kabuki theaters always were, in contrast to the nō and puppet theaters, to having their scripts published and circulated outside the theater. In fact, because Edo kabuki scripts were never meant to be circulated and thus took a form that made them eminently unsuitable for popular consumption, they actually had to be *created* as a form or genre of reading material during the early twentieth century. This process assimilated kabuki scripts, and even to a certain extent performances themselves, into a literary mode of reception.

The invention of the published, readable script as a new vehicle for the textual transmission of plays affected kabuki more fundamentally than did the various movements to reform the theater that took place during the Meiji period. Understanding the process by which this newly "textualized" approach to kabuki emerged will enable us to acquire a fuller picture both of how the location of meaning in *Yotsuya kaidan* changed and of kabuki's modernity more generally. The creation of readable texts did, after all, give kabuki a new lease on life, enabling it to function for an ever larger, national audience as a reservoir of *memories* of Edo, as a historical artifact whose role was entirely different from that of Edo kabuki, which had contributed so much through its constant invocation of the *sekai* and its special calendar to the construction of an urban community.

KABUKI ACROSS THE DIVIDE

The four decades of the Meiji period saw various attempts to reform the theaters, initiated at different levels, both from within and from without. In 1872, the new government issued edicts, published in the newspapers, calling for theaters to make the content of their productions suitable for "nobles and foreign guests."[8] In the following year, Kawatake Mokuami and Morita Kan'ya were called in and urged to avoid "wild language and embellished words" (*kyōgen kigo*).[9] These instructions had essentially two aims. The first was to get the theaters to tailor their productions to a new audience, and the second was to make the theater serve an educational purpose by privileging historical accuracy over theatrical convention. This meant, for instance, doing away with the tradition of presenting the historical Hashiba Hideyoshi using the slightly fictionalized name Mashiba Hisayoshi or jumbling the historical world of *The Chronicle of Great Peace* with characters from the contemporary Akō incident. These attempts to transform the content of performances were followed by the construction of theaters with Western seating or inspired by Western architecture, beginning with the Shintomi Theater, remodeled in 1878. In 1886, the Society for Theater Reform (Engeki Kairyō Kai) was organized by government officials—including Itō Hirobumi, Suematsu Kenchō, and Inoue Kaoru, many of whom had visited Western theaters on government missions during the early years of the Meiji period—with the participation of scholars and others who were particularly interested in theater. The society made radical suggestions concerning the content of plays and theater architecture and even advocated replacing professional, conventionally trained kabuki playwrights with elite literary figures who would assume responsibility for producing scripts. While in retrospect, the society's approach to creating a "national theater" appears rather unrealistic and its momentum did not last very long, it did result in the construction of nationally sponsored theaters and, crucial to my purposes, inspired a new attention to the script.

The prevailing scholarly narrative of the history of modern theater is rooted in a logic of substitution in which new forms are regarded as taking the place of old ones.[10] According to this narrative, the conventional kabuki acting style was jettisoned in favor of a modern style epitomized by the acting of Ichikawa Danjūrō IX, who pursued a more "realistic" approach in his "living history" (*katsureki*) plays and advocated a technique called *haragei*—literally, "stomach art" but suggesting "acting from the heart." Karatani Kōjin has described Danjūrō's technique as an inversion of the "face as concept," the exposure of "the naked face as a kind of landscape," and he sees in this shift a complete epistemological break with earlier performance.[11] Beyond the change in acting styles, kabuki itself as a form is said to have been replaced by newly created theatrical forms such as Shinpa (New School) and especially Shingeki (New Theater), which featured many successful productions of plays translated from Western languages at Osanai Kaoru's Free Theater (Jiyū gekijō) and Tsubouchi Shōyō and Shimamura Hōgetsu's Literary Arts Society (Bungei kyōkai). Shingeki's employment of the actress Matsui Sumako, in particular, has been discussed as an important move away from the all-male kabuki.

These narratives of substitution mesh well with an interpretation of the transition from early modernity to modernity that is based on a clean dichotomy between the premodern period and Westernized modernity, but it is at odds with the actual state of kabuki during the Meiji period and beyond. In reality, Danjūrō's reformed acting style was a fairly short-lived phenomenon that had little influence on other actors, and in any event *haragei* is more accurately understood as an acting style based on early modern views of characters defined by their rank and disposition that was only later reinterpreted by scholars as an art aimed at psychological expression.[12] Even after Shingeki emerged as a new theatrical form, kabuki retained pride of place as Japan's most popular theater and came to serve an important function in the construction of a national memory. As in earlier periods, kabuki's influence continued to extend beyond the theater, though in different media. Many among the first generation of popular film actors had kabuki training, and kabuki sensibilities had a profound effect on the trajectory of Japanese cinema. Indeed, film emerged in Japan from "dirt kabuki" (*doro shibai*), an originally condescending term denoting plays that starred minor kabuki actors and were staged outdoors rather than in theaters. While new plays ceased to be produced at the same pace, kabuki never acquired the somewhat ossified, classical status of theatrical forms such as nō and puppet theater. Right into the postwar period, intellectuals continued to write about the excitement of seeing contemporary kabuki actors perform; these actors, performing *now*, still served as timekeepers for a particular historical moment. In terms of the number of plays staged and the size of its audiences, kabuki is still the most vibrant theatrical form in Japan.

Perhaps kabuki had to be relegated discursively to the status of a premodern other, used as a sort of mirror to show how much Japan had progressed, because its physical embodiedness made it so much more difficult to change than were other forms—literature, for instance—and thus so much harder to incorporate into a narrative of modernization. Kabuki carried traces of its early modern existence in the most visible ways, which were all but impossible to expunge. Kabuki continued, and had to continue, with essentially the same acting lineages, playwrights, and traditions across the divide between early modern and modern. Its stubborn adherence to its old ways made it tempting to insist that it was being supplanted, and then that it had been supplanted, when in fact it was not and had not been.

The cultural field of Meiji theatrical arts might be described more accurately in terms of a *proliferation* of genres. Shinpa built on kabuki performance styles even as it strove to accommodate contemporary political drama and sentimental melodrama, which meshed poorly with conventional kabuki role-types, especially the lead male, the evil role, and the handsome male. Shingeki, for its part, invented a different style to stage works in a completely new genre: plays translated by literary figures into the vernacular, presented using female as well as male actors. Either way, kabuki was the form in contrast to which these new theatrical forms were developed and with which they were compared. Experiments on stage either attempted to expand the performative potential of kabuki or kept it at arm's length, resisting its pull.

Another shortcoming in the narrative of substitution is that it obscures the dramatic changes to which kabuki was subject for almost half a century, even before theatrical reforms began to be explicitly debated in Tokyo. As I have shown, the conventions of Edo kabuki were gradually dismantled in the early nineteenth century. The conventional historical *sekai* began to lose its importance, especially after the 1830s and following the theaters' relocation to Saruwaka-machi; the theater-affiliation system began unraveling; and the face-showing production ceased completely in 1849. During the final decade of the early modern period and in the early years of the Meiji period, political unrest forced the theaters to close.[13]

But there was more to it than this. Already during the nineteenth century, both the image of the kabuki theater as a space of fantasy and the use of "wild language and embellished words" that the Meiji government later tried to ban were beginning to fade. Nanboku sought material for his *kizewa* plays among the riffraff of Edo, and Segawa Jokō III and Kawatake Mokuami pushed this even further by staging plays featuring low-class bandits, rural farmers, and beggars. *Bakumatsu* (late Tokugawa period) playwrights, in particular, actively sought new material outside the communal memory of the historical *sekai* by incorporating sentimental tales of human-size characters from storytelling (*kōdan*) and "true accounts."[14] Their eager incorporation of real-life "documentary" sources also represented a conscious displacement of conventional struggles pursued as part of a larger communal mission. Plays featuring poor farmers suffering from unbearable financial oppression, such as *The Tale of Martyr Sakura* (*Higashiyama Sakura no sōshi*, 1851) and *Revenge at the Old Market Place* (*Katakiuchi uwasa no furuichi*, 1857), which depicts a righteous farmer named Seibei who is reduced to the status of a beggar, are good examples of hits. Known as "cotton plays" (*momen shibai*) because of the dirty costumes and the lack of color and lavishness in the stage designs, these plays explored fresh territory for kabuki and were unexpectedly well received. Their main characters, often brutally tortured and murdered, have no redemption. They are cut off from the grand old historical worlds and lack the secret blood ties that linked earlier, seemingly humble, characters to noble families; they must simply accept the fates that their social position and financial standing bring down on them. This taste for a sort of "realism" and a journalistic interest in scandal, along with a fascination with violence, eroticism, and vulgarity, persisted even after Edo became Tokyo.

Actors, for their part, had already become interested in historical accuracy by the time the Meiji period began. This trend is generally associated with Danjūrō IX's Meiji-period *katsureki* plays, for which the actor often consulted with scholars about historical customs and costumes. According to the Meiji- and Taishō-period kabuki playwright Enomoto Torahiko (1866–1916), Danjūrō had wanted to reform kabuki since he was a thirteen-year-old boy in Edo, when he studied images of samurai in Tosa-style paintings and picture scrolls as part of learning to paint. Enomoto quotes Danjūrō from a talk the two men had three months before the actor's death in 1903:

> It struck me that everything we were doing in plays in those days was a lie, and I really wanted to act with costumes and props made in this style [like the pictures], but of course at that time this would have been impossible. Just appearing on stage wearing real armor was enough to have my father punished by the Tokugawa government—he was chained up and put under house arrest—so there was no way I could stage things as they actually were.[15]

The father is Ichikawa Danjūrō VII, who played Iemon in the original production of *Yotsuya kaidan* and who ended up being targeted by the government for his extravagance. Danjūrō IX also pointed out that when he was young, class differences would have made it all but impossible for him to consult with scholars about old customs and habits, and he described how he had struggled to find a way to play samurai by studying Yamauchi Yōdō, a samurai with whom he had contact.[16] Already during the early to mid-nineteenth century, as kabuki abandoned its long-standing reliance on the *sekai*, actors were beginning to take an interest in the historical past in a new sense—as a remote, material reality. The seed for Danjūrō's pursuit of "realism" was present long before he began playing samurai characters in real armor and even—in another experiment that had been attempted and banned during the early modern period—with a beard, or exposing his unmade-up face, to the bewilderment of his audience. In short, it is questionable whether the radical paradigm shift that Karatani's narrative suggests actually took place or, at the very least, whether it was as clear-cut as Karatani makes it seem. Danjūrō IX's innovations represent a continuation into the Meiji period of an experiment begun in the late early modern period.

The notion of substitution is belied as well by the history of the theaters themselves. It is true that when Tokugawa restrictions on the size of theaters were lifted, Meiji theater producers and government officials promptly set about constructing grand new venues for performance.[17] It was in these new theater buildings, some of which were directly inspired by Western architecture, that Danjūrō IX was able to explore his acting philosophy. But this was only one strand of Meiji kabuki. Early in the modern period, kabuki split into two separate strata, each with its own audiences. The first was kabuki reimagined as a national theater, in terms of a hypothetical equivalence with Western theater. The second was kabuki as it continued to be performed in the Edo style. Performances of the first sort took place in newly constructed venues such as the Shintomi Theater and the Kabuki Theater; those of the second type were staged at small theaters such as the Miyato Theater (Miyato-za), Kotobuki Theater (Kotobuki-za), and Ryūsei Theater (Ryūsei-za).[18] Described literally as "theaters at the edge" (*basue no gekijo*), meaning that they were located in peripheral, somewhat dangerous areas, the smaller venues openly staged erotic, violent plays of the sort that had been popular during the *bakumatsu* era.[19]

A new word was created for the aspiring new theater in order to distinguish it from the old: *engeki* (theater, drama), which emerged alongside such other terms as *bijutsu* (art) and *bungaku* (literature). In contrast to the early modern concept of *shibai*—a word that literally means "a hut on the grass" but that encompassed both the play and the space in which it was performed—*engeki* had a narrower connotation centered on the act of performing a play, though precisely what it meant was not always clear. Like other such terms that have retrospectively come to inform our understanding of the genre, *engeki*'s borders were gradually demarcated through a process of negation in which it defined itself according to what it was not.

What is clear about *engeki* is that it was strongly associated with a desire for a "national theater" in a Western mold. One early, self-conscious use of the word is Danjūrō IX's invocation of it in a speech celebrating the opening of the newly remodeled Shintomi Theater in 1878: "I must emphasize that *engeki* is not a trivial pastime without merit; I expect that it will become a medium able to adorn the peaceful Meiji era."[20] When Danjūrō spoke these lines, he was standing on stage dressed in a tuxedo, with his hair cut short. Unlike the two national theaters—the Kabuki Theater, which opened in 1889, and the Imperial Theater (Teikoku gekijō), which opened in 1911, both of which were designed by architects influenced by Josiah Conder—the Shintomi Theater was private, built under the supervision of its manager, Morita Kan'ya. Nonetheless, at the opening, the entrance was decked out with national flags and a gas-lit sign, making it look like a government landmark. Danjūrō was undoubtedly conscious of his surroundings when he read his speech, which had been prepared for him by Fukuchi Ōchi, a member of several missions to America and Europe.[21] In this performance of a new beginning, the actor spoke in the language of a former government official and used the word *engeki*. But if these words were important, so too was the fact that it was Danjūrō who spoke them: the actor lent his body, and the lineage it embodied, to the cause of redefining Japanese theater. Kabuki was the most popular theatrical form, and it was deeply rooted in the city now known as Tokyo, now the capital. It was not older theatrical forms such as nō and kyōgen or Kyoto kabuki but Edo kabuki that was pressed into service as a bearer of national consciousness. The bifurcation of the meaning of kabuki and the contradictory structure of the reforms, which sought to create a new theater even as they implicitly clung to a strong local tradition, are encapsulated even in Danjūrō's presence, in the split between the words he read and his physical presence on stage as the bearer of a name in a long line of traditional actors.

Tokyo's shifting demographics, and particularly the theater's need to cater to a new class of intellectuals, also contributed to the division of kabuki into two strata. Tsubouchi Shōyō illustrates something of the complexity of these changes in an essay from 1931 in which he combines an observation about the inability of traditional Edo kabuki to satisfy audiences increasingly composed of elites from the provinces with disdainful comments about the early modern theater, in which he himself had been immersed since his childhood:[22]

From the Bunka/Bunsei periods through to the Ansei period [1854–1860]—during Ichikawa Kodanji's lifetime—plays in Edo were constructed in an urban, *sewa* style aimed exclusively as suiting the tastes of Edoites. They were presented in a manner one might describe as a "serious farce" in which the *sewa* elements, that is, depictions of everyday life in humbler areas of the city, were being made increasingly realistic. But since playwrights' and actors' knowledge of past events and the customs and so on of the middle and upper classes was less reliable than even the novels of the time, known as "reading books," the content was not only at odds with history, which it obviously was, but also extremely unnatural and illogical in every respect. The plays' plots would have been all but incomprehensible to a viewer from the provinces without the necessary knowledge [of kabuki convention], but still they were full of scenes featuring the bloody entertainment of murder, the flagrant eroticism [*ō ero ero*] of love scenes, and grotesque depictions of black magic, vengeful ghosts, and the like; they kept churning out popular young actors; and the stage settings had a formal beauty that cannot even be compared with those of today, so kabuki managed to keep attracting broad audiences until the Restoration.

But then there was the Restoration. When the capital changed to Tokyo, all of a sudden there was an incredible increase in the number of theatergoing intellectuals, particularly people from the middle and upper classes who had come to Tokyo from the provinces.[23]

Shōyō was deeply involved in Meiji- and Taishō-period theater not only as an avid theatergoer, drama critic, translator of Shakespeare, author of both kabuki and Shingeki plays, and head of the Literary Arts Society but also as the editor of the collected works of Chikamatsu Monzaemon and Tsuruya Nanboku. He thus had a very good sense of the changes taking place in the composition of theater audiences, specifically in the new or newly remodeled large theaters. It was this elite audience that required a sanitized theater. At the same time, there was still an audience for theater in the Edo style, which continued to be performed in Tokyo's small theaters and in theaters outside the capital.[24]

YOTSUYA KAIDAN ACROSS THE DIVIDE

Meiji-period productions of *Yotsuya kaidan* demonstrate the coexistence of two different strains of reception in Tokyo. During the Meiji period, Tsuruya Nanboku's plays were all but banished from the lavish new theaters, apart from a few subdued performances of *Yotsuya kaidan*, while the play thrived in small theaters. Onoe Kikugorō V played Oiwa only three times during his life, even though he was active during most of the Meiji period and was the designated inheritor of the role.[25] On the occasions when Nanboku's plays were staged in the major theaters of Tokyo, scenes now considered characteristic of his work, such as the one in *Yotsuya kaidan* in which Iemon tortures Oiwa and the servant Kohei, often fell victim to police censorship. This was true of some of the exciting special effects as well, such as those used in the presentation of Oiwa's ghost. In an essay published in *Engei gahō* in 1909, the actor Onoe Baikō VI, who inherited the role of Oiwa after Kikugorō V, describes how the Tokyo Theater (Tōkyō-za) production of *Yotsuya kaidan* that year was censored by the Tokyo Metropolitan Police Department.[26] Several warnings were issued concerning scenes that depict terrible cruelty, such as one in which Iemon pulls off the kimono that the sick Oiwa is wearing, in order to take it to a pawnshop, and then violently tears a mosquito net from her grasp, ripping out her fingernails. Fault was also found with the scene that shows Oiwa's transformation, including the climactic moment when she starts pulling out clumps of her hair. Rather than acting out these scenes, Baikō tells us, he was made to narrate them.

As Baikō complained, narrating such actions not only stripped the play of much of its interest and excitement but also was completely out of keeping with its logic: "Ghosts appear because they have been horribly wronged," he insisted. "If we don't show how Oiwa was wronged, the audience won't feel any sympathy for her. It's only natural, in such circumstances, that the ghost will fail to stir up any fear."[27] But at the same time that Baikō criticized the censors for destroying *Yotsuya kaidan*, he himself clearly felt ambivalent about the play. He made excuses for having agreed to star in it at all, saying that at first he declined "because the role is still a difficult one for me to perform, and because an old, magic-lantern-style play seems unsuited to the age in which we live. I feared people would find it ridiculous and uninteresting."[28]

This sense of the inappropriateness of Nanboku's plays to the modern age, so acutely felt by performers, theater managers, and intellectuals during most of the Meiji period, was not, however, shared by the general public, or at least that portion of it that had long enjoyed Edo kabuki. *Yotsuya kaidan* was performed repeatedly in small theaters, where the special effects remained the focus of the play. In 1903, in a production at the Engi Theater (Engi-za)—a small theater in Asakusa—in which Onoe Shōkaku played Oiwa, the actor immediately plunged into Oiwa's gruesome transformation, skipping the earlier acts that depict her death and the reasons for her change.[29] Shōkaku's Oiwa also flew across the stage riding in a burning cart—an innovative scene perhaps inspired by the preproduction print from the original production in 1825 (see figure I.1). The *Miyako shinbun*, known for its extensive coverage of the theater and the arts, commented on Shōkaku's take on *Yotsuya kaidan* in a production staged in 1907 at the Tokyo Theater (the same theater, interestingly enough, where Baikō's performance was censored two years later): "There's no point talking about how Kikugorō would have done it, just appreciate the fantastic ghost performance."[30] The reference to Kikugorō is to Kikugorō V, the natural inheritor of the role of Oiwa.[31]

The fact that Shōkaku could step in and fill the void that Baikō left in his ambivalence toward the role, and do so in a production of *Yotsuya kaidan* in the same theater in which Baikō would act in a censored version of the play just two years later, underscores the complexity of the theatrical field at this moment and the bifurcation of kabuki in the Meiji period. The conventions of Edo kabuki were carried on by relatively minor actors who continued to stage plays by Nanboku and Mokuami for longtime fans, most often in small theaters, while more important actors, inspired by a new sense of responsibility and pressed to perform in large, important theaters, maintained a certain distance from those conventions.

The traditional actor-centric mode of enjoying kabuki itself posed a problem in an age in which the script was being given unprecedented significance as the only suitable vehicle for theater redefined as *engeki*, in part because the intellectuals involved in this revaluation had no firsthand memory of Edo actors. Seisei'en discussed this issue in *From the Sajiki to the Study*, but he was by no means alone. Shōyō blamed the absence of a tradition of publishing scripts for preventing kabuki from developing into a serious art form. In his view, the historical study of kabuki had been neglected precisely because texts were generally unavailable. As Shōyō saw it, intellectuals and critics required texts to keep them interested. In Europe, theatrical works were valued "just as scholars in Japan value *The Tale of Genji*, *The Book of Odes*, *The Collection of Ten Thousand Leaves*, and *Poems Old and New*." European theater maintained a certain elevated status, he argued, "because the practice of *reading* kept intellectuals constantly tied to the world of the theater."[32]

By the late Meiji period, Shōyō had come to regard theater scripts and attitudes toward scripts as one part of Japanese literature that still had to be reformed. This reformation would consist, on the one hand, of changing the status of the script and, on the other, of making the scripts themselves interesting as literature. In fact, as I mentioned earlier, Shōyō compiled an anthology of Nanboku's works, *The Collected Works of the Great Tsuruya Nanboku* (*ŌNanboku zenshū*, 1925–1928). His preface to this collection clearly reveals how central Nanboku was becoming to the canon of Japanese playwrights: "The great Chikamatsu is considered Japan's Shakespeare, but this is incorrect. He wrote for the popular musical theater, for puppets; he was not a dramatist. The writer who is truly able to compete with Shakespeare . . . is none other than the great Nanboku."[33]

Chikamatsu had been viewed as the greatest playwright in Japan since he was rediscovered in the 1880s, and as "Japan's Shakespeare," since Shōyō himself made that comparison in 1891 in the preface to his translation of *Macbeth*.[34] But by 1924, Nanboku had acquired such cachet that Shōyō was moved to modify his ranking, reserving the ultimate praise for Nanboku rather than Chikamatsu. It was this recanonization that brought Nanboku back out of the small theaters to which he had been largely relegated in the Meiji period and assigned him a central place in modern kabuki. In this way, during the 1910s and 1920s, the bifurcation of kabuki that had begun with the onset of the modern period was finally resolved.

THEATER AS TEXT: THE REDISCOVERY OF NANBOKU

Shōyō's shift in perspective was symptomatic of a larger rediscovery of Nanboku by a younger generation of Tokyo intellectuals who became active during the Taishō period. With their graphic depictions of squalor, their extreme violence, and their unabashedly ribald humor, Nanboku's plays had conveyed the particular aesthetic of the end of the early modern period and the mood of Edo too vividly for the older generation of Meiji reformers, the "old men of the Tenpō period" (*Tenpō rōjin*) who had grown up in the early modern period and were actively trying to put it behind them.[35] Nanboku was rediscovered by intellectuals with no firsthand experience of Edo, from whose perspective he, his plays, and the age in which he had lived could be viewed as belonging to a comfortably distant past. This was particularly true after 1923, when remnants of Edo that already had been rapidly fading were wiped out by the Great Kantō Earthquake, which leveled the entire city. For people who came of age around this time, Edo had been relegated to the historical past, and Nanboku belonged to a tradition of Japanese "classical theater." At the same time, toward the end of the Taishō period, Nanboku's "classics" came to seem not merely acceptable but perfectly suited to the sensibilities of a diverse modern metropolis with a vibrant mix of high culture and subcultures.[36]

The discovery of Nanboku began with studies of the scripts of nineteenth-century playwrights by the members of the Japanese Classical Theater Study Group (Kogeki Kenkyūkai). The group was founded in 1915 by Osanai Kaoru (1881–1928), Nagai Kafū (1879–1959), Okamoto Kidō (1872–1939), Kawatake Shigetoshi (1889–1967), and others in the circle associated with the literary journal *Mita Literature* (*Mita bungaku*).[37] Participants first published a series of articles analyzing scripts in *Mita Literature* that were later collected in *The Study of Sewamono Plays* (*Sewa kyōgen no kenkyū*), published in 1916 with a preface by Osanai. According to this preface, the Classical Theater Study Group "is not dedicated to research for the sake of research; our studies are directed toward the creation of something new." Above all, the group aimed to bring about the "establishment of a new national theater" through the discovery of a true Japanese essence via reading and studying "classical plays."[38] In practice, the term "classical plays" referred almost exclusively to the works of Kawatake Mokuami and Tsuruya Nanboku.[39] Osanai contextualized the group's approach by invoking various Western theatrical traditions, from Russia to France, and their roots in their respective national cultures. Distance made it possible to incorporate Edo plays into a national past, and to see them as fresh, newly relevant, and even exotic.

The exoticism underlying the Classical Theater Study Group's discovery of Nanboku is evident not only in the group's invocation of analogies with Western literature but also in its introduction to plays sometimes by way of translations into Western languages. Osanai first became interested in *Yotsuya kaidan*, for instance, when he read James S. De Benneville's *The Yotsuya Kwaidan, or, O'Iwa Inari, Retold from the Japanese Originals*. In an essay published in *New Performance* (*Shin engei*) in June 1923, Osanai suggested that this book, which was based largely on a *kōdan* rewriting of *Yotsuya kaidan* by Shunkintei Ryūō (1826–1894), had a certain exotic attraction even before it was read. Oiwa was depicted in a highly unusual manner in the frontispiece ("even we have never seen anything like it"), dressed in the style of Otohime, the Dragon King's daughter, and standing on a rock and holding a *mani* (*hōju no tama* [wish-fulfilling jewel]) in one hand and the key to a storehouse in the other (figure 5.1).[40]

Osanai was taken with the style of De Benneville's narration as well—so taken that he used it as his model for a novel, *Oiwa*, that he serialized in the *Universal Morning Report* (*Yorozu chōhō*) from 1919 to 1920. "The whole reason I wrote *Oiwa*," he explained, "was that I liked the style of the description, and I thought it would be interesting for a Japanese person to try writing in the same way."[41] He described this process as "the reimportation from the West of a work that had been exported from Japan to the West."[42] Osanai's encounter with Nanboku thus was thoroughly mediated by a Western text and represented both a brand-new discovery and the invention of an alienated past. "I don't think anything else written by a foreigner has ever delved so deeply into a Japanese ghost story," he wrote. "It goes without saying that no Japanese has ever written anything like this. I learned a great deal about *Yotsuya kaidan* from this book. It's a very strange thing to have to say, but that's the truth."[43]

If Nanboku had been obscured during the Meiji period by intellectuals whose teleological view of history relegated Edo to a past that they were eager to escape, Osanai embraced Nanboku as a figure from a foreign past who could be made to serve the needs of his present. In his analysis of *Yotsuya kaidan* in *The Study of Sewamono Plays*, Osanai equated Nanboku's aesthetic with the "grotesque" (*das Groteske*) and "demonic" (*das Teufische*) of the controversial turn-of-the-century German avant-garde playwright Frank Wedekind, a forerunner of expressionism whose work featured grotesque characters and dramatized sexual taboos.[44] Osanai compared Nanboku's plays with Wedekind's *Earth Spirit*, *Pandora's Box*, and *Spring Awakening*, and his actors with those who had participated in Wedekind's productions. Osanai's understanding of Nanboku and his quest for a "national theater" were clearly based on a relationship to Edo mediated by translation and on a sense of the modern that was capable of reframing and thus subsuming the very past that Meiji intellectuals had needed to reject.

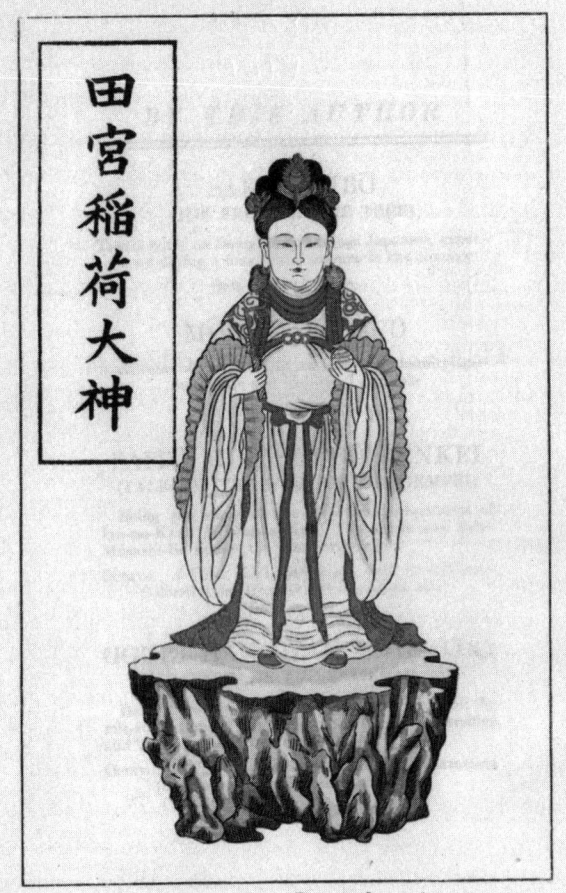

FIGURE 5.1 "The O'Iwa of the Tamiya Inari Jinja of Echizenbori, Tokyo," the frontispiece to James S. De Benneville, *The Yotsuya Kwaidan, or O'Iwa Inari, Retold from the Japanese Originals*. (Courtesy of Princeton University Library, Princeton, N.J.)

The rediscovery of Nanboku's plays was, at the same time, the discovery of the author as a mirror of his art. It was during this period that the basic vocabulary for talking about Nanboku's identity as an artist and the nature of his art began to take shape. Kamiyama Akira, a scholar of modern kabuki, has discussed the process by which an awareness of humor and wit was stripped from the appreciation of Nanboku's plays and dark psychological interpretations came to dominate.[45] This is evident, for instance, in a description of the playwright that Kusuyama Masao included in an essay published in 1916: "Nanboku peered out at life from the dark world of actors like a man in the shadows. He was used to an unnatural life that the general public would consider 'grotesque.' This is where his thoroughly grotesque, gloomy, and nihilistic tone, utterly lacking in anything bright or brilliant, comes from."[46] We see the same sentiment much later in the string of nouns that Kawatake Shigetoshi used to describe the play and its historical context in 1940: "It was an age that reveled in the thrill of the demonic," he writes. "*Yotsuya kaidan* embodies a complex, eerie desire for murder, cruelty, incest, eroticism, nihilism, and sorrow."[47]

This view of Nanboku fits in with the Taishō-period fascination with perverse psychology and sexuality as an avenue for exploring new experiences, a theme probed in the fiction of Tanizaki Jūn'ichirō, Akutagawa Ryūnosuke, and Edogawa Ranpo. Freudian psychoanalysis was introduced to Japan in 1912, and translations of Sigmund Freud and Carl Jung began to appear in the 1920s.[48] In fact, in a discussion of kabuki plays from the closing decades of the early modern period, Shōyō somewhat anxiously associated the perverse sensibilities of the end of the early modern period with the Japanese psyche. Shōyō explained that he was able to see Edo-style plays in his hometown, Nagoya, even during the Meiji period, when such plays were "largely banned in the main theaters of the capital Tokyo."[49] He discusses their "extremely erotic, bloody scenes," in comparison to which contemporary performances seem like "watered down *shōchū*."[50] Nanboku's plays, he writes, can be viewed as representing *hentai shinri* (abnormal psychology).[51] *Hentai shinri* was the title of a journal that began appearing in 1915 and contained essays by psychologists, critics, and intellectuals that lavished attention on sexual and psychological issues. Extending his discussion beyond Nanboku, Shōyō goes on to say that from "a psychoanalytic perspective," plays from the first decades of the nineteenth century constituted a conscious or an unconscious manifestation of erotic desires as well as an expression of "extreme sadism and masochism."[52]

This psychologically inflected approach to the play had an effect on performance as well. At the same time that the Classical Theater Study Group was kindling interest in Nanboku's plays from a textual perspective, a more performance-oriented theater study group called the Seven Herbs Society (Nanakusakai) worked to promote the staging of his plays in the major theaters. The membership of this group included core affiliates of the Classical Theater Study Group such as Osanai Kaoru, Nagai Kafū, and Okamoto Kidō, as well as a handful of others: Matsui Shōyō (1870–1933), who used the name Shōō after 1924; Kimura Kinka (1877–1960); and Oka Onitarō (1872–1943). These scholars, playwrights, and critics were invited by the film and theater production company Shōchiku to help prepare play scripts, both old and new, for the Shinkabuki (New Kabuki) star Ichikawa Sadanji II (1880–1940). Included among the scripts they worked on were some by Nanboku. Comparing and analyzing variant texts in order to make sure the productions of old plays were based on the most "authentic" scripts was an important part of the work done by the members of the Seven Herbs Society.

The renewed interest in Nanboku, which took the form of a fresh psychological approach to his works, inspired new interpretations of *Yotsuya kaidan*. This is evident, for instance, in Okamoto Kidō's observation in 1928 that characters such as Tamiya Iemon and Naosuke Gonbei were more interesting to the audience than the ghost of Oiwa.[53] As a result, the "Triangular House" scene (*sankaku yashiki no ba*), which has little to do with Oiwa's story and is rarely performed today, became a focus of critical attention. The scene centers on Oiwa's sister Osode, who, convinced that her husband, Yomoshichi, is dead, has married Naosuke. When Yomoshichi turns out to be alive, Osode, unable to bear the guilt she feels at having committed to two men, tricks them into killing her, making them think that they are killing each other. After Osode's death, Naosuke learns that she was in fact his sister and, to make matters worse, that a man he had killed earlier in the play, thinking he was Yomoshichi, was in fact his lord. Unable to live with his sins, Naosuke commits suicide. The intense drama of morality, perversion, and guilt that members of the Classical Theater Study Group and the Seven Herbs Society discovered in this scene, particularly when contextualized in their reading of the other acts, brought new attention to this subplot.

At the same time that Nanboku's personality was being reimagined during the 1920s, he was also being reinvented as an author. The notion of the "original," "authoritative" script and the question of Nanboku's authorial intention came to be seen as increasingly important to both reading and staging his plays. This becomes clear when we consider two productions of *Yotsuya kaidan* starring Onoe Baikō VI that were staged in 1923 and 1925.[54] The former was called *Keepsake Flower: Ghost Stories at Yotsuya* (*Katamigusa Yotsuya kaidan*), the same title that had been used for Baikō's productions in 1909 and 1918 and, indeed, for nearly every major production that had taken place in Tokyo since Baikō's foster father, Onoe Kikugorō V, starred in a production with that title in 1884. The *katamigusa* (literally, "keepsake flower") in the title is another name for the chrysanthemum, the *kiku* in Onoe Kikugorō's name—a reference to the fact that Onoe Kikugorō III had starred in the first production of *Yotsuya kaidan*. The production mounted in 1925, however—which, tellingly, marked the centennial anniversary of *Yotsuya kaidan*'s initial production—was the first in a major Tokyo theater to use the play's original title from 1825: *Tōkaidō Yotsuya kaidan*.

In a roundtable discussion transcribed in the June 1923 issue of *New Performance*, eminent kabuki scholars, playwrights, and drama critics such as Seisei'en, Osanai, and Kubota Mantarō (1889–1963) criticized a current production in reference to a number of scripts that the panelists believed reflected Nanboku's intentions better than the one that had been used. This script at least was derived from those used in Edo, which had not always been the case, but that was not enough for the panelists, who found fault with what they considered the naive use of a text that had been passed down in the Onoe family but had never been compared with other surviving scripts. Osanai concluded that "the performers and theater managers should take the utmost care in deciding which script to use, especially when the play they will be staging is an old one."[55]

In the absence of textual materials that could easily be framed as "authentic," subjective views of Nanboku's nature as an author and of his authorial intentions became guiding principles in the interpretation of his oeuvre, in the productions of his plays, and in the preparation of readable editions. Nanboku's reception was now governed by something akin to what Jerome McGann has described as the "ideology of final intentions," a perspective rooted in problematic romantic notions of the creative genius that long dominated critical editorial practice in the English-language publishing world.[56]

Matsui Shōyō, a member of the Seven Herbs Society who prepared the script for the production at the Kabuki Theater in 1925, clearly saw himself as being guided by Nanboku's "original intentions."[57] He explained his editorial process in an essay that appeared in the August 1925 issue of *New Performance*: first, he carefully compared several different sources of information about *Yotsuya kaidan*, including nine different scripts from a variety of early modern manuscripts and modern critical editions from both Tokyo and Osaka; musical notes from a Meiji-period production; a transcription of a "side" (*kakinuki*) that an actor in a Meiji-period production had used; and Meiji-period newspaper commentaries. After selecting what seemed to him the most "authentic" of the scripts, Matsui then cross-referenced it to the other sources to complete his master text. Given the time restrictions of the modern theater, in which performances last a few hours rather than an entire day, as they had in the early modern period, Matsui had to cut a number of scenes. In his essay, he detailed these and other necessary alterations and explained how he attempted to remain faithful to Nanboku's intentions even when he had to make changes. For example, he used words from Nanboku's vocabulary in places where he felt it necessary to rewrite lines, and made certain adjustments that he hoped would allow the audience to see Iemon as Nanboku had originally wanted him to be seen.

This reconstruction was possible because *Yotsuya kaidan* and Nanboku had come to be seen as residing in their texts. Throughout the early modern and Meiji periods, *Yotsuya kaidan* had been characterized by its performative aspects, particularly by the spectacular effects used in staging Oiwa's ghost. These were the very elements that led Onoe Baikō VI to describe it as "an old, magic-lantern-style play" and to fear that audiences would find it "ridiculous and uninteresting." As Osanai's fascination with De Benneville's rewriting and Wedekind's plays demonstrates—or, for that matter, Mitamura Engyo's equation of Nanboku's works with Russian novels—the Taishō turn toward a psychologically inflected appreciation of *Yotsuya kaidan* was rooted in readings of the play as a literary work. Nagai Kafū, a novelist and one of the contributors to *The Study of Sewamono Plays*, expressed this clearly when he observed that their principle was to distinguish the analysis of theater as "literature" and "art dramatique."[58]

Taishō-period intellectuals' attempt to resurrect "the true," "original" Nanboku, unsullied by the changes that Meiji-era reforms had wrought on the kabuki theater, was permeated by an attachment to and a faith in text, and, as a corollary to this, by an equally great skepticism of the validity of performance. Actors were thus a sort of necessary evil. Even as they tried to realize Nanboku's intentions through their acting, they rendered them impure. Or put in another way, for the intellectuals' view of Nanboku to have any credibility, actors and their performances ideally should have been removed from the picture. Oka Eiichirō (1890–1966) demonstrates this in explaining how Nanboku's ghost plays ought to be handled:

> Originally, the special effects were a big part of what stunned the audience in *Yotsuya kaidan*. They were also what lured the audience in. But nowadays, those same special effects tend rather to invite the audience's laughter. Thus, since you have to work with the special tricks of the Kikugorō house, on the one hand, and the script, on the other, you have to take all the more care with the script. As much as possible, you have to make sure you are conveying the brilliance of Nanboku's script... making it possible to see just how serious he is.[59]

In Oka's analysis, the script and the performance each belong to a separate domain: the ghost roles are a product of "special effects" or the "special tricks of the Kikugorō house" and are now more comic than anything else. Meanwhile, Nanboku's intentions are preserved, in all their seriousness, in the script. This distinction liberates Nanboku's authorial intention from the performative aspects of the play, especially from the interest that the ghost's appearance on stage once held for the audience.

At the same time, intellectuals who sought Nanboku's intentions took particular issue with actors such as Ichikawa Danjūrō IX and Onoe Kikugorō V, who had been very much involved in the reform movements in the major theaters during the Meiji period. These actors were criticized for having destroyed the true-to-life, lively grotesqueries that the intellectuals believed were characteristic of Nanboku's scripts.[60] The Taishō-period interest in the visceral and grotesque aspects of cultural production in Edo toward the end of the early modern period, and especially in Nanboku's plays, was a reaction to Meiji modernity, which was represented in their eyes by these two actors. Both Danjūrō IX and Kikugorō V had died near the end of the Meiji period—in 1903, just a few months apart—but their influence continued to be seen in the acting styles of those who had studied under them. Thus Nanboku could be admired in all his twisted purity, unadulterated by the interpretations of actors, only in his scripts.

TEXT AND THE CONSERVATION OF KABUKI

The Nanboku revival depended on the construction of an image of Nanboku as a person with particular creative proclivities and intentions that permeate his work—that is, as an author in the romantic sense. At the same time, the revival also depended on the construction of Nanboku as an author in another, more mundane sense: as the locus of authority, the man responsible for his creation. It depended, in other words, on the suppression of knowledge about Edo playwriting and the fluid reality of Edo kabuki production—knowledge that, needless to say, Nanboku himself had.

Scholars of Shakespeare have demonstrated how printed books from the Elizabethan period contributed to the construction of the image of Shakespeare and the persona of the author.[61] Published scripts became the locus of the romantic conception of the creative genius and provided access to his art, while performance often came to be regarded as no more than a reenactment, a product of the text. The Taishō rediscovery of Nanboku traced a similar trajectory, but it was characterized by a greater consciousness of this process of construction, since urban intellectuals, trying to dig up a Shakespeare of their own, understood the importance of the text before they had access to it. Accordingly, they first had to overcome the *absence* of the text, and thus of the author, by creating scripts that could serve as a focal point for their desire to re-create, for the present, Nanboku and early modern kabuki more generally.

As in Elizabethan England, playwriting during the early modern period in Japan was collaborative and authorship was so fluid before the invention of the modern copyright that it frequently is impossible to attribute scripts to a given playwright. This is particularly true of Nanboku's time, when it was common for several playwrights to collaborate on a given production. The head playwright would supervise the entire play, but some scenes would actually be written by second and third playwrights, based on an outline provided by the head playwright. Generally, the group responsible for the script would consist of at least five people:

the head playwright (*tatesakusha*), the second playwright (*nimaime*), the third playwright (*sanmaime*), a stage assistant (*kyōgenkata*), and an apprentice (*minarai*).[62] The second and third playwrights would compose their assigned scenes, transcribe the text in booklets known as *yokogakibon* (literally, "books written sideways"), and then pass them on to the head playwright, who would read through the entire script, make final changes, run everything by the theater manager (*zamoto*) and head actor (*zagashira*), and, finally, if time permitted, have a clean copy of the script prepared as a *tatehon* (vertical book, so-called because it was taller than it was wide).[63] This final product was known as the *shōhon* ("authentic" or "correct" script) and was intended for the head playwright's use.

Taking into account the collaborative nature of Edo theatrical production gives us a very different understanding of kabuki scripts in general and of the script of *Yotsuya kaidan* in particular. For the original production of *Yotsuya kaidan*, Tsuruya Nanboku served as the head playwright, Matsui Kōzō II (1793–1830) was the second playwright, and Katsui Genpachi (1778–1828) was the third playwright.[64] Kabuki scholars have often insisted that Nanboku took after his master, Sakurada Jisuke I (1734–1806), in the thoroughness with which he supervised his junior playwrights, giving them detailed outlines of the sections that they were to write. This may well be true, but at the same time the insistence on Nanboku's close involvement seems likely to be in part a product of the modern concern with authorial intention and integrity. Nanboku is, after all, one of only two kabuki playwrights—Mokuami being the other—whose collected works have been published. Because he is one of the central, canonical figures of kabuki theater, the definition of his style as an author has been, and still is, an academic concern.

In addition to overseeing the creation of the script, the head playwright was responsible for preparing advertisements for upcoming productions. He had to provide rough drafts of the playbills and the "parrot stones" (*ōmuseki*)—books containing a given play's catchiest, most memorable lines—and to communicate with publishers about actor prints. The playwright even had to draft the illustrations for playbills to give to the Torii School artists who would prepare the final images. He took part not only in preparing the script but also in directing, advertising, and designing the sets in an environment that was fundamentally collaborative.[65]

The extent of the difference between the understanding of the playwright's responsibilities that obtained in the early modern context and the authorial notion of the modern period can be seen in an episode that took place in 1902, when the nonprofessional kabuki playwright Okamoto Kidō and two other figures collaborated on a production at the Kabuki Theater of a play titled *A Tall Wave of Rumor for a Golden Carp Windsock* (*Kogane shachi uwasa no takanami*). Kidō recounts how he clashed with Takeshiba Kisui (1847–1923), who had been conventionally trained in kabuki playwriting and was affiliated with the theater:

> [Kisui] then said I should write the narrative advertisement [*katari*] for the playbill. I declined, pointing out that we're not businessmen and that kind of thing isn't our job. To this, Kisui replied with heavy irony that the head playwright is responsible for the narrative advertisement—Kawatake Mokuami did it, too. I'm asking you, he said, because I have no doubt that you, too, must know how to write the narrative advertisement.[66]

Kidō, of course, had no idea how to write a narrative advertisement, and, more importantly, he saw no reason why he should have that knowledge: his thoroughly modern understanding of the playwright's creative sphere was limited to creating the play script, while Kisui's more workmanlike understanding embraced all aspects of the production. The clash is emblematic of the conflict between new and old conceptions of the playwright.

Not until the Meiji period did the notion of authorship gradually crystallize. The first copyright law related to the theater, the Ordinance on Scripts and Sheet Music (Kyakuhon gakufu jōrei), was passed in 1887, along with restrictions concerning other forms of what we now know as "intellectual property." This made it difficult to produce plays in the conventional manner. The copyright law complicated the situation, since it was unclear who held the rights to existing plays and their adaptations. Mokuami's disciple Kawatake Shinshichi III (1842–1901), for instance, took issue with theaters that staged versions of his popular *A Sword Named Kagotsurube* (*Kagotsurube sato no eizame*, 1888), even though his play was itself an adaptation of a piece in the *kōdan* repertoire known as *Slaughtering Hundreds at Yoshiwara* (*Yoshiwara hyakuningiri*).[67] Many playwrights acted in a similar fashion, obtaining copyrights for old works whose origins were often ambiguous. This was especially true of plays from the closing decades of the early modern period, many of which had their origin in *kōdan*.

The coexistence of new laws and old conventions during the Meiji and even the Taishō period resulted in numerous misunderstandings and court cases dealing with these issues. Tsubouchi Shōyo served as an expert witness in several legal disputes. In one instance, he was called to court in Yokohama to say whether Katsu Genzō III's (1844–1902) *The True Record of the Hinokiyama Incident* (*Kōdan Hinokiyama jikki*, 1881) and Kawatake Shinshichi III's *Stories on Hinokiyama Heard on the Road* (*Hinokiyama tabiji no kikigaki*)—both kabuki plays based on *kōdan* material—were original works in their own right. In his testimony, Shōyo offered his opinion about how to distinguish between "adaptation" and "original creation": "Depending on how the work turns out, it could be either a rewriting or a creation. If the product of the rewriting is merely an adaptation of an existing *kōdan* or *shōsetsu* [novel] to which nothing literary or artistic has been added, then it is an adaptation and not a creation. If, however, the rewriting is skillful and expresses a style different from the original, then it is without any doubt a creation."[68] Shōyo wrote this in 1914, and he still seems unsure how to fit the complexity of early modern cultural production and authorship into a modern legal notion of property. The transformation happened only gradually, of course, because the new system was so drastically foreign.[69]

If the concept of the playwright was elaborated in the hazy realms of modern jurisprudence, the notion of the script as a fixed text—the object of the playwright's intellectual property—was largely a product of the readable edition. In order to clarify the meaning of the modern edition of the kabuki script and the ideology that underwrites it, it will be helpful to compare two versions of scripts of *Yotsuya kaidan*. The first is a hand-copied manuscript from the early nineteenth century (figure 5.2), and the second is the most widely circulated modern edition of the play's script, edited by the kabuki scholar Gunji Masakatsu and included in the series Shinchō Collection of Japanese Classics (*Shinchō Nihon koten shūsei*) (figure 5.3). Gunji's edition is a model of scholarly practice, and the editorial principles that guided its creation are clearly set out in a detailed note to the reader (*hanrei*) at the beginning of the book. It has long been, and remains, the most influential text of *Yotsuya kaidan* and was used as the base text for all English translations of the play.[70] Comparing Gunji's text with the early modern manuscript reveals, metonymically, some of the significant changes that the textualization of kabuki had brought about.

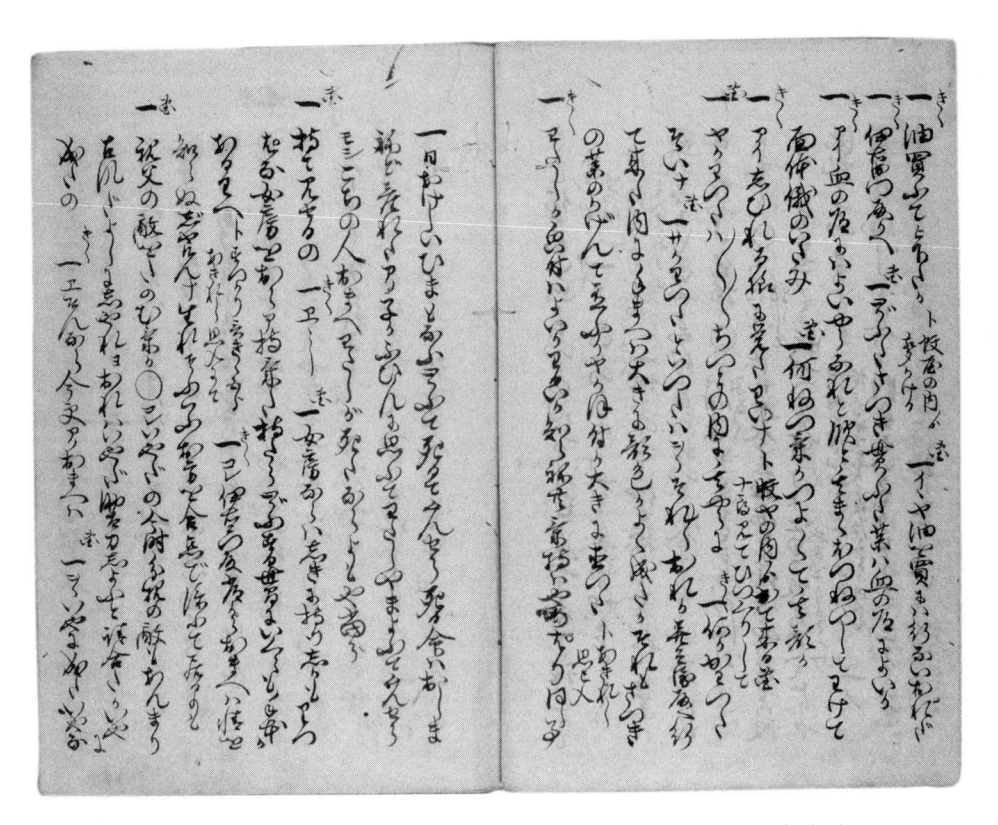

FIGURE 5.2 Suzuki Hakutō's copy of the manuscript of the script for the production of *Tōkaidō Yotsuya kaidan* at the Nakamura Theater in 1825 (fascicle 2, 20 *ura*–21 *omote*). (Courtesy of Waseda University, Tsubouchi Memorial Theater Museum, *ro* 16-332-2)

In Gunji's edition, the main text has been allotted two-thirds of the page. Brief explanations and translations into modern Japanese are provided in red ink beside unfamiliar words, so that even a reader unversed in the vernacular language of Edo is able to work through the play. The tremendous care and attention devoted to making the text easy to read reflects the occasion of its publication: the Shinchō Collection of Japanese Classics was produced to commemorate the eightieth anniversary of the publishing house Shinchōsha and was edited with the explicit purpose of making the classics accessible to everyone. The upper third of the page, which is set in a smaller type, is reserved for more detailed explanations of early modern customs and excerpts from acting notes from past productions that give a lineage of performance styles. Gunji's edition has the most elaborate notes of any published to date, and it

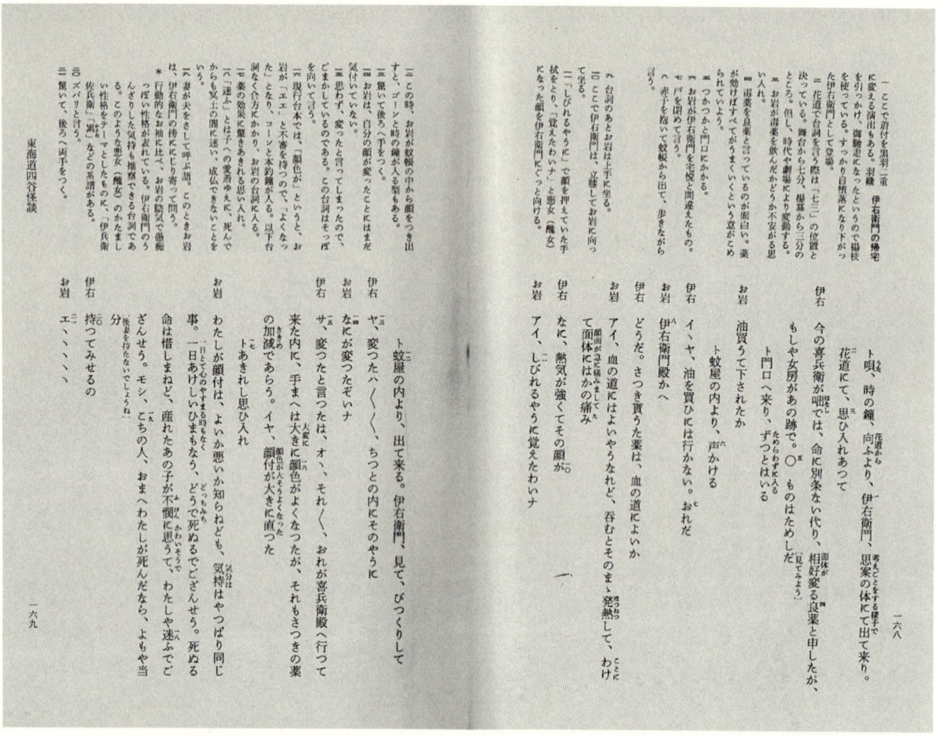

FIGURE 5.3 Gunji Masakatsu's edited version of the script of *Tōkaidō Yotsuya kaidan* (168–69). (Courtesy of the author)

includes a seventy-page essay providing background information, as well as reproductions of visual materials that contribute to a historical understanding of the play.

Figure 5.2 shows the main copy-text that Gunji consulted in preparing his edition. The manuscript was transcribed by Suzuki Hakutō (1769–1852), a one-time government commissioner of documents and an avid book collector. This copy, known as the "Hakutō book," is thought to be the closest to the script of the original production, because the dates that Hakutō included in the text indicate that with the exception of act 1 (*jomaku*) and act 4, it was copied in 1825, the same year that the play was first performed. In the absence of a script in Nanboku's hand, Gunji attempted to reconstruct the original script of *Yotsuya kaidan* through Hakutō's copy.[71]

Needless to say, there are many differences between a typeset modern edition and a hand-copied manuscript, but I would like to focus on one

THE MODERN REBIRTH OF KABUKI

in particular: while the names of the characters are given with their lines in Gunji's edition, in Hakutō's manuscript the character names are not indicated in the main body of the script. The Hakutō book uses a format called *hitotsugaki*, in which the Sino-Japanese character for the numeral 1 (*hitotsu*) is printed at the beginning of each speech, followed by an abbreviation—written using a Sino-Japanese character or in the hiragana syllabary—of the name of the actor who speaks the lines. In the enlarged section of the manuscript shown in figure 5.2, we see *Kiku* (きく) for Kikugorō III, who first played Oiwa. In the detail of the modern edition shown in figure 5.3, we see *Oiwa* (お岩) for Oiwa. This format, indicating actors and their lines, is used even in plays like *Yotsuya kaidan* in which a single actor played multiple roles, switching rapidly between them.

This erasure of the actor is perhaps the most significant change in the text. It also is the most revealing of the editorial principles behind the modern readable editions that began with the publication of Shōyō's *Collected Works of the Great Tsuruya Nanboku* in the 1920s and continues in critical editions and even in translations of *Yotsuya kaidan*, which are invariably based on Japanese critical editions. Clearly, the goal is to create a text that encapsulates or represents an imaginary world—to enable readers of the script to participate in Nanboku's vision of his characters and their interactions. Hakutō's manuscript, by contrast, is less focused on the characters than on the actors who actually performed on stage. Skilled playwrights would tailor even a well-known play to suit the particular cast of actors who would be acting in it, recognizing that the play itself, as a performance, would be realized through the actor's experience, lineage, and bodily memory. As represented in Hakutō's copy, the script is thus no more than a blueprint for the actor's art. This crucial sense of the *incompleteness* of the script as part of a particular production in the making is precisely what is eliminated from the modern edition.

Just how significant this change is becomes clear when we consider the 1825 production of *Yotsuya kaidan*. As I have demonstrated, there are various ways to think about the origins of a play like *Yotsuya kaidan*. From one perspective, the production was designed to showcase Onoe Kikugorō III, Ichikawa Danjūrō VII, and Matsumoto Kōshirō V. The part of Oiwa, for instance, was written specifically for Kikugorō. Nanboku wrote *Yotsuya kaidan* knowing that it would be the last play in which Kikugorō would appear before leaving Edo for a year to perform in Osaka. It was to be a farewell performance, and so Nanboku decided to do something special and invoke the Kikugorō lineage. First, he had the play staged as a sort of double feature with *The Treasury of Loyal Retainers*: scenes from the two plays were presented in alternation by the same actors. This is not an insignificant detail but an important aspect of the performance, since the central role of Ōboshi Yuranosuke in *The Treasury of Loyal Retainers* had been established by Kikugorō I (1717–1783), Kikugorō III's grandfather. Kikugorō I had also incorporated stunning quick changes into *The Treasury of Loyal Retainers*, in which he appeared for his own farewell performance from Edo in 1780, switching from a man to a woman as Yuranosuke and Tonase.[72] Kikugorō I had started out as a female-role actor but then switched to being a lead male-role actor, and this quick change showcased his versatility. Drawing both on Kikugorō III's grandfather's success performing quick changes and playing both male and female roles and on his foster father Matsusuke I's special talent for playing ghosts, Nanboku had Kikugorō III play both male and female ghosts and perform a quick change from one to the other.

Of course, at the same time that Nanboku was alluding to Kikugorō III's distinguished acting lineage, he also was presenting Kikugorō's own talent as a multiple-role actor and exploiting it to the fullest. In addition to playing Oiwa and Kohei, Kikugorō took on a third role as Satō Yomoshichi, a loyal retainer of Lord En'ya who ultimately kills Iemon. The actor critique *A Beaded String of All the Best Actors: Osaka* (*Yakusha tamazukushi Ōsaka*, 1826) gave a rave review to Kikugorō's performance, praising his ability to switch rapidly from one role to another: "Kikugorō did a fantastic job with Satō Yomoshichi, Oiwa's ghost, and Kohei. The horrifying scenes were even more exquisite than those of his father, creating effects so scary it made one's hair stand on end."[73]

The differences between Hakutō's manuscript and Gunji's critical edition, however, affect more than just the reader's sense of the relative importance of Nanboku vis-à-vis the actors in creating the play. Perhaps more importantly, the modern edition embodies an intention to create a universal and, in a sense, *eternal* text, whereas the early modern manuscript is marked by the presence of the actor's names as *temporally specific*. Suppressing the porousness and malleability of the script as a sort of blueprint, the modern edition represents an attempt to *con-*

serve the script as a fixed object—a timeless, unchanging figure of the playwright's intention. As I noted earlier, productions of kabuki plays during the early modern period were enmeshed in an endless process of recycling and rewriting: each production worked with fundamental elements of kabuki, starting with the *sekai*, and added the *shukō*. Following this structure, each production, even those of popular plays like *The Treasury of Loyal Retainers* that were staged again and again, was rewritten in such a way that it was haunted by earlier performances and conventions, even as it exploited the unique characteristics of its cast. As a rule, every production was a new play in the context of its lineage. Existing plays were constantly overwritten and replaced as new ideas and performance styles were introduced.

Some sense of *Yotsuya kaidan*'s fluidity, even in an age when the importance of "presenting the past" had faded, can be gleaned from playbills and other ephemera produced in connection with the production mounted in 1836. In this print, Oiwa's ghost, dressed in a fancy kimono, drifts out of Iemon's robe (figure 5.4). Oiwa and Iemon were played by the same actors as in 1825; the third character is Princess Yaegaki, depicted here in an unusual commoner style and played by Iwai Shijaku I

FIGURE 5.4 Iwai Shijaku I as Princess Yaegaki (*left*) from *Honchō nijūshi-kō*, but in a domestic setting, and Onoe Kikugorō III as the ghost of Oiwa (*center*) and Ichikawa Ebizō V (earlier Danjūrō VII) as Tamiya Iemon (*right*) in Utagawa Kunisada's triptych for the production of *Yotsuya kaidan* and *Honchō nijūshi-kō* at the Morita Theater in 1836. (Courtesy of Waseda University, Tsubouchi Memorial Theater Museum, 402-214, 215, 216)

(later Iwai Hanshirō VII, 1804–1845).[74] Princess Yaegaki, a character in the historical play *The Twenty-Four Models of Filial Piety* (*Honchō nijūshi-kō*, 1766), has been inserted among the other characters. *Yotsuya kaidan* was staged with *The Twenty-Four Models of Filial Piety* at the Morita Theater in 1836, and according to the playbills and actor critiques, the actors shown in this print performed these roles, except that Shijaku I played Princess Yaegaki only in *The Twenty-Four Models of Filial Piety* and does not appear in this commoner style in the relevant playbills. Since there is no evidence that characters in either of the two plays appeared in the other, the addition of Princess Yaegaki could reflect an early plan for the scene or a playful adaptation. The picture-book playbill for the 1836 staging of *Yotsuya kaidan* features the same scene except for the commoner version of Princess Yaegaki (figure 5.5). A description in the relevant actor critique, *A Quick Dissection of the Actors* (*Yakusha sassoku hōchō*, 1837), also confirms that this scene was part of the production: "The part in which [Kikugorō III] emerges from [Danjūrō VII's] sleeves in the ghost act of the Dream scene . . . struck me as extraordinarily spectacular."[75]

FIGURE 5.5 The picture-book playbill for the production of *Yotsuya kaidan* at the Morita Theater in 1836 (6 *omote*). (Courtesy of Waseda University, Tsubouchi Memorial Theater Museum, *ro* 23-2-179)

The production in 1836 was probably the sixth of *Yotsuya kaidan* since Nanboku had first staged it in 1825, and this scene was new—it was one of the highlights of this production. And yet, crucial as this scene was to this production, it does not appear in any modern edition of the play. Modern critical editions, for all the benefits they offer, produce a deceptive impression of fixity by privileging a particular production or, more precisely, the blueprint for that production. This illusion of fixity is achieved, moreover, only through the erasure of a desire to continually overwrite earlier plays and to see new plays be continually rewritten, which was part of the very nature of Edo kabuki.

The ideological underpinning of this fixity is a move from the actors to the author as an editorial principle. Gunji compared Hakutō's text with two other manuscripts in an attempt "to correct the omissions and mistakes that have presumably crept into Hakutō's transcription." One of the scripts he used was originally in the possession of Seisei'en and is now in the collection of the Waseda University Tsubouchi Memorial Theater Museum—this may have been the text that Seisei'en read when he said that the script was much more enjoyable than the performance at the Imperial Theater. Another script that Gunji consulted is now in the collection of the Japanese Literature Department at the University of Tokyo.[76] Gunji explained that he adopted a cautious approach to Hakutō's script because Nanboku had a habit of altering his scripts during rehearsals, inserting loose notes (*harigami*) and writing in corrections (*kakikomi*).[77] Needless to say, Gunji's edition belongs to the line of texts created after Nanboku's establishment as an author.

In this sense, the comparison that I have carried out between the two texts of *Yotsuya kaidan* is actually somewhat misleading. From the perspective of an ordinary Edoite, neither the Hakutō book nor any other script existed because they did not circulate. As a rule, in Edo, kabuki play scripts did not leave the theater and were almost never distributed in printed form. In the Kamigata region, however, scripts tended to be less tightly controlled and could be published in a fairly complete form with illustrations as so-called *eiri nehon* (illustrated scripts). In practice, hand-copied manuscripts do appear to have made their way into lending libraries even in Edo—in fact, most of the scripts that have survived seem to be from lending libraries. Even so, according to Okamoto Kidō, who wanted to become a playwright and believed that the study of scripts was a necessary part of his training, it was extremely difficult to find copies of scripts in lending libraries, even for Meiji-period performances.[78] Moreover, the nature of these texts as copies of scripts intended for theater insiders limited their readership to a rather eclectic group of those intimately familiar with the theater. Gunji's critical edition and the numerous other printed versions of *Yotsuya kaidan* that have appeared since the 1920s thus present a false appearance of equivalence: in regard to the social life of the text, they are exactly the opposite of the manuscripts they are meant to reproduce so faithfully. This difference extends to their use, as well, as a single printed edition can and will be used again and again in all sorts of contexts, for reading, staging new productions, and even creating adaptations in film, in literature, and on television.

The modern edition of the script is, in this sense, not a reproduction but an invention. Its presence on the library shelf, among all the other canonical works of the Japanese tradition, stands as a marker for an absence. This is not to say that kabuki plays did not circulate at all as printed narratives during the early modern period. As we have seen, narrative versions of plays often followed or even preceded productions, especially during the nineteenth century, appearing as lavishly illustrated *gōkan*.[79] The illustrated digest *The Flowers of Kikugorō's Farewell Performance: Ghost Stories at Yotsuya* was published, for example, in 1826—only a few months after the first production of *Yotsuya kaidan*, which ended around the fifteenth of the ninth month of the previous year.[80] In nineteenth-century Edo, *gōkan* digests of this sort, known in Japanese as "transcribed scripts" (*shōhon utsushi*), were the closest thing to a printed text of a kabuki play. Everything about this *gōkan*, however, from its attribution to its style and content, suggests how alien the literary, author-centered mode of reading encouraged by modern editions of *Yotsuya kaidan* would have been to its readers.

A signed preface to *The Flowers of Kikugorō's Farewell Performance* indicates that the book was written by Hanagasa Bunkyō I, who, as soon as he finished his work on the book, left Edo for Osaka to participate in the staging of *Irohagana Yotsuya kaidan*, the Osaka version of *Yotsuya kaidan*. Bunkyō also would have prepared rough sketches of the pictures for the artist, Keisai Eisen, to draw from, as was conventional at the time. Bunkyō was essentially a ghostwriter, however, and as such, his name does not appear on the cover on the work. From a contemporary standpoint, it would make sense for this readable version of what is now considered "Nanboku's *Yotsuya kaidan*" to be identified as Nanboku's product: Bunkyō would be Nanboku's ghostwriter. But in fact, the book is attributed not to Nanboku but to Onoe Kikugorō III, the star of the play, whose name appears on the cover alongside that of Keisai Eisen.[81] This attribution of the book to the star actor speaks volumes about how the "authorship" of plays was understood at the time.

THE MODERN REBIRTH OF KABUKI

As is typical in *gōkan* of this variety, the actors who performed in the play appear posed on each two-page spread, surrounded by scenery, as if they are standing on stage; writing fills the negative space. The text is composed in the third person and describes the actions of the characters, as in modern editions, rather than using the actor-centered *hitotsugaki* format of the early modern manuscript. Here, however, the use of the characters' names is not meant to invoke the world that Nanboku created and certainly does not indicate that the characters and their psychology, rather than the actors, were the focus of attention. Indeed, *The Flowers of Kikugorō's Farewell Performance* is characterized by its heavy reliance on visual elements—the subordination of the text to the pictures—to create a sense of the presence of the stage. Bunkyō alludes explicitly to the pictures' role in the narrative in his preface to the work:

> The publisher came and asked me to turn *Yotsuya kaidan* into a picture book. I've inserted pictures to replace the stage directions, as there are only so many pages in a *gōkan*. I've also condensed the actors' speeches, confining myself to giving an outline of the main plot. I leave the deciphering of the pictures to the kabuki fans. "Birds don't leave muddy water behind when they take off," as the saying goes, but I've got to get ready for the upcoming performance in Osaka and don't have time to go back to the performance and compare my text with it.[82]

The pictures, Bunkyō suggests, are there to be "deciphered," and to a large extent, they will take care of the narration. The stage directions are incorporated pictorially into the depictions of the actors, whose lines are preserved—but only to a certain extent—in the text; notes direct readers to look at a certain picture when there is not enough space to explain something in writing. The images, in this context, are the most important component. Indeed, this appears to have been true even in the creation of the book: Bunkyō notes that he put together *The Flowers of Kikugorō's Farewell Performance* in a rush, and the fact that the text often lags behind the pictures, sometimes for several pages, suggests that he settled on their composition first. And as the last line indicates, Bunkyō conceived of the book that he was ghostwriting in terms of its correspondence to what happened on stage, rather than to the script. On some level, his goal was not to provide a "reading experience" at all; his aim, instead, was to allow kabuki fans to experience the performance on the page.

The performance-centered nature of *gōkan* digests is clear, as well, in the fact that they were production specific. *The Flowers of Kikugorō's Farewell Performance* was reprinted again and again in later years with new titles and covers, incorporating new casts of actors and highlighting the changes that had been made on stage during new productions. These subsequent versions were printed from the same blocks as the first. While the areas of the woodblocks devoted to the text were left mostly unchanged, the pictures would frequently be altered to include portraits of the actors in the current cast and to prevent incorrect crests from appearing on their costumes. The faces of the actors would be changed, for instance, by carving their likenesses on little pieces of wood and inserting them into the old block; the old crests would simply be shaved off. Figures 5.6 and 5.7 show examples of this: figure 5.6 is from the 1826 printing, and figure 5.7 is from the 1832 printing.[83] In addition to the obvious changes made to Oiwa's face, Iemon's face has also been changed from a likeness of Danjūrō VII to a depiction of Seki Sanjūrō II (1786–1839), and a piece of wood has been inserted to

FIGURE 5.6 Onoe Kikugorō III as Oiwa (*right*) and Ichikawa Danjūrō VII as Iemon (*left*), as illustrated in Hanagasa Bunkyō (text) and Keisai Eisen (pictures), *Nagori no hana Yotsuya kaidan* (1826; fascicle 1, 13 *ura*–14 *omote*). (Courtesy of the National Institute of Japanese Literature, Tokyo)

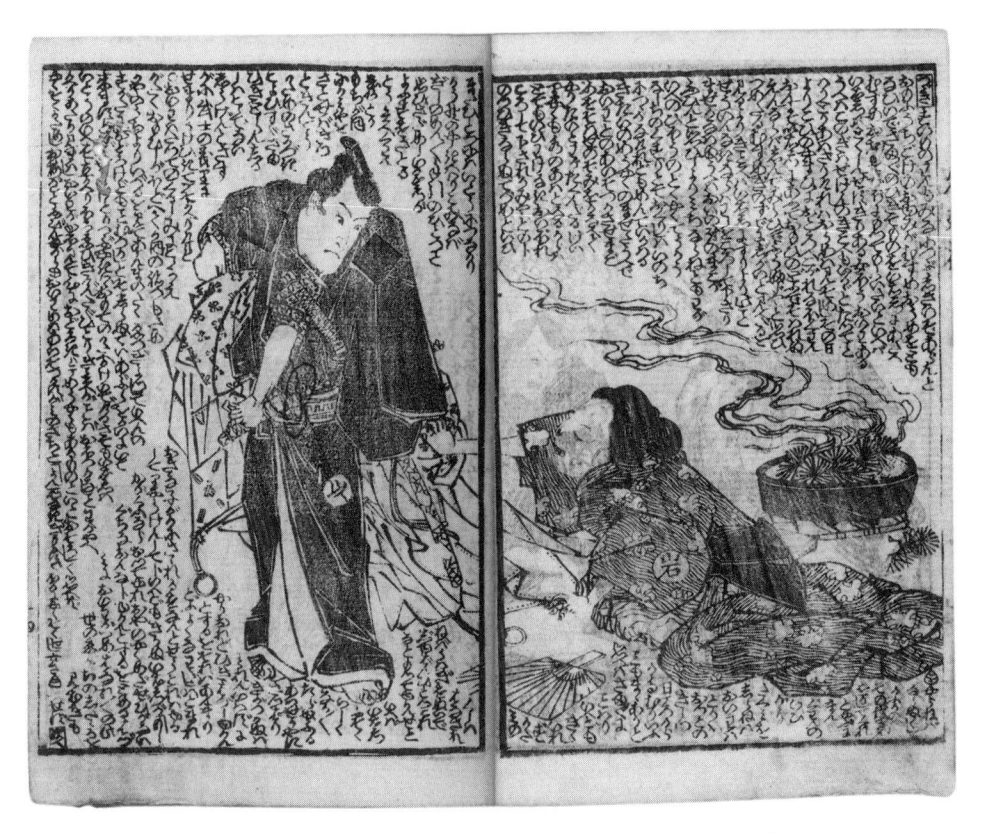

FIGURE 5.7 Onoe Kikugorō III as Oiwa (*right*) and Seki Sanjūrō II as Iemon (*left*), as illustrated in Hanagasa Bunkyō (text) and Keisai Eisen (pictures), *Tōkaidō Yotsuya kaidan* (1832; fascicle 1, 13 *ura*–14 *omote*). (Private collection)

hide the peony on Iemon's crest, since the peony was associated with Danjūrō. Sometimes the changes would be even more substantial: in the 1832 version of the *gōkan*, a brand-new picture by Utagawa Kuniyoshi (1797–1861) was commissioned and a new block was carved to replace the scene in which Oiwa appeared from a pacifying cloth with a new scene in which the ghost emerged from a lantern (figure 5.8).

Presumably, this measure was taken because, as the lavish printing in gray ink suggests, the lantern scene was very well received. Whereas pictures in *yomihon* often used gray ink, *gōkan* were generally produced more cheaply and, during this period, rarely used anything but black ink. Indeed, this is the only spread in the book that uses gray in addition to the standard ink. Clearly, the publisher was eager to capitalize on the popularity of the scene.

FIGURE 5.8 Onoe Kikugorō III as the ghost of Oiwa (*left*) and Seki Sanjūrō II as Iemon (*right*), in an illustration by Utagawa Kuniyoshi in Hanagasa Bunkyō (text) and Keisai Eisen (pictures), *Tōkaidō Yotsuya kaidan* (1832; fascicle 2, 26 *ura*–27 *omote*). (Private collection)

These *gōkan* therefore operated in a manner completely different from that of the modern critical edition and satisfied a different set of desires—especially in their focus on what we might call the "stage function," drawing on Michel Foucault's notion of the "author function." They allowed readers—those who had already seen the performance as well as those who had not, and would not—to feel as if they were really watching the actors on stage rather than just reading a story, and this desire to see, to imagine, and to know about the stage was the fundamental principle on which these books were organized. This re-creation of the stage on the page was possible not just because the actors could be visually represented through their likenesses as they would appear on stage, but because the stage function allowed the writer to leave the "deciphering of the pictures to the kabuki fans." The vast majority of the publications that grew up around the stage and its actors can be understood only if we make sense of them in this way.

In his monograph on the material history of Shakespeare's plays, *Shakespeare and the Book*, David Scott Kastan observed that "reading a play is not reading performance (the printed play as textualized drama) or even reading *for* performance (the printed play as potential drama); it is reading in the absence of performance (the printed play as . . . well, the printed play)."[84] This applies equally well to the history of modern editions of kabuki plays. We must acknowledge the ramifications of this absence. If *The Flowers of Kikugorō's Farewell Performance* is structured around, or perhaps given meaning by, the imaginary access that it offers to the world of the theater and its actors, then modern editions of *Yotsuya kaidan* remove their readers from the stage to the universal, immaterial no-place of the text: from the stage to the study.

Furthermore, to read a kabuki script in a critical edition is to read, not only in the definitive absence of performance, of the experience of being at the theater, but also, to some extent, in the absence of the innumerable printed materials that shaped the contours of the plays' early modern on- and off-stage reception. The images of Oiwa and of *Yotsuya kaidan* may continue to be refashioned in performative contexts and in contemporary visual media, but "Nanboku's script" is valued precisely to the extent that it is believed to be "original" and immutable. The presumed fixity of the text stands, indeed, as a sort of anchor for the increasingly diverse forms that performances of *Yotsuya kaidan*, and stage presentations of its characters, take.

TEXT AND THE AFTERLIFE OF *YOTSUYA KAIDAN*

Oiwa has become the paradigmatic Japanese ghost, a familiar figure whose terrifying presence is felt far beyond the kabuki stage, where Nanboku and his collaborators first conjured her. The modern Japanese writer Enchi Fumiko recalled coming across a photograph showing Onoe Baikō VI as Oiwa in the popular theater magazine *Illustrated Performance Bulletin* (*Engei gahō*) when she was a young girl, before she had ever seen the play, and being so frightened by it that she could not sleep at night (figure 5.9).[85] The terror that Baikō inspired in Enchi is hardly surprising. His Oiwa was particularly horrifying because, rather than wear a thick paper mask of the sort actors used in the early modern

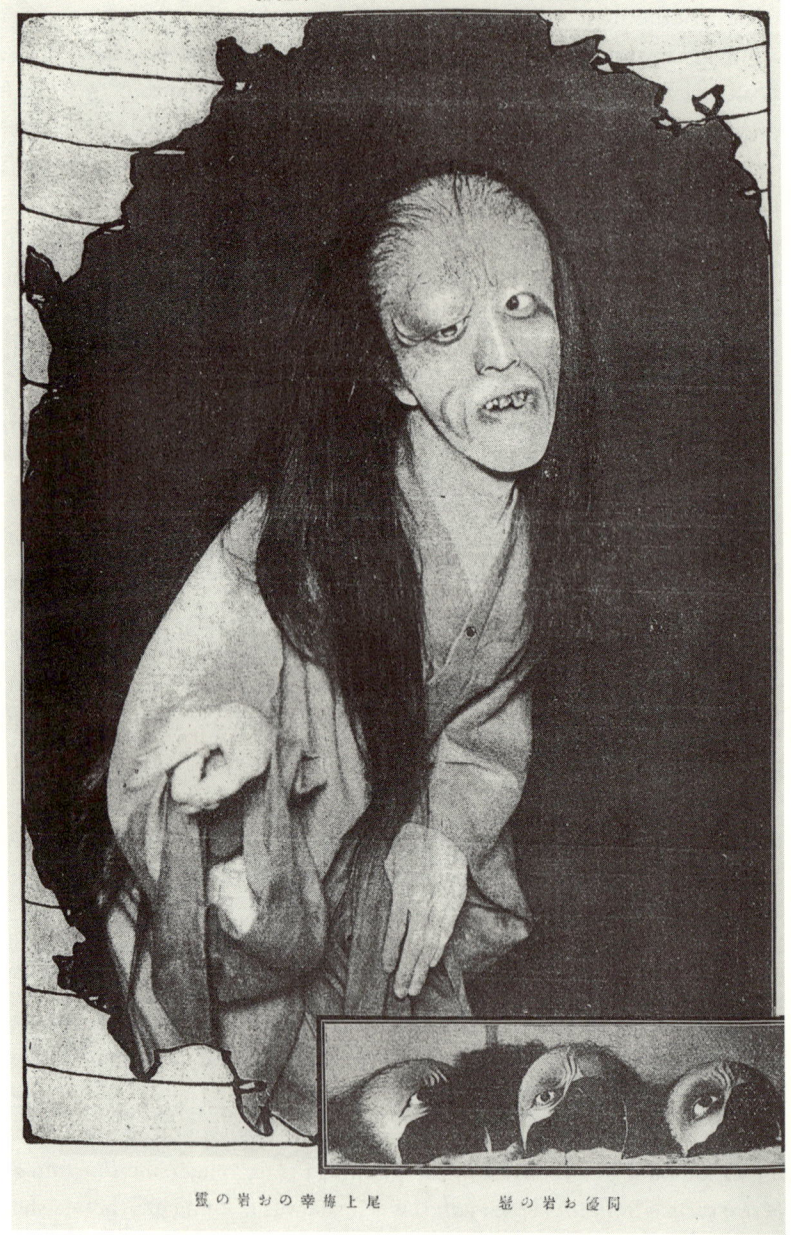

FIGURE 5.9 Onoe Baikō VI as Oiwa in the frontispiece to *Engei gahō* 3, no. 11 (1909). Judging from Enchi Fumiko's dates and photographs that were available in *Engei gahō* when she was a girl, this is most likely the photograph she saw. The three masks displayed in the inset are variations that Baikō used in different acts. (Courtesy of Waseda University Library, Tokyo)

period, he borrowed a German manual of skin diseases from a doctor friend and had a new mask fashioned, based on the illustrations.[86] And Enchi's experience was anything but unique: images of Oiwa as she would have appeared inside the theater, on stage, were able to circulate outside it, reproduced again and again. People in Japan and now around the world have continued to encounter Nanboku's Oiwa through novels, films, avant-garde theater, television dramas, "true story" specials, comic books, animated features, and translations—even, at the Moulin Rouge Shinjuku in 1937, in a musical revue that featured not one but seven "dancing Oiwas."[87]

The fact that *Yotsuya kaidan* has been preserved in textual form is a big part of what has enabled Oiwa to continue living like this—in so many different media—for almost two centuries, finding her way into new contexts and circulating freely in the visual field. She could be radically transformed precisely because the play script had acquired an aura of fixity and permanence. With the turn toward a literary mode of appreciating kabuki plays, critics came to perceive a need to establish the most "authentic" script of *Yotsuya kaidan* and to make it readily available in typeset, "readable" editions. In the 1920s, editors of the play began searching for the authentic *Yotsuya kaidan*, each claiming his source to be the original. Today, more than twenty critical editions of *Yotsuya kaidan* are available. These readable editions—works that can stand on their own as authoritative texts—turned the play into a cultural artifact that could be transplanted into other contexts, including modern media, and altered to suit new needs, always with the knowledge that the "original text" itself remained untouched.

The mediality of the readable script also generated new interpretations of the plot of *Yotsuya kaidan*. This is evident, for instance, in the perspective featured in Nakagawa Nobuo's film *Ghost Stories at Yotsuya* (*Tōkaidō Yotsuya kaidan*, 1959). The actor Amachi Shigeru, who played Iemon, reported in an interview that the director saw Naosuke as a Faust-like character and discussed their attempts to give psychological depth to Iemon's character.[88] This interest in Iemon was part of a general trend that characterized the reception of *Yotsuya kaidan* after the 1920s. In the original kabuki context, Iemon was certainly not depicted as a deeply thoughtful character. Not only does he casually murder Oiwa's father in order to get back together with Oiwa, but he abandons her without a second thought. He then goes on to nail her body to a door and takes pleasure in celebrating his wedding night with his new bride in the very room where Oiwa died earlier the same day. All this made perfect sense because Iemon was given meaning not by the structure of the play but by the Danjūrō lineage: the part was written for Ichikawa Danjūrō VII in accordance with the relatively new role type of the "erotic rogue" (*iroaku*), who was neither simply good-looking nor simply evil. The multiple lineages to which Danjūrō belonged, including that of his erotic rogue predecessors, gave the actor-as-Iemon a reason to be who he was on stage. In short, Iemon existed less in the script or even the plot than in an expansive space of theatrical memory that the audience shared. Once the play was taken out of its context and read as a text, once it began to be enacted by bodies with no connection to kabuki lineages and meanings, stage and film directors found themselves having to invent new explanations for why Iemon is who he is, a challenge that expanded the horizons of *Yotsuya kaidan*.

The text of *Yotsuya kaidan* also enabled the play to be taken up in the context of urban studies by literary scholars like Maeda Ai, who offered an analysis of the script as a "narrative," charting the urban topography in which it unfolds.[89] Only once *Yotsuya kaidan* had been detached from its performance history and given a fixed form and stable identity could it be absorbed into non-kabuki theatrical genres and used as material for literary interpretation. As I have shown, this fixing of the text became possible only through the discovery of Nanboku as an author and the broader circulation of his oeuvre through critical editions. Ishizawa Shūji, who wrote the script for a Shingeki production of *Yotsuya kaidan* in 1964 at the Haiyū Theater (Haiyū-za) and another at the National Theater (Kokuritsu Gekijō) in 1968, illustrated this point in the clearest possible manner. Noting that he based each of his two versions on Kawatake Shigetoshi's 1956 edition of *Yotsuya kaidan*, Ishizawa described his project in terms that explicitly dissociated the play from its original theatrical context: "It wasn't the kabuki play *Yotsuya kaidan* that I wanted to stage, it was Tsuruya Nanboku's *Yotsuya kaidan*."[90] Kabuki managed to survive the transition from early modern to modern only because at least some of its productions were amenable to such reinvention through the new medium of the text. *Yotsuya kaidan* proved to be particularly amenable to this sort of change. But the truth is that the productions that had formed the core of Edo kabuki—above all, the vast number of spring productions that kept building year after year on the *sekai* of the Soga brothers' revenge—were bound to fall by the wayside.

Thus the history of kabuki is not just a linear sequence of plays in chronological order, but is more accurately visualized as a current that flows both forward and backward, washing away traces of its previous existence as it goes. In that sense, this study has described a circular path, starting from the place where it ends. The very notion of "Tsuruya Nanboku's *Yotsuya kaidan*," which stands at the core of this book, is a product of the invention and canonization, beginning in the 1920s, both of Nanboku himself and of his most celebrated play, in each case through the medium of the printed script. Only by acknowledging this can we undertake a new exploration of the play and the broader history of Edo kabuki. We must remind ourselves that to some extent, the very idea of the play is an illusion; that we have access to only a fraction of the masses of printed materials that once gave form to Edo kabuki; that it was not scripts and authors who mattered but the audiences' memories of the theater, inscribed on the bodies of actors; that numerous kabuki productions never found their way into the world of text; and that in any event, individual productions were malleable and porous. Only then can we begin to understand what kabuki was, how it has changed, and how it has remained the same.

In the modern period, when the once young but now old city of Edo was reborn as Tokyo, the textualization of kabuki gradually enabled it, in its new guise as a classical form, to serve a function loosely analogous to the one it had performed in the early modern period, but for an ever larger and more diverse public. Tsuruya Nanboku IV and his plays, and kabuki in general, made Edo real and tangible as a safely, comfortably distant past—a time and place that could be claimed not only by the inhabitants of Tokyo but by all Japanese, in a modern world that, much like Edo, found itself greatly in need of a past that could be shared, that could fill the vacuum of the present. Kabuki was, we could say, reinvented as the embodiment of another, different form of history.

NOTES

INTRODUCTION

1. Kyokutei Bakin, *Niimaze no ki*. In *Nihon zuihitsu taisei*, dai ikki (Tokyo: Yoshikawa Kōbunkan, 1976), 21:495.

2. *Yanagitaru kenkyū* contains an early modern *senryū* that comments on the feeling that the smell of ink evoked in theater aficionados: "Playbills—the stronger the stench, more exciting the play" (*Yanagitaru kenkyū* [Tokyo: Yumani Shobō, 1982], 4:418). The accompanying explanation includes information about how ink was made. Kabuki fans liked the stench of the playbills, and when a playbill had a bad odor, it was said that the play would be a success, according to Okamoto Kidō, *Meiji gekidan Ranpu no moto nite*, afterword by Okamoto Keiichi (1935; repr., Tokyo: Iwanami Bunko, 1993), 62.

3. For more details about this print, see Satoko Shimazaki, "The Ghost of Oiwa in Actor Prints: Confronting Disfigurement," *Impressions* 29 (2008): 76–97.

4. Follow-up street playbill for *Tōkaidō Yotsuya kaidan*, performed at the Nakamura Theater (1825), Waseda University, Tsubouchi Memorial Theater Museum. The playbill's text is very ambiguous, and its interpretation has been debated.

5. Akama Ryō, "Kabuki no shuppanbutsu o yomu: Edo no jōen shisutemu, *Tōkaidō Yotsuya kaidan* no koto nado," in *Edo no shuppan*, ed. Nakano Mitsutoshi (Tokyo: Perikansha, 2005), 152–53.

6. J. L. Austin, *How to Do Things with Words*, 2nd ed., ed. J. O. Urmson and Marina Sbisà. (Cambridge, Mass.: Harvard University Press, 1975). I am influenced here by W. B. Worthen's analysis of "performance" in Austin and in reinterpretations of the concept by Jacques Derrida and Judith Butler, in *Shakespeare and the Force of Modern Performance* (Cambridge: Cambridge University Press, 2003), 1–27. Elin Diamond discusses the notion of performance as it is framed in texts by writers from J. L Austin to Judith Butler in

"Re: Blau, Butler, Beckett, and the Politics of Seeming," *Drama Review* 44, no. 4 (2000): 31–43.

7. Mimasuya Nisōji, *Kami kuzukago*, in *Zoku enseki jisshu*, ed. Iwamoto Kattōshi (Tokyo: Chūō Kōronsha, 1980), 3:91. This practice continued until theaters were moved to Saruwaka-machi in Asakusa, which was so remote that plays there had to begin much later.

8. Koike Shōtarō introduces some popular views of these early morning segments in *Kōshō Edo kabuki* (Tokyo: Miki Shobō, 1997), 62–65.

9. Furuido Hideo, "Ranjuku-ki no kabuki," in *Iwanami kōza Nihon bungakushi* (Tokyo: Iwanami Shoten, 1996), 10:101.

10. In contrast to the spring production, the summer and autumn productions usually concluded within the season.

11. Ihara Toshirō, *Kabuki nenpyō*, ed. Kawatake Shigetoshi and Yoshida Teruji (Tokyo: Iwanami Shoten, 1957), 2:6.

12. Roger Chartier, *Publishing Drama in Early Modern Europe* (London: British Library, 1999), 7.

13. Anthony Grafton, "How Revolutionary Was the Print Revolution?," Adrian Johns, "How to Acknowledge a Revolution," and Elizabeth L. Eisenstein, "An Unacknowledged Revolution Revisited," and "Reply, " collected as "AHR Forum," *American Historical Review* 107 no. 1 (2002): 84–128.

14. The history of print in Japan is traced in detail in Peter F. Kornicki, *The Book in Japan: A Cultural History from the Beginnings to the Nineteenth Century* (Honolulu: University of Hawai'i Press, 2000).

15. For a discussion of manuscripts in early modern culture, both private and public, see Peter F. Kornicki, "Manuscript, Not Print: Scribal Culture in the Edo Period," *Journal of Japanese Studies* 32, no. 1 (2006): 23–52.

16. Kobayashi Tadashi, *Edo no ukiyo-e* (Tokyo: Geika Shoin, 2009), 130.

17. There is a growing interest among literary scholars in integrating analyses of the visual and the textual. For Chinese literature, Robert E. Hegel explores the continuum of the arts and illustrated, printed books from the sixteenth to the nineteenth century in *Reading Illustrated Fiction in Late Imperial China* (Stanford, Calif.: Stanford University Press, 1998). More recently, Suzuki Jun and Ellis Tinios published *Understanding Japanese Woodblock-Printed Illustrated Books: A Short Introduction to Their History, Bibliography, and Format* (Leiden: Brill, 2013), a masterful introduction to print and book culture with a focus on illustration and visuality. Valuable contributions have also been made in specific areas and in relation to specific topics. Joshua S. Mostow explores the relationship of the visual to the textual in the early modern reception of Heian poetry in *Pictures of the Heart: The Hyakunin Isshu in Word and Image* (Honolulu: University of Hawai'i Press, 1996); Michael Emmerich includes a chapter on "image–text–book" relations in a work in the early modern genre known as the *gōkan* (combined booklets) in *The Tale of Genji: Translation, Canonization, and World Literature* (New York: Columbia University Press, 2013); and Adam Kern outlines the history of illustrated booklets in early modern Japan in *Manga from the Floating World: Comic Book Culture and the Kibyōshi of Edo Japan* (Cambridge, Mass.: Harvard University Press, 2006).

18. Cast and picture-book playbills usually took the form of a booklet made by folding in half and sewing together three leaves of *hanshi* paper (literally, "half size" paper, approximately 6.5 × 9 inches [16.5 × 23.5 cm]), each printed on both sides. The cast playbill was usually published after the street playbill, except in the case of spring performances.

19. Production of the picture-book playbill was supervised by the set designer (*ōdōgukata*) or the second or third playwright. See Kawatake Shigetoshi, *Kabuki sakusha no kenkyū* (Tokyo: Tōkyōdō, 1940), 388.

20. The concept of "twice-behaved behaviors" or "restored behavior" comes from Richard Schechner's framing of performativity as something that is already a reenactment, or a performance of another performance, in *Between Theater and Anthropology* (Philadelphia: University of Pennsylvania Press, 1985), and "Collective Reflexivity: Restoration of Behavior," in *A Crack in the Mirror: Reflexive Perspectives in Anthropology*, ed. Jay Ruby (Philadelphia: University of Pennsylvania Press, 1982), 39–81. They are both a repetition of meaning and a vehicle for new meaning.

21. These explorations include Julie Stone Peters, *Theater of the Book, 1480–1880: Print Text, and Performance in Europe* (Oxford: Oxford University Press, 2000); W. B. Worthen, *Print and the Poetics of Modern Drama* (Cambridge: Cambridge University Press, 2005); David Scott Kastan, *Shakespeare and the Book* (Cambridge: Cambridge University Press, 2001); and Zachery Lesser, *Renaissance Drama and the Politics of Publication: Reading in the English Book Trade* (Cambridge: Cambridge University Press, 2004).

22. Schechner, for instance, invokes nō drama in discussing performativity in "Collective Reflexivity," while Marvin Carlson uses it to think about memory and the function of "ghosting" in the theater in *The Haunted Stage: The Theater as Memory Machine* (Ann Arbor: University of Michigan Press, 2001).

23. Michel Foucault, "Two Lectures," in *Power/Knowledge: Selected Interviews and Other Writings, 1972–1977*, ed. Colin Gordon (New York: Pantheon Books, 1980), 82.

24. I have been inspired by Dwight Conquergood's articulation of the historical intervention that performance studies can make as a discipline dealing with subjugated forms of knowledge, in "Performance Studies: Intervention and Radical Research," *Drama Review* 46, no. 2 (2002): 145–56.

25. This approach is best represented by Donald H. Shively's influential "Bakufu Versus Kabuki," *Harvard Journal of Asiatic Studies* 18, nos. 3 and 4 (1955): 326–56. Our understanding of kabuki has been shaped largely by government edicts and plays whose scripts have survived. Even Eiko Ikegami's analysis in her excellent *Bonds of Civility: Aesthetic Networks and Political Origin of Japanese Culture* (Cambridge: Cambridge University Press, 2005) gives a misleadingly broad picture of kabuki by focusing on a selection of materials that conform with the subversive understanding of kabuki.

26. A few Japanese scholars have produced overarching histories of kabuki. For example, Ihara Toshirō's two-part history of early modern kabuki, *Nihon engekishi* (Tokyo: Waseda Daigaku Shuppanbu, 1904) and *Kinsei Nihon*

engekishi (Tokyo: Waseda Daigaku Shuppanbu, 1913), is organized around actors and their lineages. The focus on actors and acting patterns is important to Imao Tetsuya, *Kabuki no rekishi* (Tokyo: Iwanami Shoten, 2003); and Watanabe Tamotsu, *Edo engekishi*, 2 vols. (Tokyo: Kōdansha, 2009), which includes other early modern performance genres. Kabuki gakkai, ed., *Kabuki no rekishi: atarashii shiten to tenbō* (Tokyo: Yūzankaku Shuppan, 1998), a transcription of a panel discussion about different periods of kabuki; and Waseda Daigaku Engeki Hakubutsukan, ed., *Shibai-e ni miru Edo Meiji no kabuki* (Tokyo: Shōgakukan, 2003), which was written collaboratively by specialists in different fields, consider differences between kabuki in the Kamigata region and in Edo. Moriya Takeshi focuses on the development of legal systems and production structures in *Kinsei geinō kōgyōshi no kenkyū* (Tokyo: Kōbundō, 1985).

27. All extant scripts (as of 2003) predating the 1780s were included in the forty-five-volume *Kabuki daichō shūsei*. Most are from Kyoto and Osaka; scripts for only about ten titles have survived from Edo. See Mitsunobu Shinya, *Edo kabuki sakusha no kenkyū: Kanai Sanshō kara Tsuruya Nanboku e* (Tokyo: Kasama Shoin, 2012), 126.

28. Shively, "Bakufu Versus Kabuki," 326, 336.

29. Hirano Katsuya's study of early modern popular culture illustrates the pervasiveness of the notion that the government maintained "sustained control of the urban popular culture of Edo" by simply taking it for granted that early modern popular culture was heavily censored. He summarizes earlier scholarship as an opposition between notions of an "apolitical realm of escapist activity" and "facile concepts of 'cultural resistance'" that fail "to provide a cogent explanation of how and why putatively apolitical realms of play and pleasure or the dispersed cultural representations were a constant source of concern for the officials and intellectuals" (*The Politics of Dialogic Imagination: Power and Popular Culture in Early Modern Japan* [Chicago: University of Chicago Press, 2013], 3).

30. The casual, transhistorical use of *akusho* appears already in the Taishō-period writings of cultural historian Mitamura Engyo, such as "Nishiki-e no ōkubi," in *Mitamura Engyo zenshū* (Tokyo: Chūō Kōronsha, 1976), 12:157. The use of *akusho* in relation to power structures became common only after the publication of Hirosue's works, but it has since become a key metaphor for understanding early modern culture. *Edojidai zushi*, for instance, states that "the administrators perceived these two worlds [kabuki theaters and pleasure quarters] as evil places (*akubasho*)" (Akai Tatsurō and Nishiyama Matsunosuke, eds., *Edojidai zushi* [Tokyo: Chikuma Shobō, 1976], 5:32). This perspective has also exerted an influence on seminal English-language scholarship in the field. See, for instance, Haruo Shirane, ed., *Early Modern Japanese Literature: An Anthology, 1600–1900* (New York: Columbia University Press, 2002), 16, 21, 121; Gregory M. Pflugfelder, *Cartographies of Desire: Male-Male Sexuality in Japanese Discourse, 1600–1950* (Berkeley: University of California Press, 2007), 117; and C. Andrew Gerstle, *18th Century Japan: Culture and Society* (London: Routledge, 2000), 35.

31. It is telling that prewar dictionaries like *Daigenkai* (1932) do not even include kabuki in their definitions of *akusho* or *akujo*. See Ōtsuki Fumihiko, *Daigenkai* (Tokyo: Fuzanbō, 1954), 1:30. Nanboku's plays were adapted in the late 1960s and 1970s by Betsuyaku Minoru, Suzuki Tadashi, Ōta Shōgo, Ninagawa Yukio, and Kara Jūrō. For a history of the Nanboku boom in the 1970s, see Nakayama Mikio, *Nanboku josetsu: Tsuruya Nanboku kenkyū nyūmon* (Tokyo: Kōbundō Shuppansha, 1984), 45–51.

32. Carol Gluck, "The Invention of Edo," in *Mirror of Modernity: Invented Traditions of Modern Japan*, ed. Stephen Vlastos (Berkeley: University of California Press, 1998), 262–84.

33. Moriya Takeshi, *Genroku bunka: yugei, akusho, shibai* (Tokyo: Kōdansha, 2011), 68–115. Emoto Hiroshi, who surveyed Saikaku's works, also concludes that the usage is limited to the pleasure quarters, in "Shibai to yūri," in *Saikaku hikkei*, ed. Taniwaki Masachika, *Bessatsu kokubungaku* 45 (Tokyo: Gakutōsha, 1993), 88.

34. In Ihara Saikaku's *Kōshoku ichidai otoko*, Yonosuke asks, "Are we off to the *akusho* (the bad place) again?" (*Kōshoku ichidai otoko*, in *Ihara Saikaku shū*, ed. Teruoka Yasutaka, Shinpen Nihon koten bungaku zenshū 66 [Tokyo: Shōgakukan, 1996], 1:160). He is referring to the pleasure quarters. It is no coincidence that the allures and dangers of the pleasure quarters dominate both fictional and performative genres from this period. Kabuki plays from late-seventeenth-century Kamigata almost always featured a daimyo heir indulging himself in the pleasure quarters, neglecting his responsibilities and putting his entire household in jeopardy. Moriya pointed out that Chikamatsu's early-eighteenth-century love suicide plays, including such famous works as *Sonezaki shinjū* and *Shinjū ten no Amijima*, show young men from humble backgrounds succumbing to the same fate, falling for courtesans only to lose everything they have and come to a tragic end, as pointed out in Moriya, *Genroku bunka*, 85–86.

35. Torigoe Bunzō, "Shibai akusho no ron," *Ōkurayama bunka kaigi kenkyū nenpō* 5 (1994): 151–60. One of the earliest references to kabuki as an *akusho* appears in *Hetadangi chōmonshū* (1754): "Plays are called *kyōgen* (literally, 'crazy words') because they are like the words of a madman. Therefore, just as Yoshiwara is an evil place, so too kabuki theaters can be called *akusho*" (*Hetadangi chōmonshū*, in *Dangibonshū*, vol. 3, ed. Kashikawa Shūichi [Tokyo: Koten Bunko, 1999], 140).

36. The analysis of *kabuki-mono* as the origin of kabuki appears, for instance, in Ikegami, *Bonds of Civility*, 260–71. See also Donald H. Shively, "Popular Culture," in *Early Modern Japan*, ed. John Whitney Hall, vol. 4 of *The Cambridge History of Japan* (Cambridge: Cambridge University Press, 1991), 749.

37. Kabuki is still the most active theatrical form with a steady fan base: in addition to monthly productions in Tokyo at the Kabuki-za and Kokuritsu gekijō, plays are also staged every year at the Shinbashi enbujō, Kyoto's Minami-za, and Hakata's Hakata-za. There also are seasonal Cocoon productions, Asakusa kabuki in Tokyo, and Konpira kabuki.

38. Karatani Kōjin seems to assume that vanishing-point linear perspective was unknown in the early modern period, even though it was widely practiced, in *Nihon kindai bungaku no kigen* (Tokyo: Kōdansha, 1988), 191–95. The Maruyama shijō school in Kyoto developed a meticulous sketching practice, but even popular Edo ukiyo-e artists began working with *uki-e* (perspective prints) in the eighteenth century. The later Utagawa school artists, Hokusai, and others used more sophisticated types of perspective. While linear perspective was deployed in unorthodox ways, it was a standard method even among Edo artists. For literature on perspective in Edo prints, see Kishi Fumikazu, *Edo no enkinhō: ukie no shikaku* (Tokyo: Keisō Shobō, 1994); and Ōkubo Jun'ichi, *Hiroshige to ukiyo-e fūkeiga* (Tokyo: Tōkyō Daigaku Shuppankai, 2007).

39. Hachimonji Jishō, *Yakusha han'ei banashi: Edo* (Kyoto and Osaka: Hachimonijiya Hachizaemon and Kawachiya Tasuke, 1825), 23 *omote*–24 *ura*. At this point, Matsusuke had taken the acting name Shōroku.

40. Hattori Yukio, "Kaidan kyōgen no kuden to geidan," *Engekikai* 22, no. 8 (1964): 67–68.

41. Onoe Baikō VI, *Oyama no geidan* (Tokyo: Engeki Shuppansha, 1988), 46.

42. Mikhail M. Bakhtin, *Rabelais and His World*, trans. Hélène Iswolsky (Bloomington: Indiana University Press, 1984), 303–67, 368–436.

43. Ibid., 317.

44. For a discussion of the Tokugawa government's promotion of the Confucian relationships and especially the notion of filial piety, see Noriko Sugano, "State Indoctrination of Filial Piety in Tokugawa Japan: Sons and Daughters in the *Official Record of Filial Piety*," in *Women and Confucian Cultures in Premodern China, Korea, and Japan*, ed. Dorothy Ko, JaHyun Kim Haboush, and Joan Piggott (Berkeley: University of California Press, 2003), 170–92.

45. Ibid., 170.

46. Benedict Anderson, *Imagined Communities: Reflections on the Origin and Spread of Nationalism* (London: Verso, 1991).

47. This was also the case with *kamigata* actors, such as Nakamura Utaemon III (1778–1838), who visited Edo.

48. For details of Danjūrō VII, see Hattori Yukio, *Ichikawa Danjūrō daidai* (Tokyo: Kōdansha, 2002), 77–93. The government tried as much as possible to confine Edo kabuki and its actors to the theatrical quarters. For most of the early modern period, actors thus had to use the pretense of traveling to "take the waters" when leaving Edo to perform elsewhere. When Danjūrō V traveled to Kōfu to appear in a rural production staged at Kameya Yohei's playhouse in 1791—the first time any Danjūrō openly performed anywhere other than the official licensed theaters in Edo, Kyoto, and Osaka—his fans could hardly believe it. In the actor critique *Oedo no kazari ebi* (1792), one of the actor's fans exclaims, "Is it true that Ichikawa Danjūrō went on a trip? How can this be possible? They've always said that Mount Fuji, the Kannon in Asakusa, and Danjūrō are immobile!" In another actor critique, *Yakusha meishozue* (1792)—not to be confused with Bakin's book of the same title, published

in 1800—another fan, equally unable to fathom how Danjūrō could have left Edo, suggested that "the Danjūrō who starred in rural productions must have been either a spirit from an *ema* [a wooden tablet hung at a temple] or an actor print." For details, see Furuido Hideo, "Kinsei engeki to chihō," *Kokugo to kokubungaku* 64, no. 5 (1987): 109.

49. This idea is developed further in chapter 1. On the emergence of the licensed theaters as new venues to supplement or replace temple sites, see Ogasawara Kyōko, *Toshi to gekijō: chū-kinsei no chinkon, juraku, kenryoku* (Tokyo: Heibonsha, 1992), 139–43; and Hattori Yukio, *Ōinaru koya: Edo kabuki no shukusai kūkan* (Tokyo: Kōdansha, 2012), 34–68.

50. Tsubouchi Shōyō, *Shōyō gekidan* (Tokyo: Tenyūsha, 1919), 1–9.

51. Ibid., 3–4.

1. PRESENTING THE PAST

1. Sakurada Jisuke I, *Sukeroku yukari no Edozakura*, ed. Toita Yasuji, Meisaku kabuki zanshū (Tokyo: Tokyo Sōgensha, 1969), 18:158.

2. The love suicide, which records suggest occurred in the late seventeenth or early eighteenth century, was brought to the stage in Kamigata. Works based on the story include the puppet play *Ōsaka Sennichidera no shinjū* (1700) and the kabuki play *Sukeroku shinjū kamiko sugata* (1706). On the prehistory of the Edo version of Sukeroku, see Akama Ryō, "Sukeroku jitsu wa Soga Gorō no umareru made: Soga kyōgen jōenshi no kenkyū 1," *Geinō* 29 (1987): 8.

3. Barbara E. Thornbury, *Sukeroku's Double Identity: The Dramatic Structure of Edo Kabuki* (Ann Arbor: Center for Japanese Studies, University of Michigan, 1982), 73–74.

4. For a detailed treatment of the historical development of the Soga brothers' revenge in literary and performative genres, see Laurence R. Kominz, *Avatars of Vengeance: Japanese Drama and the Soga Literary Tradition* (Ann Arbor: Center of Japanese Studies, University of Michigan, 1995). The brothers were originally depicted in medieval military chronicles such as *Azuma kagami* (ca. 1300) and *The Tale of the Soga Brothers* (*Soga monogatari*, fourteenth century) and provided material for various oral and dramatic performances.

5. Michael Serres, with Bruno Latour, *Conversations on Science, Culture, and Time*, trans. Roxanne Lapidus (Ann Arbor, Michigan: University of Michigan Press, 1995), 58. Joseph Roach cites this passage in discussing "the deep eighteenth century" that haunts us today as "not merely a period of time, but a kind of time . . . experienced by its subjects as uneven developments and periodic returns" (*It* [Ann Arbor: University of Michigan Press, 2007], 13).

6. Serres and Latour, *Conversations*, 60.

7. The rich merchant Ōguchiya Jihei (also known as Ōguchiya Gyōu) took to walking around the Yoshiwara pleasure quarters dressed in imitation of Sukeroku's black costume. He was called "today's Sukeroku" (*ima Sukeroku*)

and booked the entire row of seats in the lower *sajiki* when Danjūrō performed Sukeroku for the third time at the Nakamura Theater. Jihei's craze for the role is noted in Mimasuya Nisōji, *Jūhachidai tsū*, in *Zoku enseki jisshu*, ed. Iwamoto Kattōshi (Tokyo: Chūō Kōronsha, 1980), 2:394.

8. Mikhail M. Bakhtin, "Forms of Time and of the Chronotope in the Novel," in *The Dialogic Imagination: Four Essays*, ed. Michael Holquist, trans. Caryl Emerson and Michael Holquist (Austin: University of Texas Press, 1981), 84.

9. Hattori Yukio, *Ōinaru koya: Edo kabuki no shukusai kūkan* (Tokyo: Kōdansha, 2012), 41–47. Matsuda Osamu has written about the association between water and utopia in the early modern visual field in "Esoragoto no Etsuraku no sono gensō," in *Nihon byōbue shūsei*, ed. Takeda Tsuneo (Tokyo: Kōdansha, 1977), 14:140. The folding screen is one of two in a set owned by the Idemitsu Museum of Art. It is thought to represent Edo during the late 1620s and 1630s. The screens are reproduced in Naitō Masato, *Edo meishozu byōbu: Ōedo gekijō no maku ga hiraku* (Tokyo: Shōgakukan, 2003).

10. Ogasawara Kyōko discusses the association of riverbanks with performance in *Toshi to gekijō: chū-kinsei no chinkon, yūraku, kenryoku* (Tokyo: Heibonsha, 1992), 88–135.

11. Steven Mullaney, *The Place of the Stage: License, Play, and Power in Renaissance England* (Ann Arbor: University of Michigan Press, 1995). Also see Steven Mullaney, "Civic Rites, City Sites: The Place of the Stage," in *Staging the Renaissance: Reinterpretations of Elizabethan and Jacobean Drama*, ed. David Scott Kastan and Peter Stallybrass (London: Routledge, 1991), 17–26.

12. The government put the theaters in Fukiyachō, Kobikichō, and other locations. On the theaters' early movements, see Ogasawara, *Toshi to gekijō*.

13. For a description and introduction of relevant sources, see Moriya Takeshi, *Kinsei geinō kōgyōshi no kenkyū* (Tokyo: Kōbundō, 1985), 169–70.

14. Yoshida Setsuko, ed., *Edo kabuki hōrei shūsei* (Tokyo: Ōfūsha, 1989), 36. Hato Yoshiaki treats this visit to Edo Castle in some detail in "Genroku kabuki no hatten to sono shūen," in *Kabuki no sekai, bi to aku no gekikūkan*, ed. Ogasawara Kyōko (Tokyo: Yūseidō Shuppan, 1988), 34.

15. Although kabuki developed into a multiact form, the acts were much more loosely strung together in Edo than in Kamigata. In the seventeenth century, kabuki theaters in Edo tended to bring in a new audience after each act, according to Torigoe Bunzō, *Genroku kabuki kō* (Tokyo: Yagi Shoten, 1991), 294–95. During most of the seventeenth century, some actors such as Ichikawa Danjūrō I also served as playwrights; professional playwrights emerged gradually over the course of the early eighteenth century. One of the earliest professional kabuki playwrights in Edo was Tsuuchi Jihei (d. ca. 1710s). For a historical overview of kabuki playwriting, see Katherine Saltzman-Li, *Creating Kabuki Plays: Context for Kezairoku, "Valuable Notes on Playwriting"* (Leiden: Brill, 2010).

16. Hachimonji Jishō, *Yarō sekisumō*, in *Kabuki hyōbanki shūsei*, ed. Kabuki hyōbanki kenkyūkai (Tokyo: Iwanami Shoten, 1972), 1:549.

17. Hachimonji Jishō, *Yakusha zensho*, in *Nihon shomin bunka shiryō shūsei*, ed. Geinōshi Kenkyūkai (Tokyo: San'ichi Shobō, 1973), 6:203.

18. Yokoyama Shigeru, ed., *Kokyōgaeri no Edo-banashi*, Kinsei bungaku shiryō ruijū: koban chishihen 10 (Tokyo: Benseisha, 1980), 316–26.

19. An edict published in the twelfth month of 1661 banned kabuki productions outside Sakai-chō, Kobiki-chō, and Fukiya-chō. See *Ofuregaki kanpō shūsei*, in *Edo kabuki hōrei shūsei*, ed. Yoshida, 49.

20. The licenses were given to the four theaters in the 1650s. See Waseda Daigaku Engeki Hakubutsukan, ed., *Shibai-e ni miru Edo Meiji no kabuki* (Tokyo: Shōgakukan, 2003), 44. By the 1660s and 1670s, all four theaters regularly staged plays.

21. For a discussion of temple productions and small theaters see Moriya, *Kinsei geinō kōgyōshi no kenkyū*, 174–77; and Ogasawara, *Toshi to gekijō*, 142. Exceptions seem to have been made for important temple venues such as the Yushima Shrine, according to Satō Katsura, *Kabuki no bakumatsu Meiji: koshibai no jidai* (Tokyo: Perikansha, 2010), 18–40. In fact, there is some evidence to suggest that the major actors may have appeared in certain productions at the Yushima Shrine during periods of governmental reform and the financial decline of the major theaters. According to *Gekijō zue*, a Meiji-period guide to theater, temple sites were able to avoid certain censors because they were controlled by a different office (*jisha bugyō*) from those that regulated the theaters. See *Gekijō zue, Sejigahō* 1, no. 8 (Tokyo: Sejigahōsha, 1898), 8.

22. For details of the correspondence between stage productions with temple ceremonies in Kamigata and Edo, see Gunji Masakatsu, *Kabuki no hassō* (Tokyo: Meicho Kankōkai, 1978), 165–85. This sort of collaboration between theaters and temples was prominent in the case of puppet theater productions. On this topic, see Hirata Sumiko, "Chikamatsu jōruri to shomin shinkō," *Gengo to bungaku* 83 (1976): 71–94.

23. Kyoto and Osaka had a strong continuity between the licensed and the small theaters, however. Small theaters called *chūu shibai* and *kodomo shibai* were basically a training ground for young actors. In some exceptional cases in Edo, small-theater actors appeared in major theaters, and major actors performed in small theaters.

24. For details of Danzaemon and his involvement in the larger world of performance in early modern society, see Yoshida Nobuyuki, *Mibunteki shūen to shakai bunka kōzō* (Kyoto: Buraku Mondai Kenkyūjo, 2003). On commercial structures of performances outside Edo in early modern Japan, see Kanda Yutsuki, *Kinsei geinō kōgyō to chiiki shakai* (Tokyo: Tōkyō Daigaku Shuppan, 1999). Exceptions to this rule appear in a 1842 document that excludes the three major temple theaters at Shiba Jinmei, Ichigaya Hachiman, and Yushima Tenjin from Danzaemon's rule until 1844, as discussed in Yoshida Nobuyuki, "Geinō to mibunteki shūsen: kotsujiki kagushi o rei toshite," *Buraku mondai kenkyū* 132 (1995): 90. Satō Katsura discusses the changes in legal restrictions placed on temple theater productions in the 1840s in *Kabuki no bakumatsu Meiji*, 28.

25. Moriya, *Kinsei geinō kōgyōshi no kenkyū*, 216. In Kyoto and Osaka, performance rights were divided among *nadai*, who had the rights for the production; *zamoto*, who organized the actors; and *shibainushi*, who owned

the theater building. *Nadai* was the only inherited position. In Edo, all three rights were concentrated in the *zamoto*. Hayashi Kimiko analyzed the gradual concentration of all authority on the theater managers in Edo in "Edo no zamoto," in *Kabuki no Sekai, bi to aku no geki kūkan*, ed. Ogasawara Kyōko (Tokyo: Yuseidō Shuppan, 1988), 224–44.

26. In accordance with a 1669 edict regarding employment, most contracts began on the fifth day of the third month. See Ōkura-shō, ed., *Nihon zaisei keizai shiryō* (Tokyo: Zaisei Keizai Gakkai, 1922), 3:1101. Kabuki was an exception to this rule. The annual contract seems to have existed earlier, judging from references to face-showing productions that appear in documents from the 1660s. See Moriya, *Kinsei geinō kōgyōshi no kenkyū*, 217.

27. This text is introduced in Morishima Chūryō, *Sunkin zattetsu*, in *Nihon zuihitsu taisei*, dai ikki (Tokyo: Yoshikawa Kōbunkan, 1982), 7:180–82. Sample legal documents are also found in Nakamura Jūsuke, *Shibai noriai banashi*, in *Nihon shomin bunka shiryō shūsei*, ed. Geinōshi Kenkyūkai (Tokyo: San'ichi Shobō, 1973), 6:274–75; and *Gekijō shinwa*, in *Enseki jisshu*, ed. Iwamoto Kattōshi (Tokyo: Chūō Kōronsha, 1979), 4:12. The documents in these other sources take roughly the same form.

28. Records show that there were exceptions, however. After the An'ei–Tenmei period, actors became more mobile. See Furuido Hideo, *Kabuki: toikake no bungaku* (Tokyo: Perikansha, 1998), 62.

29. Ayame's and Danjūrō's salaries are introduced in Katō Eibian (Genki), *Waga koromo*, in *Enseki jisshu*, ed. Iwamoto Kattōshi (Tokyo: Chūō Kōronsha, 1979), 1:167. Toward the end of the early modern period, it became fairly common for star actors to earn more than 1,000 *ryō*, and their salaries were made public on special, poster-size bills. The exception was when theater managers were able to conceal their salaries during financial difficulties.

30. Moriya, *Kinsei geinō kōgyōshi no kenkyū*, 249–51. According to Moriya, theater managers in Kyoto and Osaka had to pay to borrow the right to actually produce a play, even in licensed venues. In both Edo and Kamigata, theater managers had to find investors (*ginshu* or *kinshu*) to acquire enough funds to stage their productions during the year.

31. The content of this text is recorded, with some variation, in a number of sources. See Tatekawa Enba, *Sanza ie kyōgen narabi ni yuishogaki*, in *Enseki jisshu*, ed. Iwamoto Kattōshi (Tokyo: Chūō Kōronsha, 1979), 4:281–82; and Yoshida, ed., *Edo kabuki hōrei shūsei*, 162–65.

32. On the role of *yuisho* in the early modern period in the production of vested rights among various social groups, see Kurushima Hiroshi and Yoshida Nobuyuki, eds., *Kinsei no shakai shūdan: yuisho to gensetsu* (Tokyo: Yamakawa Shuppansha, 1995). For an overview of the historiography of *yuisho*, see Yamamoto Eiji, "Nihon chūkinseishi ni okeru yuisho-ron no sōkatsu to tenbō," in *Yuisho no hikakushi*, ed. Rekishigaku Kenkyūkai (Tokyo: Aoki Shoten, 2010), 3–27.

33. Furuido, *Kabuki: toikake no bungaku*, 59.

34. Hato, "Genroku kabuki no hatten to sono shūen," 35.

35. Cited in Sekine Shisei, *Tōto gekijō enkakushi*, in *Edo kabuki hōrei shūsei*, ed. Yoshida, 181. Moriya mentions three other theaters aside from his

own because he is including the now defunct Yamamura Theater, managed by Yamamura Chōdayū.

36. Cited from Sekine Shisei, *Tōto gekijō enkakushi*, in *Edo kabuki hōrei shūsei*, ed. Yoshida, 185. This episode is also cited in Ihara Toshirō [Seisei'en], *Kabuki nenpyō*, ed. Kawatake Shigetoshi and Yoshida Teruji (Tokyo: Iwanami Shoten, 1957), 2:221. My attention was drawn to this quotation by Furuido, *Kabuki: toikake no bungaku*, 59.

37. Yoshida, ed., *Edo kabuki hōrei shūsei*, 241–54; *Zoku Edo kabuki hōrei shūsei* (Tokyo: Ōfūsha, 1997), 177–87.

38. For details on the requests and the response, see Ihara Toshirō [Seisei'en], *Kabuki nenpyō*, ed. Kawatake Shigetoshi and Yoshida Teruji (Tokyo: Iwanami Shoten, 1960), 5:176–82.

39. This incident is explained in detail in Donald H. Shively, "The Social Environment of Tokugawa Kabuki," in *Studies in Kabuki: Its Acting, Music, and Historical Context*, ed. James R. Brandon, William P. Malm, and Donald H. Shively (Honolulu: University of Hawai'i Press, 1978), 29–36.

40. Motojima Chishin, *Getsudō kenmonshū*, in *Kinsei fūzoku kenbunshū* (Tokyo: Kokusho Kankōkai, 1912), 1:363.

41. Nagashima Imashirō and Ōta Yoshio, *Chiyodajō ōoku* (Tokyo: Chōya Shinbunsha, 1892), 72–76, 89. The author cites possibly exaggerated descriptions of the incident from an unknown source and adds his comments.

42. Ibid., 89–94. The rather novelistic depiction of the banquet Ejima and the women had at the theater, which appears in *Chiyodajō ōoku*, may include a certain amount of exaggeration, but it captures an interpretation of the incident. The contours of the incident coincide with descriptions in *Tokugawa jikki*, *Kojiruien*, and many other accounts, in *Edo kabuki hōrei shūsei*, ed. Yoshida, 120–37.

43. Ihara Toshirō, *Nihon engekishi* (Tokyo: Waseda Daigaku Shuppanbu, 1904), 444. Also see Moriya, *Kinsei geinō kōgyōshi no kenkyū*, 174–77. The incident resulted in the temporary simplification of theater architecture, with the curtains taken away from the *sajiki* boxes and the passages connecting the *sajiki* to private rooms being banned, according to Shihōshō Shomuka, ed., *Tokugawa kinreikō* (Tokyo: Kyōeki Shōsha Shoten, 1894), 5:697–98.

44. For a discussion of *yagura* and the imitation of *buke* architecture see Hattori, *Ōinaru koya*, 69–82.

45. Suwa Haruo, "Geinō no ba: yagura no keisei," *Bungaku* 55, no. 2 (1987): 47. On the symbolic meaning of *yagura* in earlier temple and shrine productions, where they were meant to fend off evil spirits, see Ogasawara, *Toshi to gekijō*, 20.

46. James L. McClain, John M. Merriman, and Kaoru Ugawa, *Edo and Paris: Urban Life and the State in the Early Modern Era* (Ithaca, N.Y.: Cornell University Press, 1997), 13. The population of Edo included many men of samurai status, according to Nishiyama Matsunosuke and Haga Tōru, *Edo sanbyakunen* (Tokyo: Kōdansha, 1975), 1:8, 42–43, 197–98.

47. Naitō Akira, *Edo to Edojō* (Tokyo: Kajima Shuppankai, 1966), 133.

48. For an analysis of Moronobu's theater prints see Matsuba Ryōko, "Edo no gekijōzu: Hishikawa-ha o chūshin ni," in *Fūzoku kaiga no bunkagaku:*

toshi o utsusu media, ed. Matsumoto Ikuyo and Idemitsu Sachiko (Kyoto: Shibunkaku Shuppan, 2009), 211–42.

49. *Yamato no kami nikki, Tottori Ikeda-han geinō shiryō, Nichijō shōnin nikki, Moriyama nikki*, and many other records include detailed information about kabuki performances at daimyo residences. For recent studies on kabuki at upper-ranking samurai and daimyo residences in Edo, see Takei Kyōzō, *Wakashu kabuki yarō kabuki no kenkyū* (Tokyo: Yagi Shoten, 2000), 307–38; Hayashi Kimiko, "Yashikikata ni okeru kabuki jōen o megutte," in *Kabuki jōruri*, ed. Suwa Haruo (Tokyo: Kokusho Kankōkai, 1993), and "Daimyo yashiki ni okeru kabuki," in *Kabuki no rekishi I*, ed. Torigoe Bunzō, Uchiyama Mikiko, and Watanabe Tamotsu, Iwanami kōza kabuki bunraku 2 (Tokyo: Iwanami Shoten, 1997); and Suzuki Hiroko, "Kyōhōki Edo kabuki ni okeru yashikikata to shibaimachi no ichiyōsō: Kaga hantei jōen kiroku o chūshin ni," *Geinōshi kenkyū* 174 (2006): 24–40.

50. According to Gunji Masakatsu, *Tōshōgū gojikki* depicts Hideyoshi's troupes enjoying nō performances during the day and performances of singing and dancing at night, the latter enjoyment accompanied by drink. A similar distinction applies to nō and kabuki in the early seventeenth century. See *Gunji Masakatsu santei shū* (Tokyo: Hakusuisha, 1991), 1:115–16.

51. Torigoe Bunzō wrote that this changed with the decline of daimyo finances during the Genroku period. See Kabuki Gakkai, ed., *Kabuki no rekishi: atarashii shiten to tenbō* (Tokyo: Yūzankaku Shuppan, 1998), 21.

52. Hayashi, "Daimyo yashiki ni okeru kabuki," 219.

53. Takei, *Wakashu kabuki yarō kabuki no kenkyū*, 320. Takei noted that Matsudaira Yamato no Kami staged kabuki plays four times and puppet plays once at his residence in one year, from 1679 to 1680, and that Ikeda Mitsunaka staged both kabuki plays and puppet plays five times from 1675 to 1676.

54. Takei, *Wakashu kabuki yarō kabuki no kenkyū*, 328–30.

55. Matsuzaki Hitoshi, "Kabuki no kankyaku," *Kokubungaku kaishaku to kyōzai no kenkyū* 37, no. 6 (1992): 43.

56. Namiki Gohei's *Haikai tsūgen*, which compares the pleasure quarters of the three cities, includes entries for different kinds of *kamuro* (child attendants), ranging from pairs of girls to boy attendants, all of whom were unique to the Yoshiwara district in Edo. In Edo, customer–courtesan relationships also were governed by their own characteristic procedures and described by special terms. A customer and a courtesan had a "first meeting" (*shokai*), then exchanged "secret promises" (*ura yakusoku*), and finally, only at their "third meeting" (*sankaime*), became physically involved, according to Namiki Gohei, *Haikai tsūgen* (Edo: Seiundō, 1809), 3 *ura*, 25 *omote*.

57. See, for example, Komatsu Kazuhiko, *Shutendōji no kubi* (Tokyo: Serika Shobō, 1997); Minobe Shigekatsu and Minobe Tomoko, *Shutendōji-e o yomu: matsurowanu mono no jikuū* (Tokyo: Miyai Shobō, 2009); and Irene H. Lin, "The Ideology of Imagination: The Tale of Shutendōji as a Kenmon Discourse," *Cahiers d'Extrême-Asie* 13 (2002): 379–410.

58. John Whitney Hall, "The *Bakuhan* System," in *Early Modern Japan*, vol. 4 of *The Cambridge History of Japan*, ed. John Whitney Hall (Cambridge: Cambridge University Press, 1991), 130–34.

59. Even the limited records that have survived from the main theaters show how important this play was in the seventeenth century. For information on productions involving Shutendōji, Kinpira, or the four guardians, see Ihara Toshirō, *Kabuki nenpyō*, ed. Kawatake Shigetoshi and Yoshida Teruji (Tokyo: Iwanami Shoten, 1956), 1:53, 95, 99, 115, 151, 157, 174, 177, 193, 203.

60. For a comprehensive outline and discussion of the cultural meaning of Kinpira puppet plays, see Janice Kanemitsu, "Guts and Tears: Kinpira Jōruri and Its Textual Transformations," in *Publishing the Stage: Print and Performance in Early Modern Japan*, ed. Keller Kimbrough and Satoko Shimazaki (Boulder: University of Colorado Center for Asian Studies, 2011), 15–35. Kinpira jōruri had wide appeal and quickly caught on in Kyoto and Osaka as well.

61. This structure is detailed in ibid., 25–30. Kamakura Keiko also found that compared with earlier jōruri, Kinpira plays tend to focus on public battles aimed at restoring peace to a much larger community, as discussed in Ogasawara Kyōko and Kamakura Keiko, "Engeki no kōryū," in *Iwanami kōza Nihon bungakushi* (Tokyo: Iwanashi Shoten, 1996), 7:70.

62. Akimoto Suzushi, "Kinpira jōruri seiritsu no kiban: Meireki Manjigoro no rensakumono no jōruri," *Gobun* 43 (1984): 25–26.

63. Yokoyama Shigeru, ed., *Kokyōgaeri no Edo-banashi*, 313.

64. *Kantō kekki monogatari*, in *Kyōkaku zenden*, ed. Tsukahara Jūshi'en (Tokyo: Hakubunkan, 1913), 14.

65. Satō Eri, "Genroku-ki Edo kabuki no seikaku: ōgiri no shinreigoto ni okeru oni no sonzai," *Engekigaku* 25 (1984): 116. A general sense of the content of plays during this period can be gleaned from the abundant secondary publications of the time, including illustrated prompt books (*eiri kyōgenbon*), actor critiques, books of actors' lines (*serifu shōhon*), musical scripts (*usumono shōhon*), as well as various types of playbills, actor prints, and books published and sold to provide entertainment offstage.

66. According to Torigoe Bunzō, there were thirty-eight different acting styles in Genroku kabuki; Mutō Junko, who surveyed actor critiques, found eighty-seven entries. See Mutō Junko, "Aragoto kō: genroku kabuki o chūshin ni shite," *Musashi daigaku jinbun gakkai zasshi* 16, no. 2 (1984): 117.

67. Satō Eri, "Aragoto to kinpira jōruri no ningyō gei: sono jiban," *Bungaku* 55, no. 4 (1984): 250–68.

68. Kinjinsai Shin'ō, *Kokon yakusha rongo sakigake*, in *Kinsei geidōron*, ed. Nishiyama Matsunosuke (Tokyo: Iwanami Shoten, 1972), 484. While in contemporary times the *aragoto* style is tied to the Danjūrō lineage, it was first cultivated even earlier by a line of Edo actors, such as Murayama Heijūrō and Nakamura Denkurō, who staged "performances depicting wild warriors" (*aramusha-goto*).

69. Nyūgatei Ganyū (Namiki Shōza II), *Sakusha shikihō kezairoku*, in *Kinsei geidōron*, ed. Nishiyama Matsunosuke, Watanabe Ichirō, and Gunji Masakatsu (Tokyo: Iwanami Shoten, 1972), 511. A translation of *Kezairoku* is included in Saltzman-Li, *Creating Kabuki Plays*, 168–226.

70. Gunji noted the connections between the *oie sōdō* plot pattern and the society of the time in *Gunji Masakatsu santei shū*, 1:157.

71. C. Andrew Gerstle, *Circles of Fantasy: Convention in the Plays of Chikamatsu* (Cambridge, Mass.: Harvard University Asia Center, 1995), 63.

72. Iterations of the story of the four guardians and their symbolic defeat of a demon are seen in many Edo kabuki plays. In *Nagoya Sanza's Meeting with the Courtesan* (*Sankai Nagoya*, 1697), Shōki—a guardian spirit from Tang-dynasty China, played by Danjūrō—kills the evil spirit of Dazainojō. At the end of the play, Shōki reveals his true identity as a guardian of the Buddha who has come to restore peace, while Dazainojō turns out to be the spirit of the historical Kusunoki Masashige, a legendary warrior who died in vain fighting to seize power from the Ashikaga shogunate (also descended from a different branch of the Seiwa Genji line) and restore it to Emperor GoDaigo. Ichikawa Danjūrō, who was associated with Fudō Myō-ō (Acala in Sanskrit) and other deities, often performed such heroic roles. While the antagonists are often referred to as resentful spirits (*onryō*), they tend to be depicted in prompt books with a horn of the sort that characterizes *oni* (demons). In the prompt book for *Nagoya Sanza's Meeting with the Courtesan*, as well, Dazainojō is depicted as a demon. A transcription of the prompt book for *Sankai Nagoya* appears in Takano Tatsuyuki and Kuroki Kanzō, *Genroku kabuki kessaku shū* (Tokyo: Waseda Daigaku Shuppanbu, 1925), 1:19–54.

73. Gunji Masakatsu, *Kabuki yōshiki to denshō* (Tokyo: Chikuma Shobō, 2005), 15–32.

74. For details on other characters from different *sekai* in *Wait a Minute!* see Furuido Hideo, "Kabuki no haru," *Kokubungaku* 52, no. 1 (2007): 27 28.

75. *Yakusha nichojamisen: Edo*, in *Kabuki hyōbanki shūsei*, ed. Kabuki Hyōbanki Kenkyūkai (Tokyo: Iwanami Shoten, 1973), 3:219. This passage is also cited in Satō Eri, "Genroku kabuki: Edo," in *Kabuki no rekishi I*, ed. Torigoe Bunzō, Uchiyama Mikiko, and Watanabe Tamotsu, Iwanami kōza kabuki bunraku 2 (Tokyo: Iwanami Shoten, 1997), 81.

76. Furuido, *Kabuki: toikake no bungaku*, 15–16.

77. An awareness of *sekai* and *shukō* emerged during the Kyōhō era (1716–1736), although the terms were not yet fixed. The ritual of *sekai sadame* was established much earlier. For a discussion of this, see Kabuki Gakkai, ed., *Kabuki no rekishi: atarashii shiten to tenbō*, 149–52.

78. Nyūgatei Ganyū, *Sakusha shikihō kezairoku*, 511–12.

79. Saltzman-Li, *Creating Kabuki Plays*, 132. Also see Gunji Masakatsu, "Kabuki no sekai kōzō ni tsuite," *Geinōshi kenkyū* 87 (1984): 1–8.

80. Nyūgatei Ganyū, *Sakusha shikihō kezairoku*, 531.

81. Gachikuken, *Hetadangi chōmonshū*, in *Dangibonshū*, vol. 3, ed. Kashikawa Shūichi [Tokyo: Koten Bunko, 1999], 140.

82. Mitsunobu Shinya, *Edo kabuki sakusha no kenkyū: Kanai Sanshō kara Tsuruya Nanboku e* (Tokyo: Kasama Shoin, 2012), 12.

83. There also are categories of *sekai* for ancient times, contemporary plays, chivalrous male parts, and religious and ceremonial categories. These entries tend to be much less significant, containing fewer characters than those listed under historical categories. See Kokuritsu Gekijō Geinō Chōsashitsu, ed., *Sekai kōmoku*, in *Kyōgen sakusha shiryōshū* (Tokyo: Kokuritsu Gekijō Chōsa Yōseibu Geinō Chōsashitsu, 1976), 1:1–84.

84. Gunji, *Gunji Masakatsu santei shū*, 1:51–52.

85. Mimasuya Nisōji, *Sakusha nenjū gyōji*, in *Nihon shomin bunka shiryō shūsei*, ed. Geinōshi kenkyūkai (Tokyo: San'ichi Shobō, 1973), 6:680.

86. For a discussion of historical variations on this act, see Kagami Kimiko, "Oniō hinka no ba no keisei to hensen: Edo kabuki ni okeru Soga kyōgen no ichi," *Geinōshi kenkyū* 143 (2008): 33–49.

87. Furuido, "Kabuki no haru," 29.

88. It is telling that Nakamura Yukihiko applies the theatrical notions of *sekai* and *shukō* to the understanding of popular literature in *Gesakuron* (Tokyo: Kadokawa Shoten, 1966), 170–213.

89. Haruo Shirane discusses the introduction of vertical and horizontal plots in the *haikai* treatise *Uda no hōshi* by Morikawa Kyoriku, one of Bashō's disciples, in *Japan and the Culture of the Four Seasons: Nature, Literature, and the Arts* (New York: Columbia University Press, 2012), 178. The poet Kikaku identifies the vertical as the set topic (*hondai*) and horizontal as the twist (*haikai*), in *Kukyōdai*, in *Takarai Kikaku zenshū*, hencho hen, ed. Ishikawa Hachirō (Tokyo: Benseisha, 1994), 227.

90. Gunji Masakatsu also noted a similarity between kabuki playmaking and *honkadori* in the way they celebrate the present while simultaneously evoking an origin, in "Gikyoku no hassō," in *Gunji Masakatsu santei shū* (Tokyo: Hakusuisha, 1991), 2:67. Nakamura Yukihiko discusses the essentially communal nature of early modern cultural production in *Gesakuron*, 169.

91. Hattori Yukio, *Kabuki no kōzō: dentō engeki no sōzō seishin* (Tokyo: Chūō Kōronsha, 1970), 204–7.

92. Furuido Hideo, *Edo kabukishū*, ed. Furuido Hideo, Torigoe Bunzō, and Wada Osamu, Shin Nihon koten bungaku taikei 96 (Tokyo: Iwanami Shoten, 1997), 414n.4. In Kamigata, the three-segment structure was customary.

93. The organic nature of the four-segment production—which moves from the presentation of evil characters who disturb the established order to a *michiyuki*, to scenes in the pleasure quarters, to the sacrifice of a child by a parent, and finally ends with the restoration of peace—is discussed in Nishizawa Ippō, *Denki sakusho*, in *Shin gunsho ruijū* (Tokyo: Kokusho Kankōkai, 1906), 1:17–18.

94. For an explanation of the production style and an example of a mid-eighteenth-century play that was staged in all four parts, see Satō Chino, "Edo kabuki no kōgyō to kyōgen," *Kinsei bungei* 69 (1999): 11–24.

95. Ibid., 22–23.

96. Tamenaga Itchō, *Kabuki jishi*, in *Kabuki sōsho*, ed. Kinkōdō Henshūbu (Tokyo: Kinkōdō Shoseki, 1910), 222.

97. See, for instance, Hattori Yukio, *Edo kabuki no biishiki* (Tokyo: Heibonsha, 1996), 237–38.

98. Thornbury discusses the calendar from the audience's perspective in *Sukeroku's Double Identity*, 3–15, while Saltzman-Li discusses it from the point of view of the playwright in *Creating Kabuki Plays*, 53–69. Thornbury abbreviates the third-month and fifth-month productions, which are part of the long spring production, and also focuses exclusively on Edo. There are some differences in the two accounts based on the sources used.

99. Face-showing playbills came to be regularly published by the late seventeenth century in all three cities. See Akama Ryō, "Kabuki no shuppanbutsu I," in *Kabuki bunka no shosō*, vol. 4 of *Iwanami kōza kabuki*, ed. Torigoe Bunzō, Uchiyama Mikiko, and Watanabe Tamotsu (Tokyo: Iwanami Shoten, 1998), 7. They were published around the tenth of the month, according to Nakamura Jūsuke, *Shibai noriai banashi*, 275. During the nineteenth century, the date of publication was pushed further back. For example, Mimasuya Nisōji states that the playbills originally came out around the nineteenth, though he also gives the date as the thirteenth, in *Gakuya suzume*, in *Nihon shomin bunka shiryō shūsei*, ed. Geinōshi Kenkyūkai (Tokyo: San'ichi Shobō, 1973), 6:647.

100. *Gekijō shinwa*, in *Enseki jisshu*, ed. Iwamoto Kattōshi (Tokyo: Chūō Kōronsha, 1979), 4:12.

101. Furuido writes that wealthy attendants at daimyo houses would pool their money to purchase the playbill. The price of the playbill is based on a crazy verse that says: "In one day, the cost goes from one *bu* to twelve *mon*" (Furuido, *Kabuki: toikake no bungaku*, 28). The *senryū* appears in Goryōken Kayū, ed., *Yanagitaru* (Edo: Hanaki Kyūjirō), fascicle 40, 12 *ura*.

102. Nakamura Jūsuke, *Shibai noriai banashi*, 276.

103. Hattori Yukio, *Kabuki no kōzō* (Tokyo: Chūō Kōronsha, 1970), 70–71. Typically this occurred on the twenty-fifth day of the tenth month.

104. Nakamura Jūsuke, *Shibai noriai banashi*, 276.

105. Different sources identify the origin of the celebration to the long run of either *Otokodate hatsugai Soga*, staged at the Nakamura Theater in 1753, or *Umewakana futaba Soga*, staged in 1756 at the Ichimura Theater. See, for instance, Hachimonji Jishō, *Yakusha zensho*, 227. For a discussion of the Soga story and its reception in kabuki, including the origin of the long spring production, see Satō Chino, "The Performing Arts Connecting the Dead with the Living: In the Case of 'Soga Legends,'" *Bulletin of Death and Life Studies* 7 (2011): 243–64. While this plot structure continued to be used into the 1880s, it became increasingly difficult to maintain interest in the Soga story through the fifth month. According to Nakamura Jūsuke, the period from the New Year production through the fifth month had always been devoted to Soga plays in the past, "but depending on the cast, this is not always the case anymore" (*Shibai noriai banashi*, 273). He mentions that by the third month, the production would be changed (*saragae* or *saragawari*) to lure the audience back.

106. Satō Chino, "Performing Arts," 259–61.

107. Typical examples are Greengrocer's Daughter Oshichi; Ume no Yoshibei, a chivalrous man who committed a murder in Osaka; and Yatsuhashi, an Edo courtesan who was brutally murdered after she insulted a samurai named Sano Jirozaemon.

108. Koike Shōtarō, *Kōshō Edo kabuki* (Tokyo: Miki Shobō, 1997), 50.

109. This tradition of planting cherry trees in Yoshiwara seems to have had its origins in 1742. Interestingly, it may have become established as an annual event only after a staging in 1749 of *The Soga Brother's Tale Written in a Male Hand* (*Otokomoji Soga monogatari*), which featured the cherry trees.

See Furuido Hideo, *Kabuki tōjō jinbutsu jiten*, comp. Kawatake Toshio (Tokyo: Hakusuisha, 2006), 459. There are many versions of this story. Another source suggests that it started earlier, in 1741, and that it was brought to the stage in Danjūrō's Sukeroku play in 1742. See Saitō Gesshin, *Tōto saijiki*, ed. Asakura Haruhiko (Tokyo: Heibonsha, 1970), 1:218–19.

110. Takamura Chikuri, *Ehon shibai nenjū kagami* (1803), in *Shibai nenjū gyōji shū*, ed. Kokuritsu Gekijō Geinō Chōsa Shitsu (Tokyo: Kokuritsu Gekijō Chōsa Yōseibu Geinō Chōsashitsu, 1976), 205–6.

111. The long summer break became customary for stars after Ichikawa Danjūrō achieved a smashing success, leading the theater managers to decide to give the actors a break.

112. This production would be quickly thrown together, since playwrights were already busy with preparations for the next face-showing production. If the farewell production proved to be sufficiently popular, it might continue right up until the first gathering on the seventeenth of the tenth month.

113. Bakhtin, "Forms of Time," 84.

114. Furuido Hideo, "Kabuki no irei: tsuizen to shūmei," in *Shiseigaku*, vol. 4, *Shi to shigo o meguru imēji to bunka*, ed. Osano Shigetoshi and Kinoshita Naoyuki (Tokyo: Tokyo Daigaku Shuppankai, 2008), 137.

115. Tatekawa Enba, *Hana no Edo kabuki nendaiki* (1811–1815), in *Kabuki nendaiki* (Tokyo: Ōtori Shuppan, 1976), 32.

116. Furuido, "Kabuki no irei," 131–35.

117. Shikitei Sanba, *Ukiyoburo*, in *Ukiyoburo, Kejō suigen maku no soto, Daisen sekai gakuya sagashi*, ed. Jinbō Kazuya, Shin Nihon koten bungaku taikei 86 (Tokyo: Iwanami shoten, 1989), 284.

118. On the population explosion in Edo, see McClain, Merriman, and Ugawa, *Edo and Paris*, 434.

119. The interiors of theaters were originally produced as "floating images" or "perspective pictures" (*uki-e*) that used loose atmospheric perspectives with more than one vanishing point to highlight the pictorial topics of interest; similar pictures were produced over and over again in printed media. For analysis of *ukie* and theater images, see Kishi Fumikazu, *Edo no enkinhō: uki-e no shikaku* (Tokyo: Keisō Shobō, 1994).

120. *Shibai kinmō zui*, ed. Kokuritsu Gekijō Chōsa Yōseibu Geinō Chōsashitsu, Kabuki no bunken 3 (Tokyo: Kokuritsu Gekijō Chōsa Yōseibu Geinō Chōsashitsu, 1976), 135–60. For an analysis of the nineteenth-century cartographic imagination of kabuki, see Jonathan Zwicker, "Stage and Spectacle in an Age of Maps: Kabuki and the Cartographic Imagination in Nineteenth Century Japan," in *Publishing the Stage: Print and Performance in Early Modern Japan*, ed. Keller Kimbrough and Satoko Shimazaki (Boulder: University of Colorado Center for Asian Studies, 2011), 215–24.

121. Buyō Inshi, *Seji kenmonroku*, ed. Honjō Eijirō and Takikawa Masajirō (Tokyo: Seiabō, 2001), 260.

122. The dates are from Yoshida, ed., *Edo kabuki hōrei shūsei*, and *Zoku Edo kabuki hōrei shūsei*. Courtesans were separated from kabuki after the Genna era (1615–1624), according to Ogasawara, *Toshi to gekijō*, 198. In comparison with Kyoto and Osaka, where restrictions were placed on female

kabuki during this period as a way of preventing the fights and quarrels that often broke out during productions, seventeenth-century Edo tended to give rise to restrictions, based on Confucian notions of morality, on productions that featured both male and female actors.

123. Entries 2685 (1652) and 2700 (1665), in *Ofuregaki kanpō shūsei*, ed. Ishii Ryōsuke and Takayanagi Shinzō (Tokyo: Iwanami Shoten, 1934), 1239, 1242.

124. This statement is based on a survey of the edicts in Yoshida, ed., *Edo kabuki hōrei shūsei*, and *Zoku Edo kabuki hōrei shūsei*.

125. Entries 2688 (1655), 2699 (1670), and 2711 (1699), in *Ofuregaki kanpō shūsei*, ed. Ishii and Takayanagi, 1239, 1242, 1245.

126. Suzuki Hiroko, "Kyōhōki Edo kabuki ni okeru yashikikata to shibaimachi no ichiyōsō," 27.

127. An abundance of examples appears in Yanagisawa Yoshiyasu, *Enyū nikki*, in *Nihon shomin bunka shiryō shūsei*, ed. Geinōshi Kenkyūkai (Tokyo: San'ichi Shobō, 1977), 13:817–942.

128. For details, see Moriya, *Kinsei geinō kōgyōshi no kenkyū*, 365–67. Miyoshi Ikkō summarizes the trend toward having less cheap seating and adding expensive new seating areas in *Edo seigyō bukka jiten* (Tokyo: Seiabō, 2002), 111–12. Records relating to the Nakamura Theater show that prices in 1790s were twice what they had been in the 1770s.

129. Hattori Yukio, *Edo kabuki ron* (Tokyo: Hōsei Daigaku Shuppan Kyoku, 1980), 171.

130. Descriptions of this incident appear in *Kabuki nenpyō*, *Gekijō nenpyō*, and *Tōto gekijō enkakushi*, in *Edo kabuki hōrei shūsei*, ed. Yoshida, 287–89. According to certain sources, the members of the Ha Group were enraged that the theater had used a particular kind of "Genji cart" (*Genjiguruma*) crest that resembled their own. An identical incident also occurred in 1835 when two men in the Su Group (Su-gumi), who had been kicked out of the theater for trying to see a play for free, brought fifty to sixty members from their group and damaged the Morita Theater. For an instructive discussion of the place of *tobi* in Tokugawa society and culture, see Steve Wills, "Fires and Fights: Urban Conflagration, Governance, and Society in Edo-Tokyo, 1657–1890" (Ph.D. diss., Columbia University, 2010).

131. Prices for this production appear in Ihara Toshio, *Kabuki nenpyō*, 5:354. My selection of equivalents is based on the nineteenth-century price of noodles given in *Morisada mankō*, which gives the cheap 16-*mon* soba in Edo. Other sources on the prices of soba in the nineteenth century introduced in *Edo bukka jiten* show a range from 16 to 48 *mon*. The price of the cheapest seats at this production was less than that in some of the small theater productions. See Ono Takeo, ed., *Edo bukka jiten* (Tokyo: Tenbōsha, 2009), 348–50, 424.

132. We know it was possible to watch only one act because there were theater workers whose job it was to sell tickets of this sort. See Nakamura Jūsuke, *Shibai noriaki banashi*, 283.

133. The prices of noodles are based on an advertisement for a shop in Koishikawa district. See Ono, ed., *Edo bukka jiten*, 349. The price of roasted eel is from *Morisada mankō*. In 1814, Ogawa Akimichi wrote in his journal that

these seats had disappeared entirely, but this statement seems to be based on a misunderstanding or misreading of his source. See Ogawa Akimichi, *Chirizuka dan*, in *Enseki jisshu*, ed. Iwamoto Kattōshi (Tokyo: Chūō Kōronsha, 1979), 1:275.

134. Masakatsu Gunji, "Kabuki and Its Social Background," in *Tokugawa Japan: The Social and Economic Antecedents of Modern Japan*, ed. Chie Nakane and Shinzaburō Ōishi, trans. Conrad D. Totman (Tokyo: University of Tokyo Press, 1990), 197.

135. The prices for these temple and small productions, as well as for sideshows, were a fraction of the cost of going to see a play at a major theater. *Edo bukka jiten* suggests that they ranged roughly from 6 to 88 *mon*. See Ono, ed., *Edo bukka jiten*, 424–25.

136. Yoshida, ed., *Edo kabuki hōrei shūsei*, 227.

137. This took place at least three times, in 1655, 1672, and 1852. See ibid., 44, 61, 566.

138. Prohibitions against staging contemporary events and love suicides were issued in 1723 and 1793. One of the most famous bans concerned the staging of the vendetta of the Akō retainers (1702), which was turned into the kabuki play *Keisei Asama Soga* for the New Year production of 1703, just a few weeks after the incident. In the second month, an edict was issued banning the staging of contemporary plays. See Umetada Misa, "Edo kabuki no ken'etsu," in *Ken'etsu media bungaku: Edo kara sengo made*, ed. Tomi Suzuki et al. (Tokyo: Shinyōsha, 2012), 31. A similar case resulted when the Nakamura Theater staged *Hanashōbu Sano no yatsuhashi* (1811), which incorporated the murder of Tanuma Okitsugu. This play, too, had to be terminated. See Yoshida, ed., *Edo kabuki hōrei shūsei*, 284.

139. Buyō Inshi, *Seji kenmonroku*, 257.

140. For details, see Umetada, "Edo kabuki no ken'etsu." My translations of the terms are based on Thomas Gaubatz's translation of Umetada's article, published together with the original in a bilingual collection of essays.

141. Onoe Kikugorō, *Onoe Kikugorō jiden* (Tokyo: Jiji Shinpōsha, 1906), 135. Yaozen was the most prestigious restaurant in Edo.

142. Buyō Inshi, *Seji kenmonroku*, 257.

143. Ihara Toshirō, *Kabuki nenpyō*, ed. Kawatake Shigetoshi and Yoshida Teruji (Tokyo: Iwanami shoten, 1958), 3:483.

144. Umetada, "Edo kabuki no ken'etsu," 35. Peter F. Kornicki wrote about the absence of a system to censor manuscripts until 1842 in *The Book in Japan: A Cultural History from the Beginnings to the Nineteenth Century* (Honolulu: University of Hawai'i Press, 2000).

2. OVERTURNING THE WORLD

1. Ihara Toshirō [Seisei'en], *Kabuki nenpyō*, ed. Kawatake Shigetoshi and Yoshida Teruji (Tokyo: Iwanami Shoten, 1960), 5:160; Moriya Takeshi, "Edo no kabuki kōgyōkai," in *Kasei bunka no kenkyū*, ed. Hayashiya Tatsusaburō (Tokyo: Iwanami Shoten, 1976), 221–25.

2. Actor's salaries were capped at 500 *ryō*, still quite a good salary but less than one-half or one-third of what star actors were earning at the time. For the text, see Tōkyō-shi, ed., *Tōkyō shishikō sangyō hen* (Tokyo: Tōkyōshi, 1996), 40:32–45.

3. This change in the meaning of the theater has been pointed out in Furuido Hideo, "Ranjukuki no kabuki," in *Iwanami kōza Nihon bungakushi* (Tokyo: Iwanami Shoten, 1996), 10:100.

4. *Sanga no tsu yakusha kyūkin narabi ni kurai sadame*, cited in Ihara Toshirō, *Kinsei Nihon engekishi* (Tokyo: Waseda Daigaku Shuppanbu, 1913), 718–19. Published information about actors' salaries often includes a certain element of fantasy. Ihara suggests that this figure is relatively reliable because it was provided by an insider and because the print was banned.

5. The Nakamura Theater managed to remain in operation for the most part, except when it was being rebuilt in the aftermath of a fire. Productions in the other two theaters were often passed along to the backup theaters, thus weakening the authority of the three main theaters. For details of the sporadic productions during the first three decades of the early modern period, see Moriya, "Edo no kabuki kōgyōkai," 221–29.

6. Mimasuya Nisōji, *Kabuki shūdan* (1851), last page (manuscript, Historiographical Institute of the University of Tokyo).

7. New Year productions of Soga continued to the end of the Tokugawa period and even into the Meiji period. However, these productions ceased to continue its proliferating structure over several seasons. Also, the plot of Soga brothers' revenge itself sometimes becomes secondary, resulting in the emptying out of the Soga world itself.

8. *Notes by Juami* (*Juami hikki*, ca. 1840). The whereabouts of *Juami hikki* are unknown today; it may have been destroyed during the Great Kantō Earthquake. The text is cited in Ihara Toshirō, *Kinsei Nihon engekishi*, 724. Juami attributes the increase in costs to his view of the decline of the theater and the pleasure quarters.

9. The price of the *sajiki* seats for *Tenjiku Tokubei ikoku banashi* (1804) is given in Ihara Toshirō, *Kabuki nenpyō*, 5:354. The price of these seats sometimes would climb to 40 *monme* for hit productions according to Mimasuya Nisōji, *Gakuya suzume*, in *Nihon shomin bunka shiryō shūsei*, ed. Geinōshi Kenkyūkai (Tokyo: San'ichi Shobō, 1973), 6:641. Playwrights are said to have earned only as much as "books for blowing their nose" (*hon no hanagamidai*). See Mimasuya Nisōji, *Sakusha nenjū gyōji*, in *Nihon shomin bunka shiryō shūsei*, ed. Geinōshi Kenkyūkai (Tokyo: San'ichi Shobō, 1973), 6:680.

10. Nanboku employed actors during the summer production for forty-five days, but he paid extra when the production was extended because of its popularity.

11. Based on a study of the narrative advertisements in playbills, Furuido Hideo has shown that quick changes involving water remained a major highlight in the first decade of the nineteenth century, in *Kabuki: toikake no bungaku* (Tokyo: Perikansha, 1998), 169–88. Yokoyama Yasuko also discusses Matsusuke's water acrobatics, in *Edo kabuki no kaidan to bakemono* (To-

kyo: Kōdansha, 2008), 12–35. For a comprehensive discussion of the use of water on the kabuki stage, see Samuel L. Leiter, *Frozen Moments: Writings on Kabuki, 1966–2001* (Ithaca, N.Y.: Cornell University East Asia Program, 2002), 86–89.

12. Tatekawa [Utei] Enba, *Hana no Edo kabuki nendaiki* (1811–1815), in *Kabuki nendaiki* (Tokyo: Ōtori Shuppan, 1976), 676–77.

13. Matsusuke walked on a lotus leaf floating on a pool of water as the ghost of Kasane, using a trick that involved placing black platforms under the leaves, according to Ihara Toshirō, *Kinsei Nihon engekishi*, 211.

14. A clearer sense of how this works is given by a diagram printed that accompanied a panel discussion on ghost plays and especially the water tricks used in Kyoto and Osaka (moderated by Hattori Yukio and with the participation of set designers and kabuki actors) when it was printed in the modern journal *Kabuki*. See Hattori Yukio et al., "Natsukyōgen ban shin *Okyōgen gakuya no honsetsu*," *Kikan zasshi kabuki* 5 (1969): 157. This diagram also is cited and elaborated on in Leiter, *Frozen Moments*, 101–2, 89.

15. Santei Shunba, *Okyōgen gakuya no honsetsu* (Edo: Tsutaya Kichizō, 1859), fascicle 4, 22 *ura*–23 *omote*. The text at the upper left of figure 2.1 explains that the actor "wipes water from his nose and face as though he is sobbing."

16. Onoe Kikugorō, *Onoe Kikugorō jiden* (Tokyo: Jiji Shinpōsha, 1906), 186.

17. Ihara Toshirō, *Kabuki nenpyō*, 5:419.

18. Hachimonji Jishō, *Yakusha daigaku: Edo* (Kyoto: Hachimonjiya Hachizaemon, 1809), 16 *ura*.

19. Nanboku's collaboration with Hiraga Gennai and Tatekawa Enba is mentioned in Mimasuya Nisōji's *Ukiyo zōdan*, cited in Furuido, *Kabuki: toikake no bungaku*, 134. On the role that Hasegawa Kanbei, and especially Tomokurō, played in sideshows, see Gunji Masakatsu, *Tsuruya Nanboku: kabuki ga unda mukyōyō no hyōgen shugi* (Tokyo: Chūō Kōronsha, 1994), 144–57.

20. Kawazoe Yū, *Edo no misemono* (Tokyo: Iwanami Shoten, 2000), 39. For details of how profits were calculated, see 30–39.

21. Kimura Yaeko introduces a print from Takezawa Tōji's tent shows that illustrates effects similar to those used in Nanboku's plays, in "Geinō to gazō shiryō," *Geinōshi kenkyū* 176 (2007): 17. Examples of tent show scenes are quite common in Nanboku's oeuvre; see, for instance, *Okuni gozen keshō no sugatami* (1809), *Ehon gappō ga tsuji* (1810), and *Kakitsubata iro mo Edozome* (1815).

22. Tamenaga Shunsui, *Iwaiburo shigure no karakasa* (1838), in *Sato no hanagasa; Futari musume; Iwaiburo shigure no karakasa; Omoto Kamematsu Otomi Mohei*, Ninjōbon kankōkai 18 (Tokyo: Ninjōbon Kankōkai, 1925), 381.

23. Andrew Markus cites the display in 1734 of whales in *Bukō nenpyō* as the earliest record of a tent show at Ryōgoku, in "The Carnival of Edo: Misemono Spectacles from Contemporary Accounts," *Harvard Journal of Asiatic Studies* 45, no. 2 (1985): 509.

24. From 1785 to 1815, many face-showing productions featured the classical worlds of the four guardians, the pre-Taiheiki, and other Genji-related topics. See Ihara Toshirō, *Kabuki nenpyō*, 5:14, 71, 121, 123, 165, 219, 288, 359, 374, 424, 446, 459, 569.

25. The Tamagawa Theater had formerly been the Miyako Theater; it had just been renamed after Tamagawa Hikojūrō became the owner (*nadai*). Both the Miyako and Tamagawa Theaters served as the backup turret for the Ichimura Theater. The Tamagawa Theater continued staging kabuki until the production license was returned to the Ichimura Theater in 1821. See Ihara Toshirō, *Kabuki nenpyō*, ed. Kawatake Shigetoshi and Yoshida Teruji (Tokyo: Iwanami Shoten, 1961), 6:52–54; and Moriya, "Edo no kabuki kōgyōkai," 224.

26. Tsuruya Nanboku IV, *Shitennō ubuyu no Tamagawa*, in *Tsuruya Nanboku zenshū*, ed. Gunji Masakatsu (Tokyo: San'ichi Shobō, 1973), 7:157–250.

27. Ibid., 235–36.

28. Ibid., 238.

29. Ibid., 243. In addition to actor prints that correspond to the picture-book playbills and the script, some preproduction prints have survived that show Kōshirō as the Chinese envoy holding Danjūrō's *Shibaraku* print, suggesting that originally the role was assigned differently and changes took place at the last minute. For details, see prints 001–1174, 001–1228, and 001–1227 at Waseda University, Tsubouchi Memorial Theater Museum.

30. Tsuruya, *Shitennō ubuyu no Tamagawa*, 250.

31. Hachimonji Jishō, *Yakusha yume awase* (Kyoto and Osaka: Hachimonjiya Hachizaemon and Kawachiya Tasuke, 1819), 41 *omote*.

32. Igusa Toshio, "Shitennō ubuyu no Tamagawa ni tsuite," *Gobun* 31 (1968): 14.

33. This is not to say that playwrights and actors lost interest in the past. Early to mid-nineteenth-century innovations went hand in hand with the rediscovery of kabuki's history, characterizing it as a time of simultaneous invention and nostalgic reflection, illustrated by a surge in publications on theater history and Ichikawa Danjūrō VII's naming of the "eighteen kabuki classics" of his lineage.

34. *San'nin Kichisa kuruwa no Hatsugai* (1860) focuses on the spirit of brotherhood that binds the three bandits together. Their lack of a true blood connection is of no importance in the play. *Azuma kudari gojūsantsugi* (1854), also known as *Gojūsantsugi Tennichibō*, incorporates the theme of fake identity by adapting the story of the mountain priest Tennichibō, who faked his identity as the son of the shogun. Hōsaku (later Tennichibō) kills an old lady so that he can fake his identity by a proof of lineage and a sword, both of which had been given to her daughter's son by Minamoto no Yoritomo.

35. Anonymous Torii-school artist, street playbill for *Yotsuya kaidan*, performed with *Kanadehon chūshingura* at the Nakamura Theater (Edo: Murayama Genbei, 1825), *sho'nichi*, Waseda University, Tsubouchi Memorial Theater Museum.

36. For a detailed analysis of the incident, see Bitō Masahide, "The Akō Incident of 1701–1703," trans. Henry D. Smith II, *Monumenta Nipponica* 58,

no. 2 (2003): 149–70; and Eiko Ikegami, *The Taming of the Samurai: Honorific Individualism and the Making of Modern Japan* (Cambridge, Mass.: Harvard University Press, 1995), 223–40.

37. Henry D. Smith II, "The Capacity of *Chūshingura*," *Monumenta Nipponica* 58, no. 1 (2003): 1–42.

38. This has been taken up by many scholars. See, for instance, Henry D. Smith II "*Chūshingura* in the 1980s: Rethinking the Story of the Forty-Seven Rōnin," in *Revenge Drama in European Renaissance and Japanese Theatre: From Hamlet to Madame Butterfly*, ed. Kevin J. Wetmore Jr. (New York: Palgrave Macmillan, 2008), 187–215, and "Capacity of *Chūshingura*"; James R. Brandon, ed., *Chūshingura: Studies in Kabuki and the Puppet Theater* (Honolulu: University of Hawai'i Press, 1982); Miyazawa Seiichi, *Kindai Nihon to Chūshingura gensō* (Tokyo: Aoki Shoten, 2001); and Chelsea Foxwell, "The Double Identity of *Chūshingura*: Theater and History in Nineteenth-Century Prints," *Impressions* 26 (2004): 22–43.

39. This line of argument was particularly common during the 1970s and 1980s when *Yotsuya kaidan* received much attention from literary and cultural critics.

40. A few representative examples are Ochiai Kiyohiko, *Hyakki yagyō no rakuen: Tsuruya Nanboku no sekai* (Tokyo: Geijutsu seikatsusha, 1975); and Tsurumi Shunsuke and Yasuda Takeshi, *Chūshingura to Yotsuya kaidan: Nihonjin no komyunikēshon* (Tokyo: Asahi Sensho, 1983).

41. For a reading of the fluidity of the 1825 production as seen through playbills, see the introduction to this book.

42. The notes are transcribed in Waseda Daigaku Engeki Hakubutsukan, ed., *Edo shibai banzuke shuhitsu kaki-ire shūsei* (Tokyo: Waseda Daigaku Engeki Hakubutsukan, 1990). For facsimiles of all of the playbills with red notes, see Torigoe Bunzō and Kikuchi Akira, eds., *Shuhitsu kaki-ire Edo shibai banzuke shū*, 3 vols. (Tokyo: Waseda Daigaku Shuppanbu, 1992).

43. Ihara Toshirō, *Kabuki nenpyō*, ed. Kawatake Shigetoshi and Yoshida Teruji (Tokyo: Iwanami Shoten, 1961), 6:550. In writing the kabuki chronology, Ihara surveyed massive numbers of playbills and actor critiques.

44. Waseda Daigaku Engeki Hakubutsukan, ed., *Edo shibai banzuke shuhitsu kaki-ire shūsei*, 154–55.

45. Ibid., 155–57. Part of the confusion may have been due to the sudden illness of Ichikawa Ebizō, the production's star actor, whose role had to be replaced by the nineteenth. Another actor injured himself, and one even died during the production.

46. Tatekawa Enba, *Hana no Edo kabuki nendaiki*, 202.

47. Ōnishi Atsuko, "Kinsei chūki ikō ni okeru ningyō jōruri no kabukika," *Kabuki kenkyū to hihyō* 12 (1993): 73–87. Ōnishi confirmed the number of Chūshingura productions by looking at playbills to add productions not included in *Kabuki nenpyō*.

48. Among the works not included are plays that head in completely different directions but involve characters from *The Treasury of Loyal Retainers*. Examples are Sakurada Jisuke's *Chūkō Ryōgoku ori* (A Loyal Ryōgoku Weave, 1790) and Tsuruya Nanboku's *Kiku no en tsuki no shiranami* (The

Chrysanthemum Bond: Bandit on a Moonlit Night, 1821), which I discuss later in this chapter.

49. Eliza Ruhamah Scidmore, *Jinrikisha Days in Japan* (New York: Harper, 1891), 100–101. The "Tokugawa's ban against the play" was actually a ban against using the real names of the historical personages involved in the Akō incident; the play itself was not banned. My attention was directed to this book by Umetada Misa, "Mokuami sakuhin gekika ni kansuru ichikōsatsu: *Katakiuchi uwasa no furuichi* o rei ni," *Engeki kenkyū sentā kiyō* 7 (2006): 59.

50. Mimasuya Nisōji wrote this sequence for *Ura omote Chūshingura* (*The Inside and Outside of The Treasury of Loyal Retainers*, 1833), which was staged at the Kawarasaki Theater in Edo in the fourth month of 1833. The sequence is usually performed today after act 4.

51. The movements are based on scenes in Kawatake Mokuami's *Shijūshichi koku chūya dokei* (*A Day-and-Night Clock with Forty-Seven Ticks*, 1871) and Kawatake Shinshichi III's *Chūshingura nenjū gyōji* (*The Treasury of Loyal Retainers Annual Events*, 1882), according to Toita Yasuji, *Chūshingura* (Tokyo: Sōgensha, 1957), 233.

52. The script dated 1891 in the collection of the Waseda University, Tsubouchi Memorial Theater Museum, seems to have been presented to censors five times during the Meiji period, three times during the Taishō period, and thirteen times during the Shōwa period (1926–1989). This was the main text used for Hattori Yukio, ed., *Kanadehon chūshingura*, Kabuki on sutēji 8 (Tokyo: Hakusuisha, 1994).

53. Hachimonji Jishō, *Kokon iroha hyōrin* (1785), in *Shin gunsho ruijū* (Tokyo: Kokusho Kankōkai, 1908), 3:92.

54. This was pointed out in both Toita, *Chūshingura*, 233; and James R. Brandon, "The Theft of Chūshingura: or The Great Kabuki Caper," in *Chūshingura: Studies in Kabuki and the Puppet Theater*, ed. James R. Brandon (Honolulu: University of Hawai'i Press, 1982), 113. In the production at the Nakamura Theater in 1749, the name Ōwashi Bungo was Ōdate Kumanosuke. In the *bunraku* performances, Ōwashi Bungo appeared with arrows rather than an ax.

55. For a discussion on Tokugawa revenge, see Ikegami, *Taming of the Samurai*, 241–64.

56. David Atherton, "Valences of Vengeance: The Moral Imagination of Early Modern Japanese Vendetta Fiction" (Ph.D. diss., Columbia University, 2013).

57. The *Handbook of Theatrical Worlds* lists revenge plays as a subcategory of "household disturbance." See Kokuritsu Gekijō Geinō Chōsashitsu, ed., *Sekai kōmoku*, in *Kyōgen sakusha shiryōshū* (Tokyo: Kokuritsu Gekijō Chōsa Yōseibu Geinō Chōsashitsu, 1976), 1:58–61.

58. Kawatake Shigetoshi, "Edo minshūgeki toshite no oiemono no tenkai," *Kikan zasshi kabuki* 4 (1969): 65. Some "household-disturbance" plots involve a disturbance on a larger scale, not limited to a specific house.

59. There also were exceptions in which female versions of the household-disturbance plot was staged, especially in the mid- to late eighteenth century. *Kagamiyama kokyō no nishikie* is a popular example.

60. Atherton, "Valences of Vengeance," 91.

61. Tsuruya Nanboku IV, *Tōkaidō Yotsuya kaidan*, ed. Gunji Masakatsu (Tokyo: Shinchōsha, 1981), 83.

62. The content of this back-and-forth changes, depending on the relationship between the actors playing Naosuke and Iemon. The reference to the actual identity of the actors breaks the fictional frame of the play, which is a popular technique in kabuki.

63. Before this binary distinction came into being, contemporary scenes of characters visiting the pleasure quarters in "historical" plays were simply considered *yatsushi* (dual identity). For a discussion of this history, see Gunji Masakatsu, "Kizewa no seritsu," in *Gunji Masakatsu santei shū* (Tokyo: Hakusuisha, 1990), 1:271–83, and "Kabuki gikyoku no kōzō to hassō," in *Gunji Masakatsu santei shū* (Tokyo: Hakusuisha, 1992), 2:75–99.

64. Gunji, "Kizewa no seritsu," 276.

65. Nishizawa Ippō, *Denki sakusho*, in *Shin gunsho ruijū* (Tokyo: Kokusho Kankōkai, 1906), 1:33.

66. Following the convention in Edo, *Godairiki koi no fūjime* was not given a separate title in 1795, but the success of this production allowed Gohei to provide separate titles for his later plays. For details, see Waseda Daigaku Engeki Hakubutsukan, ed., *Shibai-e ni miru Edo Meiji no kabuki* (Tokyo: Shōgakukan, 2003), 54–55. I have used Paul B. Kennelly's translation of *Edo sunago kichirei Soga*, which appears in Tsuruya Nanboku, "*Ehon gappō ga tsuji*: A Kabuki Drama of Unfettered Evil by Tsuruya Nanboku IV," trans. Paul B. Kennelly, *Asian Theater Journal* 17, no. 2 (2000): 187.

67. Furuido Hideo, "Kaidai," in *Fukumori Kyūsuke kyakuhon shū*, ed. Furuido Hideo et al., Sōsho Edo bunko 49 (Tokyo: Kokusho Kankōkai, 2001), 455.

68. Imao Tetsuya, *Kabuki no rekishi* (Tokyo: Iwanami Shoten, 2003), 115.

69. For a discussion of *kizewa*, see Gunji, "Kizewa no seritsu," 271–83. Suwa Haruo also notes that *kizewa* was "real" or "pure," in that Nanboku brought the lives of lower-class Edoites to the stage, in *Sei to zoku no doramatsurugi* (Tokyo: Gakugei Shorin, 1988), 263–313. This was unlike earlier contemporary plays, which were influenced heavily by characters originating in Kyoto and Osaka, where *sewa* plays first appeared. In this sense, *kizewa* also connotes the characteristically Edo-style language, customs, and character types that had been established by the late eighteenth century, as opposed to the language, customs, and character types of Kyoto and Osaka.

70. Shikitei Sanba, *Ukiyoburo*, in *Ukiyoburo, Kejō suigen maku no soto, Daisen sekai gakuya sagashi*, ed. Jinbō Kazuya, Shin Nihon koten bungaku taikei 86 (Tokyo: Iwanami Shoten, 1989), 125.

71. Kawatake Toshio, *Kabuki: Baroque Fusion of the Arts*, trans. Frank Connell Hoff and Jean Connell Hoff (Tokyo: International House of Japan, 2003), 142–43. The part of Sandakurō was originally for those in the *aichū*, a second tier of actors situated beneath the *tatemono*, or *nadai*, the first tier. There were six ranks in all, including child actors, apprentices, and assistants, but only those actors in the first tier had their names on the playbill.

72. In this production from the eighth month, Sadakurō was played by Nakamura Nakazō I. Ephemera for frequently staged plays like *The Treasury of Loyal Retainers* include publications in which the content or the attire of actors is not updated. This publication is an early type of picture-book playbill, closer to a work of illustrated fiction, and is thus called *kyōgen ezukushi*.

73. Hachimonji Jishō, *Kokon iroha hyōrin*, 78.

74. Nakamura Nakazō III, *Temae miso*, ed. Gunji Masakatsu (Tokyo: Seiabō, 1969), 38–45. Note, however, that this text was edited several times for republication in journals during the Meiji period. Furthermore, since Nakazō III was envisioning a lineage for the comparatively minor Nakazō name, it is reasonable to assume that he wanted an interesting acting-family history. Although *Temae miso* is a valuable record, it should be treated with care as a source.

75. Yamamoto Jirō, "Sadakurō no kata," *Kokubungaku kaishaku to kanshō* 32, no. 13 (1967): 97–98. For a detailed discussion of acting styles in acts 5 and 6, see Kokuritsu Gekijō Geinō Chōsashitsu, ed., *Kanadehon chūshingura godanme, rokudanme*, Kokuritsu gekijō jōen shiryō shū 288 (Tokyo: Kokuritsu Gekijō Chōsa Yōseibu Geinō Chōsashitsu, 1989).

76. For lineages of villain roles from the late eighteenth to the early nineteenth century, see Ukai Tomoko, *Yodaime Tsuruya Nanboku ron; akuningeki no keifu to shukō o chūshin ni* (Tokyo: Kazama Shobō, 2005), 11–58.

77. In act 7, Sadakurō appears disguised as Akatsuki Hoshigorō.

78. Tsuruya Nanboku IV, *Kiku no en tsuki no shiranami*, in *Tsuruya Nanboku zenshū*, ed. Gunji Masakatsu (Tokyo: San'ichi Shobō, 1974), 9:70.

79. Hachimonji Jishō and Ichimonsha Tashō, *Yakusha sokuseki ryōri: Edo* (Kyoto and Osaka: Hachimonjiya Hachizaemon and Kawachiya Tasuke, 1822), 20 *ura*.

80. Michael Goldman, *On Drama: Boundaries of Genre, Borders of the Self* (Ann Arbor: University of Michigan Press, 2000), 33.

81. In fact, a new type of play began appearing in the late eighteenth century that featured not the struggle to prove one's loyalty but the failure to do so. The puppet play *Natsumatsuri Naniwakagami* (1745), about a man who ends up murdering his father-in-law, is a good example.

82. Hachimonji Jishō, *Kokon iroha hyōrin*, 85. There is no presentation of blood in staging Hangan's suicide scene today.

83. Hattori, ed., *Kanadehon chūshingura*, 179.

84. The music played here is *Ruri no tsuya*. *Meriyasu* originated as a musical genre in Kyoto and Osaka; the name derives from the phrase *ki ga meriyasu* (my heart sinks). In Kyōden's *Edo umare uwaki no kabayaki* (1785), Enjirō is told that the first thing he needs to do in order to understand the mood of love is to learn *meriyasu*. This is probably the first reference in Edo to the musical style. For more about kabuki music, see Mochizuki Tainosuke, *Kabuki no geza ongaku* (Tokyo: Engeki Shuppansha, 1997). An identical scene appears in Nanboku's early play *Okuni gozen keshō no sugatami*, but it was not accompanied by this chanting, which must have given it a completely different feeling.

85. In Chikamatsu's later works, figures who harbor grudges are reborn when they kill themselves and their spirits fly into a woman's womb. For more examples of this theme, see Han Kyonja, "Chikamatsu no jidai jōruri ni egakareta shūjaku shūnen," *Kokugo to kokubungaku* 987 (2006): 44–57.

86. For a discussion of the social context of the Bunka and Bunsei periods, when Nanboku was active, see Paul B. Kennelly, "Realism in Kabuki: The Ghost Stories at Yotsuya on the Tōkaidō," *Journal of Oriental Studies of Australia* 27–28 (1995/1996): 136.

3. SHADES OF JEALOUSY

1. The scene of a third figure spying on a couple and finding a ghost or corpse comes from "The Peony Lantern," in Qu You's *Jiandeng xinhua*. This story was adapted and illustrated in Asai Ryōi's "Botan no tōrō," in *Otogi bōko*, and in Santō Kyōden's *Ukibotan zenden*. Nanboku had already incorporated a similar scene into *Okuni gozen keshō no sugatami*. For a history of the reception of this scene from *Jiandeng xinhua*, see Tachikawa Kiyoshi, *Botan tōki no keifu* (Tokyo: Bensei Shuppan, 1998).

2. Tsuruya Nanboku IV, *Tōkaidō Yotsuya kaidan*, ed. Gunji Masakatsu (Tokyo: Shinchōsha, 1981), 370–71.

3. Bai Juyi, "Song of Lasting Pain," in *An Anthology of Chinese Literature: Beginnings to 1911*, ed. and trans. Stephen Owen (New York: Norton, 1996), 447.

4. Barbara Creed, *The Monstrous-Feminine: Film, Feminism, Psychoanalysis* (New York: Routledge, 2007).

5. Santei Shunba, *Okyōgen gakuya no honsetsu* (Edo: Tsutaya Kichizō, 1859), fascicle 3, 7 *omote*–8 *ura*.

6. Sakurada Jisuke I, *Gohiki kanjinchō*, in *Edo kabukishū*, ed. Furuido Hideo, Torigoe Bunzō, and Wada Osamu, Shin Nihon koten bungaku taikei 96 (Tokyo: Iwanami Shoten, 1997), 337. This edition of the play is an unusual example that uses the actors' names rather than those of the characters they play. Since I am presenting the scene out of context here, I have used the character names instead.

7. Ibid., 384. The association with Dōjōji is foreshadowed on 171; see also 172n.15.

8. Unlike Umegae, Shinobu no Mae's desire is self-centered. This version echoes more directly the adaptation of the "muken no kane" in *Hatachiyama hōrai soga* (1759), in which Nakamura Tomijūrō played a jealous woman who also gets tied to a tree. See ibid., 384–85.

9. Sekine Shisei, *Tōto gekijo enkaku shiryō*, ed. Kokuritsu Gekijō Geinō Chōsashitsu, Kabuki shiryō sensho 6 (Tokyo: Kokuritsu Gekijō Geinō Chōsashitsu, 1989), 1:223–24.

10. This is a *dokugin*, which the head singer chants alone. The effect is emotional and dramatic and is often used in love scenes.

11. Hattori Yukio, *Edo kabuki ron* (Tokyo: Hōsei Daigaku Shuppan Kyoku, 1980), 2–18. Scenes of a woman combing her lover's hair had been

performed from early on, but they became extremely popular during the Kyōhō period (1716–1736). This form of expression became even richer during the Hōreki period (1751–1764), when it came to be associated with new sentimental music called *meriyasu*. See Sakurada Jisuke, *Gohīki kanjinchō*, 423–24n.49, "kamisuki."

12. R. Keller Kimbrough, trans., *Isozaki*, in *Monsters and the Fantastic: A Collection of Short Medieval Japanese Fiction*, ed. Haruo Shirane and R. Keller Kimbrough (New York: Columbia University Press, forthcoming). I am grateful to Keller Kimbrough for pointing me to this source.

13. Tsuruya, *Tōkaidō Yotsuya kaidan*, 180.

14. When Oiwa first appears on stage in act 1, she appears as a street prostitute walking around with a straw mat to use as bedding outside. Her sister Osode makes a remark about this as well.

15. Jacques Lacan, "The Mirror Stage as Formative of the *I* Function as Revealed Psychoanalytic Experience," in *Écrits: The First Complete Edition in English*, trans. Bruce Fink (New York: Norton, 2006), 75–81.

16. Ueda Akinari, *Tales of Moonlight and Rain*, trans. Anthony H. Chambers (New York: Columbia University Press, 2007), 192–94.

17. This quotation from *Kaie rakusōdan* is introduced and transcribed in Tamamuro Taijō, *Sōshiki bukkyō* (Tokyo: Daihōrinkaku, 1963), 176.

18. Caroline Hirasawa, *Hell-Bent for Heaven in Tateyama Mandara: Painting and Religious Practice at a Japanese Mountain* (Leiden: Brill, 2013), 120.

19. Hitomi Tonomura, "Birth Giving and Avoidance Taboo Women's Body Versus the Historiography of Ubuya," *Japan Review* 19 (2007): 16.

20. Taira Masayuki, "Chūsei bukkyō to josei," in *Nihon josei seikatsushi*, ed. Joseishi Sōgō Kenkyūkai (Tokyo: Tōkyō Daigaku Shuppan, 1990), 2:75–108. The five obstacles originally marked the limits of women's upward mobility but came to be redefined in the context of medieval Buddhism as an outright exclusion from Buddhahood or sacred spaces, according to Bernard Faure, *The Power of Denial: Buddhism, Purity, and Gender* (Princeton, N.J.: Princeton University Press, 2003), 63. For a different view of the five obstacles in the context of female monastic practice, see Lori Meeks, *Hokkeji and the Reemergence of the Female Monastic Orders in Premodern Japan* (Honolulu: University of Hawai'i Press, 2010); on representations of gender and the female body in *setsuwa* collections, see Hitomi Tonomura, "Black Hair and Red Trousers: Gendering the Flesh in Medieval Japan," *American Historical Review* 99, no. 1 (1994): 129–54.

21. Nishiguchi Junko, "Nihon shijō no josei to bukkyō: nyonin kyūsai to nyonin jōbutsu o megutte." *Kokubungaku kaishaku to kanshō* 56, no. 5 (1991): 19.

22. Meeks, *Hokkeji*, 14–18, 23.

23. The negative connotation of jealousy appears as early as the Nara period (710–784), but becomes pervasive only with the spread of discourse about Blood Pool Hell. For a discussion of Blood Pool Hell and the popular circulation of images of it, see D. Max Moerman, *Localizing Paradise: Kumano Pilgrimage and the Religious Landscape of Premodern Japan* (Cambridge, Mass.: Harvard University Asia Center, 2006); and Duncan Ryūken

Williams, *The Other Side of Zen: A Social History of Sōtō Zen Buddhism in Tokugawa Japan* (Princeton, N.J.: Princeton University Press, 2005).

24. On the multitude of visual representations of *yūrei*, see Takada Mamoru, "Yūrei zō wa ika ni shite seiritsu shita ka: katachi no hensen," in *Edo bungaku no kyokō to keishō* (Tokyo: Shinwasha, 2001), 271–300. Kenji Kajiya also analyzes representations of *yūrei* in relation to the iconography of dreams in paintings and print in "Reimagining the Imagined: Depictions of Dreams and Ghosts in the Early Edo Period," *Impressions* 23 (2001): 86–107.

25. A different approach, in which all supernatural representations are classified under the term *yōkai*, is common in folklore studies and anthropology. For representative works in this field, see Komatsu Kazuhiko, *Yōkaigaku shinkō: yōkai kara miru Nihonjin no kokoro* (Tokyo: Shōgakkan, 1994); and Michael Dylan Foster, *Pandemonium and Parade: Japanese Monsters and the Culture of Yōkai* (Berkeley: University of California Press, 2008).

26. The abundance of different beliefs makes representations of snakes extremely complex. W. Michael Kelsey categorizes various literary examples into five archetypes in "Salvation of the Snake, the Snake of Salvation: Buddhist-Shinto Conflict and Resolution," *Japanese Journal of Religious Studies* 8, nos. 1–2 (1981): 83–113.

27. Faure, *Power of Denial*, 60–61.

28. Tanaka Takako, *Akujo-ron* (Tokyo: Kinokuniya Shoten, 1992), 180.

29. For an interpretation of *Dōjōji* and other tales from the perspective of female salvation, see Monica Dix, "Saint or Serpent? Engendering the Female Body in Medieval Buddhist Narratives," in *The Bodies in Asia*, ed. Bryan S. Turner and Zheng Yangwen (Oxford: Berghahn Books, 2011), 43–58. Also, for discussions of serpentine proclivities of women, see Hirasawa, *Hell-Bent for Heaven*, 126–30.

30. The story of the *nāga* girl from the Lotus Sutra was a popular vehicle for speaking about female salvation, and there were many narratives and visual depictions of a monk pacifying a serpent or a woman who had turned into a serpent. For the sake of brevity, however, I will not discuss these here.

31. Baba Akiko, *Oni no kenkyū* (Tokyo: Chikuma Shobō, 1988), 252–55.

32. For an explanation of these hells, see the *kojōruri* work *Goō no hime*, in *Wondrous Brutal Fictions: Eight Buddhist Tales from the Early Japanese Puppet Theater*, ed. and trans. R. Keller Kimbrough (New York: Columbia University Press, 2013), 244. For an extensive discussion of hells, including the three gendered ones, in *Tateyama mandara* and beyond, see Hirasawa, *Hell-Bent for Heaven*, 79–135.

33. Takase Baisei, *Ruisenshūi* [*Haikai ruisenshū*] (Kyoto: Terada Yoheiji, 1676), 1:68 ura.

34. This print is cited in Takada Mamoru, *Onna to hebi: hyōchō no Edo bungakushi* (Tokyo: Chikuma Shobō, 1991), 135–38. *Hyaku monogatari* offers a playful take on famous early modern ghosts like Oiwa, who is represented as a lantern, and Koheiji, who appears as a skeleton.

35. Examples are *Semimaru* and *Kazan no in kisaki arasoi*. This type of water effect was particularly popular on the puppet stage.

36. William H. McCullough divided marriage systems into four types—"virilocal" (the woman lives with the man's family), "uxorilocal" (the man becomes part of the woman's family), "duolocal" (the husband and wife stay at their own houses), and "neolocal" (the man and woman live together apart from their in-laws)—in "Japanese Marriage Institutions in the Late Heian Period," *Harvard Journal of Asiatic Studies* 27 (1967): 105. Joan R. Piggott suggests that the "Chinese-style patriarchal family paradigm, which was characterized by male privilege, virilocality, and patrilineality" had been adopted by middle- and upper-level aristocrats in Kyoto by the mid-eleventh century ("A Comedy of Marriage and Family in Eleventh-Century Kyoto," *Nihon kodaigaku* 1 [2009]: 51–80). The virilocal marriage structure was promoted in medieval warrior society.

37. Haruko Wakita, "Marriage and Property in Premodern Japan from the Perspective of Women's History," *Journal of Japanese Studies* 10 (1984): 73–99. Wakita is building on Takamura Itsue's classic study of marital systems, *Nihon kon'inshi* (Tokyo: Shibundō, 1963). See also Hitomi Tonomura, "Women and Inheritance in Japan's Early Warrior Society," *Comparative Studies in Society and History* 32, no. 3 (1990): 592–623.

38. Chie Nakane discusses the permeation of the notion of *ie* through all classes, in "Tokugawa Society," in *Tokugawa Japan: The Social and Economic Antecedents of Modern Japan*, ed. Chie Nakane and Shinzaburō Ōishi, trans. Conrad D. Totman (Tokyo: University of Tokyo Press, 1990), 213–31. Recently, scholars have began to devote more attention to women's autonomy, noting the high proportion of women working outside the home and their responsibility for managing and running their households, but the basic picture remains rather bleak. See, for instance, Marcia Yonemoto, "Outside the Inner Quarters: Sociability, Mobility and Narration in Early Edo-Period Women's Diaries," *Japan Forum* 21, no. 3 (2010): 389–401; and Bettina Gramlich-Oka, "Neo-Confucianism Reconsidered: Family Rituals in the Rai Household," *U.S–Japan Women's Journal* 39 (2011): 7–37.

39. Mitamura Engyo, "Buke no kon'in," in *Mitamura Engyo zenshū* (Tokyo: Chūō Kōronsha, 1975), 2:340. Fujimoto Kizan notes in the section on *shō* (mistresses) in *Shikidō ōkagami* (*The Great Mirror of the Erotic Way*, late seventeenth century) that if a wife becomes jealous of a mistress, she will not be able to manage the house. See Fujimoto Kizan, *Shikidō ōkagami*, ed. Noma Kōshin (Tokyo: Yūzan Bunko, 1961), 441.

40. Ōtake Hideo, "Edo jidai no mekake," in *Bakuhan kokka no hō to shihai*, ed. Ōtake Hideo and Harafuji Hiroshi (Tokyo: Yūhikaku, 1984), 507–34. The wooden gates that separated blocks were closed at night, so people were unable to get around freely. *Hatamoto* warriors (those in the direct service of *bakufu* [tent government]), who needed permission to spend a night outside their main residences, therefore had to keep their mistresses in their own houses with their official wives. The spread of mistresses among commoners both high and low is detailed in Buyō Inshi, *Seji kenmonroku*, ed. Honjō Eijirō and Takikawa Masajirō (Tokyo: Seiabō, 2001), 271–75.

41. Mitamura Engyo, "Kakoimono no hanashi," in *Mitamura Engyo zenshū* (Tokyo: Chūō Kōronsha, 1975), 11:206.

42. Terakado Seiken, *Edo hanjōki*, in *Edo hanjōki Ryūkyō shinshi*, ed. Hino Tatsuo, Shin Nihon koten bungaku taikei 100 (Tokyo: Iwanami Shoten, 1989), 156–62. The character Yonehachi in Tamenaga Shunsui's *Shunshoku umegoyomi* is a good example.

43. Asai Ryōi, *Honchō jokan*, in *Honchō jokan*, vol. 2, ed. Kinsei Bungaku Shoshi Kenkyūkai, Kinsei bungaku shiryō ruijū, kanazōshi-hen 7 (Tokyo: Benseisha, 1972), 326. This page is a facsimile reproduction of fascicle 12, 16 *ura*.

44. *Onna daigaku takarabako* (1716), in *Onna daigaku shū*, ed. Ishikawa Matsutarō, Tōyō bunko 302 (Tokyo: Heibonsha, 1977), 34. The section on *shichikyo* is taken from the same entry in Kaibara Ekiken, "Joshi o oshiyuru hō" (vol. 5 of *Wazoku dōjikun*, 1710), in ibid, 13–14. Many works following *Onna daigaku takarabako* were published throughout the early modern period.

45. Miyako no Nishiki, *Tōsei chie kagami* (1712), 4:1 *omote*.

46. Tsutsumi Kunihiko explores this topic in *Nyonin jatai: hen'ai no Edo kaidanshi* (Tokyo: Kadokawa Shoten, 2006), 149–56.

47. Satō Eri notes that male spirits are depicted with horns in illustrated playbooks, in *Kabuki niwaka kenkyū* (Tokyo: Shintensha, 2002), 113–41. This representation derives from the motif of defeating demons (*oni*), which was important in early Edo kabuki, a topic I touch on in chapter 1.

48. Tsutsumi Kunihiko, *Nyonin jatai*, 146–47.

49. Ibid., 24. The association between the female sex and early modern pictorial depictions of serpents has also been explored in Takada, *Onna to hebi*.

50. Kondō Mizuki, "Jusha no yōkai taiji," *Nihon bungaku* 55, no. 4 (2006): 26.

51. Fuji Akio, ed., "Hayashi Razan hencho *Yūrei no koto*," in *Kinsei bungaku ronsō*, ed. Mizuno Minoru (Tokyo: Meiji Shoin, 1992), 495. Fuji transcribed a copy of a manuscript originally owned by Nagasawa Kikuya (1902–1980). The original was probably written some time in the Kanei period (1624–1644). Judging from the handwriting, Nagasawa concluded that the copy had probably been made sometime between then and the 1660s or 1670s. See Fuji, "Hayashi Razan," 474.

52. Satō Hiroo, *Shisha no yukue* (Tokyo: Iwata Shoin, 2008), 196.

53. Ibid., 190. Ishida Mizumaro also discussed the various images of hell current during the early modern period, as an image of the afterlife and as having nonreligious, metaphorical applications to everyday life, in "Kinsei ni okeru jigoku no kannen," in *Jigoku* (Kyoto: Hōzōkan, 1985), 255–72.

54. Kamakura Keiko, "Chikamatsu no jōruri ni okeru yume," *Rikkyō Daigaku Nihon bungaku* 59 (1987): 54–65, and "Kojōruri ni okeru yume," *Rikkyō Daigaku Nihon bungaku* 61 (1988): 66–80.

55. Furuido Hideo, "*Yotsuya kaidan*: yume no ba," *Nihon no bigaku* 17 (1991): 56–73.

56. Hōseidō Kisanji (text) and Katsukawa Shundō (pictures), *Ukan sandai zue*, ed. Kokuritsu Gekijō Geinō Chōsashitsu, Kabuki no bunken 4 (Tokyo: Kokuritsu Gekijō Chōsa Yōseibu Geinō Chōsashitsu, 1971), 51–53. This work was later imitated and adapted by Shikitei Sanba, and a similar depiction

appears in his *Shibai kinmō zui*, ed. Kokuritsu Geijō Chōsa Yōseibu Geinō Chōsashitsu, Kabuki no bunken 3 (Tokyo: Kokuritsu Gekijō Chōsa Yōseibu Geinō Chōsashitsu, 1976), 130.

57. Hōseidō Kisanji and Katsukawa Shundō, *Ukan sandai zue*, 51.

58. Ibid., 52.

59. We see this as well in more popular works by intellectuals that circulated widely in print, such as *Kokon hyaku monogatari hyōban* (1686). This *kanazōshi*, based on a manuscript by Yamaoka Genrin (1631–1672), also provided rational explanations from a Confucian perspective of various strange creatures and phenomena. *Kokon hyaku monogatari hyōban* includes a good example of another tendency in Confucian treatments of the supernatural: the attribution of supposed mysteries to mental weakness on the part of the observer. "When the soul (*kokoro*) is lax," the narrator notes, "fox spirits find you; if your soul is in the right place, then even a thousand-year-old fox will not come to you" (Tachikawa Kiyoshi, ed., *Zoku hyaku monogatari shūsei*, Sōsho Edo bunko 27 [Tokyo: Kokusho Kankōkai, 1993], 26).

60. Hattori Yukio, *Sakasama no yūrei: shi no Edo bunka ron* (Tokyo: Chikuma Gakugei Bunko, 2005), 120.

61. The theme of Nanboku's chaotic reversal of order is explored in "Nanboku-geki no kōzu: gyakuten to konton no kōshō to kyōfu," in ibid., 9–98. Hattori argues that Nanboku attempted to subvert the late Tokugawa period's social order and its expectations in a nonsensical farce.

62. This is evident in the three types of acting skills mentioned in praising the abilities of the top female-role actor Ikushima Daikichi in *Yakusha sansesō*: "Whatever he does—*shosa*, *maigoto*, or *onryōgoto*—the Edo audience is charmed" (Kabuki Hyōbanki Kenkyūkai, ed., *Kabuki hyōbanki shūsei* [Tokyo: Iwanami Shoten, 1973], 4:66).

63. *Yakusha itchō zutsumi: Kyoto*, in *Kabuki hyōbanki shūsei*, ed. Kabuki Hyōbanki Kenkyūkai (Tokyo: Iwanami Shoten, 1973), 3:319.

64. For a discussion of the symbolism of upside-down ghosts, see Hattori, *Sakaksama no yūrei*. This play was staged at the Hayakumo Theater in Kyoto as a New Year performance (*ni no kawari*). My summary of this scene is based mainly on the description in Ihara Toshirō [Seisei'en], *Kabuki nenpyō*, ed. Kawatake Shigetoshi and Yoshida Teruji (Tokyo: Iwanami Shoten, 1956), 1:342. *Kabuki jishi* states that Koshirō perfected six different acting styles, including dance. See Tamenaga Itchō, *Kabuki jishi*, in *Kabuki sōsho*, ed. Kinkōdō Henshūbu (Tokyo: Kinkōdō Shoseki, 1910), 270–71. For a detailed discussion of this actor, see Ihara Toshirō, *Nihon engekishi* (Tokyo: Waseda Daigaku Shuppanbu, 1904), 489–91.

65. *Yakusha mai ōgi*, in *Kabuki hyōbanki shūsei*, ed. Kabuki Hyōbanki Kenkyūkai (Tokyo: Iwanami Shoten, 1973), 3:539.

66. Gunji Masakatsu, "Kabuki no yakugara: hassei, kaitai," in *Gunji Masakatsu santei shū* (Tokyo: Hakusuisha, 1991), 2:201.

67. The earliest account of *kumomai* appears in the notes (*okugaki*) to the Kōfukuji Temple's 1549 copy of *Daihannyakyō*. See the entry on *kumo*, in Asakura Musei, *Misemono kenkyū* (Kyoto: Shibunkaku Shuppan, 1977), 28–31.

68. *Shokoku yūri kōshoku yuraizoroe*, in *Kinsei bungei sōsho* (Tokyo: Kokusho Kankōkai, 1911), 10:23.

69. Iwahashi Koyata, "Kumomai kō," in *Nihon geinōshi: chūsei kabu no kenkyū* (Tokyo: Geiensha, 1951), 159.

70. According to *Tokugawa jikki*, Kanzaburō was invited to the Ninomaru palace on the twenty-fifth and twenty-seventh of the second month of Keian 4. The entry for the twenty-seventh reports that "Kanzaburō and Hikosaku's kabuki troupes were invited to the Ninomaru palace, and [Iemitsu] watched magic tricks and acrobatics involving the use of wooden pillows" (*Tokugawa jikki*, ed. Kuroita Katsumi and Kokushi Taikei Henshūkan, Kokushi taikei: shintei zōho kansei kinen ban 40 [Tokyo: Yoshikawa Kōbunkan, 1964], 3:685).

71. Gunji Masakatsu, "Karuwaza no keifu," in *Gunji Masakatsu santei shū*, 2:291–314.

72. The first production was staged at the Hayakumo Theater in Kyoto. Nakamura Shichisaburō I, an Edo-based actor visiting Kyoto, played Tomoenojō. He immediately brought part of the play back to Edo as *Kyō miyage Asamagatake* (A Souvenir from Kyoto, Asama Mountain, 1699), according to Ihara Toshirō, *Kabuki nenpyō*, vol. 1. For a transcription, see Takano Tatsuyuki and Kuroki Kanzō, eds., *Keisei Asamagatake*, in *Genroku kabuki kessakushū* (Tokyo: Waseda Daigaku Shuppanbu, 1925), 2:389–464. The text is a transcription of a nineteenth-century reprinting of an *eiri kyōgenbon* issued by the publisher Hachimonjiya in 1698. For a detailed summary of the play that focuses on the lead male actor, Nakamura Shichisaburō I, see Holly A. Blumner, "Nakamura Shichisaburō I and the Creation of Edo Style *Wagoto*," in *A Kabuki Reader: History and Performance*, ed. Samuel L. Leiter (Armonk, N.Y.: Sharpe, 2002), 60–75.

73. *Keisei Asamagatake*, 9 *omote*. I consulted the copy at the Tōkyō University of Arts Library.

74. For a discussion of *sabaki*, see Kimura Yūnosuke, *Katsura* (Tokyo: Bunka Shinkōkai, 1974), 1:155.

75. This translation is based on one by Holly A. Blumner, though I have made slight changes to fit it into the context of my discussion. For the original translation, see Blumner, "Nakamura Shichisaburō I and the Creation of Edo-Style *Wagoto*," 65–66. For the original, see Takano and Kuroki, *Keisei Asamagatake*, 413–14.

76. For details of the conflated visual representations of the two hells, see Hirasawa, *Hell-Bent for Heaven*, 97–100. I am grateful to one of my anonymous reviewers for pointing out this gender reversal.

77. *Yakusha yatsushijō: Kyoto*, in *Kabuki hyōbanki shūsei*, ed. Kabuki Hyōbanki Kenkyūkai (Tokyo: Iwanami Shoten, 1973), 3:49. Sennojō is categorized here as a *kashagata* (actor of middle-aged women's roles).

78. *Yakusha gozen kabuki: Kyoto*, in *Kabuki hyōbanki shūsei*, ed. Kabuki Hyōbanki Kenkyūkai (Tokyo: Iwanami Shoten, 1973), 3:378. Kiyosaburō is categorized as a *waka onnagata* (actor of young women's roles).

79. Ibid. For details of Mizuki's cat performance, see Satoko Shimazaki, "Strange Encounters: Performing *Genji* on the Kabuki Stage" (paper presented at the conference "*The Story of the Stone* and *The Tale of Genji* in Modern

China and Japan: Issues in Media, Technology, Gender, and National Identity," Columbia University, New York, November 19–20, 2010).

80. This shift is evident in the performance history of various Dōjōji-related kabuki plays, as Mizuta Kayano demonstrated in "*Dōjōji*-mono ni okeru jigei to shosagoto: Tomijūrō ni yoru 'shitto no zendan' kakuritsu made," *Engekigaku* 29 (1988): 54–73.

81. The transformative power of jealous women's blood is also seen in *Sesshū gappō ga tsuji*.

82. For a survey of ghost plays by Onoe Matsusuke and Onoe Kikugorō, see Yokoyama Yasuko, *Edo Tōkyō no kaidan bunka no seiritsu to hensen* (Tokyo: Kazama Shobō, 1997), 66–257.

83. Tsutsumi Kunihiko introduced early Tokugawa plays representing jealous male figures turning into serpents and has suggested the possibility that during the early Tokugawa period, the distinction between male and female might not have been very rigid in performance, in *Nyonin jatai*, 138–39.

84. Examples of works featuring Kohada Koheiji are Tsuruya Nanboku's *Iroeiri otogizōshi* (1808), Santō Kyōden's *yomihon*, *Fukushū kidan Asaka no numa* (1803), and Santō Kyōden's *gōkan*, *Asaka no numa gonichi no Adauchi* (1807).

85. Sanyūtei Enchō, *Shinkei Kasane ga fuchi* (Tokyo: Iwanami Shoten 2007), 82.

86. Futabatei Shimei, *Ukigumo* (Tokyo: Iwanami Shoten, 1941), 147.

87. Ibid., 150.

4. THE END OF THE WORLD

1. The snowfall is suggested by the beating of the drum.

2. Tsuruya Nanboku IV, *Tōkaidō Yotsuya kaidan*, ed. Gunji Masakatsu (Tokyo: Shinchōsha, 1981), 382–84. This edition is based on a manuscript by Suzuki Hakutō (1767–1851), who is thought to have had access to some of the script used in the 1825 production. In this passage from the script, Oume is referred to as Kihei's daughter and Kihei as Iemon's father-in-law. To avoid confusion in my translation, since Kihei's daughter (Oume's mother) also is mentioned, I have made the relationships among the characters consistent with those in the rest of the play.

3. Santei Shunba, *Okyōgen gakuya no honsetsu* (Edo: Tsutaya Kichizō, 1858), 1:16 *ura*. For a transcription of the text, see Santei Shunba, *Okyōgen gakuya no honsetsu*, ed. Kokuritsu Gekijō Geinō Chōsashitsu, Kabuki no bunken 2 (Tokyo: Kokuritsu Gekijō Chōsa Yōseibu Geinō Chōsashitsu, 1967). For a discussion of other ghost-related effects taken up by the work, see Samuel L. Leiter, *Frozen Moments: Writings on Kabuki 1966–2001* (Ithaca, N.Y.: Cornell University East Asia Program, 2002), 92–109.

4. Scholars such as Tsutsumi Kunihiko, Tamamuro Taijō, Kōdate Naomi, and, more recently, Hank Glassman have situated the *ubume* in the context of beliefs and practices associated with the Ketsubonkyō (Blood Bowl Sutra) and religious salvation for women. Sasaki Kōshō, Shinmura Taku, and Yasui

Manami have shed light on medical practices that competed with Buddhist means of pacifying the *ubume*.

5. In an insightful analysis of Nanboku's ghost plays, Takahashi Noriko argued that Nanboku superimposed images of female suffering and grief onto the ghosts by presenting them as *ubume*, in "Tsuruya Nanboku to ubume: Tenjiku Tokubei ikokubanashi no menoto Iohata kara Yotsuya kaidan no Oiwa e no henbō," *Bungaku* 53, no. 9 (1985): 80–88. Kitashiro Nobuko, who has written on popular Buddhism and *ubume* in the nineteenth century, noted that from the late eighteenth century, the monk Yūten, who was well known for pacifying the ghost of Kasane, came to be even more famous for his ability to ensure safe childbearing, and temples frequently held pacification rituals alongside kabuki productions featuring *ubume*. See Kitashiro Nobuko, "Hen'yō suru jisha engi: kinsei shōdō to bungei, geinō," in *Jisha engi no bunkagaku*, ed. Tsutsumi Kunihiko and Tokuda Kazuo (Tokyo: Shinwasha, 2005), 111–32. For a general discussion of *ubume* in literature, see Nishida Kōzō, "Ubume nōto: bungei ga toraeta ubume to sono shūhen," *Kumamoto Daigaku kyōyōbu kiyō: jinbun shakai gakka* 15 (1980): 124–32, and "Ubume nōto: zoku," *Kumamoto Daigaku kyōyōbu kiyō: jinbun shakai gakka* 24 (1989): 107–12. For an analysis of images of *ubume* in Santō Kyōden's studies of Buddhist hells and ghosts, see Inoue Keiji, *Kyōden kōshōgaku to yomihon no kenkyū* (Tokyo: Shintensha, 1997).

6. Mabuchi Kazuo, Kunisaki Fumimaro, and Inagaki Taiichi, eds., *Konjaku monogatarishū*, Shinpen Nihon koten bungaku zenshū 38 (Tokyo: Shōgakukan, 2002), 4:134–38.

7. Ibid., 138.

8. The title of this work is given as *Konjaku monogatari* on the outside and inside covers, and the title *Kōtei konjaku monogatari* appears, strictly speaking, only in the preface. See Izawa Nagahide [Banryō], *Konjaku monogatari* [*Kōtei konjaku monogatari*] (Kyoto: Ryūshiken, 1820), National Institute of Japanese Literature. I have used *Kōtei konjaku monogatari* to avoid confusion with the Heian-period text and to accord with standard academic practice. Inagaki Taiichi's facsimile publication of the work, for instance, is titled *Kōtei konjaku monogatari*.

9. For example, it falsely attributed the original *Konjaku monogatarishū* to Minamoto no Takakuni, thus initiating a long-lived misapprehension. The compiler of *Konjaku monogatarishū* is unknown. For background on *Kōtei konjaku monogatari*, see Inagaki Taiichi, "Kaisetsu to kenkyū," in *Kōtei konjaku monogatari* (Tokyo: Shintensha, 1990), 2:553–606; Ueda Setsuo, "*Kōtei Konjaku monogatari* no setsuwa sekai: Izawa Banryō no setsuwa kyōju o megutte," *Kokugo kokubun* 60, no. 12 (1991): 19–32; and Katō Yūichirō, "*Kōtei konjaku monogatari* to Konjaku monogatarishū," *Chūō kokubun* 37 (1995): 91–101. For a facsimile of the text, see Izawa Nagahide, *Kōtei konjaku monogatari*, 2 vols., ed. Inagaki Taiichi (Tokyo: Shintensha, 1990).

10. Izawa, *Kōtei konjaku monogatari*, 1:25–27.

11. Katayose Masayoshi, *Konjaku monogatarishū no kenkyū* (Kamakura: Geirinsha, 1974), 1:205.

12. Inagaki, "Kaisetsu to kenkyū," 557.

13. Toriyama Sekien (text and pictures), *Gazu hyakki yagyō* (Edo: Izumoji Izuminojō, 1776), Tokyo University of the Arts Library. For a reproduction and transcription, see Toriyama Sekien, *Gazu hyakki yagyō*, in *Toriyama Sekien, Gazu hyakki yagyō*, ed. Takada Mamoru, Inada Atsunobu, and Tanaka Naohi (Tokyo: Kokusho Kankōkai, 1992). The copy from 1776 that I consulted at the Tokyo University of the Arts Library has been rebound, and the pages are out of order. A smaller digital view of the text is available at http://images.lib.geidai.ac.jp/.

14. Tamamuro Taijō, *Sōshiki bukkyō* (Tokyo: Daihōrinkaku, 1963), 202–3; Caroline Hirasawa, *Hell-Bent for Heaven in Tateyama Mandara: Painting and Religious Practice at a Japanese Mountain* (Leiden: Brill, 2013), 138–39.

15. Narikiyo Hirokazu, *Josei to kegare no rekishi* (Tokyo: Hanawa Shobō, 2003). See also Minamoto Junko, *Bukkyō to sei: erosu eno ifu to sabetsu* (Tokyo: San'ichi Shobō, 1996). The menstruation taboo is set out in *Kōninshiki* (*Procedures of the Kōnin Era*, ninth century) and *Engishiki* (*Procedures of the Engi Era*, 907–927). This does not, however, indicate that notions of blood defilement circulated as widely as they did in the late medieval period.

16. For more information about these hells, see Tsutsumi Kunihiko, *Kinsei bukkyō setsuwa no kenkyū: shōdō to bungei* (Tokyo: Kanrin Shobō, 1996); and Kawamura Mitsukuni, "Onna no jigoku to sukui," in *Onna to otoko no ran: chūsei*, ed. Okano Haruko, Onna to otoko no jikū: Nihon joseishi saikō 3 (Tokyo: Fujiwara Shoten, 1996), 31–80.

17. The Blood Bowl Sutra appeared in the context of tenth-century popular beliefs in China and became extremely popular in the Ming and Qing periods, according to Kōdate Naomi, "Aspects of Ketsubonkyō Belief," trans. Susanne Formanek, in *Practicing the Afterlife: Perspectives from Japan*, ed. Susanne Formanek and William R. LaFleur (Vienna: Verlag der Österreichischen Akademie der Wissenschaften, 2004), 121–43, and "Chi no ike jigoku," in *Tōyō ni okeru shi no shisō*, ed. Yoshihara Hiroto (Tokyo: Shunjūsha, 2006), 231–47.

18. Hank Glassman, "At the Crossroads of Birth and Death: The Blood Pool Hell and Postmortem Fetal Extraction," in *Death and the Afterlife in Japanese Buddhism*, ed. Jacqueline I. Stone and Mariko Namba Walter (Honolulu: University of Hawai'i Press, 2008), 184.

19. Duncan Ryūken Williams, *The Other Side of Zen: A Social History of Sōtō Zen Buddhism in Tokugawa Japan* (Princeton, N.J.: Princeton University Press, 2005), 51. For a discussion of the use of sutras, amulets, and certificates used to save women from Blood Pool Hell in Tateyama, see Hirasawa, *Hell-Bent for Heaven*, 137–81.

20. The Blood Bowl Sutra exists in many forms. Some Japanese adaptations associated the origin of Blood Pool Hell with the sins of a jealous woman, so that women who had turned into serpents out of jealousy were depicted as residing there as well. Most often the sutra was invoked for the sake of deceased mothers.

21. According to two articles by Minakata Kumagusu, first published in *Kyōdo kenkyū* in September 1931 and August 1936, this practice also is

mentioned in early Chinese texts, such as *Yiyuan* (*Garden of Marvels*, fifth century) and Hong Mai's *Yijian zhi* (*Records of the Listener*). See Minakata Kumagusu, "Ninpu no shikabane yori taiji o hikihanasu koto," in *Sōsō bosei kenkyū shūsei*, vol. 1, *Sōhō*, ed. Doi Takuji and Satō Yoneshi (Tokyo: Meicho Shuppan, 1979), 296–98.

22. Onshi Zaidan Boshi Aiiku Kai, ed., *Nihon san'iku shūzoku shiryō shūsei* (Tokyo: Daiichi Hōki Shuppan, 1975).

23. Shinmura Taku, *Shussan to seishokukan no rekishi* (Tokyo: Hōsei Daigaku Shuppan Kyoku, 1996), 151–52. The surgery was performed using a sickle. For an analysis of this practice from the perspective of folklore studies, see Katsurai Kazuo, "Kama no e ni kansuru kinki: Taiji bunri no koshū nōto," and Yamaguchi Yaichirō, "Shitai bunri maisō jiken: Ninpu sōsō girei," both in *Sōsō bosei kenkyū shūsei*, vol. 1, *Sōhō*, ed. Doi Takuji and Satō Yoneshi (Tokyo: Meicho shuppan, 1979), 291–95, 299–303.

24. Tsutsumi Kunihiko, "Kosodate yūreitan no genfūkei: sōsō girei o tegakari to shite," in *Kinsei setsuwa to zensō* (Osaka: Izumi Shoin, 1999), 133–52.

25. Kondō Naoyoshi, *Tassei zusetsu* (Edo: Kitsushidō, 1858), fascicle 3, 39 *ura*–40 *omote*.

26. *Kōya monogatari*, in *Muromachi monogatarishū*, ed. Ichiko Teiji, Shin Nihon koten bungaku taikei 54 (Tokyo: Iwanami Shoten, 1979), 1:339.

27. Quoted in Nishida, "Ubume nōto: zoku," 107–8.

28. Kuroda Hideo, "Dōji no shi to takai," in *Emaki kodomo no tōjō: chūsei shakai no kodomo zō* (Tokyo: Kawade Shobō Shinsha, 1989), 106–13.

29. Takada Mamoru, ed., *Shiryō gedatsu monogatari kikigaki*, in *Kinsei kidan shūsei*, Sōsho Edo bunko 26 (Tokyo: Kokusho Kankōkai, 1992), 1:374–85. For a detailed analysis of this work, see Takada Mamoru, *Edo no ekusoshisuto* (Tokyo: Chikuma Shobō, 1991).

30. Not surprisingly, this shift is reflected in literary depictions of ubume. Late-seventeenth-century *kanazōshi* works were very much concerned with the situation of the woman herself, focusing on her sins, her suffering, her efforts to attain Buddhahood, and, finally, her salvation by a monk. In one of the tales in the *katakana* edition of *Inga monogatari* (*Tales of Retribution*, 1661), a collection attributed to the monk Suzuki Shōsan, a young woman whose lower body is "drenched in blood" appears to a traveling monk in a dream. She provides specific instructions for him to rewrite the text on her stupa and to copy the sutra to help lighten her suffering. She turns out to be the daughter of the proprietor of the inn where the monk is staying, and she had died in childbirth. Again, the blood serves as both a reminder of the woman's suffering during childbirth and an indication of her current suffering in Blood Pool Hell. It is no coincidence, of course, that the authors of texts like this one, with their emphasis on the efficacy of religious practice, were often monks. For the text of the relevant section of *Inga monogatari* (*katakana* ed.), see Asakura Haruhiko, ed., *Kanazōshi shūsei* (Tokyo: Tōkyōdō Shuppan, 1983), 4:294.

31. Yasui Manami, "Taiji bunri maisō no shūzoku to shussan o meguru kaii no fōkuroa: sono seisei to shōmetsu ni kansuru kōsatsu," in *Nihon yōkaigaku taizen*, ed. Komatsu Kazuhiko (Tokyo: Shōgakukan, 2003), 498.

32. The teacher probably cites directly from *Bencao gangmu*, in which *yexing younü* is written 夜行游女, using the character 游. Almost all early modern Japanese texts seem to substitute the character 遊.

33. Yamaoka Genrin, *Kokon hyaku monogatari hyōban*, in *Zoku hyakumonogatari kaidan shūsei*, ed. Tachikawa Kiyoshi, Sōsho Edo bunko 27 (Tokyo: Kokusho Kankōkai, 1993), 32.

34. Yamada Keiji, *Yoru naku tori: igaku, jujutsu, densetsu* (Tokyo: Iwanami Shoten, 1990), 1–51.

35. Okami Masao and Takahashi Kiichi, eds., *Shintōshū*, Shintō taikei: bungaku hen 1 (Tokyo: Shintō Taikei Hensankai, 1988), 36. The section is from "Kumano gongen no koto," 31–42.

36. Kitagawa Morisada, *Kinsei fūzokushi: Morisada mankō*, ed. Usami Hideki (Tokyo: Iwanami Shoten, 2002), 5:143.

37. For a summary of the household-disturbance plot by Kawatake Shigetoshi, see chapter 2.

38. Tominaga Heibei, *Tanba Yosaku tazuna obi*, in *Genroku kabuki kessaku shū*, ed. Takano Tatsuyuki and Kuroki Kanzō (Tokyo: Rinsen Shoten, 1973) 2:35–68. The depiction of the mistress's ghost in a so-called illustrated kabuki text (*e-iri kyōgenbon*) for this play shows her not in the familiar visual form of the *ubume* but dressed in ordinary clothes and riding a horse.

39. This play was popular in the Kamigata region but was performed infrequently in Edo.

40. This was first pointed out by Furuido Hideo, "Kaidai," in *Fukumori Kyūsuke kyakuhon shū*, ed. Furuido Hideo et al., Sōsho Edo bunko 49 (Tokyo: Kokusho Kankōkai, 2001), 453–77. See also Furuido Hideo, ed., *Kabuki tōjō jinbutsu jiten*, comp. Kawatake Toshio (Tokyo: Hakusuisha, 2006), 108–11.

41. Fukumori Kyūsuke, *Hana to mimasu yoshino no miyuki*, in *Fukumori Kyūsuke kyakuhon shū*, ed. Furuido Hideo et al., Sōsho Edo bunko 49 (Tokyo: Kokusho kankōkai, 2001), 155.

42. Ibid., 156.

43. For an interpretation of this scene, see Hirano Hidetoshi, "Nihon buyō de no Kyūsuke saku, kiyomoto 'Onnadayū' no kaitei jōen to tokiwazu *Ubume no kowakare* no fukkatsu jōen," in *Fukumori Kyūsuke kyakuhon shū*, Monthly Report 49 (Tokyo: Kokusho kankōkai, 2001), 1–5. My own analysis draws on the script and illustrations in playbills from the 1798 production.

44. This was the case until Kawatake Mokuami's productions in the last decades of the early modern period began explicitly moving away from conventional historical drama. See Furuido, "Kaidai," 453–77.

45. Unfortunately, the script of *Tenjiku Tokubei ikoku banashi* seems not to have survived, and it is unclear from existing playbills and records of the play whether or not Iohata was cradling an infant. Numerous variant texts are available, however, that aid our understanding, such as Namiki Gohei's *Nami makura ikoku no kikigaki* (The Pillow of Waves, Anecdotes from a Foreign Land, 1806), in which Onoe Matsusuke I performed the same roles, and Tsuruya Nanboku IV's *Tenjiku Tokubei banri no irifune* (Tokubei from India, Ship from a Thousand Li, 1841).

46. Tsuruya Nanboku IV, *Iroeiri otogizōshi*, in *Tsuruya Nanboku zenshū*, ed. Gunji Masakatsu (Tokyo: San'ichi Shobō, 1971), 1:172.

47. Ibid., 179.

48. Gunji Masakatsu, "Jisuke, Kyōden, Nanboku," in *Gunji Masakatsu santei shū* (Tokyo Hakusuisha, 1991), 1:294–310. Kyōden was close to the playwright Sakurada Jisuke I, under whom Nanboku worked early in his career. Gunji shows that Nanboku adapted the ghost scene from Kyōden's *yomihon*, *Ukibotan zenden* (*The Tale of the Floating Peony*, 1809), in his play *Okuni gozen keshō no sugatami*, which was then readapted by Kyōden in his *gōkan*, *Kabuki no hana botan dōrō* (*The Flower of Kabuki, the Peony Lantern Ghost Story*, 1810), the following year.

49. Gunji, "Jisuke, Kyōden, Nanboku," 309.

50. Shikitei Sanba (text) and Ogawa Yoshimaru (pictures), *Hara no uchi gesaku no tanehon* (Edo: Tsuruya Kiemon, 1811), National Diet Library, 7 *ura*–8 *omote*.

51. Ibid., 8 *omote*.

52. Ibid., 13 *omote*.

53. Ibid., 10 *omote*.

54. After 1806, most historians of Japanese literature agree, *kibyōshi* were supplanted by *gōkan*. For a historical overview of the history of *kibyōshi*, see Adam Kern, *Manga from the Floating World: Comic Book Culture and the Kibyōshi of Edo Japan* (Cambridge, Mass.: Harvard University Press, 2006), 181–250. The *yomihon* was a more expensive form than the *gōkan* and was published in much smaller numbers, but in the first decades of the nineteenth century, some *yomihon* were published in the *gōkan* size, and some of these were more image oriented than were ordinary late *yomihon*. This special variety of *yomihon* is known as *chūhongata yomihon* (middle-size reading books). They are heavily theater oriented and may represent an intermediate stage between the two genres.

55. Koike Tōgorō discusses these developments, with special reference to Kyōden, in *Santō Kyōden no kenkyū* (Tokyo: Iwanami Shoten, 1935). My own survey of early-nineteenth-century *gōkan*, principally in the Waseda University Library's collection, indicates that ghosts in these works function largely as they do in the theater.

56. This work was republished with the title *Matsu no midori Takasagobanashi*. When the first two Sino-Japanese characters in the title are combined, the combination is read as "Shōroku" (Matsusuke's name at this point), so the title could also be translated as "Shōroku's Takasago Story," emphasizing his presence in the text.

57. Chikamatsu Monzaemon, *Kako no Kyōshin nanahaka meguri*, in *Chikamatsu zenshū*, ed. Chikamatsu Zenshū Kankōkai (Tokyo: Iwanami Shoten, 1988), 9:272–73.

58. Takagi Gen, *Edo yomihon no kenkyū: jūkyū seiki shōsetsu yōshiki kō* (Tokyo: Perikansha, 1995), 13.

59. The *yomihon* consists less of a linear narrative than of a series of climaxes that often fuse communally shared story paradigms. In Bakin, the

framework is often identified as karmic retribution (*inga ōhō*), which in some cases involves women's grudges. See, for instance, Tokuda Takeshi, "*Nansō Satomi hakkenden*: ingaritsu no hatten," in *Inga*, ed. Konno Tōru, Iwanami kōza Nihon bungaku to bukkyō 2 (Tokyo: Iwanami Shoten, 1994), 131–56; and Tanaka Norio, "Inga ōhō: chōhen shōsetsu ni naizai suru rinen," *Edo bungaku* 34 (2006): 123–33. Ōtaka Yōji, a scholar of nineteenth-century *yomihon*, suggested that whereas the theatrical framework centered on the vengeance plot or the household struggle, the *yomihon* developed a different structure:

> Usually a key figure or item appears early in the narrative—it could be a human, animal, immaterial object, or even a word—and although it does not surface in the narrative, the element keeps on affecting the development of the story either directly or indirectly. Closure comes to historical *yomihon* once that string vanishes: when, for example, an angry ghost attains salvation, or with the disappearance of past karmic ties, or the discovery of the meaning of a mystery word. ("Kyōwa san, yonen no Bakin yomihon," *Nihon bunka ronsō* 38 [2000]: 348)

60. Santō Kyōden (text) and Utagawa Toyokuni (pictures), *Sakurahime zenden akebonozōshi* (Edo: Bunkeidō, 1805), Waseda University Library. For transcriptions of the text, see Santō Kyōden, *Sakurahime zenden akebonozōshi*, in *Santō Kyōden zenshū*, ed. Mizuno Minoru et al. (Tokyo: Perikansha, 1997), 16:9–171, and *Baika hyōretsu*, in *Santō Kyōden shū*, ed. Satō Miyuki, Sōsho Edo bunko 18 (Tokyo: Perikansha, 1987), 237–347. Toward the end of the early modern period, Kyōden and other writers, such as Bakin, published texts known as *kōshō zuihitsu* (antiquarian miscellanies) describing their research into earlier customs and objects. Kyōden showed a particularly keen interest in all sorts of issues related to women, from the belief in women's hells to pregnancy and childrearing—all themes that he included in his literary oeuvre. Kyōden's concern with the contention between the wife and the mistress is reflected in *Kottōshū* (*Collection of Ancient Matters*), which includes a detailed explanation and illustration of *uwanari uchi* (beating the second wife), a practice from the medieval period and the beginning of the early modern period in which a first wife orchestrated an attack on a second. See Santō Kyōden, *Kottōshū* (1814–1815; Edo: Bunkeidō, 1836), 4:4 *omote*–6 *omote*, Waseda University Library.

61. *Sakurahime zenden akebonozōshi* draws on many sources, including the Buddhist *kangebon* (wide varieties of Buddhist books for preaching and popular enlightenment) *Kanzen Sakurahime den* (*The Complete Legend of Sakurahime*, 1765), and the lineage of stories about Sakurahime and the monk Seigen that derives from the *kojōruri* play *Isshin niga byakudō* (*White Path Between the Two Rivers*, 1673), which was rewritten in 1698 for kabuki by Chikamatsu Monzaemon.

62. Tsuruya, *Tōkaidō Yotsuya kaidan*, 184.

63. Various manuscript and printed editions of these true accounts survive. The oldest is *Yotsuya zōdanshū* (1727) in the Yaguchi Tanba Kinen

Bunko collection. For information about the various editions, see Konita Seiji, "Kaidan mono jitsuroku no isō: 'Yotsuya zōdan' saikō," in *Kinsei bungaku fukan*, ed. Hasegawa Tsuyoshi (Tokyo: Kyūko Shoin, 1997), 275–94; and Takada Mamoru, *Oiwa to Iemon: Yotsuya kaidan no shinsō* (Tokyo: Yōsensha, 2002).

64. *Umazume jigoku*, the hell for women who did not bear children, is also written using the character for "stone." A similar juxtaposition of stone and flower is seen in the episode in the *Kojiki* (*Record of Ancient Matters*, 712) about the ugly Iwanagabime (Stone Princess), resented by Ninigi, who loves her sister Konohana no Sakuyabime (Flower-Blossoming Princess). Konohana no Sakuyabime becomes pregnant with Ninigi's baby after their first night together. See Yamaguchi Yoshinori, ed., *Kojiki*, Shinpen Nihon koten bungaku zenshū 1 (Tokyo: Shōgakukan, 1997), 121–23. In the *Nihon shoki* (*Chronicles of Japan*, 720), Iwanagabime even places a curse on Konohana no Sakuyabime's baby. See Kojima Yoshinori, ed., *Nihon shoki*, Shinpen Nihon koten bungaku zenshū 2 (Tokyo: Shōgakukan, 1994), 1:141.

65. It is telling, in this sense, that in later productions of *Yotsuya kaidan*, Oiwa stops appearing as an *ubume* at all; the effect is replaced by her appearance inside a lantern. Sawamura Gennosuke IV emerged from the consecration cloth as Oiwa in the August 1905 production at the Miyato Theater. It is interesting to find him explaining in an apologetic tone that he was not following the "authentic" manner of appearing from a lantern because it was his first time performing Oiwa and he did not want anything to go wrong. See Sawamura Gennosuke IV, "Hatsuyaku no Oiwa ni tsuite," *Kabuki* (Kabuki Hakkōjo) 65 (1905): 43–44.

66. This phenomenon is analyzed in detail in Imao Tetsuya, "Kabuki ni okeru 'sekai' no hōkai," in *Kabuki "tsūsetsu" no kenshō* (Tokyo: Hōsei Daigaku Shuppan Kyoku, 2010), 47–86.

5. ANOTHER HISTORY

1. Ihara Seisei'en [Toshirō], "P fujin e," in *Sajiki kara shosai e* (Tokyo: Shin Engei Sōsho, 1924), 3–4. This chapter originally appeared in the journal *Kabuki* (Kabuki Hakkōjo) 168 (1914): 19–27.

2. Zoë Kincaid to Ihara Seisei'en, February 17, 1917.

3. Ibid.; Zoë Kincaid to Ihara Seisei'en, June 15 and 22, 1917.

4. Zoë Kincaid, *Kabuki: The Popular Stage of Japan* (1925; New York: Blom, 1965), v.

5. Ihara Seisei'en, *Sajiki kara shosai e*, 327.

6. Ibid, 303.

7. Mitamura Engyo, "*Yotsuya kaidan* wa obake shibai ka," *Kikan zasshi kabuki* 1, no. 3 (1925): 57.

8. "Shibai osatoshi," *Shinbun zasshi*, no. 36 (1872), in *Meiji bunka zenshū*, ed. Meiji Bunka Kenkyūkai (Tokyo: Nihon Hyōronsha, 1967), 24:484.

9. "Engeki shushi no setsuyu," *Shinbun zasshi*, no. 40 (1872), in *Meiji bunka zenshū*, ed. Meiji Bunka Kenkyūkai, 24:485.

10. Several scholarly works have analyzed the shift in the understanding of theater during the Meiji and Taishō periods, especially among elites. Excellent works in this field include Indra A. Levy, *Sirens of the Western Shore: The Westernesque Femme Fatale, Translation, and Vernacular Style in Modern Japanese Literature* (New York: Columbia University Press, 2006), 195–266; M. Cody Poulton, "Meiji Drama Theory Before Ibsen" and "The Rise of Modern Drama," in *A Beggar's Art: Scripting Modernity in Japanese Drama, 1900–1930* (Honolulu: University of Hawai'i Press, 2010), 1–25, 29–45; Harue Tsutsumi, "Kabuki Encounters the West: Morita Kan'ya's Shintomi-za Productions, 1878–79" (Ph.D. diss., Indiana University, 2004); and Ōzasa Yoshio, *Nihon gendai engekishi: Meiji, Taishō hen* (Tokyo: Hakusuisha, 1985). Brian Powell offers a thorough survey of Japanese theater from the Meiji period to recent times, including the revival of kabuki after the 1930s, in *Japan's Modern Theater: A Century of Change and Continuity* (London: Japan Library, 2002).

11. Karatani Kōjin, *Nihon kindai bungaku no kigen* (Tokyo: Kōdansha, 1988), 67–68.

12. For an analysis of Danjūrō's *haragei*, see Sasayama Keisuke, "Kudaime Danjūrō no hara to kao," in *Engijutsu no Nihon kindai* (Tokyo: Shinwasha, 2012), 21–56.

13. Gunji Masakatsu, "Kabuki: Edo kara Meiji," *Bungaku* 53, no. 11 (1985): 178.

14. Imaoka Kentarō, "Bakumatsu no kabuki," in *Kabuki no rekishi II*, ed. Torigoe Bunzō, Uchiyama Mikiko, and Watanabe Tamotsu, Iwanami kōza kabuki bunraku 3 (Tokyo: Iwanami Shoten, 1997), 53; Waseda Daigaku Engeki Hakubutsukan, ed., *Shibai-e ni miru Edo Meiji no kabuki* (Tokyo: Shōgakukan, 2003), 98–99.

15. Enomoto Torahiko, *Ōchi koji to Ichikawa Danjūrō* (Tokyo: Kokkōsha, 1903), 17.

16. Ibid., 19–20.

17. For details of the new movements during the Meiji period, see Tsutsumi, "Kabuki Encounters the West."

18. On the different grades of Meiji theaters, I consulted *Gekijō zue*, a Meiji-period guide to theater and theater culture, and confirmed the information that I found there in guidebooks to Tokyo. In 1890, ten theaters were classified as major theaters and twelve as small theaters, according to *Gekijō zue*, *Sejigahō* 1, no. 8 (Tokyo: Sejigahōsha, 1898), 8–9; Tōkyō shi, ed., *Tōkyō an'nai*, 2 vols. (Tokyo: Shōkabō, 1907); and Yomiuri Shinbunsha, *Tōkyō an'nai* (Tokyo: Yomiuri Shinbunsha, 1906). For a comprehensive study of small theaters in Meiji-period Tokyo, see Satō Katsura, *Kabuki no bakumatsu Meiji: koshibai no jidai* (Tokyo: Perikansha, 2010).

19. Kamiyama Akira, " 'Bikutorian Japan' (Meiji Nihon) no gekijō," *Kabuki* (Kabuki gakkai) 39 (2007): 34.

20. Quoted in Sekine Shisei, *Tōto gekijō enkaku shiryō*, ed. Kokuritsu Gekijō Geinō Chōsashitsu. Kabuki shiryō sensho 6 (Tokyo: Kokuritsu Gekijō Geinō Chōsashitsu, 1984), 2:683. For a discussion of the use of the term *engeki* during the Meiji period, see Kamiyama Akira, *Kindai engeki no raireki: kabuki no isshin nisei* (Tokyo: Shinwasha, 2006), 7–10.

21. Fukuchi Ōchi also served in the government and later became the editor of *Tokyo nichinichi shinbun*, one of the first journalistic newspapers.

22. Tsubouchi Shōyō grew up in Nagoya, where theaters had more freedom to stage kabuki in the early modern style even during the Meiji period, so he was immersed in the old style of kabuki as a child.

23. Tsubouchi Shōyō, "Katsureki geki *Momoyamatan* no konjaku," in *Kaki no heta* (Tokyo: Chūō Kōronsha, 1933), 99.

24. Shōyō wrote repeatedly about the vulgarity of plays in his hometown Nagoya. See, for example, Tsubouchi Shōyō, "Akarui shibai tai kurai shibai," in *Shōyō senshū* (Tokyo: Shunyōdō, 1927), 10:325–35. For a modern production history of kabuki, including the small theaters, see Komiya Kiichi, ed., *Kabuki shinpa shinkokugeki jōen nenpyō*, dai 6-han (Privately printed, 2007).

25. During the Meiji period, Nanboku's plays survived mainly in the Kamigata region and in small theaters in Tokyo. In the small theaters, *Yotsuya kaidan* would be staged by actors who had no firsthand knowledge of acting the part.

26. Tōkyō-za was a new brick building constructed in 1897, and according to the *Tōkyō an'nai* of 1907, it was one of Tokyo's major theaters. See Tōkyō shi, *Tōkyō an'nai*, 1:546. The price per person for box seats in the theater was less than half the price of similar seats at the Kabuki-za. The Tōkyō-za staged *Yotsuya kaidan* twice during the Meiji period, with a different actor playing Oiwa each time. See Komiya, *Kabuki shinpa shinkokugeki jōen nenpyō*, 275.

27. Onoe Baikō VI, "Oiwa," *Engei gahō* 12 (1909): 135.

28. Ibid., 134. Baikō gives a detailed account of which scenes had to be taken out because of censorship, his ambivalence reflecting the larger intellectual climate of the Meiji era. For a larger discussion of the supernatural and modernity among the elites, see Gerald Figal, *Civilization and Monsters: Spirits of Modernity in Meiji Japan* (Durham, N.C.: Duke University Press, 1999); and Michael Dylan Foster, *Pandemonium and Parade: Japanese Monsters and the Culture of Yōkai* (Berkeley: University of California Press, 2008), 77–159.

29. *Miyako shinbun*, September 10, 1903. According to *Ninki yakusha no koseki shirabe*, Onoe Shōkaku (Shinohara Takendo) was an actor born in Osaka who, after debuting in that city, became popular as a traveling actor in regional productions. A Tokyo actor of the sixth degree, the lowest rank of actors named on billboards, he was "still popular among lowly educated audiences" (Takazawa Shofū, ed., *Ninki yakusha no koseki shirabe* [1919], Meiji–Shōwa shoki haiyū meikan shūsei, vol. 3 [Tokyo: Yumani Shobō, 2005], 44). Shōkaku was known as "Ghost Shōkaku" (obake no Shōkaku) for the ghost roles, especially Oiwa and Kohei, that he performed in regional productions and small theaters, according to Abe Yūzō, *Tōkyō no koshibai* (Tokyo: Engeki Shuppansha, 1970), 297.

30. *Miyako shinbun*, September 20, 1907. This production moved to the Kokka-za (the former Asakusa-za) the month after the Tokyo-za production.

31. Sawamura Gennosuke IV, who played Oiwa at the Miyato Theater in 1905, also called his performance an "imitation" (*ukeuri*) of a role that properly belonged to the Onoe house, in "Hatsuyaku no Oiwa ni tsuite,"

Kabuki 65 (1905): 44. According to *Miyako shinbun*, August 8, 1905, Gennosuke's production was a hit, and all the seats were sold.

32. Tsubouchi Shōyō, "Bungaku toshite no waga zairai kyakuhon," in *Shōyō senshū* (Tokyo: Shunyōdō, 1927), 10:221–22.

33. Tsubouchi Shōyō, "Shogen," in *ŌNanboku zenshū* (Tokyo: Shunyōdō, 1925), 1:1. The title of the anthology is also read as *Dai Nanboku zenshū* today.

34. William Lee, "Chikamatsu and Dramatic Literature in the Meiji Period," in *Inventing the Classics: Modernity, National Identity, and Japanese Literature*, ed. Haruo Shirane and Tomi Suzuki (Stanford, Calif.: Stanford University Press, 2000), 188.

35. For a discussion of this generational change, see Kamiyama, *Kindai engeki no raireki*, 229.

36. The changing reception of the theater audience is discussed in Miyake Shūtarō, *Engeki gojūnenshi* (Tokyo: Masu Shobō, 1942), 166–75.

37. The formation of the Kogeki Kenkyūkai was announced in the February 1915 issue of the journal *Mita bungaku*. The original members listed here were Osanai Kaoru, Nagai Kafū, Kinoshita Mokutarō, Yoshii Isamu, Kusuyama Masao, Osada Hideo, and Kubota Mantarō. Many of the men were also taking part in the Pan no kai (Association of Pan, 1908–1912). See Mita bungakukai, "Shōsoku," *Mita bungaku* 6, no. 2 (1915): 134.

38. Osanai Kaoru, "Jo," in *Sewa kyōgen no kenkyū*, ed. Kogeki Kenkyūkai (Tokyo: Tengendō, 1916), 1.

39. Aside from one play by Namiki Gohei I, no other playwrights' works were considered in the book.

40. Osanai Kaoru, "Do Beruniuru no *Yotsuya kaidan* ni tsuite," *Shin engei* 8, no. 6 (1923): 55. On Osanai's reading of James De Benneville, see Kamiyama Akira, "Taishōki no Nanboku juyō," *Taishō engeki kenkyū* 4 (1993): 14–28.

41. Osanai, "Do Beruniuru no *Yotsuya kaidan* ni tsuite," 55.

42. Ibid., 54.

43. Ibid., 57.

44. For a discussion of Wedekind, see David Kuhns, "Palimpsestus: Frank Wedekind's Theater of Self-Performance," *New Theater Quarterly* 12, no. 45 (1996): 50–64.

45. Kamiyama, "Taishōki no Nanboku juyō," 4. Kawatake Toshio discusses the Taishō-period reception of Nanboku in "Taishōki nisei Sadanji no Nanboku," *Kikan zasshi kabuki* 10, no. 1 (1977): 50–59.

46. Kusuyama Masao, "*Yotsuya kaidan* oyobi Nanboku ni tsukite," in *Sewakyōgen no kenkyū*, ed. Kogeki Kenkyūkai (Tokyo: Tengendō, 1916), 197–98.

47. Kawatake Shigetoshi, *Kabuki sakusha no kenkyū* (Tokyo: Tōkyōdō, 1940), 189.

48. Nina Cornyetz and Vincent, J. Keith, "Introduction: Japan as Screen Memory: Psychoanalysis and History," in *Perversion and Modern Japan: Psychoanalysis, Literature, Culture*, ed. Nina Cornyetz and J. Keith Vincent (London: Routledge, 2010), 3.

49. Tsubouchi Shōyō, *Shōnenji ni mita kabuki no tsuioku* (Tokyo: Nihon Engei Gasshi Geisha Shuppanbu, 1920), 1.
50. Ibid., 177.
51. Shōyō, "Akarui shibai tai kurai shibai," 335.
52. Shōyō, *Shōnenji ni mita kabuki no tsuioku*, 181, 183.
53. Okamoto Kidō, "Muzukashii kaidangeki," *Engei gahō* 22, no. 7 (1928): 47.
54. The 1909, 1918, and 1923 productions were all titled *Katamigusa Yotsuya kaidan*, following Onoe Kikugoro V's production in 1884.
55. Quoted in Ihara Seisei'en et al., "Ichimura-za shinkyōgen *Katamigusa Yotsuya kaidan*" [panel discussion], *Shin engei* 8, no. 6 (1923): 76.
56. Jerome J. McGann, *Critique of Modern Textual Criticism* (Chicago: University of Chicago Press, 1983), 37.
57. Matsui Shōyō, "*Yotsuya kaidan* no jōen shōhon sakusei to sono jōen suru ni tsuite," *Engei gahō* 75, no. 19 (1925): 54–62.
58. Nagai Kafū, "*Sannin Kichisa kuruwa no hatsugai* ni tsukite," ed. Kogeki Kenkyūkai (Tokyo: Tengendō, 1916), 2.
59. Oka Eiichirō, "*Yotsuya kaidan* to *Omatsuri Sashichi*," *Kabuki* (Kabuki Hakkōjo) 1, no. 3 (1925): 41.
60. Osanai Kaoru points this out in "Kaseiki Edo engeki no fukuen ni kansuru aru anji," *Kabuki kenkyū* 26 (1928): 1–13. His view is shared by figures like Kusuyama Masao and Matsui Shōyō.
61. On the relationship of text, performance, and the constructions of authorship, see David Scott Kastan, *Shakespeare and the Book* (Cambridge: Cambridge University Press, 2001); and W. B. Worthen, *Print and the Poetics of Modern Drama* (Cambridge: Cambridge University Press, 2005).
62. Around the 1840s, role divisions among the playwrights became somewhat ambiguous, according to Mimasuya Nisōji, *Sakusha nenjū gyoji*, in *Nihon shomin bunka shiryō shūsei*, ed. Geinōshi Kenkyūkai (Tokyo: San'ichi Shobō, 1973), 6:677. The head playwright would delegate too much responsibility for rehearsal to the *kyōgenkata*, to the extent that he would allow the actors to rewrite the play and it would be ruined. His disappointment in and anxiety about the changing status of playwrights would have been unthinkable in Nanboku's time.
63. The text of *yokogakibon* was actually written vertically, and the name reflects the fact that the booklets were wider than they were tall. On the different bibliographic formats of the scripts, see Kawatake Shigetoshi, *Kabuki sakusha no kenkyū*, 376–78.
64. Information about the playwrights is included on the final page of the cast playbill. The name of the head playwright is printed larger than the others.
65. My description of the job of the playwright in the later decades of the early modern period draws on Kawatake Shigetoshi, *Kabuki sakusha no kenkyū*; and Mimasuya, *Sakusha nenjū gyōji*. The role of the playwright is not consistent and differs throughout the early modern period and also from city to city.

66. Okamoto Kidō, "Jisaku shoen no omoide," in *Meiji geidan ranpu no moto nite*, afterword by Okamoto Keiichi (1935; repr., Tokyo: Iwanami Bunko, 1993), 292.

67. Cited in Kurata Yoshihiro, *Shibaigoya to yose no kindai: yugei kara bunka e* (Tokyo: Iwanami Shoten, 2006), 175.

68. Tsubouchi Shōyō, "*Hinokiyama* jiken no kanteisho," *Kabuki* (Kabuki Hakkōjo) 163 (1914): 15. My attention was drawn to this incident by Kurata, *Shibaigoya to yose no kindai*, 180.

69. All this has had an impact on the style of playmaking. In fact, theater history from the Meiji period is characterized by a gradual decline in the traditional style, in which playwrights also served as directors. As we saw earlier, educated literary figures such as Okamoto Kidō began to overpower conventional playwrights like Takeshiba Kisui. The same thing happened in many other performing arts. For example, during the Meiji period, stories told by *kōdan* storytellers were transcribed in shorthand and serialized in *Kōdan kurabu* (*Kōdan Club*) until the storytellers went on strike to protest the fact that their work was being serialized alongside transcriptions of the chanted tales of *naniwabushi* (Naniwa chanting) masters (low-ranking street performers during the early modern period who borrowed *kōdan* materials). This ultimately led the magazine to replace the storytellers' tales with works by intellectual writers like Mori Ōgai. See Shashi Hensan Iinkai, ed., *Kōdansha no ayunda gojū-nen: Meiji Taishō hen* (Tokyo: Kōdansha, 1901), 175–78.

70. Translations include Mark Oshima, *Ghost Stories at Yotsuya*, in *Early Modern Japanese Literature: An Anthology, 1600–1900*, ed. Haruo Shirane (New York: Columbia University Press, 2002), 844–84; Paul B. Kennelly, *The Ghost Stories at Yotsuya on the Tōkaidō / Tōkaidō Yotsuya kaidan*, in *Darkness and Desire, 1804–1864*, vol. 3 of *Kabuki Plays on Stage*, ed. James R. Brandon and Samuel L. Leiter (Honolulu: University of Hawai'i Press, 2002), 135–63; and Faith Bach, *Epic Yotsuya Ghost Tale*, in *An Edo Anthology: Literature from Japan's Mega-City, 1750–1850*, ed. Sumie Jones and Kenji Watanabe (Honolulu: University of Hawai'i Press, 2013), 168–82.

71. Furuido Hideo writes that two groups of scripts for the first production have survived, one unedited and the other edited, in "Tōkaidō Yotsuya kaidan," in *Nihon koten bungaku daijiten* (Tokyo: Iwanami Shoten, 1984), 4:401. The Hakutō copy seems to incorporate edits that were done before or during the first production. There are different theories, however. Ogita Kiyoshi notes in "Ikeda Bunko no *Yotsuya kaidan* zakkan," *Kanpō Ikeda bunko* 3 (1993): 6–8, that the Hakutō text is suspiciously well organized and polished.

72. Ihara Toshirō [Seisei'en], *Nihon engekishi* (Tokyo: Waseda Daigaku Shuppanbu, 1904), 650.

73. Hachimonji Jishō, *Yakusha tamazukushi: Osaka* (Kyoto and Osaka: Hachimonjiya Hachizaemon and Kawachiya Tasuke, 1826), 11 *ura*. Kikugorō III appears in the Osaka volume of the 1826 edition because he signed a contract with a theater there after performing in his "farewell production."

5. ANOTHER HISTORY

74. Iemon was played by Ichikawa Ebizō, who was the former Danjūrō VII.

75. Hachimonji Jishō and Shimonsha Namimaro, *Yakusha sassoku hōchō: Edo* (Osaka: Hachimonjiya Hachizaemon and Kawachiya Tasuke, 1837), 74 *omote*. I use the name Danjūrō VII for clarity; the actor already had taken the name Ebizō.

76. The Waseda text, which served as the basis for an edition of *Tōkaidō Yotsuya kaidan* that Kawatake Shigetoshi edited in 1956, belongs to a different line of manuscripts from the Tokyo University text, which is closer to Suzuki Hakutō's copy. The Tokyo University text was used as the base text for *Tōkaidō Yotsuya kaidan* edited by Suwa Haruo in 1999. Both Hakutō's manuscript and Tokyo University's manuscript are large *hanshibon*, which indicates that they were probably made at the theater for transmission or were personal copies, rather than initial drafts or books that circulated among playwrights and actors.

77. Gunji Masakatsu, "Hanrei," in *Tōkaidō Yotsuya kaidan*, ed. Gunji Masakatsu, Shinchō Nihon koten shūsei 45 (Tokyo: Shinchōsha, 1981), 3.

78. Okamoto Kidō, *Meiji no engeki* (Tokyo: Daitō Shuppan, 1942), 77.

79. During the 1850s, as *gōkan* digests began to be regularly produced to accompany kabuki plays, they also began to precede the stage production. For further information, see Akama Ryō, *Edo no engekisho* (Tokyo: Yagi Shoten, 2003), 157. In 1861, the production of the play was preceded by the publication of the *gōkan* version of the play: Segawa Jokō III (text) and Utagawa Kunisada (pictures), *Tōkaidō Yotsuya kaidan* (Edo: Kōeidō, 1861).

80. The dates here are from Ihara Toshirō, *Kabuki nenpyō*, ed. Kawatake Shigetoshi and Yoshida Teruji (Tokyo: Iwanami Shoten, 1961), 6:129.

81. As with *Nagori no hana Yotsuya kaidan*, most actors had ghost writers: Hanagasa Bunkyō frequently served as Onoe Kikugorō III's ghost writer, just as Goryūtei Tokushō wrote many of the works published under Ichikawa Danjūrō VII's name. But even though readers may well have been aware that Kikugorō III had not actually composed the text, the work was neither Bunkyō's nor Nanboku's.

82. Hanagasa Bunkyō, *Nagori no hana Yotsuya kaidan* (Edo: Wakasaya Yoichi, 1826), 1 *omote*. Bunkyō was involved as a script writer in the Osaka production he mentions here.

83. For a thorough analysis of several editions, see Takahashi Noriko, "*Yotsuya kaidan* nigao-e zōgan no gōkan," in *Kusazōshi to engeki* (Tokyo: Kyūko shoin, 2004), 391–413.

84. Kastan, *Shakespeare and the Book*, 8 (italics in original).

85. Enchi Fumiko, *Edo bungaku towazugatari* (Tokyo: Kōdansha, 1978), 19. This episode is mentioned in Yokoyama Yasuko, *Yotsuya kaidan wa omoshiroi* (Tokyo: Heibonsha, 1997). These photographs from *Engei gahō* must have been memorable; Miyamoto Yuriko (1899–1951) described a similar episode of seeing photos of ghosts like Oiwa in "Dōkan'yama," in *Miyamoto Yuriko zenshū* (Tokyo: Shin Nihon Shuppansha, 1981), 17:738.

86. Onoe Baikō's explanation of the mask first appeared in "Oiwa to Okon," *Kabuki* (Kabuki Hakkōjo) 112 (1909): 77–81, and "Oiwa" (1909).

It is cited in Onoe Baikō VI, "Oiwa," in *Tōkaidō Yotsuya kaidan*, ed. Kokuritsu Gekijō Geinō Chōsashitsu, Kokuritsu gekijō jōen shiryō shū 68 (Tokyo: Kokuritsu Gekijō Chōsa Yōseibu Geinō Chōsashitsu, 1971), 105–8.

87. "Odoru Oiwa sama," *Yomiuri shinbun*, July 10, 1937.

88. Suzuki Kensuke, *Jigoku de yōi hai! Nakagawa Nobuo kyōfu eiga no gyōka* (Tokyo: Waizu Shuppan, 2000), 24–25.

89. MaedaAi, *Toshikūkan no naka no bungaku* (Tokyo: Chikuma Shobō, 1982).

90. Ishizawa Shūji, "*Yotsuya kaidan* no gendaisei," *Kikan zasshi kabuki* 1 (1968): 172.

BIBLIOGRAPHY

Abe Yūzō. *Tokyō no koshibai*. Tokyo: Engeki Shuppansha, 1970.
Akai Tatsurō and Nishiyama Matsunosuke, eds. *Edojidai zushi*. Vol. 5. Tokyo: Chikuma Shobō, 1976.
Akama Ryō. *Edo no engekisho*. Tokyo: Yagi Shoten, 2003.
——. "Kabuki no shuppanbutsu I." In *Kabuki bunka no shosō*, edited by Torigoe Bunzō, Uchiyama Mikiko, and Watanabe Tamotsu, 1–26. Iwanami kōza kabuki bunraku 4. Tokyo: Iwanami Shoten, 1998.
——. "Kabuki no shuppanbutsu o yomu: Edo no jōen shisutemu, *Tōkaidō Yotsuya kaidan* no koto nado." In *Edo no shuppan*, edited by Nakano Mitsutoshi, 131–55. Tokyo: Perikansha, 2005.
——. "Sukeroku jitsu wa Soga Gorō no umareru made: Soga kyōgen jōenshi no kenkyū 1." *Geinō* 29 (1987): 8–20.
Akimoto Suzushi. "Kinpira jōruri seiritsu no kiban: Meireki Manji-goro no rensakumono no jōruri." *Gobun* 43 (1984): 10–28.
Anderson, Benedict. *Imagined Communities: Reflections on the Origin and Spread of Nationalism*. London: Verso, 1991.
Asai Ryōi. *Honchō jokan*. In *Honchō jokan*. Vol. 2. Edited by Kinsei Bungaku Shoshi Kenkyūkai, Kinsei bungaku shiryō ruijū, kanazōshi-hen 7. Tokyo: Benseisha, 1972.
——. *Otogi bōko*. Edited by Matsuda Osamu, Watanabe Morikuni, and Hanada Fujio. Shin Nihon koten bungaku taikei 75. Tokyo: Iwanami Shoten, 2001.
Asakura Haruhiko. *Kanazōshi shūsei*. Vol. 4. Tokyo: Tōkyōdō Shuppan, 1983.
Asakura Musei. *Misemono kenkyū*. Kyoto: Shibunkaku Shuppan, 1977.
Atherton, David. "Valences of Vengeance: The Moral Imagination of Early Modern Japanese Vendetta Fiction." Ph.D. diss., Columbia University, 2013.
Austin, J. L. *How to Do Things with Words*. 2nd ed. Edited by J. O. Urmson and Marina Sbisà. Cambridge, Mass.: Harvard University Press, 1975.
Baba Akiko. *Oni no kenkyū*. Tokyo: Chikuma Shobō, 1988.

Bai Juyi. "Song of Lasting Pain." In *An Anthology of Chinese Literature: Beginnings to 1911*, edited and translated by Stephen Owen, 442–47. New York: Norton, 1996.

Bakhtin, Mikhail M. *The Dialogic Imagination: Four Essays*. Edited by Michael Holquist. Translated by Caryl Emerson and Michael Holquist. Austin: University of Texas Press, 1981.

———. *Rabelais and His World*. Translated by Hélène Iswolsky. Bloomington: Indiana University Press, 1984.

Banritei Fukoku. *Yakusha meibutsu sode nikki*. In *Nihon shomin bunka shiryō shūsei*. Vol. 6, *Kabuki*. Edited by Geinōshi Kenkyūkai, 243–46. Tokyo: San'ichi Shobō, 1973.

Barthes, Roland. *Image—Music—Text*. Translated by Stephen Heath. New York: Hill, 1977.

Berry, Mary Elizabeth. *Japan in Print: Information and Nation in the Early Modern Period*. Berkeley: University of California Press, 2006.

Bitō Masahide. "The Akō Incident of 1701–1703." Translated by Henry D. Smith II. *Monumenta Nipponica* 58, no. 2 (2003): 149–70.

Blumner, Holly A. "Nakamura Shichisaburō I and the Creation of Edo-Style Wagoto." In *A Kabuki Reader: History and Performance*, edited by Samuel L. Leiter, 60–75. Armonk, N.Y.: Sharpe, 2002.

Brandon, James R., ed. *Chūshingura: Studies in Kabuki and the Puppet Theater*. Honolulu: University of Hawai'i Press, 1982.

———. "The Theft of *Chūshingura*: Or the Great Kabuki Caper." In *Chūshingura: Studies in Kabuki and the Puppet Theater*, edited by James R Brandon, 111–46. Honolulu: University of Hawai'i Press, 1982.

Brandon, James R., and Samuel L. Leiter, eds. *Kabuki Plays on Stage*. 4 vols. Honolulu: University of Hawai'i Press, 2002–2003.

Burns, Susan L. *Before the Nation: Kokugaku and the Imagining of Community in Early Modern Japan*. Durham, N.C.: Duke University Press, 2003.

Buyō Inshi. *Seji kenmonroku*. Edited by Honjō Eijirō and Takikawa Masajirō. Tokyo: Seiabō, 2001.

Carlson, Marvin. *The Haunted Stage: The Theater as Memory Machine*. Ann Arbor: University of Michigan Press, 2001.

Chartier, Roger. *Publishing Drama in Early Modern Europe*. London: British Library, 1999.

Chikamatsu Monzaemon. *Kako no Kyōshin nanahaka meguri*. In *Chikamatsu zenshū*, edited by Chikamatsu Zenshū Kankōkai, 9:225–338. Tokyo: Iwanami Shoten, 1988.

Conquergood, Dwight. "Performance Studies: Intervention and Radical Research." *Drama Review* 46, no. 2 (2002): 145–56.

Cornyetz, Nina, and J. Keith Vincent. "Introduction: Japan as Screen Memory: Psychoanalysis and History." In *Perversion and Modern Japan: Psychoanalysis, Literature, Culture*, edited by Nina Cornyetz and J. Keith Vincent, 1–21. London: Routledge, 2010.

Creed, Barbara. *The Monstrous Feminine: Film, Feminism, Psychoanalysis*. New York: Routledge, 2007.

De Benneville, James. S. *The Yotsuya kwaidan, or, O'Iwa Inari, Retold from the Japanese Originals*. Philadelphia: Lippincott, 1917.

Diamond, Elin. "Re: Blau, Butler, Beckett, and the Politics of Seeming." *Drama Review* 44, no. 4 (2000): 31–43.

Dix, Monica. "Saint or Serpent? Engendering the Female Body in Medieval Buddhist Narratives." In *The Bodies in Asia*, edited by Bryan S. Turner and Zheng Yangwen, 43–58. Oxford: Berghahn, 2011.

Doi Takuji and Satō Yoneshi, eds. *Sōsō bosei kenkyū shūsei*. Vol. 1, *Sōho*. Tokyo: Meicho Shuppan, 1979.

Eisenstein, Elizabeth. "An Unacknowledged Revolution Revisited." *American Historical Review* 107, no. 1 (2002): 87–105.

———. "Reply." *American Historical Review* 107, no. 1 (2002): 126–28.

———. *The Printing Revolution in Early Modern Europe*. Cambridge: Cambridge University Press, 1983.

Emmerich, Michael. *The Tale of Genji: Translation, Canonization, and World Literature*. New York: Columbia University Press, 2013.

Emoto Hiroshi. "Shibai to yūri." In *Saikaku hikkei*, edited by Taniwaki Masachika, 88–91. Bessatsu Kokubungaku 45. Tokyo: Gakutōsha, 1993.

Enchi Fumiko. *Edo bungaku towazugatari*. Tokyo: Kōdansha, 1978.

Enomoto Torahiko. *Ōchi koji to Ichikawa Danjūrō*. Tokyo: Kokkōsha, 1903.

Face-showing playbill at the Nakamura Theater, 1822. Tokyo University Library, A1-10-14.

Faure, Bernard. *The Power of Denial: Buddhism, Purity, and Gender*. Princeton, N.J.: Princeton University Press, 2003.

Figal, Gerald. *Civilizations and Monsters: Spirits of Modernity in Meiji Japan*. Durham, N.C.: Duke University Press, 1999.

Foucault, Michel. *Power/Knowledge: Selected Interviews and Other Writings, 1972–1977*. Edited by Colin Gordon. New York: Pantheon Books, 1980.

Foster, Michael Dylan. *Pandemonium and Parade: Japanese Monsters and the Culture of Yōkai*. Berkeley: University of California Press, 2008.

Foxwell, Chelsea. "The Double Identity of *Chūshingura*: Theater and History in Nineteenth-Century Prints." *Impressions* 26 (2004): 22–43.

Fuji Akio, ed. "Hayashi Razan hencho *Yūrei no koto*." In *Kinsei bungaku ronsō*, edited by Mizuno Minoru, 459–95. Tokyo: Meiji Shoin, 1992.

Fujimoto Kizan. *Shikidō ōkagami*. Edited by Noma Kōshin. Tokyo: Yūzan bunko, 1961.

Fukumori Kyūsuke. *Hana to mimasu yoshino no miyuki*. In *Fukumori Kyūsuke kyakuhon shū*, edited by Furuido Hideo et al., 3–158. Sōsho Edo bunko 49. Tokyo: Kokusho Kankōkai, 2001.

Furuido Hideo. *Kabuki: toikake no bungaku*. Tokyo: Perikansha, 1998.

———. "Kabuki no haru." *Kokubungaku* 52, no. 1 (2007): 26–31.

———. "Kabuki no irei: tsuizen to shūmei." In *Shiseigaku*. Vol. 4, *Shi to shigo o meguru imēji to bunka*, edited by Osano Shigetoshi and Kinoshita Naoyuki, 129–61. Tokyo: Tōkyō Daigaku Shuppankai, 2008.

———, ed. *Kabuki tōjō jinbutsu jiten*. Compiled by Kawatake Toshio. Tokyo: Hakusuisha, 2006.

———. "Kaidai." In *Fukumori Kyūsuke kyakuhon shū*, edited by Furuido Hideo et al., 453–77. Sōsho Edo bunko 49. Tokyo: Kokusho Kankōkai, 2001.

———. "Kinsei engeki to chihō." *Kokugo to kokubungaku* 64, no. 5 (1987): 109–19.

———. "Nihon ni okeru engeki kenkyū no genjō to kadai: kabuki no fukugen kenkyū o chūshin ni." *Engeki kenkyū sentā kiyō* 3 (2004): 307–9.

———. "Ranjuku-ki no kabuki." In *Iwanami kōza Nihon bungakushi*. Vol. 10, *Jūkyūseiki no bungaku*, 97–124. Tokyo: Iwanami Shoten, 1996.

———. "Tōkaidō Yotsuya kaidan." In *Nihon koten bungaku daijiten*. Vol. 4. 400–401. Tokyo: Iwanami Shoten, 1984.

———. "*Yotsuya kaidan*: yume no ba." *Nihon no bigaku* 17 (1991): 56–73.

Futabatei Shimei. *Ukigumo*. Tokyo: Iwanami Shoten, 1941.

Gachikuken. *Hetadangi chōmonshū*. In *Dangibonshū*. Vol. 3. Edited by Kashikawa Shūchi, 129–230. Tokyo: Koten Bunko, 1999.

Gekijō shinwa. In *Enseki jisshu*, edited by Iwamoto Kattōshi, 4:5–59. Tokyo: Chūō Kōronsha, 1979.

Gekijō zue, Sejigahō 1, no. 8. Tokyo: Sejigahōsha, 1898.

Gerstle, C. Andrew. *Circles of Fantasy: Convention in the Plays of Chikamatsu*. Cambridge, Mass.: Harvard University Asia Center, 1995.

———. *18th Century Japan: Culture and Society*. London: Routledge, 2000.

Glassman, Hank. "At the Crossroads of Birth and Death: The Blood Pool Hell and Postmortem Fetal Extraction." In *Death and the Afterlife in Japanese Buddhism*, edited by Jacqueline I. Stone and Mariko Namba Walter, 175–206. Honolulu: University of Hawai'i Press, 2008.

Gluck, Carol. "The Invention of Edo." In *Mirror of Modernity: Invented Traditions of Modern Japan*, edited by Stephen Vlastos, 262–84. Berkeley: University of California Press, 1998.

Goldman, Michael. *On Drama: Boundaries of Genre, Borders of the Self*. Ann Arbor: University of Michigan Press, 2000.

Goryōken Kayū, ed. *Yanagitaru*. Fascicle 40. Edo: Hanaki Kyūjirō, 1765–1832. Waseda University Library.

Grafton, Anthony. "How Revolutionary Was the Print Revolution?" *American Historical Review* 107, no. 1 (2002): 84–86.

Gramlich-Oka, Bettina. "Neo-Confucianism Reconsidered: Family Rituals in the Rai Household." *U.S–Japan Women's Journal* 39 (2011): 7–37.

Gunji Masakatsu. *Gunji Masakatsu santei shū*. 6 vols. Tokyo: Hakusuisha, 1990–1992.

———. "Hanrei." In *Tōkaidō Yotsuya kaidan*, edited by Gunji Masakatsu, 3–7. Shinchō Nihon koten shūsei 45. Tokyo: Shinchōsha, 1981.

———. "Kabuki: Edo kara Meiji." *Bungaku* 53, no. 11 (1985): 171–80.

———. "Kabuki and Its Social Background." In *Tokugawa Japan: The Social and Economic Antecedents of Modern Japan*, edited by Chie Nakane and Shinzaburō Ōishi, translated by Conrad D. Totman, 192–212. Tokyo: University of Tokyo Press, 1990.

———. *Kabuki no hassō*. Tokyo: Meicho Kankōkai, 1978.

———. "Kabuki no sekai kōzō ni tsuite." *Geinōshi kenkyū* 87 (1984): 1–8.

———. *Kabuki yōshiki to denshō*. Tokyo: Chikuma Shobō, 2005.

———. "Kaisetsu." In *Tōkaidō Yotsuya kaidan*, edited by Gunji Masakatsu, 401–39. Shinchō Nihon koten shūsei 45. Tokyo: Shinchōsha, 1981.

———. *Tsuruya Nanboku: kabuki ga unda mukyōyō no hyōgen shugi*. Tokyo: Chūō Kōronsha, 1994.

Hachimonji Jishō. *Kokon iroha hyōrin*. 1785. In *Shin gunsho ruijū*. Vol. 3, Engeki 1. Edited by Kokusho Kankōkai, 49–110. Tokyo: Kokusho Kankōkai, 1908.

———. *Yakusha daigaku: Edo*. Kyoto: Hachimonjiya Hachizaemon, 1809.

———. *Yakusha han'ei banashi: Edo*. Kyoto and Osaka: Hachimonjiya Hachizaemon and Kawachiya Tasuke, 1814.

———. *Yakusha tamazukushi: Ōsaka*. Kyoto and Osaka: Hachimonjiya Hachizaemon and Kawachiya Tasuke, 1826.

———. *Yakusha yume awase*. Kyoto and Osaka: Hachimonjiya Hachizaemon and Kawachiya Tasuke, 1819.

———. *Yakusha zensho*. 1774. In *Nihon shomin bunka shiryō shūsei*. Vol. 6, Kabuki. Edited by Geinōshi Kenkyūkai, 199–242. Tokyo: San'ichi Shobō, 1973.

———. *Yarō sekisumō*. In *Kabuki hyōbanki shūsei*, edited by Kabuki Hyōbanki Kenkyūkai, 1:527–49. Tokyo: Iwanami Shoten, 1972.

Hachimonji Jishō and Ichimonsha Tashō. *Yakusha sokuseki ryōri: Edo*. Kyoto and Osaka: Hachimonjiya Hachizaemon and Kawachiya Tasuke, 1822.

Hachimonji Jishō and Shimonsha Namimaro. *Yakusha sassoku hōchō: Edo*. Osaka: Hachimonjiya Hachizaemon and Kawachiya Tasuke, 1837.

Hall, John Whitney. "The *Bakuhan* System." In *Early Modern Japan*, edited by John Whitney Hall, 128–82. Vol. 4 of *The Cambridge History of Japan*. Cambridge: Cambridge University Press, 1991.

———, ed. *Early Modern Japan*. Vol. 4 of *The Cambridge History of Japan*. Cambridge: Cambridge University Press, 1991.

Han Kyonja. "Chikamatsu no jidai jōruri ni egakareta shūjaku shūnen." *Kokugo to kokubungaku* 987 (2006): 44–57.

Hanagasa Bunkyō, Onoe Baikō (nominal author of text), and Keisai Eisen (pictures). *Nagori no hana Yotsuya kaidan*. Edo: Wakasaya Yoichi, 1826.

———. *Tōkaidō Yotsuya kaidan*. Edo: Shōeidō, 1832.

Hato Yoshiaki. "Genroku kabuki no hatten to sono shūen." In *Kabuki no sekai, bi to aku no gekikūkan*, edited by Ogasawara Kyōko, 33–44. Tokyo: Yūseidō Shuppan, 1988.

Hattori Yukio. *Edo kabuki no biishiki*. Tokyo: Heibonsha, 1996.

———. *Edo kabuki ron*. Tokyo: Hōsei Daigaku Shuppan Kyoku, 1980.

———. *Ichikawa Danjūrō daidai*. Tokyo: Kōdansha, 2002.

———. *Kabuki no kōzō*. Tokyo: Chūō Kōronsha, 1970.

———. "Kaidan kyōgen no kuden to geidan." *Engekikai* 22, no. 8 (1964): 67–71.

———, ed. *Kanadehon chūshingura*. Kabuki on sutēji 8. Tokyo: Hakusuisha, 1994.

———, ed. *Kanadehon chūshingura o yomu*. Tokyo: Yoshikawa Kōbunkan, 2008.

———. *Ōinaru koya: Edo kabuki no shukusai kūkan*. Tokyo: Kōdansha, 2012.

———. *Sakasama no yūrei: shi no Edo bunka ron*. Tokyo: Chikuma Gakugei Bunko, 2005.

———. "Yuranosuke to Okaru Kanpei: *Kanadehon chūshingura* no kosumosu." *Kokubungaku* 31, no. 15 (1986): 67–76.

Hattori Yukio et al. "Natsukyōgen ban shin *Okyōgen gakuya no honsetsu*." *Kikan zasshi kabuki* 5 (1969): 150–77.

Hayashi Kimiko. "Daimyō yashiki ni okeru kabuki." In *Kabuki no rekishi I*, edited by Torigoe Bunzō, Uchiyama Mikiko, and Watanabe Tamotsu, 213–27. Iwanami kōza kabuki bunraku 2. Tokyo: Iwanami Shoten, 1997.

———. "Edo no Zamoto." In *Kabuki no Sekai, bi to aku no geki kūkan*, edited by Ogasawara Kyōko, 224–44. Tokyo: Yūseidō Shuppan, 1988.

———. "Yashikikata ni okeru kabuki jōen o megutte." In *Kabuki jōruri*, edited by Suwa Haruo, 214–30. Tokyo: Kokusho Kankōkai, 1993.

Hegel, Robert E. *Reading Illustrated Fiction in Late Imperial China*. Stanford, Calif.: Stanford University Press, 1998.

Hirano, Katsuya. *The Politics of Dialogic Imagination: Power and Popular Culture in Early Modern Japan*. Chicago: University of Chicago Press, 2013.

Hirano Hidetoshi. "Nihon buyō de no Kyūsuke saku, kiyomoto 'Onnadayū' no kaitei jōen to, tokiwazu *Ubume no kowakare* no fukkatsu jōen." In *Fukumori Kyūsuke kyakuhon shū*, 1–5. Monthly Report 49. Tokyo: Kokusho Kankōkai, 2001.

Hirasawa, Caroline. *Hell-Bent for Heaven in Tateyama Mandara: Painting and Religious Practice at a Japanese Mountain*. Leiden: Brill, 2013.

Hirata Sumiko. "Chikamatsu jōruri to shomin shinkō." *Gengo to bungaku* 83 (1976): 71–94.

Hirosue Tamotsu. *Akubasho no hassō*. 1970. Vol. 6 of *Hirosue Tamotsu chosakushū*. Tokyo: Kage Shobō, 2000.

———. *Henaki no akusho*. Tokyo: Heibonsha, 1973.

Hōseidō Kisanji (text) and Katsukawa Shundō (pictures). *Ukan sandai zue*. Edited by Kokuritsu Gekijō Geinō Chōsashitsu. Kabuki no bunken 4. Tokyo: Kokuritsu Gekijō Chōsa Yōseibu Geinō Chōsashitsu, 1971.

Igusa Toshio. "Shintennō ubuyu no Tamagawa ni tsuite: kaomise kyōgen toshite." *Gobun* 31 (1968): 12–21.

Ihara Saikaku. *Kōshoku ichidai otoko*. In *Ihara Saikaku shū*, edited by Teruoka Yasutaka, 1:15–250. Shinpen Nihon koten bungaku zenshū 66. Tokyo: Shōgakukan, 1996.

Ihara Seisei'en [Toshirō]. *Engeki dangi: zuihitsu shū*. Tokyo: Okakura Shobō, 1934.

———. "P fujin e." *Kabuki* (Kabuki Hakkōjo) 168 (1914): 19–27.

———. "P fujin e." In *Sajiki kara shosai e*, 1–64. Tokyo: Shin Engei Sōsho, 1924.

———. *Sajiki kara shosai e*. Tokyo: Shin Engei Sōsho, 1924.

Ihara Seisei'en et al. "Ichimura-za shinkyōgen *Katamigusa Yotsuya kaidan*" [panel discussion]. *Shin engei* 8, no. 6 (1923): 70–81.

Ihara Toshirō [Seisei'en]. *Kabuki nenpyō*. 8 vols. Edited by Kawatake Shigetoshi and Yoshida Teruji. Tokyo: Iwanami Shoten, 1956–1963.

———. *Kinsei Nihon engekishi*. Tokyo: Waseda Daigaku Shuppanbu, 1913.

———. *Nihon engekishi*. Tokyo: Waseda Daigaku Shuppanbu, 1904.

Iijima Kyoshin. *Kawanabe Kyōsai-ō den*. Edited by Kawanabe Kusumi. Tokyo: Perikansha, 1984.
Iizuka Yūichirō. *Kabuki saiken*. Tokyo: Daiichi Shobō, 1926.
Ikegami, Eiko. *Bonds of Civility: Aesthetic Networks and Political Origin of Japanese Culture*. Cambridge: Cambridge University Press, 2005.
———. *The Taming of the Samurai: Honorific Individualism and the Making of Modern Japan*. Cambridge, Mass.: Harvard University Press, 1995.
Illustrated play summary for *Kanadehon chūshingura*, performed at the Morita Theater in 1779. Edo: Kyūya Kohei, 1779. Nihon Daigaku Sōgō Gakujutsu Jōhō Sentā.
Imao Tetsuya. "Kabuki ni okeru 'sekai' no hōkai." In *Kabuki "tsūsetsu" no kenshō*, 47–86. Tokyo: Hōsei Daigaku Shuppan Kyoku, 2010.
———. *Kabuki no rekishi*. Tokyo: Iwanami Shoten, 2003.
Imaoka Kentarō. "Bakumatsu no kabuki." In *Kabuki no rekishi II*, edited by Torigoe Bunzō, Uchiyama Mikiko, and Watanabe Tamotsu, 53–77. Iwanami kōza kabuki bunraku 3. Tokyo: Iwanami Shoten, 1997.
Inagaki Taiichi. "Kaisetsu to kenkyū." In *Kōtei konjaku monogatari*, 2:553–606. Tokyo: Shintensha, 1990.
Inoue Keiji. *Kyōden kōshōgaku to yomihon no kenkyū*. Tokyo: Shintensha, 1997.
Ishida Mizumaro. *Jigoku*. Kyoto: Hōzōkan, 1985.
Ishii Ryōsuke and Takayanagi Shinzō, eds. *Ofuregaki kanpō shūsei*. Tokyo: Iwanami Shoten, 1934.
Ishizawa Shūji. "*Yotsuya kaidan* no gendaisei." *Kikan zasshi kabuki* 1 (1968): 172–74.
Ishizuka Hōkaishi. *Hana no Edo kabuki nendaiki zokuhen*. In *Shin gunsho ruijū*. Vol. 4, Engeki 4. Edited by Kokusho Kankōkai. Tokyo: Kokusho Kankōkai, 1907.
Iwahashi Koyata. "Kumomai kō." In *Nihon geinōshi: chūsei kabu no kenkyū*, 154–66. Tokyo: Geiensha, 1951.
Izawa Nagahide [Banryō]. *Konjaku monogatari* [*Kōtei konjaku monogatari*]. 15 vols. Kyoto: Ryūshiken, 1820. National Institute of Japanese Literature.
———. *Kōtei konjaku monogatari*. 2 vols. Edited by Inagaki Taiichi. Tokyo: Shintensha, 1990.
Johns, Adrian. "How to Acknowledge a Revolution." *American Historical Review* 107, no. 1 (2002): 106–25.
Jones, Sumie, and Kenji Watanabe, eds. *An Edo Anthology: Literature from Japan's Mega-City, 1750–1850*. Honolulu: University of Hawai'i Press, 2013.
Kabuki Gakkai, ed. *Kabuki no rekishi: atarashii shiten to tenbō*. Tokyo: Yūzankaku Shuppan, 1998.
Kabuki Hyōbanki Kenkyūkai, ed. *Kabuki hyōbanki shūsei*. 10 vols. Tokyo: Iwanami Shoten, 1972–1976.
Kagami Kimiko. "Oniō hinka no ba no keisei to hensen: Edo kabuki ni okeru Soga kyōgen no ichi." *Geinōshi kenkyū* 143 (2008): 33–49.
Kaibara Ekiken. "Joshi o oshiyuru hō." In *Onna daigaku shū*, edited by Ishikawa Matsutarō, 1–26. Tōyō bunko 302. Tokyo: Heibonsha, 1977.

Kajiya, Kenji. "Reimagining the Imagined: Depictions of Dreams and Ghosts in the Early Edo Period." *Impressions* 23 (2001): 86–107.

Kamakura Keiko. "Chikamatsu no jōruri ni okeru yume." *Rikkyō Daigaku Nihon bungaku* 59 (1987): 54–65.

———. "Kojōruri ni okeru yume." *Rikkyō Daigaku Nihon bungaku* 61 (1988): 66–80.

Kamiyama Akira. "'Bikutorian Japan' (Meiji Nihon) no gekijō." *Kabuki* (Kabuki gakkai) 39 (2007): 31–41.

———. *Kindai engeki no raireki: Kabuki no isshin nisei*. Tokyo: Shinwasha, 2006.

———. "Taishōki no Nanboku juyō." *Taishō engeki kenkyū* 4 (1993): 14–28.

Kanda Yutsuki. *Kinsei geinō kōgyō to chiiki shakai*. Tokyo: Tōkyō Daigaku Shuppan, 1999.

Kanemitsu, Janice. "Guts and Tears: Kinpira Jōruri and Its Textual Transformations." In *Publishing the Stage: Print and Performance in Early Modern Japan*, edited by Keller Kimbrough and Satoko Shimazaki, 15–35. Boulder: University of Colorado Center for Asian Studies, 2011.

Kantō kekki monogatari. In *Kyōkaku zenden*, edited by Tsukahara Jūshi'en, 1–74. Tokyo: Hakubunkan, 1913.

Karatani Kōjin. *Nihon kindai bungaku no kigen*. Tokyo: Kōdansha, 1988.

Kastan, David Scott. *Shakespeare and the Book*. Cambridge: Cambridge University Press, 2001.

Katayose Masayoshi. *Konjaku monogatarishū no kenkyū*. 2 vols. Kamakura: Geirinsha, 1974.

Katō Eibian [Genki]. *Waga koromo*. In *Enseki jisshu*, edited by Iwamoto Kattōshi, 1:159–226. Tokyo: Chūō Kōronsha, 1979.

Katō Yūichirō. "*Kōtei konjaku monogatari* to *konjaku monogatari shū*." *Chūō kokubun* 37 (1995): 91–101.

Katsurai Kazuo. "Kama no e ni kansuru kinki: Taiji bunri no koshū nōto." In *Sōsō bosei kenkyū shūsei*. Vol. 1, *Sōhō*, edited by Doi Takuji and Satō Yoneshi, 291–95. Tokyo: Meicho Shuppan, 1979.

Kawamura Mitsukuni. "Onna no jigoku to sukui." In *Onna to otoko no ran: chūsei*, edited by Okano Haruko, 31–80. Onna to otoko no jikū: Nihon joseishi saikō 3. Tokyo: Fujiwara Shoten, 1996.

Kawatake, Toshio. *Kabuki: Baroque Fusion of the Arts*. Translated by Frank Connell Hoff and Jean Connell Hoff. Tokyo: International House of Japan, 2003.

———. "Taishōki Nisei Sadanji no Nanboku." *Kikan zasshi kabuki* 10, no. 1 (1977): 50–59.

Kawatake Shigetoshi. "Edo minshūgeki toshite no oiemono no tenkai." *Kikan zasshi kabuki* 4 (1969): 65–76.

———. *Kabuki sakusha no kenkyū*. Tokyo: Tōkyōdō, 1940.

Kawazoe Yū. *Edo no misemono*. Tokyo: Iwanami Shoten, 2000.

Keisei Asamagadake. 1698. Tokyo University of Arts Library, special collection.

Keisei Motomezuka. Kyoto: Shōhonya Kyūbei, 1706. Tenri University Library, special collection.

Kelsey, W. Michael. "Salvation of the Snake, the Snake of Salvation: Buddhist-Shinto Conflict and Resolution." *Japanese Journal of Religious Studies* 8, nos. 1–2 (1981): 83–113.

Kennelly, Paul B. "Realism in Kabuki: The Ghost Stories at Yotsuya on the Tōkaidō." *Journal of Oriental Studies of Australia* 27–28 (1995/1996): 132–45.

Kern, Adam. *Manga from the Floating World: Comic Book Culture and the Kibyōshi of Edo Japan*. Cambridge, Mass.: Harvard University Press, 2006.

Kikaku. *Kukyōdai*. In *Takarai Kikaku zenshū*, hencho hen, edited by Ishikawa Hachirō, 213–54. Tokyo: Benseisha, 1994.

Kimbrough, R. Keller, trans. *Isozaki*. In *Monsters and the Fantastic: A Collection of Short Medieval Japanese Fiction*, edited by Haruo Shirane and R. Keller Kimbrough. New York: Columbia University Press, forthcoming.

——, ed. and trans. *Wondrous Brutal Fictions: Eight Buddhist Tales from the Early Japanese Puppet Theater*. New York: Columbia University Press, 2013.

Kimura Yaeko. "Geinō to gazō shiryō." *Geinōshi kenkyūkai* 176 (2007): 3–19.

Kimura Yūnosuke. *Katsura*. 3 vols. Tokyo: Bunka Shinkōkai, 1974.

Kincaid, Zoë [Zoë Kincaid Penlington]. *Kabuki: The Popular Stage of Japan*. 1925. New York: Blom, 1965.

——. Letters to Ihara Seiseien. Waseda University Library, special collection, *Ihara Seisei'en ate shokan*, nos. 3866–3874.

Kinjinsai Shin'ō. *Kokon yakusha rongo sakigake*. In *Kinsei geidōron*, edited by Nishiyama Matsunosuke, 463–92. Tokyo: Iwanami Shoten, 1972.

Kishi Fumikazu. *Edo no enkinhō: uki-e no shikaku*. Tokyo: Keisō Shobō, 1994.

Kitagawa Morisada. *Kinsei fūzokushi: Morisada mankō*. Edited by Usami Hideki. 5 vols. Tokyo: Iwanami Shoten, 1996–2002.

Kitashiro Nobuko. "Hen'yō suru jisha engi: kinsei shōdō to bungei, geinō." In *Jisha engi no bunkagaku*, edited by Tsutsumi Kunihiko and Tokuda Kazuo, 111–32. Tokyo: Shinwasha, 2005.

Kobayashi Tadashi. *Edo no ukiyo-e*. Tokyo: Geika Shoin, 2009.

Kōdate Naomi. "Aspects of Ketsubonkyō Belief." Translated by Susanne Formanek. In *Practicing the Afterlife: Perspectives from Japan*, edited by Susanne Formanek and William R. LaFleur, 121–43. Vienna: Verlag der Österreichischen Akademie der Wissenschaften, 2004.

——. "Chi no ike jigoku." In *Tōyō ni okeru shi no shisō*, edited by Yoshihara Hiroto, 231–47. Tokyo: Shunjūsha, 2006.

Kogeki Kenkyūkai, ed. *Sewa kyōgen no kenkyū*. Tokyo: Tengendō, 1916.

Koike Shōtarō. *Kōshō Edo kabuki*. Tokyo: Miki Shobō, 1997.

——. *Tsuruya Nanboku no sekai*. Tokyo: Miki Shobō, 1981.

Koike Tōgorō. *Santō Kyōden no kenkyū*. Tokyo: Iwanami Shoten, 1935.

Kojima Yoshinori, ed. *Nihon shoki*. Vol. 1. Shinpen Nihon koten bungaku zenshū 2. Tokyo: Shōgakukan, 1994.

Kokuritsu Gekijō Geinō Chōsashitsu, ed. *Kanadehon chūshingura godanme, rokudanme*. Kokuritsu gekijō jōen shiryō shū 288. Tokyo: Kokuritsu Gekijō Chōsa Yōseibu Geinō Chōsashitsu, 1989.

——, ed. *Sekai kōmoku*. In *Kyōgen sakusha shiryōshū*, 1:1–84. Tokyo: Kokuritsu Gekijō Chōsa Yōseibu Geinō Chōsashitsu, 1976.

——, ed. *Tōkaidō Yotsuya kaidan*. Kokuritsu gekijō jōen shiryō shū 68. Tokyo: Kokuritsu Gekijō Chōsa Yōseibu Geinō Chōsashitsu, 1971.

Komatsu Kazuhiko. *Shutendōji no kubi*. Tokyo: Serika Shobō, 1997.

——. *Yōkaigaku shinkō: yōkai kara miru Nihonjin no kokoro*. Tokyo: Shōgakukan, 1994.

Kominz, Laurence R. *Avatars of Vengeance: Japanese Drama and the Soga Literary Tradition*. Ann Arbor: Center for Japanese Studies, University of Michigan, 1995.

Komiya Kiichi, ed. *Kabuki shinpa shinkokugeki jōen nenpyō*. Dai 6-han. Privately printed, 2007.

Kondō Mizuki. "Jusha no yōkai taiji." *Nihon bungaku* 55, no. 4 (2006): 19–28.

Kondō Naoyoshi. *Tassei zusetsu*. 3 fascicles. Edo, Osaka, and Kyoto: Kitsushidō, 1858.

Konita Seiji. "Kaidan mono jitsuroku no isō: 'Yotsuya zōdan' saikō." In *Kinsei bungaku fukan*, edited by Hasegawa Tsuyoshi, 275–94. Tokyo: Kyūko Shoin, 1997.

Kornicki, Peter F. *The Book in Japan: A Cultural History from the Beginnings to the Nineteenth Century*. Honolulu: University of Hawai'i Press, 2000.

——. "Manuscript, Not Print: Scribal Culture in the Edo Period." *Journal of Japanese Studies* 32, no. 1 (2006): 23–52.

Kōya monogatari. In *Muromachi monogatarishū*, edited by Ichiko Teiji, 1:325–50. Shin Nihon koten bungaku taikei 54. Tokyo: Iwanami Shoten, 1979.

Ku Yū. "Botan dōrō." Translated by Iizuka Akira. In *Sentō shinwa, yowa, seiko kawa tōin hiji*, 42–47. Chūgoku koten bungaku taikei 39. Tokyo: Heibonsha, 1969.

Kuhns, David. "Palimpsestus: Frank Wedekind's Theater of Self-Performance." *New Theater Quarterly* 12, no. 45 (1996): 50–64.

Kurata Yoshihiro. *Shibaigoya to yose no kindai: yugei kara bunka e*. Tokyo: Iwanami Shoten, 2006.

Kuroda Hideo. "Dōji no shi to takai." In *Emaki kodomo no tōjō: chūsei shakai no kodomo zō*, 106–13. Tokyo: Kawade Shobō Shinsha, 1989.

Kuroishi Yōko. "Hōreki kabuki: Edo." In *Kabuki no rekishi I*, edited by Torigoe Bunzō, Uchiyama Mikiko, and Watanabe Tamotsu, 163–84. Iwanami kōza kabuki bunraku 2. Tokyo: Iwanami Shoten, 1997.

Kurushima Hiroshi and Yoshida Nobuyuki, eds. *Kinsei no shakai shūdan: yuisho to gensetsu*. Tokyo: Yamakawa Shuppansha, 1995.

Kusuyama Masao. "*Yotsuya kaidan* oyobi Nanboku ni tsukite." In *Sewa kyōgen no kenkyū*, edited by Kogeki Kenkyūkai, 195–208. Tokyo: Tengendō, 1916.

Kyokutei Bakin. *Bei bei kyōdan*. Kyoto, Edo, and Osaka: Kawachiya Tōshirō, Suharaya Mohei, etc., 1858. Hōsa bunko, Nagoya.

———. *Niimaze no ki*. In *Nihon zuihitsu taisei*. Dai ikki 21. Tokyo: Yoshikawa Kōbunkan, 1976.
Lacan, Jacques. "The Mirror Stage as Formative of the *I* Function as Revealed in Psychoanalytic Experience." In *Écrits: The First Complete Edition in English*, 75–81. Translated by Bruce Fink. New York: Norton, 2006.
Lee, William. "Chikamatsu and Dramatic Literature in the Meiji Period." In *Inventing the Classics: Modernity, National Identity, and Japanese Literature*, edited by Haruo Shirane and Tomi Suzuki, 179–98. Stanford, Calif.: Stanford University Press, 2000.
Leiter, Samuel L. *Frozen Moments: Writings on Kabuki, 1966–2001*. Ithaca, N.Y.: Cornell University East Asia Program, 2002.
———, ed. *A Kabuki Reader: History and Performance*. Armonk, N.Y.: Sharpe, 2002.
———. *New Kabuki Encyclopedia: A Revised Adaptation of* Kabuki jiten. Westport, Conn.: Greenwood Press, 1997.
Lesser, Zachary. *Renaissance Drama and the Politics of Publication: Reading in the English Book Trade*. Cambridge: Cambridge University Press, 2004.
Levy, Indra A. *Sirens of the Western Shore: The Westernesque Femme Fatale, Translation, and Vernacular Style in Modern Japanese Literature*. New York: Columbia University Press, 2006.
Lin, Irene H. "The Ideology of Imagination: The Tale of Shutendōji as a Kenmon Discourse." *Cahiers d'Extrême-Asie* 13 (2002): 379–410.
Mabuchi Kazuo, Kunisaki Fumimaro, and Inagaki Taiichi, eds. *Konjaku monogatarishū*. Vol. 1. Shinpen Nihon koten bungaku zenshū 35. Tokyo: Shōgakukan, 1999.
———. *Konjaku monogatarishū*. Vol. 4. Shinpen Nihon koten bungaku zenshū 38. Tokyo: Shōgakukan, 2002.
Maeda Ai. *Toshikūkan no naka no bungaku*. Tokyo: Chikuma Shōbo, 1982.
Markus, Andrew. "The Carnival of Edo: Misemono Spectacles from Contemporary Accounts." *Harvard Journal of Asiatic Studies* 45, no. 2 (1985): 499–541.
Matsuba Ryōko. "Edo no gekijōzu: Hishikawa-ha o chūshin ni." In *Fūzoku kaiga no bunkagaku: toshi o utsusu media*, edited by Matsumoto Ikuyo and Idemitsu Sachiko, 211–42. Kyoto: Shibunkaku Shuppan, 2009.
Matsuda Osamu. "Esoragoto no *etsuraku no sono* gensō." In *Nihon byōbue shūsei*, edited by Takeda Tsuneo, 14:137–42. Tokyo: Kōdansha, 1977.
Matsui Shōyō. "*Yotsuya kaidan* no jōen shōhon sakusei to sono jōen suru ni tsuite." *Engei gahō* 75, no. 19 (1925): 54–62.
Matsuzaki Hitoshi. "Kabuki no kankyaku." *Kokubungaku kaishaku to kyōzai no kenkyū* 37, no. 6 (1992): 41–46.
McClain, James L., John M. Merriman, and Kaoru Ugawa, eds. *Edo and Paris: Urban Life and the State in the Early Modern Era*. Ithaca, N.Y.: Cornell University Press, 1997.
McCullough, William H. "Japanese Marriage Institutions in the Late Heian Period." *Harvard Journal of Asiatic Studies* 27 (1967): 103–67.
McGann, Jerome J. *A Critique of Modern Textual Criticism*. Chicago: University of Chicago Press, 1983.

McKenzie, D. F. *Bibliography and the Sociology of Texts*. Cambridge: Cambridge University Press, 1999.
McLuhan, Marshall. *The Gutenberg Galaxy: The Making of Typographic Man*. Toronto: University of Toronto Press, 1962.
Meeks, Lori. *Hokkeji and the Reemergence of the Female Monastic Orders in Premodern Japan*. Honolulu: University of Hawai'i Press, 2010.
Meiji Bunka Kenkyūkai, ed. *Meiji bunka zenshū*. Vol. 24, Bunmei kaika hen. Tokyo: Nihon Hyōronsha, 1967.
Mimasuya Nisōji. *Gakuya suzume*. In *Nihon shomin bunka shiryō shūsei*. Vol. 6, *Kabuki*. Edited by Geinōshi Kenkyūkai, 617–68. Tokyo: San'ichi Shobō, 1973.
———. *Jūhachidai tsū*. In *Zoku enseki jisshu*, edited by Iwamoto Kattōshi, 2:391–403. Tokyo: Chūō Kōronsha, 1980.
———. *Kabuki shūdan*. 1851. Manuscript. Historiographical Institute of the University of Tokyo, 4187-3.
———. *Kami kuzukago*. In *Zoku enseki jisshu*, edited by Iwamoto Kattōshi, 3:61–95. Tokyo: Chūō Kōronsha, 1980.
———. *Sakusha nenjū gyōji*. In *Nihon shomin bunka shiryō shūsei*. Vol. 6, *Kabuki*. Edited by Geinōshi Kenkyūkai, 669–716. Tokyo: San'ichi Shobō, 1973.
———. *Shibai hidenshū*. In *Nihon shomin bunka shiryō shūsei*. Vol. 6, *Kabuki*. Edited by Geinōshi Kenkyūkai, 717–30. Tokyo: San'ichi Shobō, 1973.
Minakata Kumagusu. "Ninpu no shikabane yori taiji o hikihanasu koto." In *Sōsō bosei kenkyū shūsei*. Vol. 1, *Sōhō*. Edited by Doi Takuji and Satō Yoneshi, 296–98. Tokyo: Meicho Shuppan, 1979.
Minamoto Junko. *Bukkyō to sei: erosu eno ifu to sabetsu*. Tokyo: San'ichi Shobō, 1996.
Minobe Shigekatsu and Minobe Tomoko. *Shutendōji-e o yomu: matsurowanu mono no jikuū*. Tokyo: Miyai Shobō, 2009.
Mita bungakukai. "Shōsoku." *Mita bungaku* 6, no. 2 (1915).
Mitamura Engyo. "Buke no kon'in." In *Mitamura Engyo zenshū*, 2:335–62. Tokyo: Chūō Kōronsha, 1975.
———. "Kakoimono no hanashi." In *Mitamura Engyo zenshū*, 11:199–215. Tokyo: Chūō Kōronsha, 1975.
———. "Nishiki-e no ōkubi." In *Mitamura Engyo zenshū*, 12:156–78. Tokyo: Chūō Kōronsha, 1976.
———. "Yotsuya kaidan wa obake shibai ka." *Kikan zasshi kabuki* 1, no. 3 (1925): 57–61.
Mitsunobu Shinya. *Edo kabuki sakusha no kenkyū: Kanai Sanshō kara Tsuruya Nanboku e*. Tokyo: Kasama Shoin, 2012.
Miyake Shūtarō. *Engeki gojūnenshi*. Tokyo: Masu Shobō, 1942.
Miyako no Nishiki [Ōkaishi]. *Tōsei chie kagami*. 1712.
Miyako shinbun. 1889–1942. Miyako shinbun fukkokuban. Edited by Chūnichi Shinbunsha. Tokyo: Kashiwa Shobō, 1994–.
Miyamoto Yuriko. "Dōkan'yama." In *Miyamoto Yuriko zenshū*, 17:734–44. Tokyo: Shin Nihon Shuppansha, 1981.

Miyazawa Seiichi. *Kindai Nihon to Chūshingura gensō*. Tokyo: Aoki Shoten, 2001.

Miyoshi Ikkō. *Edo seigyō bukka jiten*. Tokyo: Seiabō, 2002.

Mizuta Kayano. "*Dōjōji*-mono ni okeru jigei to shosagoto: Tomijūrō ni yoru 'shitto no zendan' kakuritsu made." *Engekigaku* 29 (1988): 54–73.

Mochizuki Tainosuke. *Kabuki no geza ongaku*. Tokyo: Engeki Shuppansha, 1997.

Mocrman, D. Max. *Localizing Paradise: Kumano Pilgrimage and the Religious Landscape of Premodern Japan*. Cambridge, Mass.: Harvard University Asia Center, 2006.

Morishima Chūryō. *Sunkin zattetsu*. In *Nihon zuihitsu taisei*. Dai ikki 7. Tokyo: Yoshikawa Kōbunkan, 1982.

Moriya Takeshi. "Edo no kabuki kōgyōkai." In *Kasei bunka no kenkyū*, edited by Hayashiya Tatsusaburō, 217–54. Tokyo: Iwanami Shoten, 1976.

———. *Genroku bunka: yugei, akusho, shibai*. 1987. Tokyo: Kōdansha, 2011.

———. *Kinsei geinō kōgyōshi no kenkyū*. Tokyo: Kōbundō, 1985.

Mostow, Joshua S. *Pictures of the Heart: The* Hyakunin Isshu *in Word and Image*. Honolulu: University of Hawai'i Press, 1996.

Motojima Chishin. *Getsudō kenmonshū*. In *Kinsei fūzoku kenbunshū*, 1:242–494. Tokyo: Kokusho Kankōkai, 1912.

Mullaney, Steven. "Civic Rites, City Sites: The Place of the Stage." In *Staging the Renaissance: Reinterpretations of Elizabethan and Jacobean Drama*, edited by David Scott Kastan and Peter Stallybrass, 17–26. London: Routledge, 1991.

———. *The Place of the Stage: License, Play, and Power in Renaissance England*. Ann Arbor: University of Michigan Press, 1995.

Murasaki Shikibu. *The Tale of Genji*. Translated by Royall Tyler. New York: Penguin Books, 2001.

Mutō Junko. "Aragoto kō: genroku kabuki o chūshin ni shite." *Musashi daigaku jinbun gakkai zasshi* 16, no. 2 (1984): 115–40.

Nagai Kafū. "*Sannin Kichisa kuruwa no hatsugai* ni tsukite." Edited by Kogeki Kenkyūkai. Tokyo: Tengendō, 1916.

Nagashima Imashirō and Ōta Yoshio. *Chiyodajō ōoku*. Tokyo: Chōya Shinbunsha, 1892.

Naitō Akira. *Edo to Edojō*. Tokyo: Kajima Shuppankai, 1966.

Naitō Masato. *Edo meishozu byōbu: Ōedo gekijō no maku ga hiraku*. Tokyo: Shōgakukan, 2003.

Nakamura Jūsuke. *Shibai noriaki banashi*. In *Nihon shomin bunka shiryō shūsei*. Vol. 6, *Kabuki*. Edited by Geinōshi Kenkyūkai, 265–92. Tokyo: San'ichi Shobō, 1973.

Nakamura Nakazō III. *Temae miso*. Edited by Gunji Masakatsu. Tokyo: Seiabō, 1969.

Nakamura Yukihiko. *Gesakuron*. Tokyo: Kadokawa Shoten, 1966.

Nakane, Chie. "Tokugawa Society." In *Tokugawa Japan: The Social and Economic Antecedents of Modern Japan*, edited by Chie Nakane and

Shinzaburō Ōishi, translated by Conrad D. Totman, 213–31. Tokyo: University of Tokyo Press, 1990.

Nakayama Mikio. *Nanboku josetsu: Tsuruya Nanboku kenkyū nyūmon.* Tokyo: Kōbundō Shuppansha, 1984.

Namiki Gohei. *Haikai tsūgen.* Edo: Seiundō, later printing of the edition with the 1809 preface. Waseda University Library, special collection.

Narikiyo Hirokazu. *Josei to kegare no rekishi.* Tokyo: Hanawa Shobō, 2003.

Nihon koten bungaku daijiten henshū iinkai, ed. *Nihon koten bungaku daijiten.* 6 vols. Tokyo: Iwanami Shoten, 1983–1986.

Nishida Kōzō. "Ubume nōto: bungei ga toraeta ubume to sono shūhen." *Kumamoto daigaku kyōyōbu kiyō: jinbun shakai gakka* 15 (1980): 124–32 (25–33).

———. "Ubume nōto: zoku." *Kumamoto Daigaku kyōyōbu kiyō: jinbun shakai gakka* 24 (1989): 107–12 (11–16).

Nishiguchi Junko. "Nihon shijō no josei to bukkyō: nyonin kyūsai to nyonin jōbutsu o megutte." *Kokubungaku kaishaku to kanshō* 56, no. 5 (1991): 19–25.

Nishiyama Matsunosuke and Haga Tōru. *Edo sanbyakunen.* Vol. 1, Tenka no chōnin. Tokyo: Kōdansha, 1975.

Nishizawa Ippō. *Denki sakusho.* In *Shin gunsho ruijū.* Vol. 1, Engeki 1, 1–478. Edited by Kokusho kankōkai. Tokyo: Kokusho kankōkai, 1906.

Nyūgatei Ganyū [Namiki Shōza II]. *Sakusha shikihō kezairoku.* In *Kinsei geidōron*, edited by Nishiyama Matsunosuke, Watanabe Ichirō, and Gunji Masakatsu, 493–532. Tokyo: Iwanami Shoten, 1972.

Ochiai Kiyohiko. *Hyakki yagyō no rakuen: Tsuruya Nanboku no sekai.* Tokyo: Geijutsu Seikatsusha, 1975.

Ogasawara Kyōko. *Toshi to gekijō: chū-kinsei no chinkon, yūraku, kenryoku.* Tokyo: Heibonsha, 1992.

Ogasawara Kyōko and Kamakura Keiko. "Engeki no kōryū." In *Iwanami kōza Nihon bungakushi*, 7:65–98. Tokyo: Iwanashi Shoten, 1996.

Ogawa Akimichi. *Chirizuka dan.* In *Enseki jisshu*, edited by Iwamoto Kattōshi, 1:263–309. Tokyo: Chūō Kōronsha, 1979.

Ogita Kiyoshi. "Ikeda Bunko no *Yotsuya kaidan* zakkan." *Kanpō Ikeda bunko* 3 (1993): 6–8.

Oka Eiichirō. "*Yotsuya kaidan* to *Omatsuri Sashichi*." *Kabuki* (Kabuki Hakkōjo) 1, no. 3 (1925): 40–43.

Okami Masao and Takahashi Kiichi, eds. *Shintōshū.* Shintō taikei: bungaku hen 1. Tokyo: Shintō Taikei Hensankai, 1988.

Okamoto Kidō. *Meiji gekidan Ranpu no moto nite.* Afterword by Okamoto Keiichi. 1935. Reprint, Tokyo: Iwanami bunko, 1993.

———. *Meiji no engeki.* Tokyo: Daitō Shuppan, 1942.

———. "Muzukashii kaidangeki." *Engei gahō* 22, no. 7 (1928): 47–48.

Ōkubo Jun'ichi. *Hiroshige to ukiyo-e fūkeiga.* Tokyo: Tōkyō Daigaku Shuppankai, 2007.

Ōkura-shō, ed. *Nihon zaisei keizai shiryō.* Vol. 3. Tokyo: Zaisei Keizai Gakkai, 1922.

Ong, Walter J. *Orality and Literacy: The Technologizing of the World.* 1982. Reprint, London: Routledge, 2002.

Ōnishi Atsuko. "Kinsei chūki ikō ni okeru ningyō jōruri no kabukika." *Kabuki kenkyū to hihyō* 12 (1993): 73–87.
Onna daigaku takarabako. 1716. In *Onna daigaku shū*, edited by Ishikawa Matsutarō, 27–60. Tōyō bunko 302. Tokyo: Heibonsha, 1977.
Ono Takeo, ed. *Edo bukka jiten*. Tokyo: Tenbōsha, 2009.
Onoe Baikō VI. "Oiwa." *Engei gahō* 12 (1909): 134–38.
———. "Oiwa." In *Tōkaidō Yotsuya kaidan*, edited by Kokuritsu Gekijō Geinō Chōsashitsu, 105–8. Kokuritsu gekijō jōen shiryō shū 68. Tokyo: Kokuritsu Gekijō Chōsa Yōseibu Geinō Chōsashitsu, 1971.
———. "Oiwa to Okon." *Kabuki* (Kabuki Hakkōjo) 112 (1909): 77–81.
———. *Oyama no geidan*. Tokyo: Engeki Shuppansha, 1988.
Onoe Kikugorō V. *Onoe Kikugorō jiden*. Tokyo: Jiji Shinpōsha, 1906.
Onshi Zaidan Boshi Aiiku Kai, ed. *Nihon san'iku shūzoku shiryō shūsei*. Tokyo: Daiichi Hōki Shuppan, 1975.
Osanai Kaoru. "Do Beruniuru no *Yotsuya kaidan* ni tsuite." *Shin engei* 8, no. 6 (1923): 54–57.
———. "Jo." In *Sewa kyōgen no kenkyū*, edited by Kogeki Kenkyūkai, 1–4. Tokyo: Tengendō, 1916.
———. "Kaseiki Edo engeki no fukuen ni kansuru aru anji." *Kabuki kenkyū* 26 (1928): 1–13.
Ōtaka Yōji. "Kyōwa san, yonen no Bakin yomihon." *Nihon bunka ronsō* 38 (2000): 347–84.
Ōtake Hideo. "Edo jidai no mekake." In *Bakuhan kokka no hō to shihai*, edited by Ōtake Hideo and Harafuji Hiroshi, 507–34. Tokyo: Yūhikaku, 1984.
Ōtsuki Fumihiko. *Daigenkai*. Tokyo: Fuzanbō, 1954.
———, ed. *Genkai*. Tokyo: Fuzanbō, 1932.
Owen, Stephen, ed and trans. *An Anthology of Chinese Literature: Beginnings to 1911*. New York: Norton, 1996.
Ōzasa Yoshio. *Nihon gendai engekishi: Meiji, Taishō hen*. Tokyo: Hakusuisha, 1985.
Peters, Julie Stone. *Theater of the Book, 1480–1880: Print Text, and Performance in Europe*. Oxford: Oxford University Press, 2000.
Pflugfelder, Gregory M. *Cartographies of Desire: Male-Male Sexuality in Japanese Discourse, 1600–1950*. Berkeley: University of California Press, 2007.
Picture-book playbill for *Kiku no en tsuki no shiranmi*, performed at the Kawarasaki Theater in 1824. Edo: Ogawa Hansuke, 1824. Waseda University, Tsubouchi Memorial Theater Museum.
Picture-book playbill for *Shitennō ubuyu no Tamagawa*, performed at the Tamagawa Theater. Edo: Yamamoto Jūgorō, 1818. Waseda University, Tsubouchi Memorial Theater Museum.
Picture-book playbill for *Tōkaidō Yotsuya kaidan*, performed with *Honchō nijūshi-kō* at the Morita Theater in 1836. Edo: Ogawa Hansuke, 1836. Waseda University, Tsubouchi Memorial Theater Museum.
Picture-book playbill for *Tōkaidō Yotsuya kaidan*, performed with *The Treasury of Loyal Retainers* at the Nakamura Theater in 1825. Sho'nichi and

gojitsu. Edo: Sawamuraya Rihei, 1825. Waseda University, Tsubouchi Memorial Theater Museum.

Piggott, Joan R. "A Comedy of Marriage and Family in Eleventh-Century Kyoto." *Nihon kodaigaku* 1 (2009): 51–80.

Poulton, M. Cody. *A Beggar's Art: Scripting Modernity in Japanese Drama, 1900–1930*. Honolulu: University of Hawai'i Press, 2010.

Powell, Brian. *Japan's Modern Theater: A Century of Change and Continuity*. London: Japan Library, 2002.

Roach, Joseph. *It*. Ann Arbor: University of Michigan Press, 2007.

Saitō Gesshin. *Tōto saijiki*. Edited by Asakura Haruhiko. Vol. 1. Tokyo: Heibonsha, 1970.

Sakurada Jisuke I. *Gohīki kanjinchō*. In *Edo kabukishū*, edited by Furuido Hideo, Torigoe Bunzō, and Wada Osamu, 75–399, 441–74. Shin Nihon koten bungaku taikei 96. Tokyo: Iwanami Shoten, 1997.

———. *Sukeroku yukari no Edozakura*. In *Meisaku kabuki zenshū*, edited by Toita Yasuji. Vol. 18, Ie no gai shū, 125–80. Tokyo: Tōkyō Sōgensha, 1969.

Saltzman-Li, Katherine. *Creating Kabuki Plays: Context for Kezairoku, "Valuable Notes on Playwriting."* Leiden: Brill, 2010.

Santei Shunba. *Okyōgen gakuya no honsetsu*. Edited by Kokuritsu Gekijō Geinō Chōsashitsu. Kabuki no bunken 2. Tokyo: Kokuritsu Gekijō Chōsa Yōseibu Geinō Chōsashitsu, 1967.

Santei Shunba (text) and Utagawa Kunitsuna (pictures). *Okyōgen gakuya no honsetsu*. Nihen. Fascicles 3 and 4. Edo: Tsutaya Kichizō, 1859.

Santei Shunba (text) and Utagawa Kunisada and Utagawa Yoshitsuya (pictures). *Okyōgen gakuya no honsetsu*. Ippen. Fascicles 1 and 2. Edo: Tsutaya Kichizō, 1858.

Santō Kyōden. *Asaka no numa gonichi no Adauchi*. In *Santō Kyōden zenshū*, edited by Mizuno Minoru, 6:103–44. Tokyo: Perikansha, 1995.

———. *Baika hyōretsu*. In *Santō Kyōden shū*, edited by Satō Miyuki, 237–347. Sōsho Edo bunko 18. Tokyo: Perikansha, 1987.

———. *Fukushū kidan Asaka no numa*. In *Santō Kyōden zenshū*, edited by Mizuno Minoru, 15:267–392. Tokyo: Perikansha, 1995.

———. *Kottōshū*. Jōhen. 4 vols. 1814–1815. Edo: Bunkeidō, 1836. Waseda University Library, special collection.

———. *Sakurahime zenden akebonozōshi*. In *Santō Kyōden zenshū*, edited by Mizuno Minoru et al., 16:9–171. Tokyo: Perikansha, 1997.

———. *Ukibotan zenden*. In *Santō Kyōden zenshū*, edited by Mizuno Minoru et al., 17:9–138. Tokyo: Perikansha, 2003.

Santō Kyōden (text) and Utagawa Toyokuni (pictures). *Sakurahime zenden akebonozōshi*. 5 fascicles. Edo: Bunkeidō, 1805. Waseda University Library, special collection.

Sanyūtci Enchō. *Shinkei Kasane ga fuchi*. Tokyo: Iwanami Shoten, 2007.

Sasaki Kōshō. "Nagare kanjō to minzoku." In *Kōza Nihon no minzoku shūkyō*. Vol. 2, Bukkyō minzokugaku. Edited by Gorai Shigeru, 68–82. Tokyo: Kōbundō, 1980.

Sasayama Keisuke. "Kudaime Danjūrō no hara to kao." In *Engijutsu no Nihon kindai*, 21–56. Tokyo: Shinwasha, 2012.

Satō Chino. "Edo kabuki no kōgyō to kyōgen." *Kinsei bungei* 69 (1999): 11–24.

———. "The Performing Arts Connecting the Dead with the Living: In the Case of 'Soga Legends.'" *Bulletin of Death and Life Studies* 7 (2011): 243–64.

Satō Eri. "Aragoto to kinpira jōruri no ningyō gei: sono jiban." *Bungaku* 55, no. 4 (1984): 250–68.

———. "Genrokuki Edo kabuki no seikaku: ōgiri no shinreigoto ni okeru oni no sonzai." *Engekigaku* 25 (1984): 115–33.

———. "Genroku kabuki: Edo." In *Kabuki no rekishi I*, edited by Torigoe Bunzō, Uchiyama Mikiko, and Watanabe Tamotsu, 79–104. Iwanami kōza kabuki bunraku 2. Tokyo: Iwanami Shoten, 1997.

———. *Kabuki niwaka kenkyū*. Tokyo: Shintensha, 2002.

Satō Hiroo. *Shisha no yukue*. Tokyo: Iwata Shoin, 2008.

Satō Katsura. *Kabuki no bakumatsu Meiji: koshibai no jidai*. Tokyo: Perikansha, 2010.

Sawamura Gennosuke IV. "Hatsuyaku no Oiwa ni tsuite." *Kabuki* (Kabuki Hakkōjo) 65 (1905): 43–44.

Schechner, Richard. *Between Theater and Anthropology*. Philadelphia: University of Pennsylvania Press, 1985.

———. "Collective Reflexivity: Restoration of Behavior." In *A Crack in the Mirror: Reflexive Perspectives in Anthropology*, edited by Jay Ruby, 39–81. Philadelphia: University of Pennsylvania Press, 1982.

Scidmore, Eliza Ruhamah. *Jinrikisha Days in Japan*. New York: Harper, 1891.

Segawa Jokō III (text) and Utagawa Kunisada (pictures). *Tōkaidō Yotsuya kaidan*. 3 fascicles. Edo: Kōeidō, 1861.

Sekine Shisei. *Tōto gekijō enkaku shiryō*. Edited by Kokuritsu Gekijō Geinō Chōsashitsu. 2 vols. Kabuki shiryō sensho 6. Tokyo: Kokuritsu Gekijō Geinō Chōsashitsu, 1983, 1984.

Serres, Michael, with Bruno Latour. *Conversations on Science, Culture, and Time*. Translated by Roxanne Lapidus. Ann Arbor: University of Michigan Press, 1995.

Shashi Hensan Iinkai. *Kōdansha no ayunda gojū-nen: Meiji Taishō hen*. Tokyo: Kōdansha, 1901.

Shihōshō Shomuka, ed. *Tokugawa kinreikō*. Vol. 5. Tokyo: Kyōeki Shōsha Shoten, 1894.

Shikitei Sanba. *Hara no uchi gesaku no tanehon*. In *Sakusha tainai totsuki no zu*, edited by Hayashi Yoshikazu, 36–79. Edo gesaku bunko 10. Tokyo: Kawade Shobō Shinsha, 1987.

———. *Shibai kinmō zui*. Edited by Kokuritsu Geijō Chōsa Yōseibu Geinō Chōsashitsu. Kabuki no bunken 3. Tokyo: Kokuritsu Gekijō Chōsa Yōseibu Geinō Chōsashitsu, 1976.

———. *Ukiyoburo*. In *Ukiyoburo, Kejō suigen maku no soto, Daisen sekai gakuya sagashi*, edited by Jinbō Kazuya, 3–293. Shin Nihon koten bungaku taikei 86. Tokyo: Iwanami Shoten, 1989.

Shikitei Sanba (text) and Ogawa Yoshimaru (pictures). *Hara no uchi gesaku no tanehon*. Edo: Tsuruya Kiemon, 1811. National Diet Library. Microfilm YD-*ko*-3399.

Shimazaki, Satoko. "The Ghost of Oiwa in Actor Prints: Confronting Disfigurement." *Impressions* 29 (2008): 76–97.

——. "Strange Encounters: Performing *Genji* on the Kabuki Stage." Paper presented at the conference "*The Story of the Stone* and *The Tale of Genji* in Modern China and Japan: Issues in Media, Technology, Gender, and National Identity," Columbia University, New York, November 19–20, 2010.

Shinmura Taku. *Shussan to seishokukan no rekishi*. Tokyo: Hōsei Daigaku Shuppan Kyoku, 1996.

Shirane, Haruo, ed. *Early Modern Japanese Literature: An Anthology, 1600–1900*. New York: Columbia University Press, 2002.

——. *Japan and the Culture of the Four Seasons: Nature, Literature, and the Arts*. New York: Columbia University Press, 2013.

Shively, Donald H. "Bakufu Versus Kabuki." *Harvard Journal of Asiatic Studies* 18, nos. 3–4 (1955): 326–56.

——. "The Social Environment of Tokugawa Kabuki." In *Studies in Kabuki: Its Acting, Music, and Historical Context*, edited by James R. Brandon, William P. Malm, and Donald H. Shively, 1–62. Honolulu: University of Hawai'i Press, 1978.

Shokoku yūri kōshoku yuraizoroe. In *Kinsei bungei sōsho*. Vol. 10, Fūzoku, 1–30. Tokyo: Kokusho Kankōkai, 1911.

Smith, Henry D., II "The Capacity of *Chūshingura*." *Monumenta Nipponica* 58, no. 1 (2003): 1–42.

——. "*Chūshingura* in the 1980s: Rethinking the Story of the Forty-Seven Rōnin." In *Revenge Drama in European Renaissance and Japanese Theatre: From Hamlet to Madame Butterfly*, edited by Kevin J. Wetmore Jr., 187–215. New York: Palgrave Macmillan, 2008.

——. "Geinō no ba: yagura no keisei." *Bungaku* 55, no. 2 (1987): 39–55.

Street playbill for *Iroeiri otogizōshi*, performed at the Ichimura Theater in 1808. Edo: Yamamoto Jūgorō. Waseda University, Tsubouchi Memorial Theater Museum.

Street playbill for *Komochi yamanba*, performed at the Kawarasaki Theater in 1826. Edo: Ogawa Hansuke, 1826. Nihon Daigaku Sōgō Gakujutsu Jōhō Sentā.

Street playbill for *Yotsuya kaidan*, performed with *Kanadehon chūshingura* at the Nakamura Theater in 1825. Edo: Murayama Genbei, 1825. *Sho'nichi* and *gojitsu*. Waseda University, Tsubouchi Memorial Theater Museum.

Sugano Noriko. "State Indoctrination of Filial Piety in Tokugawa Japan: Sons and Daughters in the *Official Record of Filial Piety*." In *Women and Confucian Cultures in Premodern China, Korea, and Japan*, edited by Dorothy Ko, JaHyun Kim Haboush, and Joan Piggott, 170–92. Berkeley: University of California Press, 2003.

Suwa Haruo. "Geinō no ba: yagura no keisei." *Bungaku* 55, no. 2 (1987): 39–55.

——. *Nihon no yūrei*. Tokyo: Iwanami Shoten, 1988.

——. *Sei to zoku no doramatsurugī*. Tokyo: Gakugei Shorin, 1988.

Suzuki, Jun, and Ellis Tinios, eds. *Understanding Japanese Woodblock-Printed Illustrated Books: A Short Introduction to Their History, Bibliography, and Format*. Leiden: Brill, 2013.

Suzuki Hakutō. *Tōkaidō Yotsuya kaidan*. 4 fascicles. Acts 2, 3, and 5 copied 1825; act 1 copied 1826; act 4 date unknown. Waseda University, Tsubouchi Memorial Theater Museum.

Suzuki Hiroko. "Kyōhōki Edo kabuki ni okeru yashikikata to shibaimachi no ichiyōsō: Kaga hantei jōen kiroku o chūshin ni." *Geinōshi kenkyū* 174 (2006): 24–40.

Suzuki Kensuke. *Jigoku de yōi hai! Nakagawa Nobuo kyōfu eiga no gōka*. Tokyo: Waizu Shuppan, 2000.

Tachikawa Kiyoshi. *Botan tōki no keifu*. Tokyo: Bensei Shuppan, 1998.

———, ed. *Zoku hyaku monogatari shūsei*. Sōsho Edo bunko 27. Tokyo: Kokusho Kankōkai, 1993.

Taguchi Akiko. "Kanpei no kata no genryū: gashō shiryō o tsukatte." In *Ferisu Jogakuin Daigaku kokubungaku ronsō: Nihon bungakuka sōsetsu sanjisshūnen kinen*, edited by Mitamura Masako, 168–93. Yokohama: Ferisu Jogakuin Daigaku Bungakubu Nihon Bungakuka, 1995.

Taira Masayuki. "Chūsei bukkyō to josei." In *Nihon josei seikatsushi*, edited by Joseishi Sōgō Kenkyūkai, 2:75–108. Tokyo: Tōkyō Daigaku Shuppan, 1990.

Takada Mamoru. *Edo bungaku no kyokō to keishō*. Tokyo: Shinwasha, 2001.

———. *Edo no ekusoshisuto*. Tokyo: Chikuma Shobō, 1991.

———. *Oiwa to Iemon: Yotsuya kaidan no shinsō*. Tokyo: Yōsensha, 2002.

———. *Onna to hebi: hyōchō no Edo bungakushi*. Tokyo: Chikuma Shobō, 1991.

———, ed. *Shiryō gedatsu monogatari kikigaki*. In *Kinsei kidan shūsei*, 1:333–89. Sōsho Edo bunko 26. Tokyo: Kokusho Kankōkai, 1992.

Takagi Gen. *Edo yomihon no kenkyū: jūkyū seiki shōsetsu yōshiki kō*. Tokyo: Perikansha, 1995.

Takahashi Noriko. *Kusazōshi to engeki*. Tokyo: Kyūko Shoin, 2004.

———. "Tsuruya Nanboku to ubume: *Tenjiku Tokubei ikokubanashi* no menoto Iohata kara *Yotsuya kaidan* no Oiwa e no henbō." *Bungaku* 53, no. 9 (1985): 80–88.

Takamura Chikuri. *Ehon shibai nenjū kagami*. 1803. In *Shibai nenjū gyōji shū*, edited by Kokuritsu Gekijō Geinō Chōsa Shitsu, 27–180, 185–242. Kabuki no bunken 7. Tokyo: Kokuritsu Gekijō Chōsa Yōseibu Geinō Chōsashitsu, 1976.

Takamura Itsue. *Nihon kon'inshi*. Tokyo: Shibundō, 1963.

Takano Tatsuyuki and Kuroki Kanzō, eds. *Keisei Asamagatake*. In *Genroku kabuki kessakushū*. Vol. 2, Kamigata no bu, 389–464. Tokyo: Waseda Daigaku Shuppanbu, 1925.

———. *Sankai Nagoya*. In *Genroku kabuki kessaku shū*. Vol. 1, Edo no bu, 19–54. Tokyo: Waseda Daigaku Shuppanbu, 1925.

Takase Baisei. *Ruisenshūi* [*Haikai ruisenshū*]. 7 vols. Kyoto: Terada Yoheiji, 1676.

Takazawa Shofū, ed. *Ninki yakusha no koseki shirabe*. 1919. Meiji–Shōwa shoki haiyū meikan shūsei, vol. 3. Tokyo: Yumani Shobō, 2005.

Takei Kyōzō. *Wakashu kabuki yarō kabuki no kenkyū*. Tokyo: Yagi Shoten, 2000.

Tamamuro Taijō. *Sōshiki bukkyō*. Tokyo: Daihōrinkaku, 1963.

Tamenaga Itchō. *Kabuki jishi*. In *Kabuki sōsho*, edited by Kinkōdō Henshūbu, 159–294. Tokyo: Kinkōdō Shoseki, 1910.

Tamenaga Shunsui. *Iwaiburo shigure no karakasa*. 1838. In *Sato no hanagasa; Futari musume; Iwaiburo shigure no karakasa; Omoto Kamematsu Otomi Mohei*, 269–477. Ninjōbon Kankōkai 18. Tokyo: Ninjōbon Kankōkai, 1925.

———. *Shunshoku umegoyomi*. Nihon koten bungaku taikei 64. Tokyo: Iwanami Shoten, 1962.

Tanaka Norio. "Inga ōhō: chōhen shōsetsu ni naizai suru rinen." *Edo bungaku* 34 (2006): 123–33.

Tanaka Takako. *Akujo-ron*. Tokyo: Kinokuniya Shoten, 1992.

Tatekawa [Utei] Enba. *Hana no Edo kabuki nendaiki*. 1811–1815. In *Kabuki nendaiki*. Tokyo: Ōtori Shuppan, 1976.

———. *Sanza ie kyōgen narabi ni yuishogaki*. In *Enseki jisshu*, edited by Iwamoto Kattōshi, 4:255–92. Tokyo: Chūō Kōronsha, 1979.

Terakado Seiken. *Edo hanjōki*. In *Edo hanjōki Ryūkyō shinshi*, edited by Hino Tatsuo, 1–332. Shin Nihon koten bungaku taikei 100. Tokyo: Iwanami Shoten, 1989.

Thornbury, Barbara E. *Sukeroku's Double Identity: The Dramatic Structure of Edo Kabuki*. Ann Arbor: Center for Japanese Studies, University of Michigan, 1982.

Toita Yasuji. *Chūshingura*. Tokyo: Sōgensha, 1957.

Tokuda Takeshi. "*Nansō Satomi hakkenden*: ingaritsu no hatten." In *Inga*, edited by Konno Tōru, 131–56. Iwanami kōza Nihon bungaku to bukkyō 2. Tokyo: Iwanami Shoten, 1994.

Tokugawa jikki. Vol. 3. Kokushi taikei shintei zōho kansei kinen ban 40. Edited by Kuroita Katsumi and Kokushi Taikei Henshūkan. Tokyo: Yoshikawa Kōbunkan, 1964.

Tōkyō shi, ed. *Tōkyō an'nai*. 2 vols. Tokyo: Shōkabō, 1907.

———. *Tōkyō shishikō sangyō hen*. Vol. 40. Tokyo: Tōkyōshi, 1996.

Tominaga Heibei. *Tanba Yosaku tazuna obi*. In *Genroku kabuki kessaku shū*. Vol. 2, Kamigata no bu. Edited by Takano Tatsuyuki and Kuroki Kanzō, 35–68. Tokyo: Rinsen Shoten, 1973.

Tonomura, Hitomi. "Birth Giving and Avoidance Taboo: Women's Body Versus the Historiography of Ubuya." *Japan Review* 19 (2007): 3–45.

———. "Black Hair and Red Trousers: Gendering the Flesh in Medieval Japan." *American Historical Review* 99, no. 1 (1994): 129–54.

———. "Women and Inheritance in Japan's Early Warrior Society." *Comparative Studies in Society and History* 32, no. 3 (1990): 592–623.

Torigoe Bunzō. *Genroku kabuki kō*. Tokyo: Yagi Shoten, 1991.

———. "Shibai akusho no ron." *Ōkurayama bunka kaigi kenkyū nenpō* 5 (1994): 151–60.

Torigoe Bunzō and Kikuchi Akira, eds. *Shuhitsu kaki-ire Edo shibai banzuke shū*. 3 vols. Tokyo: Waseda Daigaku Shuppanbu, 1992.
Torii Kiyonobu II (pictures). *Kokusen'ya kassen*. Edo: Murataya, ca. 1715–1756.
Toriyama Sekien (text and pictures). *Gazu hyakki yagyō*. 3 vols. Edo: Izumoji Izuminojō, 1776. Tokyo University of the Arts Library, special collection.
———. *Gazu hyakki yagyō*. In *Toriyama Sekien, Gazu hyakki yagyō*, edited by Takada Mamoru, Inada Atsunobu, and Tanaka Naohi. Tokyo: Kokusho Kankōkai, 1992.
Tsubouchi Shōyō [Yūzō]. "Akarui shibai tai kurai shibai." In *Shōyō senshū*, 10:325–35. Tokyo: Shunyōdō, 1927.
———. "Bungaku to shiteno waga zairai kyakuhon." In *Shōyō senshū*, 10:221–22. Tokyo: Shunyōdō, 1927.
———. "*Hinokiyama* jiken no kanteisho." *Kabuki* (Kabuki Hakkōjo) 163 (1914): 11–16.
———. *Kaki no heta*. Tokyo: Chūō Kōronsha, 1933.
———, ed. *Kinsei jitsuroku zensho*. Vol. 4. Tokyo: Waseda Daigaku Shuppankyoku, 1929.
———. "Shogen." In *ŌNanboku zenshū*, 1:1–4. Tokyo: Shunyōdō, 1925.
———. *Shōnenji ni mita kabuki no tsuioku*. Tokyo: Nihon Engei Gasshi Geisha Shuppanbu, 1920.
———. *Shōyō gekidan*. Tokyo: Tenyūsha, 1919.
Tsurumi Shunsuke and Yasuda Takeshi. *Chūshingura to Yotsuya kaidan: Nihonjin no komyunikēshon*. Tokyo: Asahi Sensho, 1983.
Tsuruya Nanboku IV. "*Ehon gappō ga tsuji*: A Kabuki Drama of Unfettered Evil by Tsuruya Nanboku IV." Translated by Paul B. Kennelly. *Asian Theater Journal* 17, no. 2 (2000): 149–89
———. *Epic Yotsuya Ghost Tale*. Translated by Faith Bach. In *An Edo Anthology: Literature from Japan's Mega-City, 1750–1850*, edited by Sumie Jones and Kenji Watanabe, 168–82. Honolulu: University of Hawai'i Press, 2013.
———. *Ghost Stories at Yotsuya*. Translated by Mark Oshima. In *Early Modern Japanese Literature: An Anthology, 1600–1900*, edited by Haruo Shirane, 844–84. New York: Columbia University Press, 2002.
———. *The Ghost Stories at Yotsuya on the Tōkaidō / Tōkaidō Yotsuya kaidan*. Translated by Paul B. Kennelly. In *Darkness and Desire, 1804–1864*, 135–63. Vol. 3 of *Kabuki Plays on Stage*, edited by James R. Brandon and Samuel L. Leiter. Honolulu: University of Hawai'i Press, 2002
———. *Iroeiri otogizōshi*. In *Tsuruya Nanboku zenshū*, edited by Gunji Masakatsu, 1:143–213. Tokyo: San'ichi Shobō, 1971.
———. *Kiku no en tsuki no shiranami*. In *Tsuruya Nanboku zenshū*, edited by Gunji Masakatsu, 9:7–109. Tokyo: San'ichi shobō, 1971.
———. *Shitennō ubuyu no Tamagawa*. In *Tsuruya Nanboku zenshū*, edited by Gunji Masakatsu, 7:157–250. Tokyo: San'ichi shobō, 1973.
———. *Tōkaidō Yotsuya kaidan*. Edited by Gunji Masakatsu. Shinchō Nihon koten shūsei 45. Tokyo: Shinchōsha, 1981.
———. *Tōkaidō Yotsuya kaidan*. Edited by Kawatake Shigetoshi. Tokyo: Iwanami Shoten, 1956.

———. *Tōkaidō Yotsuya kaidan*. Edited by Suwa Haruo. Kabuki on sutēji 18. Tokyo: Hakusuisha, 1999.

———. *Tsuruya Nanboku zenshū*. Edited by Gunji Masakatsu et al. 12 vols. Tokyo: San'ichi Shobō, 1971–1974.

———. [Uba Jōsuke] (text) and Utagawa Kunisada (pictures). *Katakiuchi kokoro wa takasago*. 1 fascicle. Publication information unknown.

Tsutsumi Harue. "Kabuki Encounters the West: Morita Kan'ya's Shintomi-za Productions, 1878–79." Ph.D. diss., Indiana University, 2004.

Tsutsumi Kunihiko. *Kinsei bukkyō setsuwa no kenkyū: shōdō to bungei*. Tokyo: Kanrin Shobō, 1996.

———. "Kosodate yūreitan no genfūkei: sōsō girei o tegakari to shite." In *Kinsei setsuwa to zensō*, 133–52. Ōsaka: Izumi Shoin, 1999.

———. *Nyonin jatai: hen'ai no Edo kaidanshi*. Tokyo: Kadokawa Shoten, 2006.

Uchiyama Mikiko. *Jōrurishi no jūhasseiki*. Tokyo: Benseisha, 1989.

Ueda Akinari. *Tales of Moonlight and Rain*. Translated by Anthony H. Chambers. New York: Columbia University Press, 2007.

———. *Ugetsu monogatari*. Edited by Nakamura Yukihiko, Takada Mamoru, and Nakamura Hiroyasu. Shinpen Nihon koten bungaku zenshū 78. Tokyo: Shōgakukan, 1995.

Ueda Setsuo. "*Kōtei konjaku monogatari* no setsuwa sekai: Izawa Banryō no setsuwa kyōju o megutte." *Kokugo kokubun* 60, no. 12 (1991): 19–32.

Ukai Tomoko. *Yodaime Tsuruya Nanboku ron; akuningeki no keifu to shukō o chūshin ni*. Tokyo: Kazama Shobō, 2005.

Umetada Misa. "Censorship in Edo Kabuki." Translated by Thomas Gaubatz. In *Ken'etsu media bungaku: Edo kara sengo made*, edited by Tomi Suzuki et al., 33–43. Tokyo: Shin'yōsha, 2012.

———. "Edo kabuki no ken'etsu." In *Ken'etsu media bungaku: Edo kara sengo made*, edited by Tomi Suzuki et al, 29–37. Tokyo: Shin'yōsha, 2012.

———. "Mokuami sakuhin gekika ni kansuru ichikōsatsu: *Katakiuchi uwasa no furuichi* o rei ni." *Engeki kenkyū sentā kiyō* 7 (2006): 51–63.

Wakita, Haruko. "Marriage and Property in Premodern Japan from the Perspective of Women's History." *Journal of Japanese Studies* 10 (1984): 73–99.

Waseda Daigaku Engeki Hakubutsukan, ed. *Edo shibai banzuke shuhitsu kaki-ire shūsei*. Tokyo: Waseda Daigaku Engeki Hakubutsukan, 1990.

———, ed. *Engeki hyakka daijiten*. 6 vols. Tokyo: Heibonsha, 1983.

———, ed. *Shibai-e ni miru Edo Meiji no kabuki*. Tokyo: Shōgakukan, 2003.

Watanabe Tamotsu. *Edo engekishi*. 2 vols. Tokyo: Kōdansha, 2009.

Williams, Duncan Ryūken. *The Other Side of Zen: A Social History of Sōtō Zen Buddhism in Tokugawa Japan*. Princeton, N.J.: Princeton University Press, 2005.

Wills, Steve. "Fires and Fights: Urban Conflagration, Governance, and Society in Edo-Tokyo, 1657–1890." Ph.D. diss., Columbia University, 2010.

Worthen, W. B. *Print and the Poetics of Modern Drama*. Cambridge: Cambridge University Press, 2005.

———. *Shakespeare and the Force of Modern Performance*. Cambridge: Cambridge University Press, 2003.

Yamada Keiji. *Yoru naku tori: igaku, jujutsu, densetsu.* Tokyo: Iwanami Shoten, 1990.
Yamaguchi Yaichirō. "Shitai bunri maisō jiken: Ninpu sōsō girei." In *Sōsō bosei kenkyū shūsei*. Vol. 1, *Sōhō*. Edited by Doi Takuji and Satō Yonesi, 299–303. Tokyo: Meicho Shuppan, 1979.
Yamaguchi Yoshinori, ed. *Kojiki.* Shinpen Nihon koten bungaku zenshū 1. Tokyo: Shōgakukan, 1997.
Yamamoto Eiji. "Nihon chūkinseishi ni okeru yuisho-ron no sōkatsu to tenbō." In *Yuisho no hikakushi*, edited by Rekishigaku Kenkyūkai, 3–27. Tokyo: Aoki Shoten, 2010.
Yamamoto Jirō. "Sadakurō no kata." *Kokubungaku kaishaku to kanshō* 32, no. 13 (1967): 97–98.
Yamaoka Genrin. *Kokon hyaku monogatari hyōban.* In *Zoku hyakumonogatari kaidan shūsei*, edited by Tachikawa Kiyoshi, 5–77. Sōsho Edo bunko 27. Tokyo: Kokusho Kankōkai, 1993.
Yanagisawa Yoshiyasu. *En'yū nikki.* In *Nihon shomin bunka shiryō shūsei*. Vol. 13, Geinō kiroku Bekkan. Edited by Geinōshi Kenkyūkai. Tokyo: San'ichi Shobō, 1975–1977.
Yanagitaru kenkyū 4, no. 6 (1928). In *Yanagitaru kenkyū*. Vol. 4. Tokyo: Yumani Shobō, 1982.
Yasui Manami. "Research Notes: On Burial Customs, Maternal Spirits, and the Fetus in Japan." *U.S–Japan Women's Journal* 24 (2003): 102–14.
———. "Taiji bunri maisō no shūzoku to shussan o meguru kaii no fōkuroa: sono seisei to shōmetsu ni kansuru kōsatsu." In *Nihon yōkaigaku taizen*, edited by Komatsu Kazuhiko, 479–509. Tokyo: Shōgakukan, 2003.
Yokoyama Shigeru, ed. *Kokyōgaeri no Edo-banashi.* Kinsei bungaku shiryō ruijū: koban chishihen 10. Tokyo: Benseisha, 1980.
Yokoyama Yasuko. *Edo kabuki no kaidan to bakemono.* Tokyo: Kōdansha, 2008.
———. *Edo Tōkyō no kaidan bunka no seiritsu to hensen.* Tokyo: Kazama Shobō, 1997.
———. *Yotsuya kaidan wa omoshiroi.* Tokyo: Heibonsha, 1997.
Yomiuri Shinbunsha, ed. *Tōkyō an'nai.* Tokyo: Yomiuri Shinbunsha, 1906.
Yonemoto, Marcia. "Outside the Inner Quarters: Sociability, Mobility and Narration in Early Edo-Period Women's Diaries." *Japan Forum* 21, no. 3 (2010): 389–401.
Yoshida Nobuyuki. "Geinō to mibunteki shūen: kotsujiki kagushi o rei toshite." *Buraku mondai kenkyū* 132 (1995): 79–109.
———. *Mibunteki shūen to shakai bunka kōzō.* Kyoto: Buraku Mondai Kenkyūjo, 2003.
Yoshida Setsuko, ed. *Edo kabuki hōrei shūsei.* Tokyo: Ōfūsha, 1989.
———, ed. *Zoku Edo kabuki hōrei shūsei.* Tokyo: Ōfūsha, 1997.
Zwicker, Jonathan. "Stage and Spectacle in an Age of Maps: Kabuki and the Cartographic Imagination in Nineteenth Century Japan." In *Publishing the Stage: Print and Performance in Early Modern Japan*, edited by Keller Kimbrough and Satoko Shimazaki, 215–24. Boulder: University of Colorado Center for Asian Studies, 2011.

INDEX

Numbers in italics refer to pages on which illustrations appear.

Accompanying Boat (Haikai ruisenshū), 168
acrobatics (*karuwazagoto*), 182–85, 188, 215
actor critiques (*yakusha hyōbanki*), 15, 30, 101, 289n.65; examples of, 26, 46, 59, 68, 103, 110, 124, 135, 142, 262, 264, 282n.48; on jealousy, 183, 187
actors: and audience, 24–25, 83–84; and authorship, 122–23, 265, 266, 284n.15; boy (*wakashu*), 45, 48, 86, 87, 183; censorship of, 86–88, 91, 92–93; and characters, 267, 301n.62; child, 301n.71; and class, 48, 91, 240; and community, 31, 42, 81–82, 84; contract system for, 22, 49–50, 53, 76, 86, 97–98, 110–11, 286n.26; crests of, 13, 14, 30, 268; in double production, 149; and Edo, 30–31, 282n.48; in fiction, 219, 221; in film, 238; and ghost roles, 26, 182–83, 189–90, 199, 215–16; ghostwriters for, 266, 323n.81; in *gōkan*, 268–71; hierarchy of, 15, 48, 76, 99, 301n.71; and historical accuracy, 240–41; images of, 4, 8, 13, *14*, 14–15, 22, 30–31, *109*, 125, *139*, 139, 140, *141*, 256–57, 263, 263–64, 266–69, 268, 269, 270, 289n.65, 298n.29; and kabuki calendar, 25, 76–80, 101–2; from Kyoto, 76, 80, 81, 110; lineages of, 15–17, 31, 35, 81–86, 110, 234, 280n.26, 319n.31; male, 45, 48, 86, 87, 88, 183, 293n.122; in Meiji period, 232–45; minor, 108, 238, 245; from Osaka, 76, 80, 81, 110, 262, 322n.73; patrons (*hiiki*) of, 2, 58, 59, 77; and playwrights, 16, 17, 80, 261, 284n.15, 321n.62; popularity of, 13, 238, 243; premodern, 24, 25; and presenting the past, 42, 81–86, 298n.33; in puppet theater, 62; role types (*yakugara*) of, 33, 46, 83, 239, 308n.62, 309n.77; salaries of, 50, 53, 59, 98, 99, 286n.29, 296n.2, 296n.4, 296n.10; and samurai, 81, 87–88, 240–41; and scripts, 6–7, 122, 232, 233–34, 245, 254, 255, 256, 261, 262–63, 275; styles of, 63, 123, 124, 237, 238, 239, 289nn.66–68, 308nn.62–64; in Taishō period,

349

actors (*continued*)
234, 254–55; in tent shows, 104; and theater managers, 50, 80–82; travel by, 30, 282n.48. *See also* playbills
  FEMALE, 105, 237, 239; banning of, 48, 86, 87, 88, 293n.122; and early kabuki, 21, 45, 46–47, 52
  FEMALE-ROLE, 108, 111, 172; and acrobatics, 185, 188; as ghosts, 182, 183, 199; vs. male-role, 188–89, 199; and *ubume*, 215–16; in *Yotsuya kaidan*, 32, 32, 189, 262
  MALE-ROLE, 33, 212, 262; vs. female-role, 188–89, 199; as ghosts, 146–48, 182, 183, 189–90, 199, 215–16
Actor's Book of Great Learning, An (*Yakusha daigaku*), 103
Actors' Dancing Fan, An (*Yakusha mai ōgi*), 183
Actors' Double Shamisen, The (*Yakusha nichōjamisen*), 68
Actor's Vocal Shamisen, The (*Yakusha kuchijamisen*), 59
Adult Male Actor's Sumo (*Yarō sekisumō*), 46
advertisements, 8, 102, 296n.11; and fluidity of productions, 74–75, 120–21; and playwright, 256–57. *See also* playbills
Aigo no Waka, 40
Akama Ryō, 5, 120
Akimoto Suzushi, 61
Akō incident (*Akō jiken*), 113–14, 129, 148, 236–37, 295n.138, 300n.49
akuba (chivalrous bad woman), 33
akusho (evil place), 19–21, 280n.30, 281nn.31–34
Akutagawa Ryūnosuke, 250
All About the Actors (*Yakusha zensho*), 46
alternate attendance (*sankin kōtai*) system, 56
Amachi Shigeru, 273

Amorous Origins of the Various Pleasure Quarters, The (*Shokoku yūri kōshoku yuraizoroe*), 183
Analysis of a Hundred Ghost Stories Old and New, An (*Kokon hyaku monogatari hyōban*), 208, 209
Anderson, Benedict, 29
Another Story of the Giant Princess Osakabe by Shōroku (*Matazoro Shōroku Osakabe banashi*), 26–27
Antoku, Emperor, 105
aragoto (rough style), 62, 63, 65, 66, 124–26, 289n.68
Arajishi Otokonosuke, 65
Arashi Kiyosaburō I, 182, 187, 309n.78
Arashi Koroku I, 124
Asada Itchō, 169
Asai Ryōi, 59, 173
Asakusa, 45, 111, 227, 245
Asama plays (*Asama-mono*), 64, 185–87
Ashikaga Yoshimasa, 65
Association of Pan (Pan no kai), 320n.37
Atherton, David, 127, 128
audience, 79, 100, 113; and actors, 24–25, 83–84; and censorship, 86–93; changes in, 231–32, 234, 236, 238, 242, 243, 275; classes in, 19, 34, 42, 56–58, 65–66, 73, 88–89, 90; and evil characters, 142–43; and fluidity of productions, 75, 120; and prices, 89–90
Austin, J. L., 6
authorship: and actors, 122–23, 232, 265, 266, 284n.15; collaborative, 255–58; and copyright laws, 72, 257; of Nanboku, 256, 274, 275. *See also* playwrights

Baba Akiko, 166
Bai Juyi, 154
Bakhtin, Mikhail, 26–27, 42, 81
Bakin. *See* Kyokutei Bakin

INDEX

350

"Bakufu Versus Kabuki" (Shively), 19, 22
Bandō Mitsugorō III, 84
Basket's Ears, The (*Kago mimi*), 168
Bathhouse of the Floating World, The (*Ukiyoburo*; Shikitei Sanba), 83–84, 137
Battle of Coxinga, The (*Kokusen'ya kassen*; Chikamatsu Monzaemon), 9, 212–13, *213*
Beaded String of All the Best Actors: Osaka (*Yakusha tamazukushi Ōsaka*), 262
Before the Nation (Burns), 29
Berry, Mary Elizabeth, 12, 29
Big Business on Leech Island (*Ōakinai hiru ga kojima*; Sakurada Jisuke), 67
"Black Hair" (*Kurokami*; music), 159
Black Hand Gang and the Fight in the Pleasure Quarters, The (*Kurotegumi kuruwa no tatehiki*), 40
Blood Bowl Sutra (*Ketsubonkyō*), 205, 310n.4, 312nn.17–20
blood defilement, 163, 188, 190, 201, 204, 225, 312n.15
Blood Pool Hell, 162, 166, *167*, 201, 204–6, 208, 304n.23, 312n.20, 313n.30
"Blue Hood, The" (*Aozukin*; Ueda Akinari), 161–62, 163
Bodhisattva Jizō, 197, 226
body, female: and blood and hair, 145–46, 155–59; and changing concepts, 176–77; and emotions, 27, 28, 33, 155–63, 190, 193; in fiction, 219, 223; and ghosts, 25, 33–34, 112–13, 150–93; and grotesque, 26–27, 33; and jealousy, 174, 182–83, 190; and male-role actors, 190; in modern period, 191–93; and Nanboku, 100, 131; and selfhood, 27–29, 155, 193; stigma of, 173; transformations of, 163–68

Book in Japan, The (Kornicki), 12
Book of Dawn: The Whole Story of Princess Sakura (*Sakurahime zenden akebonozōshi*; Santō Kyōden and Utagawa Toyokuni), 223, 224
Buddhism: and actor contracts, 49, 50; and birds, 209; books of, 316n.61; and consecration cloth in *Yotsuya kaidan*, 195–98; and serpent imagery, 165–66, 175, 305n.30; and *ubume*, 198, 204, 227; and women, 27, 33, 161, 162–63, 168, 169, 173, 174, 189, 204–7, 304n.20, 313n.30
Bunka period, 20, 21–22, 101, 235
Bunsei period, 20, 21, 101, 235
Bunzō (character), 192–93
burial practices, 177, 180, 206
Burns, Susan L., 29
Buyō Inshi, 85–86

calendar, kabuki, 1, 22, 29, 31, 46, 99; and actors, 25, 76–80, 101–2; decline of, 97, 106–11, 239; eleventh month in, 8; flexibility of, 7–8; and fluidity of plays, 8–9; and Nanboku, 101, 111; open-endedness in, 75–81; and presenting the past, 42, 81; vs. textualization, 236. *See also* face-showing productions; productions
"Capacity of Chūshingura, The" (Smith), 113
Carlson, Marvin, 82
censor (*nanushi*), 76, 124
censorship, 86–93; of contemporary events, 30, 43, 295n.138; and presenting the past, 41, 43; of scripts, 295n.144, 300n.52; targets of, 40, 90–91, 92–93, 244, 319n.28; and types of kabuki inspection, 92. *See also* government, Tokugawa
Ceremonial Gentle Soga (*Shikirei yawaragi Soga*), 40

INDEX

351

chanting, 17, 138, 303n.10, 322n.69
characters: and actors, 267, 301n.62; class of, 63, 69, 80, 106, 111, 116, 128, 136, 239–40; in Edo kabuki, 39–40, 60, 66, 70, 138–39, 226, 261; in fiction and theater, 219–22, 220; of Nanboku, 100, 216–18, 225–26; psychology of, 273–74; and role types, 33, 46, 83, 130, 140, 238, 239–40, 274, 308n.62, 309n.77
   FEMALE, 66, 112, 127, 155, 182; in household-disturbance plays, 34, 144–45; of Nanboku, 100, 216–18; and spring production, 79–80. *See also* ghosts: female; specific characters
Chartier, Roger, 10
Chikamatsu Monzaemon, 169, 181, 243, 281n.34, 303n.85, 316n.61; vs. Nanboku, 246; works by, 9, 182, 212, 221–22
children, 207–8, 209, 212–13, 225, 226, 301n.71
China, 171, 176, 205; *ubume* in, 208–9, 211
choreography, 26, 62, 123, 233
Chronicles of Great Peace, The (*Taiheiki*), 65, 67, 70, 213, 236
Chrysanthemum Bond: Bandit on a Moonlit Night (*Kiku no en tsuki no shiranami*), 142, 143
class structure: and actors, 48, 91, 240; and architecture, 54; of audience, 19, 34, 42, 56–58, 65–66, 73, 88–89, 90; and censorship, 86–93; changes in, 148, 242, 243; and characters, 69, 106, 111, 116, 136, 239–40; in Edo, 20, 287n.46; and emotions, 155, 190; and female ghosts, 189, 190; and kabuki, 19, 22–23, 31, 56–66; and marriage, 171–72; and presenting the past, 66–68, 71, 72, 93; in Russian novels, 235; and vendettas, 127; and women, 27, 174

Classical Theater Study Group (Kogeki Kenkyūkai), 247, 251, 320n.37
clothing, 42, 66; censorship of, 91, 92–93; of evil characters, 139–40, 142; serpent imagery on, 174–75
Collected Essays on Kabuki (*Kabuki shūdan*; Mimasuya Nisōji), 99
Collected Illustrations of the Three Realms, Japanese and Chinese (*Wakan sansai zue*; Terajima Ryōan), 179, 209
Collected Works of the Great Tsuruya Nanboku, The (*ŌNanboku zenshū*), 246, 261
Collection of Old and New Japanese Poems (*Kokin wakashū*), 151
Collection of Tales from Uji, A (*Uji shūi monogatari*), 200
Collection of the Way of the Gods (*Shintōshū*), 209
Collections of Rumors in Yotsuya (*Yotsuya zōdanshū*), 225
Collections of Tales Old and New (*Kokon chomonjū*), 165, 200
commoners: and *akusho*, 20, 21; in audience, 18, 19, 56–58, 65–66, 90; and censorship, 86, 87; as characters, 63, 80, 106, 111, 128; culture of, 41–42, 172; in fiction, 219; and presenting the past, 41, 42, 69, 71, 72
community, 24, 29–32, 97; and actors, 42, 81–82, 84; changes in, 148, 239; Edo as, 29–31; and Nanboku, 132; nation-state as imagined, 29, 34; and Oiwa, 161, 226; and presenting the past, 40–42, 67, 72, 93; and print, 12, 236; and selfhood, 27, 28; and women, 150, 161, 218
Compendium of Materia Medica (*Bencao gangmu*), 208, 314n.32
Compilation of Birth-Related Practices in Japan (*Nihon san'iku shūzoku shiryō shūsei*), 206
Conder, Josiah, 242

INDEX

352

Confucianism: and government, 282n.44; and supernatural, 27–28, 150, 176, 308n.59; and women, 27, 150, 161, 174, 293n.122
Conquergood, Dwight, 279n.24
consecration cloth (*nagare kanjō*), 204, 206; in *Yotsuya kaidan*, 195–98
Contemporary Mirror of Wisdom (*Tōsei chie kagami*; Miyako no Nishiki), 173
copyright laws, 72, 257
Country Tale of Two Sisters, A (*Bei Bei kyōdan*; Kyokutei Bakin), 210, 210
Courtesan and the Great Buddhist Service at Mibu, The (*Keisei Mibu dainenbutsu*; Chikamatsu), 182
Courtesan of Asama Mountain, The (*Keisei Asamagatake*), 64, 185–87, *186*
Creed, Barbara, 155
Critique of The Treasury of Loyal Retainers Old and New (*Kokon iroha hyōrin*), 124, 138–39
Cultivation of Ladies, The (*Fujin yashinaigusa*; Baiu Sanjin), 169, 170, 175
culture: early modern, 20, 30, 100; of Edo, 22, 60, 63; and history, 20, 24–25, 111; of kabuki, 18–19, 21, 22, 24, 31–32, 100; local vs. national, 232; manuscript, 12; print, 14–15, 22; regional, 18, 29–31, 59–60, 61, 63; samurai, 28, 41–42
POPULAR, 22, 41–42, 172; and community, 30; subversiveness of, 19–20, 181; and women, 33, 175, 180

daimyo, 42, 54, 56; and actors, 87–88, 91, 93; performances at homes of, 58–59, 72, 88, 288n.53; in plots, 63, 65, 71, 108, 126, 281n.34; and *sekai*, 211–12; women of, 79–80, 172
dances, 7, 46, 47, 48, 123, 185–86; and female-role actors, 182, 188, 189; and *ubume*, 213–14, 215
Danzaemon, 48
Danzō hayagawari (print; Utagawa Toyokuni), *141*
De Benneville, James S., 247–48, 253
Demon Shutendōji, The (play), 61
demons, 60–65, 106, 110, 152, 160–62, 290n.72, 307n.47; female, 25, 164, 166, 178, 182, 192; and female ghosts, 163, 174, 187; male, 163, 175, 192
Diary of Izu (*Izu nikki*), 67, 70, 71
"Document Requesting a Decision Regarding Regulation of the Three Kabuki Theaters" (San-shibai kyōgenza torishimari hōgi sadame shōmon), 53, 98
Dōjōji (*Dōjō Temple*) genre, 158, 165, 166, 169, 171, 174, 310n.80
Dream Team of Actors, A (*Yakusha yume awase*), 110–11
dreams, 67, 150–52, 179
Drifting Clouds (*Ukigumo*; Futabatei Shimei), 192–93
Dupont, Florence, 10
Dustheap Stories (*Chirizukadan*), 90

Earth Spirit (Wedekind), 248
Edo: actors in, 30–31, 97, 282n.48; censorship in, 87, 91; changing kabuki of, 97–100; characters of, 39–40, 60, 66, 70, 138, 226, 261; class structure in, 20, 287n.46; as community, 29–31, 97; culture of, 22, 60, 63; demographics of, 56, 59–60, 62, 231, 242; female actors in, 293n.122; fires in, 45; history of, 20, 34; vs. Kamigata, 314n.39; vs. Kyoto, 23, 30, 31, 61, 63, 65, 242; and military tales, 56, 60, 62, 63, 64–65; and national theater, 31, 97, 232, 238, 248; vs. Osaka, 30, 61, 63, 65; playwriting

Edo (*continued*)
   style in, 136; pleasure quarters in (Yoshiwara), 21, 45, 47, 60, 76, 79, 288n.56; print culture in, 16, 22; samurai in, 31, 56–66, 287n.46; *sekai* in, 32, 34, 64, 65, 71, 73, 211–12, 215; as Tokyo, 231, 242, 243, 275; townsmen of, 39, 42; types of plays in, 185, 301n.69. See also Tokyo
Edo in Bloom: A Kabuki Time Line (*Hana no Edo kabuki nendaiki*; Tatekawa Enba I), 82, 102, 121–22, 214, *214*
Edo Shichidayū, 52
Edogawa Ranpo, 250
Eisenstein, Elizabeth, 11
Ejima Kiseki, 187
Ejima-Ikushima incident (1714), 53–54, 74
Emended Tales of Times Now Past (*Kōtei konjaku monogatari*; Izawa Banryō), 200–201, 202, 204, 210, 215
emotions, inner: and female body, 27, 28, 33, 155–63, 181, 190, 193; and female ghosts, 174, 175–80; in fiction, 219, 223; and male jealousy, 190–93; and Oiwa as *ubume*, 226
Emperor Yōmei and the Mirror of Craftsmen (*Yōmei tennō shokunin kagami*), 169, 181
Enchi Fumiko, 271, 273
engeki (performance), 241–42, 245
Engi Theater (Engi-za), 245
Enomoto Torahiko, 240
Enya, Lord (Asano Naganori; character), 113–14, 129–30, 144, 145, 146, 160
Evaluating The Treasury of Loyal Retainers' Characters (*Chūshingura jinbutsu hyōron*; Hatanaka Kansai), 138
Evil Places on the Peripheries (*Henkai no akusho*; Hirosue Tamotsu), 19

face-showing productions (*kaomise kyōgen*), 8, 52, 53, 65, 74–78, 80, 157; censorship of, 92; decline of, 106–11, 239; end of, 98–99; and Nanboku, 101, 110; prices of, 89
Fallen Leaves of Precept Ceremonies (*Kaie rakusōdan*), 162, 164
Famous Sites of Edo (*Edo meishoki*; Asai Ryōi), 59
Famous Views of Actors (*Yakusha meisho zue*; Utagawa Toyokuni and Kyokutei Bakin), 85
Fast-Food Take on the Actors, A (*Yakusha sokuseki ryōri*), 142–43
Faure, Bernard, 165
Feng Menglong, 171
festivals, 70, 76, 78–79, 151, 178
fiction, 32, 168, 210; characters in, 219–22, 220; female body in, 219, 223; ghosts in, 25, 219, 220–21, 223, 224–25; pregnancy in, 206–7, 219, 223; sentimental (*ninjōbon*), 173; sources for, 201; *ubume* in, 194, 198, 218–23
filial piety, 150, 282n.44
film, 20, 238, 273–74
Five Powers That Secure Love (*Godairiki koi no fūjime*; Namiki Gohei), 135–36
Flower of Kabuki, the Peony Lantern Ghost Story, The (*Kabuki no hana botan dōrō*; Santō Kyōden), 315n.48
Flowers of Kikugorō's Farewell Performance: Ghost Stories at Yotsuya (*Nagori no hana Yotsuya kaidan*; Hanagasa Bunkyō I and Keisai Eisen), 194–95, *195*, 266–67, 268, 271
Folding Screens of Famous Places in Edo (*Edo meishozu byōbu*), 43–44, *44*, 56, 84
Foucault, Michel, 17, 270
Four Guardians: A New Splash at Tamagawa River (*Shitennō ubuyu no Tamagawa*), 106–10, *109*, *111*

INDEX

Free Theater (Jiyū gekijō), 237
Freud, Sigmund, 250
From the Sajiki to the Study (*Sajiki kara shosai e*; Ihara Seisei'en), 232–34, 245
Fukuchi Ōchi, 242, 319n.21
Fukumori Kyūsuke, 213
Furuido Hideo, 51, 68, 72, 102, 136, 179
Futabatei Shimei, 192

gender, 112, 131, 155, 162. *See also* body, female; women
Genji (clan), 22, 60–61, 70, 71
Genroku period, 21, 45–48, 62–64, 66, 74, 175; actors in, 182, 189; in Kamigata, 127
Gerstle, Andrew, 64
Getsudō's Collection of Things Seen and Heard (*Getsudō kenmonshū*), 53
ghost plays, 1, 231, 297n.14; of Nanboku, 21, 25–28, 93, 100, 106; *Treasury of Loyal Retainers* as, 143–48; *Yotsuya kaidan* as, 148, 235
ghost stories, 168, 176, 208–9, 248
Ghost Stories at Yotsuya (*Tōkaidō Yotsuya kaidan*; film), 273
ghosts (*yūrei*): actors of, 146–47, 182, 183, 189–90, 199, 215–16; and censorship, 244; and changing concepts, 176–77, 178, 180; and Chikamatsu, 303n.85; and female body, 25, 33, 112–13, 150–93; in fiction, 25, 219, 220–21, 223, 224–25; male, 144–48, 150, 154, 177, 190–93, 216–18, 220, 222; male vs. female, 164, 175; music for, 214; in nō, 25, 154; *qi* of, 208; and serpent imagery, 174–80, 186, 191, 310n.83; and special effects, 25, 103, 178–79, 197, 218; and Taishō kabuki, 254; in *Yotsuya kaidan*, 33–34, 190–91
FEMALE, 24–29, 32–34, 150–93, 231; actors of, 189–90, 199, 215–16; depictions of, *153*, *163*, *164*, *197*; and emotions, 174, *175*–80; history of, 181–89; in household-disturbance plays, 216; as inversion, 181–82; and jealousy, 154, 155–63; in literature, 218–23, 224–25; and male surrogates, 144–45; and Nanboku, 199, 227; and revenge plays, 133; and samurai, 28, 29, 189; and *sekai*, 27–29, 190; and serpent imagery, 174–80, 186; and *ubume*, 194, 198–223, 225–26, 311n.5; in *Yotsuya kaidan*, 33–34, 262. *See also* Oiwa
Gilded and Auspicious Soga in Edo, The (*Edo sunago kichirei Soga*; Namiki Gohei), 135–36
gishi (loyal retainer), 129–30, 133
Glassman, Hank, 205, 310n.4
Gluck, Carol, 20
Go Sankei (character), 212, 213
Go-Daigo, Emperor, 290n.72
gōkan (combined booklets), 32–33, 142, 218–22, 315n.54, 323n.79; and actors, 268–71; ghosts in, 25; and performance vs. script, 266, 268; sources for, 225; *ubume* in, 218, 219; and *yomihon*, 315n.48
Goldman, Michael, 143
Goryūtei Tokushō, 323n.81
government, Meiji, 236, 244, 258
government, Tokugawa: and actors, 48, 86, 87–88, 91–92, 282n.48; bans by, 48, 86, 87–88, 285n.19, 300n.49; and Confucianism, 282n.44; and culture, 29–30; documents of, 18, 21; kabuki as resistance to, 18–22, 28, 31–32, 87, 93, 308n.61; regulation by, 19, 22–23, 56, 99; and theater managers, 50–51, 52, 53–54; and theaters, 31–32, 43–56, 99, 285n.19. *See also* censorship
Great Favorite Subscription List, The (*Gohīki kanjinchō*), 157–58, 159, 164

INDEX

355

Great Hawk, the Splendor of the Soga Brothers, The (*Ōtaka nigiwai Soga*), 8–9
Great Kantō Earthquake, 34, 247
grotesque, 26–27, 33, 248, 254
guardians, four, 106–10, 290n.72, 298n.24
Gunji Masakatsu, 64, 90, 105, 135, 185, 196, 219, 258–63, 265
Gutenberg, Johannes, 11
Gutenberg Galaxy, The (McLuhan), 11

haikai (popular linked verse), 67, 70, 72, 168
Haiyū Theater (Haiyū-za), 274
Hakutō book (hand-copied edition), 260–61, 265; vs. modern edition, 262–63
Hanagasa Bunkyō, 195, 266–67, 323n.81
Hanashōbu Sano no yatsuhashi (play), 295n.138
Handbook of Theatrical Worlds, The (*Sekai kōmoku*; Kanai Sanshō), 69–70
haragei (stomach art) technique, 237
Hasegawa Kanbei XI, 104
Hashiba Hideyoshi, 236
Hatanaka Kansai (Henkutsu Dōjin), 138
Hattori Yukio, 43, 73, 89, 90, 181–82, 189
Hayano Kanpei (character), 114–15, 123, 137, 138, 146; suicide of, 144–45
Hayashi Razan, 176–77
Heian period, 61, 68, 163, 171
hells, 307n.53; for women, 162, 166, 167, 168, 169, 187, 201, 204–6, 208, 215, 304n.23, 312n.20, 313n.30
Hentai shinri (Abnormal Psychology; journal), 250
Hikosaku, 309n.70
Hiraga Gennai, 104
Hirasawa, Carolyn, 162

Hirosue Tamotsu, 19, 21
Hishikawa Moronobu, 56, 58, 220
historical contemporaneity (*jidai sewa*), 68
history: accuracy in, 236, 240–41; and culture, 20, 24–25, 111; in early modern plays, 243; living history (*katsureki*), 34, 123, 237, 240. *See also* past, presenting the; *sekai*; time
History of Japanese Theater (*Nihon engekishi*; Ihara Seisei'en), 53
Hōei period, 45
Hokusai. *See* Katsushika Hokusai
Homecoming Stories of Edo (*Kokyōgaeri no Edobanashi*), 47, 62
horror plays (*kaidan kyōgen*), 7, 25, 101–2, 104, 106, 189
Hōseidō Kisanji, 85, 180
Hot-Blooded Tales of the Kantō Region (*Kantō kekki monogatari*), 62
House of Flowers: Aigo's Cherry Blossom (*Hanayakata Aigo no sakura*), 40
household (*ie*), 111, 127, 306n.38; and female ghosts, 27, 28, 150; in fiction, 223; jealousy in, 169–74; in *Yotsuya kaidan*, 33, 34, 225–26
household-disturbance (*oie sōdō*) plays, 300n.58; in Edo, 65–66; female ghosts in, 216; in fiction, 221, 223–24; in Kamigata, 63–64; and revenge plays, 128, 131–32; and *sekai*, 70, 226; and spring production, 79–80; *ubume* in, 34, 198–99, 216, 219; women in, 131–32, 144–46, 188, 212, 300n.59; vs. *Yotsuya kaidan*, 126–33, 224–25
"How Yorimitsu's Attendant Taira no Suetake Encountered a Woman Who Had Given Birth" (*Yorimitsu no rōdō Taira no Suetake ubume ni au koto*), 199–200

INDEX
356

humor (*okashimi*), 105, 219, 246, 250

Ichikawa Danjūrō, lineage of, 81, 82–83; and *aragoto* style, 62, 289n.68
Ichikawa Danjūrō I, 62, 66, 82–83, 284n.15, 290n.72
Ichikawa Danjūrō II, 8, 40, 50, 53, 81–84, 91, 124
Ichikawa Danjūrō IV, 83, 123, 140, *141*
Ichikawa Danjūrō V, 85, 282n.48
Ichikawa Danjūrō VII (Ebizō), 30, 233, 299n.45, 322n.74, 323n.81; in *Four Guardians*, 106, 107–8, *109*, 110; images of, 3, 4, *195*, 263, 268, *268*; and presenting the past, 81, 298n.33; and Sukeroku, 81, 123; in *Treasury of Loyal Retainers*, 126; in *Yotsuya kaidan*, 3–4, 7, 130, 140, 195, 240, 261–62, 274
Ichikawa Danjūrō IX (Kawarasaki Gonjūrō I), 122–25, 232–33, 237–38, 240–42, 254
Ichikawa Danzō IV, 123
Ichikawa Kodanji, 242
Ichikawa Sadanji II, 251
Ichimura Takenojō, 52
Ichimura Theater (Ichimura-za), 26, 47, 74, 98, 139, 227, 298n.25
Ichimura Uzaemon IX, 83, 84
ichiyazuke (overnight pickles; fill-in plays), 80
Idea of the Evil Place, The (*Akubasho no hassō*; Hirosue Tamotsu), 19
identity, dual (*yatsushi*), 39–40, 42, 46, 67, 81, 298n.34, 301n.63
Iemon. See Tamiya Iemon
Iga Jutarō, 108
Ihara Saikaku, 172
Ihara Seisei'en (Toshirō), 53, 120, 232–36, 245–46, 252, 265
Ikeda Mitsunaka, 288n.53
Ikushima Daikichi, 308n.62

Ikushima Koheiji, 49–50
Ikushima Shingorō, 53–54
Illustrated Encyclopedia of Childbirth (*Tassei zusetsu*; Kondō Naoyoshi), 206
Illustrated Encyclopedia of the Three Stages of Edo, An (*Ukan sandai zue*; Hōseidō Kisanji and Katsukawa Shundō), 85, 179, *179*, 180
Illustrated Encyclopedia of Theater, The (*Shibai kinmō zui*; Shitikei Sanba, Katsukawa Shun'ei, and Utagawa Toyokuni I), 54, *55*, 85, 152, *153*
Illustrated Mirror of the Theatrical Calendar, An (*Ehon shibai nenjū kagami*; Takamura Chikuri), 80
Illustrated Performance Bulletin (*Engei gahō*), 271, 272
illustrations, book, 179–80, 219; serpentine imagery in, *170*, *175*; of theaters, 84–85; of *ubume*, 200, 201–2, 209, 213; and ukiyo-e prints, 12–13, 32, 282n.38. See also *gōkan*; playbills
Imperial Theater (Teikoku gekijō), 242, 265
Inner Chambers of Edo Castle, The (*Chiyodajō ōoku*; Nagashima Imashirō and Ōta Yoshio), 53
Inoue Kaoru, 237
"Invention of Edo, The" (Gluck), 20
iroaku (erotic rogue), 33, 130, 140, 274
Irohagana Yotsuya kaidan (Osaka version of *Yotsuya kaidan*), 266
"Is *Yotsuya kaidan* Just a Ghost Play?" (*Yotsuya kaidan wa obake shibai ka*; Mitamura Engyo), 235
Ise Taira Clan: The Divine Wind of the Devotees (*Ise Heiji hiiki no kamikaze*), 110
Ishizawa Shūji, 274
Isozaki (*otogizōshi* play), 160

INDEX

357

It Looks Like Flowers: The Deep Snows of Yoshino (*Hana to mimasu Yoshino no miyuki*; Fukumori Kyūsuke), 213–14
Itō Hirobumi, 237
Itō Kihei (character), 133, 155, 160
Iwai Bathhouse: Umbrella in a Light Rain (*Iwaiburo shigure no karakasa*; Tamenaga Shunsui), 105
Iwai Hanshirō, 30
Iwai Hanshirō IV, 213
Iwai Hanshirō V, 106, 110–11
Iwai Hanshirō VII, 264
Iwai Kumesaburō II, 4
Iwai Sagenta, 186
Iwai Shijaku I, 263, 263–64
Izawa Banryō (Nagahide), 200–201, 215

"Japan: The Island of Women" (*Nihon nyōgo no shima*; song), 207
Japan in Print (Berry), 12, 29
Japanese Classical Theater Study Group (Kogeki Kenkyūkai), 247
Japanese Ghosts (*Nihon no yūrei*; Suwa Haruo), 163–64
Japanese Miracles of the Lotus Sutra (*Dai Nihon hokke genki*), 165
jealousy, 25, 27–28, 66, 150–93, 169–74; and acrobatics, 185; and birds, 210; and female body, 174, 182–83, 190; and female ghosts, 154, 155–63; and female transformation, 191–92; and female-role actors, 188; in fiction, 223; male, 190–93; in modern period, 191–93; in popular culture, 180; and serpent imagery, 168, 169, 174–75; warnings against, 173
Jinrikisha Days in Japan (Scidmore), 122
Jōdo sect (Buddhism), 205
Jōkyō period, 45
Journal of Matsuya (*Matsuya hikki*), 209
Jung, Carl, 250

Kabuki: The Popular Stage of Japan (Penlington), 233
kabuki, characters for, 46–47, 219–21, 220
kabuki, types of: *doro shibai* (dirt), 238; Shinkabuki (New Kabuki), 251; *wakashu* (boy actors), 45, 48, 86, 87, 183; *yarō* (older men), 45, 48–49, 86–87; *yūjo* (courtesan), 45; *zashiki shibai* (residential), 58–59, 61
Kabuki Chronology (*Kabuki nenpyō*; Ihara Seisei'en), 120, 121
Kabuki Theater (Kabuki-za), 10, 241, 242, 253, 257
kabuki-mono ("deviants"), 21
Kako no Kyōshin Makes the Rounds of Seven Graves (*Kako no Kyōshin nanahaka meguri*; Chikamatsu), 221
Kamakura, 136
Kamakura Keiko, 179, 289n.61
Kameya Yohei, 282n.48
Kamigata: actors of, 30, 32; vs. Edo, 314n.39; Nanboku in, 319n.25; pleasure quarters in, 281n.34; plots in, 63–64, 68–69, 127; productions in, 22, 35, 75, 135, 136, 138, 284n.15, 291n.92; theaters in, 46
Kamiyama Akira, 250
Kanai Sanshō, 69–70, 136, 140
Kanawa (nō play), 174
kanazōshi (*kana* booklets), 169, 174, 208, 313n.30
Kanpei. *See* Hayano Kanpei
Kanpō-Era Compilation of Legal Documents (*Ofuregaki Kanpō shūsei*), 88
Kansei period, 101
Kansei reforms, 51, 219, 221
Kanzaburo. *See* Nakamura Kanzaburō
Kaoyo (character), 113, 137
Karatani Kōjin, 23–24, 237–38, 241
Kasane (character), 191, 207, 218, 219

INDEX

358

Kastan, David, 11, 271
Katayose Masayoshi, 200
Katsu Genzō III, 258
Katsui Genpachi, 256
Katsukawa Shundō, 85
Katsukawa Shun'ei, 54, 152
katsureki (living history) movement, 34, 123, 237, 240
Katsushika Hokusai, 168, 175, 210, 220; linear perspective in, 282n.38
Kawarasaki Gonjūrō I (Ichikawa Danjūrō IX), 124, *125*
Kawarasaki Theater, 47, 89, 98, 142
Kawatake Mokuami, 34, 123, 232, 236, 245, 247, 256, 257; and *sekai*, 111, 226–27, 239, 314n.44
Kawatake Shigetoshi, 127, 247, 250, 274, 323n.76
Kawatake Shinshichi III, 123, 257, 258
Kawazoe Yū, 104
Keepsake Flower: Ghost Stories at Yotsuya (*Katamigusa Yotsuya kaidan*), 252
Keisai Eisen, 195, 266
Keisei Asama Soga, 295n.138
Ketsubonkyō. *See* Blood Bowl Sutra
kibyōshi (yellow covers) genre, 219, 221, 315n.54
Kikugorō. *See* Onoe Kikugorō
Kimura Kinka, 251
Kinoshita Mokutarō, 320n.37
Kinpira's Visit to the Pleasure Quarters (*Kinpira rokujōgayoi*), 66
Kira Yoshinaka (character), 113
Kiri Ōkura, 51–52
Kiri Theater, 47, 98
Kitagawa Morisada, 212
Kitashiro Nobuko, 311n.5
Kiyokawa Shigeharu, 120, 121
Kiyosaburō I. *See* Arashi Kiyosaburō I
kizewa (raw *sewa*) plays, 21, 105, 136, 137, 239, 301n.69
Koai Eitarō, 191
Kobayashi Tadashi, 12
Kobotoke Kohei (character), 4, 14, *14*, 146, 189, 190–91, 262

kōdan (storytelling), 239, 248, 322n.69; *rakugo* (oral), 191; as source for kabuki, 257–58
Kōdan kurabu (*Kōdan Club*; magazine), 322n.69
Kōdate Naomi, 310n.4
Kohada Koheiji (character), 146, 190, 191, 218, 220, 310n.84
Kohei. *See* Kobotoke Kohei
Koheiji. *See* Kohada Koheiji
Kondō Kenzan, 206
Kondō Mizuki, 176
Kondō Naoyoshi, 206
Kōno Moronao (character), 113, 116, 137, 144
konpaku (ghost, spirit), 176–77, 179–80
Kornicki, Peter, 12
Kotobuki Theater (Kotobuki-za), 241
Kōzaki (character), 216–18, *217*
Kubota Mantarō, 252, 320n.37
Kurata Yoshihiro, 258
Kureha no Mae (character), 213–15, *214*
Kusunoki Masashige, 290n.72
Kusuyama Masao, 250, 320n.37
Kyoden. *See* Santō Kyōden
Kyōhō reforms, 51
Kyokutei Bakin, 2, 85, 194, 201, 210, 315n.59, 316n.60
Kyoto: actors from, 76, 80, 81, 110; and *akusho*, 21; censorship in, 87, 91; vs. Edo, 23, 30, 31, 61, 63, 242; female actors in, 293n.122; influence of, 39, 45, 65; patronage in, 59; pleasure quarters in, 66; plots in, 71, 212; scripts in, 16; *sekai* in, 71, 211–12, 215; theater managers in, 50, 285n.25, 286n.30; theaters in, 285n.23; types of plays in, 105, 136, 185, 301n.69

Lacan, Jacques, 161
Lady Aoi (*Aoi no ue*; nō play), 166, 174

Lady Okuni's Makeup Mirror (*Okuni gozen keshō no sugatami*; Tsuruya Nanboku IV), 215
Latour, Bruno, 41
laws: ban on using real names, 91; copyright, 72, 257; regulatory, 19, 22–23, 48–49, 56, 86–88, 90–91; and revenge, 127; sumptuary, 91, 92–93; on women, 163
Legend of Narukami from the Genpei War, The (*Genpei Narukami denki*), 66
Life of a Sensuous Woman, The (*Kōshiku ichidai onna*; Ihara Saikaku), 172
lineages: of samurai, 31, 64, 111; shoguns, 22–23, 28, 41, 60–61, 70, 71, 97; of theaters, 51–52
OF ACTORS, 15–17, 31, 35, 81–86, 110, 234, 280n.26, 319n.31; and *aragoto* style, 62, 289n.68; beginnings of, 46; and community, 42, 81–82, 84; in modern period, 238, 242, 259; in *Yotsuya kaidan*, 262
Literary Arts Society (Bungei kyōkai), 237, 243
literature (*bungaku*), 6, 31, 161, 177; premodern, 23–24; and text, 10–11. See also fiction
Liu, Lydia, 234
Lotus Sutra, 165, 305n.30
love, concept of, 27, 154, 192. See also jealousy; sexuality
love suicides, 91, 281n.34, 283n.2, 295n.138

"Madam White Eternally Subjugated Under the Leifeng Pagoda" (Bainiangzi yongzheng Leifengta; Feng Menglong), 171
Maeda Ai, 274
Mandala of Tateyama (*Tateyama mandara*), 166
Mandala of the Heart and Ten Worlds of Kumano (*Kumano kanjin jikkai mandara*), 166, 167

manuals, kabuki, 69–70
Maples and Deer: The Long Sleeves of the Soga Brothers (*Momiji ni shika furisode Soga*; Tsuruya Nanboku IV), 135
marriage, 171–73, 306n.36
Maruyama Ōkyo, 163
Masago Theater (Masago-za), 191
masks, 160, 166, 271, 272, 273
Matsuda Osamu, 284n.9
Matsudaira Yamato no Kami, 288n.53
Matsui Kōzō II, 256
Matsui Shōyō (Shōō), 251, 253
Matsui Sumako, 237
Matsumoto Kōshirō, 30
Matsumoto Kōshirō II, 83
Matsumoto Kōshirō V, 7, 106, 108, 109, 115, 126, 130, 140–41, 219, 261
Matsusuke I. See Onoe Matsusuke I
Matsuzaki Hitoshi, 59
McGann, Jerome, 252
McLuhan, Marshall, 11
medical beliefs, 204–8, 209, 212; and separative surgery, 206–8, 213
Meeks, Lori, 163
Meiji period, 18, 236–43; actors in, 232–45; and Edo kabuki, 31; jealousy in literature of, 191–93; scripts in, 234, 245–46, 258; theater reform in, 236, 254; *Yotsuya kaidan* in, 243–46
merchants, 59, 89, 172
military tales (*gunki*), 23, 41, 56, 60, 62, 63, 64–65, 66, 67, 72, 73
Mimasuya Nisōji, 7, 71, 80, 99, 123
Minamoto no Takakuni, 311n.9
Minamoto no Yorimitsu, 60, 61, 106, 108
Minamoto no Yoritomo, 40, 64, 67, 71
Minamoto no Yoriyoshi, 61
Minamoto no Yoshiie, 61
Minamoto no Yoshitsune, 157–58, 161, 164

Mirror Mountain: A Woman's Treasury of Loyalty (*Kagamiyama kokyō no nishikie*), 80, 144
Miscellany of Precious Things (*Sunkin zattetsu*; Morishima Chūryō), 49
Miscellany of Ten Maxims, A (*Jikkin shō*), 200
Mita Literature (*Mita bungaku*; journal), 247
Mitamura Engyo, 171, 172, 235, 253
mitate (seeing as), 67
Miyako no Nishiki, 173
Miyako shinbun (newspaper), 245
Miyako Theater, 47, 70, 98, 298n.25
Miyato Theater (Miyato-za), 241
Miyazaki Denkichi, 82
Mizuki Tatsunosuke, 188
Models of Women from Japan (*Honchō jokan*; Asai Ryōi), 173
Modern Genji in Sixty Chapters, A (*Ima Genji rokujūjō*), 188
Modern Ghost Story on a Starry Night, A (*Kinsei kaidan shimoyo no hoshi*; Ryūtai Tanehiko), 175
modernity: vs. early modernity, 237–38; and kabuki, 18, 24, 34, 226–27, 236; in Meiji period, 254–55; Western, 238
Mokuami. See Kawatake Mokuami
Mokuren Sonja, 205
Monk Karukaya (*Karukaya dōshin*), 169
Monk Karukaya, Souvenirs from Tsukushi (*Karukaya dōshin Tsukushi no iezuto*; puppet play), 169
Morisada's Miscellaneous Notes (*Morisada mankō*; Kitagawa Morisada), 212
Morishima Chūryō, 49
Morita Kan'ya, 52, 82, 236, 242
Morita Theater (Morita-za), 9, 47, 52, 74, 85, 98, 138
Moriya Takeshi, 20, 48, 49
Moronao. See Kōno Moronao

Motojima Chishin, 53
Motomiya Sandayū (character), 118
Mount Imo and Mount Se: An Exemplary Tale of Womanly Virtue (*Imoseyama onna teikin*), 188
Mountain Witch with a Child, The (*Komochi yamanba*), 146, 147
Moving the Capital to Heian (*Heianjō miyako sadame*), 82
Mullaney, Steven, 44
Murayama Heijūrō, 289n.68
Muromachi period, 60, 163, 166, 204, 207
music: *meriyasu* style, 302n.84, 303n.11; and *ubume*, 214

Nagai Kafū, 247, 251, 253, 320n.37
Nagashima Imashiro, 53
Nagashima Juami, 101
Nagoya, 30, 319n.22, 319n.24
Nakagawa Nobuo, 273
Nakamura Denkurō, 289n.68
Nakamura Jūsuke II, 80
Nakamura Kanzaburō, 45, 49–50, 51–52, 82, 309n.70
Nakamura Nakazō I, 123, *139*, 139–40, 142, 219, 302n.72
Nakamura Nakazō III, 139, 302n.74
Nakamura Shichisaburō I, 309n.72
Nakamura Shikaku II, 26
Nakamura Theater (Nakamura-za), 47, 61, 89, 296n.5; and actors, 49–50, 111; closing of, 98, 227; illustrations of, 54, *55*, *57*, *58*; lineage of, 51–52; playbills from, *13*, 13–14, *14*, 76–77, *77*, *114*, 114–15, *210*; productions at, *57*, *58*, 74, 110, 148, 157; *Yotsuya kaidan* at, 1, 4, 5, 13–14, 112
Nakamura Utaemon III, 99
Nakamura Yukihiko, 291n.88
Nakazō. See Nakamura Nakazō I
Namiki Gohei, 70–71, 135–36, 215, 320n.39
Namiki Senryū, 123
Namiki Sōsuke, 169

INDEX

361

naniwabushi (Naniwa chanting), 322n.69

Naosuke Gonbei (character), 116, 130, 251, 273

National Theater (Kokuritsu Gekijō), 274

nationalism: and community, 29, 31; vs. local tradition, 232; and national theater, 31, 97, 148–49, 232, 237, 238, 241, 247, 248; and Western-style theater, 241

nativist studies (*kokugaku*), 29

neo-Confucianism, 208

New Performance (*Shin engei*; journal), 247–48, 252, 253

New Tales Under the Lamplight (*Jiandeng xinhua*; Qu You), 176, 303n.1

Night Parade of a Hundred Monsters, Illustrated, The (*Gazu hyakki yagyō*; Toriyama Sekien), 201, 203, 213, 215

Nightingale Tomb: An Old Tale of a Spear (*Uguisuzuka nagara no furugoto*), 120–21

Nishizawa Ippō, 135

Nitta Yoshisada, 61

nō theater, 54, 58, 187, 238; ghosts in, 25, 154; vs. kabuki, 242, 288n.50; presenting the past in, 67–68; scripts in, 16–17, 236; serpent imagery in, 166, 174

Notes by Juami (*Juami hikki*; Nagashima Juami), 101

Notes on Playmaking (*Sakusha shikihō kezairoku*; Nyūgatei Ganyū), 63, 68, 69, 72

nuns, traveling (*Kumano bikuni*), 168, 205

Nyūgatei Ganyū (Namiki Shōza II), 63, 68

Ōboshi Yuranosuke (character), 114, 128, 144, 262

Ōguchiya Jihei (Gyōu), 283n.7

Oiwa (character): and birds, 210, 211; blood and hair of, 145–46, 155–57; and community, 161, 226; in consecration-cloth scene, 195–98; in dream scene, 151–52, 178, 263, 263, 264; emotions of, 190–92; and female body, 155, 190; and female ghosts, 25, 28, 33, 150, 188; in hair-combing scene, 155, 156–157, 157, 159–60; images of, 4, 14, 14, 157, 163, 195, 211, 263, 263, 268, 268, 269, 269, 270, 271, 272, 273; and inversion, 181–82, 189; male-role actors as, 182, 188–89; modern versions of, 243–45, 248, 251, 253, 271, 272, 273, 317n.65; and Otowaya and Onoe Kikugorō lineage, 26, 146, 189, 235, 244, 245, 252, 262, 319n.31; power of, 144–46; and samurai, 130, 131–32, 160–61; as *ubume*, 34, 194, 198, 224–27, 317n.65; in *Yotsuya kaidan*, 3–6, 116–18, 144–47, 150–55, 156–157, 157, 159–60, 195–98, 261–62

Oiwa (novel; Osanai Kaoru), 248

"O'Iwa of the Tamiya Inari Jinja of Echizenbori, Tokyo" (frontispiece to *Yotsuya kaidan*, De Benneville), 248, 249

Oka Eiichirō, 254

Oka Onitarō, 251

Okamoto Kidō, 247, 251, 257, 265, 322n.69

Okaru (character), 131, 137, 145

Okuda Shōzaburō (character), 116

Okuni (dancer), 45, 46

On Drama: Boundaries of Genre, Borders of the Self (Goldman), 143

On Ghosts (*Yūrei no koto*; Hayashi Razan), 176–77

"On the Power to Construct" (*Kōseiryoku ni tsuite*, Karatani Kōjin), 23–24

One Hundred Ghost Stories (*Hyakumonogatari*; print series; Hokusai), 168

INDEX

362

Ong, Walter, 11
Oniō Shinzaemon, 71
"Oniō's Hovel" (Oniō hinka no ba; scene), 71
Ono Sadakurō (character), 114, 115, 123, *138*, 138–41, *139*, *141*, *142*
Onoe Baikō VI, 26, 244, 245, 252, 253, 271, 272, 273, 319n.28
Onoe Kikugorō, lineage of (Otowaya lineage), 26, 146, 189, 235, 245, 252, 262, 319n.31
Onoe Kikugorō I, 144, 152, 262
Onoe Kikugorō III, 115, 123, 142, 144, 252, 323n.81; in Edo, 30; farewell production of, 194–95, 266–67, 268, 271, 322n.73; ghost roles for, 25, 26, 215; images of, *4*, *195*, *263*, *268*, *269*, *270*; in scripts, 261; and special effects, 101–3; in *Yotsuya kaidan*, 1, 3, 5, 7, 15, 120, 126, 146, 189, 194, 225, 235, 261–62
Onoe Kikugorō V, 92, 102, 123, 232, 244, 245, 252, 254
Onoe Matsusuke I (Onoe Shōroku I), 25, 26, 101–3, 189, 215, 216, 262, 297n.13
Onoe Shōkaku (Shinohara Takendo), 245, 319n.29
onryōgoto (performances of resentful spirits), 175, 181, 182, 183
Ōoka Echizen, 52
oral performances, 11, 41, 191
Orality and Literacy (Ong), 11
Ordinance on Scripts and Sheet Music (Kyakuhon gakufu jōrei), 257
Origins of Kabuki, The (Kabuki jishi), 75
Origins of Modern Japanese Literature, The (Kindai Nihon bungaku no kigen), 23
Osada Hideo, 320n.37
Osaka: actors from, 76, 80, 81, 110, 262, 322n.73; and *akusho*, 21; censorship in, 87, 91; in contemporary plays, 136; vs. Edo, 30, 61, 63, 65; female actors in, 293n.122; and open-endedness, 75; plots in, 71, 212; scripts in, 16; *sekai* in, 211–12, 215; theater managers in, 50, 285n.25, 286n.30; theaters in, 285n.23; types of plays in, 105, 128, 301n.69; *Yotsuya kaidan* in, 196, 266
Osanai Kaoru, 237, 247–48, 251, 252, 253, 320n.37
Oshioda Matanojō (character), 117, 118, 129
Ōshū (character), *186*, 186–87
Osode (character), 4, 116–18, 130, 251
Ōtaka Yōji, 315n.59
otogizōshi, 160, 165, 176
Otogizōshi in Color (Iroeiri otogizōshi; Tsuruya Nanboku IV), 103, 215, 216 217, 220
Otowa no Mae (character), 186
Otowaya guild, 26
Ōwashi Bungo (character), 124, *125*, 300n.54

Pandora's Box (Wedekind), 248
past, presenting the, 39–93, 97; and actors, 42, 81–86, 298n.33; and calendar, 42, 81; and class structure, 66–68, 71, 72, 93; and commoners, 41, 42, 69, 71, 72; and community, 40–42, 67, 72, 93; decline of, 149, 231; and fluidity of productions, 263; and Nanboku, 110; and two-part productions, 134–35; and *ubume*, 211, 226
Penlington, John N., 233
Penlington, Zoë Kincaid, 232–34
"Peony Lantern, The" (Mudan dengji; Qu You), 176
performance, 277n.6, 279n.20; communal space for, 24; and culture, 31–32; as *engeki*, 241–42, 245; vs. text, 5–17, 24, 120, 122, 123–24, 134, 137, 148, 232, 246–55, 266, 268, 271. *See also* productions

playbills, 289n.65, 298n.29; cast (*yakuwari banzuke*), 8, 13, *13*, 264; and Edo actors, 30; evil characters in, 138–39, 142, *143*; face-showing (*kaomise banzuke*; *yakusha-zuke*), 76–77, *77*, 292n.99; and fluidity of productions, 74, 120–21, 263; follow-up (*oi banzuke*), 5, 9; ink/odor of, 2–3, 277n.2; for Nanboku's plays, 102, 106, 108, *109*; picture-book (*ehon banzuke*), 13–14, *14*, *109*, 114, 114–15, 142, *143*, 279nn.18–19, 302n.72; and playwright, 256–57; prices of, 77, 292n.101; and samurai, 88; street (*tsuji banzuke*), 2–3, 5, 9, 147, 210, 211, 216, 217, 277n.2; for *Treasury of Loyal Retainers*, 13, *14*, 114, 114–15, 119–20; *ubume* in, 216, 217; for *Yotsuya kaidan*, 13, 13–14, *14*, 112, 114, 114–15, 119–20, 210, 211, 264, *264*

plays (*shibai*, *kyōgen*), types of, 241; Asama (*Asama-mono*), 64, 185–87; ceremonial dances and skits (*waki kyōgen* or *bandachi*), 7; chivalrous commoner, 80; contemporary (*sewa*), 105, 134–37, 211, 243, 247, 248, 253; cotton (*momen shibai*), 239–40; Dōjōji, 158, 165, 166, 169, 171, 174, 310n.80; historical (*jidai kyōgen*), 134–37; horror (*kaidan kyōgen*), 7, 25, 101–2, 104, 106, 189; house (*ie kyōgen*), 7; ichiyazuke (overnight pickles; fill-in plays), 80; *kizewa* (raw *sewa*), 105, 136, 137, 239, 301n.69; multi-act (*tsuzuki kyōgen*), 46; noble in exile (*kishu ryūritan*), 61; *otogizōshi*, 160, 165, 176; *sekkyō*, 165; Shimabara, 47; Zeami's dream plays (*mugen nō*), 67. *See also* household-disturbance plays; revenge/vendetta plays; Soga brothers; *Treasury of Loyal Retainers, The*; *Wait a Minute!*; *Yotsuya kaidan*

playwrights, 46, 101, 135, 188; and actors, 16, 17, 80, 261, 284n.15, 321n.62; as ghostwriters, 266, 323n.81; modern concept of, 34, 232, 237, 255–58; and presenting the past, 72, 298n.33; and publicity, 256–57; roles of, 321n.62, 322n.69; and textualization, 235. *See also* authorship; *specific individuals*

pleasure quarters: as *akusho*, 19–21, 281n.34; architecture of, 54; and censorship, 86, 87; culture of, 42, 60; depictions of, 43, 44; and early kabuki, 19, 45, 46; in Edo (Yoshiwara), 21, 45, 47, 60, 76, 79, 288n.56; and kabuki calendar, 76, 79; in Kamigata, 281n.34; in Kyoto, 39–40, 66; in Nanboku's plays, 105, 115, 160; relocation of, 45, 47

Plum Flower and the Cracking of Ice (*Baika hyōretsu*; Santō Kyōden), 172, 223

poetry: *haikai*, 67, 70, 72, 168; *honkadori* (classical), 72, 291n.90; *renga* (linked), 73–74; in *Yotsuya kaidan*, 151

Pre-Chronicle of Great Peace (*Zentaiheiki*), 106

pregnancy, 199, 207, 209, 212, 225; in fiction, 206–7, 212–13, 219, 223; and separative surgery, 206–8

Prescriptions for Fifty-Two Ailments (*Wushier bing fang*), 209

print culture, 12, 14–15, 22

Printing Revolution in Early Modern Europe, The (Eisenstein), 11

printing technology, 11–12, 16, 34

prints, woodblock: of actors, 4, 15, 16, 22, *109*, 125, 139, *139*, *140*, *141*, 256–57, 263, 263–64, 268, 268–69, 269, 270, 289n.65, 298n.29; and artists, 12–13; in

INDEX

364

Edo, 22, 30–31; likeness (*nigao-e*) technique in, 3, 16; linear perspective in, 282n.38, 293n.119; vs. movable type, 11–12, 16; preproduction, 3–5, 13, 245, 298n.29; serpent imagery in, 168; ukiyo-e, 12–13, 32, 282n.38

productions: and actors, 78–79, 101; in Edo, 51; farewell, 293n.112; first (*ichibanme*) vs. second (*nibanme*) parts of, 134–35, 212, 215; hundred-day (*hyakunichi shibai*), 47–48; major vs. minor, 47; opening performance (*jobiraki*), 7; prices of, 89–90, 294nn.131–33, 295nn.134–35, 296nn.8–9, 319n.26; small (*koshibai*), 47, 90; spring (*hatsuharu kyōgen*), 8–9, 64, 70, 71, 74–80, 92, 99, 101, 106, 274–75; structure of, 291nn.92–93; summer, 89, 101–2, 104, 106, 278n.10; temple and shrine (*miyachi shibai*), 47–48, 90, 104, 183, 285nn.21–24; two-play, 135–36. See also calendar, kabuki; face-showing productions

prompt books, illustrated (*eiri kyōgenbon*), 18–19, 174, *184*, 289n.65, 290n.72, 314n.38

prostitution. See pleasure quarters

psychology: in film, 273–74; in Taishō period, 250–51, 253

Publishing Drama in Early Modern Europe (Chartier), 10

puppet theater (*jōruri*): chanting in, 138; classical status of, 238; and fiction, 221–22; jealous women in, 169, 188; and kabuki, 9, 80, 121, 246; in Kamigata, 69; Kinpira, 61–62, 289n.61; *kojōruri*, 165, 316n.61; plots of, 62, 64, 65, 127, 212–13, 302n.81; special effects in, 179, 305n.35; and text, 17, 236; *Treasury of Loyal Retainers* in, 112, 124, 140; venues for, 59, 88, 285n.22

Qu You, 176, 303n.1

Questioning the Rare Things of Heaven and Earth (*Tenchi waku monchin*), 209

Quick Dissection of the Actors, A (*Yakusha sassoku hōchō*), 264

Rabelais and His World (Bakhtin), 26–27

rakugo (oral storytelling), 191

ranjuku taihai (overripe and decadent) period (early nineteenth century), 100–101

realism, 136, 237, 240–41, 243

Record of Mysterious Creatures (*Xuanzhong ji*), 208

Records of a Flourishing Edo (*Edo hanjōki*; Terakado Seiken), 172–73

regionalism, 18, 29–31, 59–60, 61, 63

Reins of Yosaku of Tanba Province, The (*Tanba Yosaku tazuna obi*; Tominaga Heibei), 212

renribiki (pull of affection), 152–54, 164, 181

Revenge at the Old Market Place (*Katakiuchi uwasa no furuichi*), 239

revenge/vendetta plays (*katakiuchimono*): and early modern law, 127; female ghosts in, 133, 216; and fiction, 221, 222; and household-disturbance plays, 128, 131–32; as overnight pickles (fill-in plays), 80; and *sekai*, 226; and Soga brothers, 40, 67, 69–72, 78–79, 275, 292n.105, 296n.7; *ubume* in, 34, 198–99, 216, 219, 224–25; and women, 112, 131, 222; vs. *Yotsuya kaidan*, 126–33. See also *Treasury of Loyal Retainers, The*

Rise and Fall of the Heike and Genji: A Beginner's Version (*Hiragana seisuiki*), 120–21, 158

Rokujō, Lady (character), 166, 174

Russian novels, 235, 253

INDEX

365

Ryōgoku Bridge, 104, 105
Ryūsei Theater (Ryūsei-za), 241
Ryūtai Tanehiko, 175

Sadakurō. *See* Ono Sadakurō
Sakakiyama Koshirō I, 183, *184*
Sakata Kinpira, 61–62, 289n.61
Sakata Tōjūrō, 81
Sakurada Jisuke I, 67, 100, 136, 256, 315n.48
Sakurahime (character), 80, 219, 223, 316n.61
Saltzman-Li, Katherine, 69, 76
samurai: and actors, 81, 87–88, 240; as audience, 19, 22–23, 56–66, 89; and censorship, 87; culture of, 28, 41–42; decline of, 148; in Edo, 31, 55–66, 287n.46; and female ghosts, 28, 29, 189; and household-disturbance plays, 112, 127, 128; lineages of, 31, 64, 111; and marriage, 171–72, 306n.40; masterless, 129–30, 139; and Nanboku, 107, 110, 130, 131–32; and Oiwa, 130, 131–32, 160–61; and presenting the past, 41, 42; and *sekai*, 28–29, 40, 69, 112
Santō Kyōden, 172, 194, 219, 220, 222–25, 315n.48, 316n.60
Sanyūtei Enchō, 191
Saruwaka-machi, 227, 239
Sasaki Kōsho, 310n.4
Satō Eri, 62
Satō Hiroo, 177
Satō Yomoshichi (character), 116–18, 189, 251, 262
Sawamura Gennosuke IV, 317n.65, 319n.31
Scales of Dōjōji, a Modern Adaptation, The (*Dōjōji genzai uroko*; Asada Itchō and Namiki Sōsuke), 169
Scidmore, Eliza, 122
Screen Depicting a Kabuki Performance (*Kabuki-zu byōbu*; Hishikawa Moronobu), 56–57, *57*, 58

Screen Painting of the Shijō Riverbank District (*Shijō kawara yūrakuzu byōbu*), 183, *185*
scripts, written: and actors, 6–7, 122, 232, 233–34, 245, 254–56, 261, 262–63, 275; authentic (*shōhon*), 252–53, 254, 256; censorship of, 295n.144, 300n.52; consecration-cloth scene in, 195–98; and Edo kabuki, 18, 22, 34; as fixed texts, 258, 273–75; fluidity of, 2, 8, 255, 261–65, 271; hand-copied, 258, 259; illustrated (*eiri nehon*), 265; modern editions of, 258–65, 271; in modern period, 231–36, 245–46, 247; in nō, 16–17, 236; vs. performance, 5, 6, 8, 9, 122, 123–24, 137, 148, 232, 246–55, 266, 268, 271; printed, 11, 12, 16, 275; published, 255; reading of, 235, 236, 245, 265; reconstruction of, 5, 253; survival of, 16, 280n.27; and textualization, 237, 258–59; transcribed (*shōhon utsushi*), 266; translations of, 259, 261; typeset editions (*kokatsujiban*) of, 12; in West, 15–16, 255; of *Yotsuya kaidan*, 10, 32, 258–61, 259, 260. *See also* text
Secret Letter About the Actors, A (*Yakusha yatsushijō*; Ejima Kiseki), 187
Segawa Jokō III, 226, 239
Segawa Kikunojō II, 92–93
Segawa Kikunojō III, 85, 91–92
Segawa Kikunojō V, 106, *109*
Segawa Rokō I, 172
Seigen (character), 80, 146, 190, 223, 316n.61
Seisei'en. *See* Ihara Seisei'en
Seiwa Genji lineage, 22, 60–61
sekai (worlds; historical frameworks): categories of, 69–70, 290n.83; and contemporaneity, 68, 99, 111; and culture, 23, 24–25, 111; decline of, 24–25,

INDEX

366

97, 99, 106–11, 148, 149, 226–27, 239, 240, 275; and early kabuki, 28–29, 40, 42, 46; in Edo, 31–32, 34, 40, 42, 64, 65, 71, 73, 211–12, 215; and female body, 33, 193; and female ghosts, 27–28, 29, 190; in fiction, 222; and fluidity of productions, 72, 75, 263; and kabuki calendar, 78, 80–81; in Kyoto, 71, 211–12, 215; and Nanboku, 69, 110, 227; and shared culture, 111; and *shukō*, 66–72, 99; vs. textualization, 236; in two-part productions, 134–35; and *ubume*, 198, 199, 211–12, 215; and *Yotsuya kaidan*, 34, 112
Seki Sanjūro II, 268, 269, 270
Sekien. *See* Toriyama Sekien
Sekigahara, battle of (1600), 60
selfhood, 112, 127, 128, 132, 161; and female body, 27–29, 155, 193
serpent, imagery of, 163–68; and Buddhism, 165–66, 175, 305n.30; in China, 171; and ghosts, 174–80, 178, 186, 191, 310n.83; and jealousy, 168, 169, 174–75, 176; and masks, 166; and men, 190, 191, 192, 310n.83; in popular culture, 180; and sexuality, 165–68; and women, 164–65, 174–80, 186
"Serpent's Lust, A" (Jasei no in; Ueda Akinari), 171
Serres, Michel, 41
setsuwa (anecdotes), 175–76
Seven Herbs Society (Nanakusakai), 251, 253
sexuality, 45, 240, 241, 243, 248, 250–51; in male roles, 33, 126, 130, 139, 140, 274; and serpents, 165–68. *See also* pleasure quarters
Shakespeare, William, 11, 16, 18, 246, 255, 271
Shakespeare and the Authority of Performance (Worthen), 11
Shakespeare and the Book (Kastan), 11, 271

sharebon (book of wit and fashion), 221
Shikitei Sanba, 54, 83, 137, 152, 194, 219–21
Shimamura Hōgetsu, 237
Shinchō Collection of Japanese Classics (Shinchō Nihon koten shūsei), 258, 259
Shingeki (New Theater), 237, 239, 243
Shinmura Taku, 310n.4
Shinobu no Mae (character), 157–59, 160, 161, 164, 303n.8
Shinozuka Iganokami, 65
Shinpa (New School), 237, 238–39
Shinran (as character), 91
Shinto, 204
Shintomi Theater, 237, 242
Shirane, Haruo, 291n.89
Shively, Donald H., 19, 22
Shōchiku (production company), 251
shogun, 72; lineage of, 22–23, 28, 41, 60–61, 70, 71, 97. *See also* government, Tokugawa
Shōkajo (character), 107–8, 109
shōsetsu (novel), 258
Shōtoku period, 45
Shōyō. *See* Tsubouchi Shōyō
shukō (theatrical twist on plot), 68–72, 80–81, 263
Shunkintei Ryūō, 248
Shutendōji (demon), 60, 61
Singing My Own Praises (Temae miso; Nakamura Nakazō III), 139
Slaughtering Hundreds at Yoshiwara (Yoshiwara hyakuningiri), 257–58
Sloppy Comic Sermon on Things Heard (Hetadangi chōmonshū, Gachikuken), 69, 281n.35
Smith, Henry D., II, 113
Society for Theater Reform (Engeki Kairyō Kai), 237
Soga brothers, 40, 67, 69–72, 78–79, 275, 292n.105, 296n.7
Soga Gorō, 40, 42, 67, 81

INDEX

367

Soga Jūrō, 40
"Song of Lasting Pain" (Chang hen ge; Bai Juyi), 152, 154
Sono'o no Mae (character), 221–22, 222
Sōtō Zen sect (Buddhism), 205, 206
Sought-After Grave, The (*Keisei motomezuka*), 183, *184*
"Sparkle of Glass, The" (Ruri no tsuya; song), 159
special effects, 245, 253, 254; and blood and hair, 156–57, *157*; censorship of, 244; and consecration-cloth scene, 195–98; and ghosts, 25, 26, 178–79, *197*, 218; and Nanboku, 100–105, 156; in puppet theater, 179, 305n.35; and stage construction, 25, 48; and tent shows, 104; with water, 296n.11, 297nn.12–14, 305n.35
spider stunts (*kumomai*), 183, *185*
Spring Awakening (Wedekind), 248
Stories Heard and Written Down About the Salvation of Dead Spirits (*Shiryō gedatsu monogatari kikigaki*), 207
Stories on Hinokiyama Heard on the Road (*Hinokiyama tabiji no kikigaki*, Kawatake Shinshichi III), 258
storytelling. See *kōdan*
Strange Transmissions on Composing Plays (*Denki sakusho*; Nishizawa Ippō), 135
Study of Sewamono Plays, The (*Sewa kyōgen no kenkyū*), 247, 248, 253
subjugated knowledge, 17–24
Suematsu Kenchō, 237
Sugawara no Michizane, 150
Sukeroku (character), 39–42, 67, 79, 283n.2, 283n.7; and Danjūrō, 81, 123; secret identity of, 39–40
Sukeroku: The Flower of Edo (*Sukeroku yukari no Edozakura*), 39, 40, 81

sumptuary laws, 91, 92–93. See also clothing
supernatural, 61–62, 64–66, 162, 305n.25, 308n.59, 319n.28. See also ghosts
Sutoku, Emperor, 150
Suwa Haruo, 55, 163, 323n.76
Suzuki Hakutō, 260, 310n.2
Suzuki Shōsan, 313n.30
Sword Named Kagotsurube, A (*Kagotsurube sato no eizame*), 257

Taira no Masakado, 106
Taira no Suetake (character), 199–200
"Taira no Suetake Meets an *Ubume*" (Taira no Suetake ubume ni au hanashi), 201, *202*
Taishō period, 18, 258; actors in, 234, 254–55; text vs. performance in, 246–55
Takahashi Noriko, 311n.5
Takamura Chikuri, 80
Takeda Izumo, 112, 123
Takei Kyōzō, 59
Takeshiba Kisui, 257, 322n.69
Takezawa Tōji, 297n.21
Tale of Kōya, The (*Kōya monogatari*), 206–7, 210
Tale of Martyr Sakura, The (*Higashiyama Sakura no sōshi*), 239
Tale of the Floating Peony, The (*Ukibotan zenden*), 315n.48
Tale of the Soga Brothers, The (*Soga monogatari*), 40
Tale of Yoshitsune, The (*Gikeiki*), 70, 71
Tales of Moonlight and Rain (*Ugetsu monogatari*; Ueda Akinari), 161, 171
Tales of Retribution (*Inga monogatari*; Suzuki Shōsan), 313n.30
Tales of the Heike, The (*Heike monogatari*), 65, 70, 71
Tales of Times Now Past (*Konjaku monogatarishū*), 199–201

INDEX

368

Tall Wave of Rumor for a Golden Carp Windsock, A (*Kogane shachi uwasa no takanami*), 257
Tamagawa Hikojūrō, 298n.25
Tamagawa Sennojō, 187, 309n.77
Tamagawa (Miyako) Theater, 106, 107, 111, 298n.25
Tamakoto (character), 223, 224
Tamamuro Taijō, 310n.4
Tamenaga Shunsui, 105
Tamiya Iemon (character), 5–6, 116–18, 155, 192; censorship of, 244; in consecration-cloth scene, 195–96, 197; in dream scene, 151–52, 178–79, 263, 263, 264; as erotic rogue (*iroaku*), 130, 140; images of, 4, 14, *14*, *195*, 263, 263, 268, 268, 269, 270; and Oiwa as *ubume*, 226; in playbills, 263; psychology of, 160, 273–74; in Taishō period, 251, 253
Tanaka Takako, 165
Tanba Izumidayū, 62
Tanizaki Jūn'ichirō, 250
Tanuma Okitsugu, 295n.138
Tatekawa (Utei) Enba I, 82, 104, 121, 214
temples, 53, 75, 311n.5; productions at, 47–48, 58, 90, 104, 183, 285nn.21–24; and theater architecture, 54
Tenmei period, 101
Tenpō period, 101, 246
Tenpō reforms, 51, 93, 227
tent shows (*misemono*), 104, 105, 106, 297n.21
Terajima Ryōan, 179, 209
Terakado Seiken, 172–73
text: censorship of, 92, 93; and community, 12, 29; and conservation, 255–71; and lineage, 41, 82; as monument, 10–11, 18, 24; vs. performance, 5–17, 24, 120, 122, 123–24, 134, 137, 148, 232, 246–55, 266, 268, 271; and visual media, 6, 10, 13–14, 17–18; in West, 15–16, 255; and *Yotsuya kaidan*, 32, 273–75. *See also* scripts, written
textualization, 9, 10, 23, 31; and modern editions of scripts, 258–59; in modern period, 231–36
theater: adaptations of, 258; classical, 247, 259; culture of, 18, 22; narratives of substitution in, 237–38, 239, 241; national, 97, 148–49, 232, 237, 238, 242, 247, 248; and print culture, 14–15; reforms of, 236, 242, 254; in urban landscape, 43–44, 84; as utopia, 84; in vernacular, 239; Western, 15–16, 31, 234, 237, 245, 247–48
theater managers (*zamoto*), 49–51, 76, 78–79, 98, 256; and actors, 80, 82; and censors, 92; and government, 53–54; in Kyoto and Osaka, 50, 285n.25, 286n.30
theater pictures (*gekijōzu*), 84–85
theater-affiliation system (*zakakae sei*): contracts in, 22, 49–50, 53, 76, 86, 97–98, 110–11, 286n.26; decline of, 97–98, 239
Theaterland (*kejōkoku*), 85
theaters: architecture of, 22, 54–55, 91, 237, 241, 287n.43; backup, 98, 99, 296n.5, 298n.25; and censorship, 87, 88; and community, 29–30; Elizabethan, 43–44; finances of, 52–53; fires in, 91, 99; and government, 31–32, 43–56, 99, 285n.19; interiors of, 84–85, 293n.119; licensed, 43–56; licensed vs. unlicensed, 48, 52; lineages (*yuisho*) of, 51; locations of, 42, 284n.12; and reforms, 51; relocation of, 111, 227; rural, 282n.48; small, 243, 244, 285n.23, 318n.18; social diversity at, 57, 58; subsidiary (*hikae yagura*), 47; Western-style, 237, 241. *See also specific theaters*
Thornbury, Barbara, 39, 76

Three Acting Houses, The (*Yakusha mitokoro setai*), 135
Three Generations of Dōjōji (*Sanze Dōjōji*), 174
time: and actors' lineages, 81–82; and community, 93; cyclical, 72–81, 113, 132; layered, 66–72; and Nanboku, 107, 112, 132; and open-endedness, 73–74. *See also* past, presenting the
Tokiyuki (character), 146, 147
Tokubei from India: A Tale from Foreign Lands (*Tenjiku Tokubei ikoku banashi*; Tsuruya Nanboku IV), 89, 102, 215, 218, 219
Tokugawa Iemitsu, 45, 309n.70
Tokugawa Ietsugu, 53
Tokugawa Ietsuna, 45
Tokugawa Ieyasu, 56, 60
Tokyo (Edo), 231, 242, 243, 275
Tokyo Theater (Tōkyō-za), 244, 245, 319n.26
Tominaga Heibei, 212
Tomokurō (wig maker), 104, 156
Torii Kiyonobu II, 213
Torii School, 256, 298n.35
Toriyama Sekien, 201, 213, 215
Treasure Box of Women's Learnings, The (*Onna daigaku takarabako*), 173
Treasury of Loyal Retainers, The (*Kanadehon chūshingura*), 3, 5, 7, 9, 262; battle scenes in, 123; canonization of, 149; censorship of, 90–91; characters in, 124, 125, 129–33, 138, 138–39, 139, 140, 141; in double production, 134, 136–37, 143–44, 147, 149; evolution of, 137–43; fluidity of, 119–26, 142, 149, 263; as ghost play, 143–48; illustrated summary of, 138, 138; inversion of, 126–33; modern productions of, 123, 126; as national epic, 148–49; playbills for, 13, 14, 114, 114–15, 211; summary of, 113–15; as traditional revenge play, 128, 149; variations on, 299n.48; and *Yotsuya kaidan*, 32–33, 100, 111–19, 114, 126–33, 134, 137, 143
True Record of the Hinokiyama Incident, The (*Kōdan Hinokiyama jikki*; Katsu Genzō III), 258
True View at Kasane Marsh, The (*Shinkei Kasane ga fuchi*; Sanyūtei Enchō), 191
Tsubouchi Shōyō, 34–35, 237, 242, 245–46, 250–51, 258, 261, 319n.22
Tsuga Teishō, 201
Tsuruya Nanboku IV: authorship of, 256, 274, 275; and changes to kabuki, 93, 97, 100–106, 199, 227; and class, 239; and evil characters, 140–41, 142–43; and female ghosts, 32–34, 133, 150; and female-role actors, 189; ghost plays of, 21, 25–28, 93, 100, 106; *gōkan* of, 221–22; income of, 104; and interiority, 193; and Kyōden, 219, 224; modern views of, 243, 245, 254; and printed script, 275; psychology of, 250, 252; rediscovery of, 246–55; revenge plays of, 20, 124, 133; and *sekai*, 69, 110, 227; special effects of, 100–105, 156; as subversive, 308n.61; summer productions of, 89, 101–2, 104; textualization of, 231–36; and traditional values, 129–30; and two-part productions, 135, 136–37, 149; and *ubume*, 194, 204, 208, 210, 211, 215–18, 221–22, 226, 227. *See also Yotsuya kaidan*
Tsutsumi Kunihiko, 175, 206, 310n.4
Tsuuchi Jihei, 100, 284n.15
Twenty-Four Models of Filial Piety, The (*Honchō nijūshi-kō*), 263, 263–64
Two-Women Hell, 166, 167, 168, 169, 205

INDEX

370

ubume (female ghost who died during pregnancy or childbirth), 33–34, 194–227; as bird, 201, 208–11, *210*; and blood defilement, 201, 204; and burial practices, 206; kanji for, 201, 204, 209; images of, *202*, *203*, *214*, *216*, *217*, 221–22, *222*; in literature, 218–23; and medical practice, 204–8; Nanboku's new use of, 198–99; Oiwa as, 33–34, 194, 198, 224–27, 317n.65; origins of, 199–224; in theater, 211–18
Ueda Akinari, 161, 171
ukie (perspective pictures), 293n.119
ukiyo (floating world), 20–21; books of (*ukiyozōshi*), 21, 168; pictures of (ukiyo-e), 12–13, 33, 282n.38
Universal Morning Report (*Yorozu chōhō*), 248
Usui no Sadamitsu (character), 108
Utagawa Kunisada, 220, 222, 224
Utagawa Kuniyasu, 3, 4, *13*
Utagawa Kuniyoshi, *269*, *270*
Utagawa school, 3, 282n.38
Utagawa Toyokuni I, 54, 84, *107*, 108, *140*, *152*
Utagawa Yoshitsuya, *178*

Vengeance: This Is Takasago (*Katakiuchi kokoro wa Takasago*; Tsuruya Nanboku IV), 221–22, *222*

wagoto (gentle, delicate) style, 63
Wait a Minute! (*Shibaraku*), 65–66, 74, 78, 79, 99, *109*; and Nanboku, 107, 108, 110
wakashu (boy actors), 45, 48, 86, 87, 183
Wakita Haruko, 171
Warning Words to Penetrate the Age (*Jingshi tongyan*), 171
Watanabe Kisō, 65
Wedekind, Frank, 248, 253
West: architecture of, 237, 241; geography in, 85; vs. Japan, 10–12,
15–16; modernity of, 238; theater of, 15–16, 31, 234, 237, 242, 245, 247–48. *See also* Shakespeare, William
whale pantomime (*kujira no danmari*), 105
What Goes On in Shikitei Sanba's Mind: A Gesaku Sourcebook (*Hara no uchi gesaku no tanehon*; Shikitei Sanba), 219–21, *220*
What Really Happens Backstage (*Okyōgen gakuya no honsetsu*; Santei Shunba and Utagawa Kunitsuna), 102, *103*, 156, *157*, *178*, *178*, 197, 197–98
White Path Between the Two Rivers (*Isshin niga byakudō*), 316n.61
wigs, 104, 156–57
Woman's Fan: The Essence of Loyalty (*Onna ōgi chūshin kaname*), 142
women: and blood, 155–59, 162, 163, 164, 166, 188, 190, 201, 204, 225, 312n.15; and Buddhism, 27, 33, 161, 162–63, 168, 169, 173, 174, 189, 204–7, 304n.20, 313n.30; and early kabuki, 46–47; emotions of, 27, 28, 33, 155–63, 174–75, 180, 181, 190, 193; hair of, 155–59, 164, 225, 303n.11; hells for, 162, 166, *167*, 168, 169, 187, 201, 205–6, 208, 215, 304n.23, 312n.20, 313n.30; as heroes, 66; and household (*ie*), 306n.38; impurity of, 162–63; instructional literature for, 169, 173; and inversion, 181–82, 189; and Kyōden, 316n.60; and marriage, 171–73, 306n.36, 306n.40, 316n.60; and monstrous-feminine, 155, 157; and Nanboku, 130; productions for, 88; and revenge, 112, 131, 222; rivalry between, 169–74, 223–24, 225; and serpents, 164–65, 166, 168, 174–80, 186;

INDEX

371

women (*continued*)
and spring production, 79–80;
transformations of, 163–68, 173,
182, 190, 191–92; in *Treasury
of Loyal Retainers*, 137, 142.
See also actors: female; actors:
female-role; body, female; characters: female; ghosts: female;
jealousy; *ubume*
Worthen, W. B., 11, 277n.6

Yaegaki, Princess (character), 263, 263–64
yagura (turret), 50, 51, 54–56
Yamada Keiji, 209
Yamamura Chōdayū, 52, 54
Yamamura Theater (Yamamura-za), 47, 286n.35; closing of, 51, 54, 74; scandal at, 53–54
Yamaoka Genrin, 208, 308n.59
Yamato shinbun (newspaper), 191
Yamauchi Yōdō, 240
Yanagita Kunio, 206
Yasui Manami, 207, 310n.4
Yoichibei (character), 138, *138*, 140, *141*
yomihon (reading books), 172, 269, 315n.48, 315n.54, 315n.59; ghosts in, 25; and kabuki productions, 219, 220–21; and *sekai*, 222; serpent imagery in, 174; sources for, 201, 225; *ubume* in, 218, 219
Yomoshichi. *See* Satō Yomoshichi
Yorozuya Sukeroku, 39. *See also* Sukeroku
Yoshii Isamu, 320n.37
Yoshitsune and the Thousand Cherry Trees (*Yoshitsune senbonzakura*), 9
Yoshizawa Ayame, 50, 53, 81, 188
Yotsuya kaidan (*Tōkaidō Yotsuya kaidan*; *Eastern Seaboard High-*
way Ghost Stories at Yotsuya; Tsuruya Nanboku IV), 1–10, 15; adaptations of, 266; and birds, 210, *211*; canonization of, 24; consecration-cloth scene in, 195–98; and decadent period, 101; in double production, 134, 136–37, 143–44, 147; dream scene (*yume no ba*) in, 150–52, 178–79, 263, *263*, 264; first production of, 1–5, 24, 32, 34, 99–100, 112, 210, 227, 231, 252, 261–62; fluidity of, 32, 33, 264; as ghost play, 148, 235; ghosts in, 33–34, 190–91; hair-combing scene (*kamisuki*) in, 159–60, 175; vs. household-disturbance plays, 126–33, 224–25; lantern scene in, 269; in Meiji period, 243–46; modern editions of, 265–66, 268, 268–70, 269, 270, 273; in modern period, 17, 231–75; in other media, 271–75; playbills for, *13*, 13–14, *14*, 112, 210, *211*, 264, *264*; playwrights for, 256; script of, 10, 32, 258–61, *259*, *260*; summary of, 116–18; translations of, 247–48, 261; and *Treasury of Loyal Retainers*, 13, 14, 32–33, 100, 111–19, 126–33, 134, 137, 143; and *ubume*, 194, 204, 224–27
Yotsuya kaidan, or, O'Iwa Inari, Retold from the Japanese Originals (De Benneville), 247–48, *249*
Yotsuya Samon (character), 116
yūrei. *See* ghosts
Yūrei-zu (scroll; Maruyama Ōkyo), 164
Yushima Shrine, 285n.21
Yūten, 207, 311n.5

Zeami, 67, 177

DEC 2 1 2016

14

HEWLETT-WOODMERE PUBLIC LIBRARY

3 1327 00625 3181

28 Day Loan

Hewlett-Woodmere Public Library
Hewlett, New York 11557

Business Phone 516-374-1967
Recorded Announcements 516-374-1667
Website www.hwpl.org